Penitentiaries, Punishment, and Military Prisons

Familiar Responses to an Extraordinary

Peniten

Punish

Military

The Kent State University Press ✠ Kent, Ohio

Crisis during the American Civil War

tiaries, ment, & Prisons

Angela M. Zombek

© 2018 by The Kent State University Press, Kent, Ohio 44242

All rights reserved

ISBN 978-1-60635-355-4

Manufactured in the United States of America

Cataloging information for this title is available at the Library of Congress.

22 21 20 19 18   5 4 3 2 1

Contents

Acknowledgments

I first thank God for surrounding me with extraordinary colleagues, friends, and family who encouraged me throughout the course of this project, which started as my dissertation at the University of Florida. I owe an enormous debt of gratitude to my dissertation committee chairs, William Link and Matt Gallman, for their direction, encouragement, and insightful feedback. I am also grateful to committee members Louise Newman, Jeff Adler, and Sevan Terzian for their thoughtful questions and commentary, which shaped my thinking as I revised the project from dissertation to book.

Numerous colleagues read and commented on drafts of this project, either as conference papers or independent chapters. My sincere thanks to Glenn Robbins, Bill Blair, Aaron Sheehan-Dean, Mark Grimsley, Peter Carmichael, Lesley Gordon, Greg Downs, Christina Bon, and Joyce Harrison for their feedback. Thank you to Gerry Wolfson-Grande, who combed through the manuscript and footnotes, and to Kevin Morrow, who helped me access collections at the National Archies. Will Underwood, my editor at Kent State University Press, and reviewers Michael Gray and Richard Bell offered invaluable suggestions for revision that pushed me to improve the manuscript.

My colleagues at St. Petersburg College have provided significant support over the years. I would especially like to thank my dean, Joseph Smiley, colleagues Greg Byrd, Nan Morelli-White, Linda Yakle, and my colleagues in the Social and Behavioral Sciences Department on the Clearwater Campus. I also owe a debt of gratitude to my students at SPC, especially those in the American History Research Club who served as research assistants. They include Shannon Johnson, Drew Tharaldson, Christina Stomper, Ramsey

Kwajaha, Hadley Koontz, Audrey Shaw, and Youstina Ebaid. I could not have completed the research for this project without the invaluable, expedient, and continuous help of St. Petersburg College's Interlibrary Loan staff. They include Wanda McCawthan, Danery Pacheco, Melinda McBride, and Joanne Arthur. I received generous funding to complete research for this project from numerous organizations, including the Mellon Research Fellowship Program at the Virginia Historical Society, the St. Petersburg College Center for Excellent Teaching and Learning Travel Grant Program, the North Caroliniana Society Archie K. Davis Fellowship Program, and the Friends of Andersonville POW Research Grant Program. Many thanks to Eric Leonard and Chris Barr for the time and knowledge that they shared with me while I was at the Andersonville National Historic Site.

This project would have been impossible without the support of friends and family members. I would especially like to thank the members of the North Pinellas YMCA who have, over the past six years, regularly attended the Cycle and Abs class that I teach. They have consistently provided me with much-needed mental breaks and laughter, which bolstered my energy to keep researching and writing. My brother, Joe, and sister-in-law, Lindsay, have provided invaluable love and encouragement throughout the course of this project. While working on this project, I met and married Theo Lorentzos and am grateful every day for his love, support, and encouragement. None of this would have been possible without the love and support of my parents, Frank and Nancy Zombek. They not only provided a second set of eyes on every word I have written, but have been my biggest cheerleaders throughout the entire course of my life. Words cannot express my appreciation and I dedicate this work to them.

Portions of this work appeared in earlier form in *Ohio History* 118 (2011), and in *Civil War History* 63, no. 3 (September 2017). Copyright © 2011 and 2017 by Kent State University Press. Reprinted with permission.

Introduction

In 1864, John King weighed the option of escape while he languished in an overcrowded Ohio prison. King knew that harsh punishment awaited failure. Guards could suspend inmates by their thumbs, which could cause insanity; compel hard labor with a ball and chain attached to the ankle; or buck and gag offenders for hours in a cold, solitary cell.[1] At first glance, it would appear that King wanted out of the Ohio Penitentiary—nineteenth-century contemporaries knew that penitentiary discipline included hard labor and physical punishments. In reality, King wanted to escape from Camp Chase, a Union military prison located a few miles from the Ohio Penitentiary. His recollections indicate that penitentiaries and Civil War military prisons shared much in common.

Almost forty years ago, historian Blake McKelvey, without explanation, stated that the Civil War "helped to coordinate in time and character the scattered strands of normal penological development."[2] McKelvey's assertion seemed calculated to incite inquiry and this study answers that call. It reveals that both military and civil officials drew on ideas about imprisonment that emerged with the establishment of antebellum penitentiaries to meet the war's crisis of imprisonment as they pressed existing penitentiaries into use, commandeered abandoned factories and warehouses, and constructed stockades and barracks to hold wartime offenders. It demonstrates that the civil and military disciplinary programs were intimately connected since antebellum penal reformers drew on military discipline to formulate the penitentiary program and wartime military officials directed the operation of military prisons by incorporating aspects of the penitentiary program into military discipline.

A comprehensive story of Civil War military prisons can be told only when viewed in proper context since wartime officials relied heavily on antebellum practices to manage thousands of captives. Antebellum assumptions about prison administration, the proper treatment of inmates, inmates' identity, and methods of punishment born in penitentiaries shaped the administration of both Union and Confederate military prisons. Wartime prison officials and inmates reflected awareness of the penitentiary program in their writing as they conceptualized the relationship between administrators and inmates, as they implemented or experienced punishment, and as prisoners and prison administrators interacted with the outside world. The nature of Civil War military prisons was complex and it is impossible to extract these institutions from trends in nineteenth-century penal development, especially in a republic devoid of a standing army and largely immune from military conflicts.

Placing Civil War military prisons in the broader narrative of the development of nineteenth-century imprisonment reveals that concerns wartime contemporaries voiced about military prisons were, in fact, similar to those that surrounded penitentiaries before, during, and after the Civil War. Antebellum, wartime, and postwar officials worried about the cost of imprisonment, overcrowding, supply shortages, physical punishment, and inmates' psychological and physical distress. The Civil War magnified these problems since almost every household had a family member or close friend who fought, died, or was imprisoned during the conflict. Thus, wartime imprisonment attracted more widespread attention since many inmates were middle- and upper-class citizen-soldiers or civilians who, in ordinary circumstances, would likely have never experienced military service or imprisonment. The development of the penitentiary program in the antebellum period shaped Americans' interpretations of the Civil War's crisis of imprisonment since penitentiaries established expectations for prison operation and framed inmates' identity.

This work does not evaluate claims of intentional maltreatment or the degree to which prisoners suffered in each type of institution since Civil War scholars have already told this story. Rather, it focuses on how the Civil War's crisis of imprisonment elicited discussion among prison officials, inmates, and the general public about many long-standing problems, procedures, and relationships born from antebellum ideas about imprisonment. Military prisons were highly visible and widely discussed temporary holding facilities that Union and Confederate authorities hastily established to meet the war's unanticipated crisis of imprisonment. The only basis that Civil War contemporaries had to interpret these new institutions and the prisoner-of-war crisis came from ideas that informed the penitentiary program. These concepts manifested themselves in military prison officials' administrative practices, in prisoners' self-perception and behavior, and in public commentary on military prisons and wartime penitentiaries.

War-inspired claims of morality and accusations of inhumanity stemmed from antebellum assumptions about the proper function of imprisonment and ideas about how inmates should be treated. These emerged at the turn of the nineteenth century when middle-class reformers created the penitentiary program. The advent of long-term imprisonment as punishment inspired states to construct imposing penitentiaries that, unlike jails, were sanitary, cost-effective, and detained inmates from a period of months to many years. Penitentiary officials stressed cost-effectiveness, the merits of labor, the value of silence, the necessity of religious and educational instruction, the benefits of physical punishment, and, ultimately, the idea that humane incarceration could reform offenders into productive civilians.

Civil War contemporaries believed that if penitentiary officials treated criminals humanely, then military officials should afford military prison inmates comparable, if not better, treatment. Antebellum ideas about imprisonment applied to all types of Union and Confederate military prisons from commandeered factories and abandoned warehouses, to hastily constructed barracks and stockades, and to penitentiaries and jails.[3] They also applied to each type of prisoner held during wartime.

Federal officials categorized captives in three ways: prisoners of war, who were captured enemy soldiers or sailors; United States prisoners, who were military men held for crimes, like theft and murder; and prisoners of state/political prisoners, who were civilians suspected of treason defined by the Constitution as "levying war" against the United States or "adhering to their Enemies, giving them aid and comfort." Despite classifications, wartime prisoners—and Union and Confederate officials—could not fully disassociate incarceration from criminality, especially since the Federal Government reserved the right to try Rebel leaders and even prisoners of war for treason, a civil offense punishable by civil courts.[4]

Civil War contemporaries routinely echoed antebellum concerns and arguments about imprisonment, but thus far scholars of both antebellum penitentiaries and Civil War military prisons have considered each institutional type in isolation. Scholars of the antebellum period pause penitentiary studies in 1860 and resume in 1865, while Civil War scholars analyze military prisons solely within the context of the war, often focus on individual military prisons, analyze the magnitude of prisoners' suffering, and debate the extent to which Northern and Southern officials retaliated against enemy prisoners.[5]

Retaliation, however, was not surprising given the broader legal context. As John Fabian Witt has noted, Enlightenment-inspired eighteenth-century jurists built retaliation into the laws of war. Later, Francis Lieber, noted political theorist and author of General Orders No. 100, simultaneously condemned and condoned retaliation. The order codified the antebellum emphasis on morality by asserting that warfare does not negate the fact that men are moral beings "responsible to one another, and to God." It directed that prisoners should be spared from cruel treatment, want of food, mutilation, death, or "any other barbarity," but immediately stated that prisoners remained liable to "the infliction of retaliatory measures." Lieber also left open the possibility of justifiable cruelty by allowing captors to modify treatment of prisoners according to the demands of safety.[6] The laws of war were confusing and elicited the questions of how Civil War contemporaries determined notions of proper prison management and proper treatment of inmates. The key lies in looking to the antebellum period to witness how state officials administered, inmates experienced, and the public perceived the advent and operation of the penitentiary program.

The penitentiary became a physical reality in several states, but it was first and foremost an idea. States, both in the North and South, established penitentiaries in two waves—the first around 1790 and the second around 1820. Only Florida, North Carolina, and South Carolina were without a penitentiary by 1861.[7] States constructed penitentiaries on either the Pennsylvania system of constant solitary confinement and individual labor, or the Auburn system of congregate labor by day and solitary confinement by night. Regardless of differences in how inmates worked, both organizational programs emphasized that sentences should be just, that is, tailored to the offense; that inmates should be well provisioned; that labor, physical activity, education, and religious instruction benefited inmates; and that corporal punishment and suffering should be tempered.

These ideas about imprisonment and punishment born in penitentiaries transcended institutional type and were apparent in military prisons.

Americans, in both the antebellum and Civil War years, clung to these ideals. Reformers demanded change before the war and prisoners and their acquaintances clamored for justice during the war. David Rothman has argued that American elites established penitentiaries to ensure the safety of the republic.[8] Penitentiaries were supposed to reform criminals into responsible citizens, and middle-class reformers initially expressed confidence in inmates' ability to change. But this optimism and the penitentiary's reform agenda, which failed by midcentury, rendered penitentiaries holding pens for criminals who, in the antebellum period, were mostly lower class and/or immigrants.[9] Scholars, such as Michael Ignatieff, Erving Goffman, Mary Gibson, David Garland, and L. Mara Dodge, consequently contended that the imprisonment's purpose was punishment.[10] Instead of focusing on reform, penitentiary officers lamented inadequate supply, poor discipline, and overcrowding, and these problems later plagued military prison officials.

Since the reform program failed, the role and the practical operation of penitentiaries and military prisons were similar. Both penitentiaries and military prisons served the same function in nineteenth-century American society—punishment. They detained malefactors to protect the community from dangers, be they criminals, enemy combatants, or treason suspects.[11] Union and Confederate officials established military prisons for much the same reason that led to the establishment of penitentiaries—to ensure social order amid change.

Penitentiaries and military prisons thus conform to David Garland's assertion that punishment was historically determined. Penitentiary punishment resulted from the turn-of-the-century notion that the state should assume responsibility for criminals while military prisons emerged to chastise enemies and preserve loyalty during wartime.[12] Penitentiaries and military prisons were central to social order since they sequestered criminals, prevented prisoners of war from bolstering enemy forces, and discouraged treason by detaining individuals who were suspected of and/or guilty of subversion.[13]

The wartime crisis of imprisonment necessitated federal involvement with prisons, but national authorities had little experience with criminal justice given the system of federalism and decentralized control over punishment in the antebellum period. The Weberian notion of state formation, which contends that the central government gains authority by securing a monopoly on the legitimate use of force and establishing institutions like prisons, does not apply easily to the United States. Criminality, pauperism, and insanity were, in the late colonial and early national periods, problems with which families and local communities dealt first. In the antebellum period, state governments bore responsibility for imprisonment and state legislatures and governors directed penitentiary funding and oversight.[14] The development of carceral institutions came from the bottom up—first, with the construction of local and county jails; second, with the establishment of state penitentiaries; and third, with national authorities' hasty creation of wartime military prisons.

The Federal Government remained relatively weak in the antebellum period while state governments passed numerous criminal laws and controlled imprisonment. Instead of creating federal prisons beyond the Penitentiary of the District of Columbia, Congress directed that state penitentiaries house federal offenders. The Federal Government did not assume an active role in criminal justice until the Civil War. Then Congress created military tribunals that tried civilians for numerous offenses (ranging from treason to sabotage to moral offenses and fraud), Allan Pinkerton's detective agency became the secret service branch of the Union Army, the Bureau of Internal Revenue enforced tax laws, and military prisons detained enemy combatants and treason suspects.[15] But these national developments gave the Federal Government only temporary power. Military tribunals faded during Reconstruction, the federal income tax was repealed in 1872, and military prisons shut their doors a few years after war's end.

The Civil War necessitated that federal officials assume greater control over imprisonment and this development occurred, in many cases, much to the chagrin of state politicians, who were accustomed to overseeing prisons and prisoners within state borders. The states created the only blueprint for prison management available to national officials, and this ideal guided the response to the Civil War's prisoner-of-war crisis. As Union and Confederate officials suspended habeas corpus, incarcerated treason suspects, and held enemy captives, the national governments exercised centralized power over imprisonment that was unheard of in the antebellum period.[16] As Union and Confederate officials assumed responsibility for imprisonment, they relied on antebellum practices to manage newly established military prisons and existing penitentiaries that held prisoners of war. But they often crossed lines with state politicians in the process.

The United States had no overarching prison system and national authorities relied on the states to hold and discipline federal offenders, so Union and Confederate officials logically imitated penitentiary practices to operate military prisons. State governors, meanwhile, assumed that they maintained control over any prison within their state's borders and often authorized their own inspections of military prisons or demanded that national officials inspect the sites. During the war years, federal and state officials even shared some of the same foibles apparent in antebellum prison administration. State officials appointed to oversee penitentiaries and federal officials appointed to oversee military prisons were, like others involved in criminal justice, including public defenders and attorneys, without experience and professional training.[17]

Federal oversight of imprisonment in the North and the South was controversial since civilians were more comfortable with state authorities running prisons. Many antebellum Americans felt, as historian Lawrence Friedman has noted, that it was "important" to restrain "the national government" in criminal matters.[18] This sentiment remained during the war as the Union and Confederate governments established military prisons and assumed responsibility for prisoners in numbers that far exceeded penitentiary populations. Imprisonment, however, leveled distinctions between inmates, regardless of whether state or federal officials oversaw a prison, and regardless of whether they found themselves in a military prison or in a penitentiary.[19] Many wartime prisoners, including many in military prisons, often thought of themselves as felons since penitentiaries solidified the association of imprisonment with criminality.

This study demonstrates how ideas about penitentiary operation influenced the practical operation of Civil War military prisons by focusing on both types of institutions located in the District of Columbia and in four states: Ohio, Virginia, Georgia, and North Carolina. Analysis rests primarily on the war years, 1861–65, but inquiry also highlights the antebellum establishment, operation, and public perception of penitentiaries in these locations. The study concludes in 1870, the year that prison reformers gathered in Cincinnati, Ohio, and formed the National Prison Association. This provides an opportunity to assess the Civil War's immediate impact on imprisonment, to examine the operation and closing of military prisons during Reconstruction, and to analyze how familiar concerns regarding penitentiaries influenced North Carolinians as they debated penitentiary construction in the late 1860s.

Analysis of these sites fills gaps in scholarship on both penitentiaries and military prisons. First, this study's focus on the District of Columbia, Ohio,

Virginia, Georgia, and North Carolina breaks with the extant scholarly focus on penitentiaries and imprisonment in the Northeast since that region witnessed the birth of the Auburn and Pennsylvania systems.[20] Instead, this study illuminates similarities and differences in penal administration in the three major geographic regions of the nineteenth-century United States: The industrialized North, the agricultural West (Old Northwest), and the slave-holding South.[21] Washington, D.C., Ohio, Virginia, Georgia, and North Carolina represent these regions and facilitate analysis of imprisonment in the seat of federal power, the seat of Confederate power, and the locus of state power in the burgeoning Old Northwest and in the slaveholding upper and lower South. This model also allows for comparison of Northern and Southern imprisonment, which remains largely absent in scholarship.[22]

All sites in question, with the exception of North Carolina, established penitentiaries before the Civil War. Many antebellum North Carolinians argued that the state legislature should have authorized penitentiary construction before the Civil War given the success of other state penitentiaries. State legislators did not answer this call until after the war, providing an excellent opportunity to analyze how antebellum impulses, the Civil War, and its aftermath informed the debates surrounding authorization of the North Carolina Penitentiary.

This study also adds significantly to scholarship on Civil War prisons since it directly compares the operation of penitentiaries and military prisons within the U.S. capital; the Confederate capital; a state capital, Columbus, Ohio; and in two Southern states—Georgia, where the state penitentiary was located in the state capital of Milledgeville, with Andersonville far-removed in Americus; and North Carolina, whose town of Salisbury was said to have been home to one of the first "penitentiaries" in the new Confederacy. Focusing on these states and on the Federal District facilitates analysis of military prisons in light of broader trends of nineteenth-century imprisonment and examination of how the state and national governments either shared or disputed control over military prisons.

The study focuses on five penitentiaries and six military prisons. In Ohio, analysis centers on the Ohio Penitentiary, Camp Chase Prison, and Johnson's Island Prison; in Washington, the Penitentiary for the District of Columbia (D.C. Penitentiary) and Old Capitol Prison; in Virginia, the Virginia Penitentiary and Castle Thunder Prison; in Georgia, the Georgia Penitentiary and Andersonville Prison; and in North Carolina, Salisbury

Prison and the North Carolina Penitentiary as a proposal before the war and as reality after the war. Throughout the century, these penitentiaries detained not only common criminals, but also prisoners of war and soldiers guilty of crime. Likewise, the six military prisons held prisoners of war, treason suspects, spies, and other enemies of the state in addition to criminals, signaling commonalities between the two types of institutions and underscoring the difficulty of classifying and separating inmates.

It is important to note how authorities classified individuals held in penitentiaries and in military prisons, but this study does not focus on the causes of crime and its changing patterns over time. Primary interest rests on administrative practices, punishments, inmates' experiences and identity formation, and public perception of imprisonment. The crimes that individuals committed did not impact prisoners' treatment or confinement since imprisonment was a leveling experience. Research on the antebellum and war years, with the exception of Andersonville, revealed scant evidence that race influenced inmates' treatment and experiences since the majority of inmates incarcerated before and during the Civil War were white or poor immigrants.[23] Gender and class, especially during the Civil War, are the only significant variables found in evidence pertaining to the selected sites that influenced administrative decisions and inmates' experiences.

The military prisons under consideration also illuminate how antebellum assumptions about imprisonment informed administrators and influenced inmates at numerous military prisons regardless of their physical construction and population. Old Capitol Prison and Castle Thunder were commandeered buildings, Camp Chase and Johnson's Island were barracks enclosed by high fences, Salisbury was a combination of brick buildings surrounded by a high fence, and Andersonville was a hastily constructed open-air stockade. Inmates in four military prisons under consideration—Old Capitol Prison, Castle Thunder, Camp Chase, and Johnson's Island—represent the average population of military prisons. According to Lonnie Speer, the maximum capacity and most inmates held at these prisons was as follows: Old Capitol Prison, capacity of 500, most held 2,673; Castle Thunder, capacity of 1,400, most held 3,000+; Camp Chase, capacity of 4,000, most held 9,423; and Johnson's Island, capacity of 1,000, most held 3,256. Salisbury and Andersonville were exceptional since the highest number of inmates held exceeded 10,000 at each facility. Andersonville's maximum capacity was 10,000, but prison population peaked at 32,899; Salisbury's maximum capacity was 2,000, a figure comparable to Castle Thunder and lower than Camp Chase, but Salisbury's population peaked at 10,321.

In his study, Speer recorded 117 total Confederate and 106 Union military prisons. Of the known population totals, Speer listed one Confederate and eight Union prisons holding under one hundred inmates; twenty-two Confederate and twenty-five Union prisons holding from one hundred to 999 prisoners; six Confederate and five Union prisons holding 1,000 to 1,999 inmates; one Confederate and three Union prisons holding from 2,000 to 2,999 captives; three Confederate and three Union prisons holding from 3,000 to 3,999 prisoners; and three Confederate and one Union prison(s) holding from 4,000 to 4,999 inmates. The number of military prisons holding over 5,000 prisoners was nominal, and extremely large prisons that held over 10,000 were few. They include Camp Douglas (Chicago) at 12,082, Fort Delaware (Delaware) at 12,600, Point Lookout (Maryland) at 22,000, Belle Isle (Richmond) at 10,000, Salisbury (North Carolina) at 10,321, and Andersonville (Georgia) at 32,899.[24]

This study shifts the focus from overcrowding and prisoners' consequent suffering to the common experience of confinement, which includes how prison officials and inmates administered and experienced punishment, how inmates and guards constructed their identity, how they experienced life in captivity, interacted with the outside world, and reacted to each other amid the prison's shifting power dynamics.[25] It follows Larry Goldsmith's call to view the prison "from the inside out," focusing on the internal world of the prison from the perspective of officials and, perhaps more significantly, prisoners, who, especially in the case of penitentiary inmates, left few records.[26]

The study begins in the antebellum period and analyzes the interplay of civil and military law. Chapter 1: "Shared Theories: Commonalities among Federal, State, Civil, and Military Punishments," examines how military law and punishments, and military personnel themselves, envisioned, shaped, and implemented the penitentiary program as the United States developed in the antebellum period. Penitentiaries and the Regular Army were established to control the unruly lower classes. Criminals filled both penitentiaries and the ranks of the largely despised, but numerically small, Regular Army. Individuals in both of these institutions were the first to experience military and penitentiary discipline, and these reprimands, which included physical punishment and solitary confinement, were the same in both institutions. Middle-class penal reformers, including the famed Francis Lieber, represented a small group that gave much thought to these punishments and the inmates who bore the brunt of them. Nonetheless, reformers shaped assumptions about imprisonment, and signaled the problems apparent with it, prior to the war.

The establishment of the penitentiaries and military prisons under consideration is the subject of Chapter 2: "Penitentiaries and Military Prisons: Built on Common Ground." This chapter traces the antebellum foundations of the Ohio, Virginia, District of Columbia, and Georgia penitentiaries, and highlights the debate among North Carolina politicians over establishing their own state penitentiary. It also examines the establishment of Camp Chase, Johnson's Island, Old Capitol Prison, Castle Thunder, Salisbury, and Andersonville. The chapter details the purpose of penitentiaries and military prisons, and concentrates on the common characteristics found in both types of institutions, which include the mixing of civilian and military prisoners, the goal of institutional self-sufficiency, the emphasis on religious instruction, and the role of prison labor as an economic, punitive, and/or reformatory tool. Chapter 2 ultimately underscores the shift in the basic tenet of early nineteenth-century incarceration from reform to punitive detention.

Chapter 3: "Regulating Operation: Penitentiary and Military Prison Officials' Quest for Order," demonstrates how the state government officials assumed primary responsibility for incarceration during the antebellum period, but during the Civil War the central government—both North and South—increased involvement in imprisonment through the creation of military prisons and use of state penitentiaries to punish military offenders. National officials relied heavily on penitentiary practices to oversee military prisons and administer punishment. By focusing on administration, regulations, infractions, and punishments, Chapter 3 clearly shows the commonalities between military prisons and penitentiaries. The chapter also highlights debate that surrounded controversial forms of corporal punishment—whippings and lethal force.

Prison officials wielded much power, but inmates were far from powerless. Chapter 4: "The Internal World of the Prison: Inmates' Identity and Disobedience," highlights the administration, regulations, infractions, and punishments in penitentiaries and military prisons, but traces how inmates manipulated rules and shaped the internal dynamics of prisons. The chapter examines how penitentiary inmates forged their identity and how the stigma of imprisonment shaped the self-perception of military prison inmates as they compared themselves to criminals. The focus of Chapter 4 is on the words and actions of the inmates themselves, shifting from administrative policies to the personal worlds and actions of male inmates. It also looks at how inmates endured punishments, revealing striking similarities between penitentiaries and military prisons.

Chapter 5: "Life Out There: Inmates' Communications with the Outside World," looks at the basic human need for communication and social interaction through the accounts of administrators, inmates, and family members. Inmates at both penitentiaries and military prisons tried to overcome isolation by turning to established avenues such as social standing and political connections when seeking pardon. They also invoked traditional values such as good character, family obligation, and male duty to strengthen their pleas. Overriding all, however, was the need for communication and human interaction. Chapter 5 reveals both positive and negative communications as inmates confronted guards and officials, or undertook more docile forms of interaction such as letter writing and longed-for visits with family members.

Chapter 6: "Shifting Power Dynamics: Abused Privileges and Escape Attempts," continues the focus on inmates' identity by looking at how their desire for freedom inspired escape attempts. Outsiders fretted over escaped prisoners, whether criminals or prisoners of war. But prisoners of war and the laws of war considered escape to be a right, albeit potentially deadly, since guards could shoot at prisoners in flight. This chapter details how inmates in both penitentiaries and military prisons used privileges to free themselves, attempted escape individually, or planned escape en masse. It also details the methods that guards employed to prevent or thwart breakouts.

Chapter 7: "Fallen from Grace: The Experience of Female Inmates," examines how the few women incarcerated in the antebellum period shaped their identity even though polite society deemed them incapable of reform. It highlights how antebellum journalists judged their state's morality on the number of female inmates and details how the Civil War brought about an increase in confined women, which elicited similar discussion about female morality and the behavior of female prisoners. Women in the antebellum and Civil War years behaved in much the same way as their male counterparts when they challenged prison regulations, interacted with each other, plotted escape, yearned for connections with those at home, and clamored for release.

Chapter 8: "War's Legacy: Closing Military Prisons and Rethinking Penitentiaries," examines the period 1865–70, when the Federal Government took over Southern military prisons, used them to punish high-ranking Confederate officials, slowly released enemy prisoners, and then shut down both Northern and Southern military prisons as civilians demanded restoration of civil authority and cessation of military authority after the war. It examines how the rhetoric of reform, which was so important to the creation of the penitentiary program, influenced the closing of military prisons, inspired postwar investigations into military prisons and penitentiaries, and shaped the deliberations of North Carolina politicians and journalists as they debated construction of a state penitentiary. Those debates echoed the ideas of the original penitentiary proponents, who argued for a humane solution to crime at the turn of the nineteenth century.

The Conclusion comments on the legacy of the Civil War's crisis of imprisonment, and the postwar debates over—and failure of—reform. None of these discussions would have been possible had not the civil and military sectors been so intertwined in the nineteenth century as military punishments informed the penitentiary program and as penitentiary operation, in turn, shaped how military officials dealt with imprisonment during the nation's largest internecine conflict.

Shared Theories

Commonalities among Federal, State, Civil, and Military Punishments

Thirty-one months of war seemed more like an eternity and gave Northerners and Southerners plenty of time to realize that their soldiers were suffering in enemy prisons. In late November 1863, after inspecting Richmond's military prisons with a group of six other U.S. Army and Navy surgeons, Daniel Meeker disgustedly reported that each man firmly believed that "no prison or penitentiary ever seen . . . in a Northern State equaled, in cheerlessness, unhealthiness, and paucity of rations issued, either of the military prisons of Richmond, Virginia."[1] As Meeker's complaint indicates, Civil War contemporaries judged the function of and conditions in military prisons according to the same standards as the penitentiary program.

Historian Leslie Patrick has noted that scholars view nineteenth-century institutions, including penitentiaries and the military, in isolation from one another thereby obscuring commonalities and missing an opportunity to analyze the larger social and political purposes of confinement.[2] The Civil War inspired a crisis of imprisonment never before seen, but contemporaries judged wartime incarceration by their understanding of antebellum imprisonment and punishment. The interplay between civil and military punishments was enormous throughout the nineteenth century. It informed the establishment of penitentiaries, shaped the notions that reformers used to evaluate imprisonment, inspired humanitarian concerns, and guided how Americans handled prisoners of war. This interplay provides the appropriate context for full understanding of the Civil War's crisis of imprisonment as the Federal Government, for the first time, took charge of prisons and employed lessons from state oversight of penitentiaries, and as Americans echoed concerns about incarceration that antebellum civilians commonly raised.

Since imprisonment as punishment developed in the antebellum period, Civil War contemporaries associated imprisonment with criminality and military prison inmates often felt stigmatized by captivity. Public concern for prisoners' plight magnified as the prisoner-of-war crisis escalated and the Lieber Code defined the Civil War as a war of imprisonment. Penitentiary and military prison inmates had similar experiences of incarceration since it stripped all inmates of independence. Civilians and soldiers confined in military prisons and penitentiaries during wartime lamented that they were treated the same as, or worse than, criminals.[3] But this wartime outcry would not have been as great if not for popular knowledge of the penitentiary program, which gripped public imagination and established the expectation that imprisonment should be humane.

Outcries against mass incarceration heightened during the Civil War when volunteer citizen-soldiers flooded the ranks in 1861 and 1862, undertaking a military life they otherwise would never have considered. The United States was a young nation in 1861 and the development of institutions like penitentiaries and the Regular Army were in their infancy, but the organizational and punitive structure of both were cut from the same cloth. Civil War contemporaries were familiar with the underlying philosophy of imprisonment and army officials understood the system of military punishment. Physical punishment and mental control were central to both, since members of the Regular Army and penitentiary inmates, men who shared the distinction of being lower class and/or criminals, needed paternal guidance.

Despite the Federal Government's attempts to separate Regular Army units from volunteer forces, they could not—and did not—exclude volunteers from military punishment. Military discipline was often physical and involved isolation and reduced rations, as did penitentiary punishments. These reprimands, routine in military life and at penitentiaries, were abhorred by the polite society from which Northern and Southern citizen-soldiers came.

The Civil War's crisis of imprisonment and the concerns that dominated discussions about military prisons echoed familiar antebellum refrains. It is impossible to fully comprehend the administration of, inmates' experiences in, and public perception of Civil War military prisons without con-

sidering the ideological underpinnings and shortcomings of the penitentiary program; the organization, public perception, and disciplinary system
of the Regular Army; and America's handling of prisoners of war during the
Revolution, the War of 1812, and the Mexican War. Penitentiary program
founders borrowed from military punishment and thought the new institutions could reform criminals. Penitentiaries fell short of humanitarian ideals by midcentury, but they set the expectation that prison officials should
afford inmates humane treatment. Despite the failure of reform, antebellum reformers continued to judge penitentiaries on their founding ideals,
thereby establishing a precedent on which to judge other institutions of
confinement throughout the Civil War era.

The Enlightenment and Penitentiary Establishment

The penitentiary program resulted from the Enlightenment, stressed humane treatment of inmates, and reflected late eighteenth- and early nineteenth-century reformers' belief that institutions could transform criminals
into productive citizens.[4] After the Revolution, American reformers entered
the discussion, already underway in Europe, about how best to discipline
criminals and concluded that states should control reformatory institutions.[5]

American reformers wanted to establish new institutions of confinement
that would be free of the problems that plagued local and county jails in the
North and the South. Localities and counties erected jails haphazardly and
hastily, using whatever materials that were readily available—usually lumber and logs. Inmates consequently suffered from infectious diseases that
spread through the jails' stagnant air. Local officials, however, cared little
for captives and ignored these problems. In the colonial period, jails held
the dregs of society—prisoners awaiting trial, debtors, and individuals who
failed to pay restitution. In the nineteenth century, local and county jails
continued to hold these offenders and remained unsecure, filthy, degraded,
degrading, poorly run, and cruel.[6] Reformers, imbued with Enlightenment
optimism and hope for the New Republic at the turn of the nineteenth century, demanded an alternative.

Americans' philosophies about crime changed as the Revolutionary period
faded into the Early National period. Colonials dealt with crime, illiteracy,
poverty, and insanity on an individual level, but Jacksonians believed that

institutions such as penitentiaries, asylums, orphanages, and schools, which reflected democratic values and promoted social stability, could solve social problems and ensure community cohesion.[7] Nineteenth-century reformers believed that the penitentiary program would reform the minds and souls of criminals through solitude, education, labor, and religious instruction. State penitentiaries adopted either the Pennsylvania system of constant solitary confinement and individual labor, or the Auburn system, in which inmates labored in congregate shops by day and spent nights in solitude.[8] Penitentiaries in Virginia, Georgia, Ohio, and the District of Columbia, among others, adopted the latter model, believing it would yield countless benefits.

Optimistic penitentiary architects and proponents extolled the seemingly limitless virtues of the institutions. North Carolina inspectors monitored the Virginia Penitentiary as they pondered constructing their own and deemed the Virginia facility an immediate success. In 1810, a North Carolina investigative committee praised the Virginia Penitentiary's superintendent, Mr. Douglas, who transformed the prison into "not only an excellent mean for the reformation of criminals, but likewise a source of considerable profit to the State." Positive assessments were contagious, and penitentiary supporters in Georgia likewise expressed nothing but hope for their prison. Even before the Georgia Penitentiary opened its doors, the *Georgia Journal,* in 1816, praised it as a magnificent sight and "a proud monument of the wisdom, public spirit, and humane policy of our state." The penitentiary's potential was boundless. "Independent of its humanity," stated the *Journal,* "the Penitentiary system promises . . . a handsome annual revenue."[9] Prison labor would relieve law-abiding citizens from the financial burden of detaining criminals and would repay society as reformed, industrious civilians left the penitentiary at the end of their sentences.

Penitentiary proponents, reformers, and newspapermen continued to extol penitentiaries as time progressed. In 1837, the *Alton Telegraph* (Illinois) confidently stated that the Ohio Penitentiary was "superior to any institution of the kind in the United States" and credited the penitentiary's esteemed officers for its good order. Correspondents of the Baltimore *Sun* felt the same about the D.C. Penitentiary. They boasted in 1852 that it was "one of the best arranged prisons in this country" and contended that "none can surpass it in regard to neatness and cleanliness." The *Sun* echoed these sentiments the following year, claiming that the penitentiary was yet in the "best condition" under the management of an "excellent warden," Mr. Jonas B. Ellis. Seven years earlier, the New Orleans *Times Picayune* trumpeted reformer Dorothea Dix's overwhelming satisfaction with the Georgia Penitentiary. Dix claimed that the penitentiary's arrangement and management were "unsurpassed by anything of the sort in the country."[10]

Problems in Penitentiaries

All of these reviews were positive, and the fact that newspapers printed stories about penitentiaries outside of their home states evidenced widespread public interest in them. But these glowing reviews also contained a dark side. They hinted that penitentiary supporters were, by the 1840s and 1850s, on the defensive as deteriorating conditions inspired inquiry into penitentiary operation. Circumstances in Georgia became so dire that the state House of Representatives passed a bill in 1832 to abolish penitentiary discipline in the state.[11] Perhaps penitentiary conditions honestly improved by the time of Dix's visit the following decade, but either way, the conflicting reports on the merits of the penitentiary program indicate how difficult it was to get an accurate, unbiased idea of what went on behind prison walls. The public knew only what penitentiaries *should* be—sites of humanity, morality, education, improvement, and reform just as penitentiary program architects had envisioned. Americans continued to judge imprisonment by these ideals despite the fact that the penitentiary program failed by midcentury.

By 1860, public optimism faded and the reform system crumbled as a result of dwindling state funds, corruption, lack of trained guards, and overcrowding, but the general public disregarded the plight of criminals. Only a handful of reformers voiced concern. Religious instruction, moral guidance, solitude, and silence were supposed to be pillars of the penitentiary program, but resident chaplains, Sunday services, and Bible study either never materialized or fell by the wayside, as did solitary confinement. The Ohio Penitentiary provides a good example. Some penitentiary committee members immediately doubted the institution's success and complained that it betrayed the founding goal of guaranteeing moral discipline. In January 1831, a decade during which many reformers praised the penitentiary program, one Ohio Penitentiary Committee member railed, in an article from the *Huron Reflector* of Norwalk, Ohio, that the prison failed "in every object for which it was designed." The journalist contended that the penitentiary was "not even a place of safe keeping, and much less for the punishment and profitable employment of the convicts." This assessment, and the *Reflector*'s evaluation of the Ohio Penitentiary twelve years later, contradicted the praise that the institution garnered in the late 1830s and raised the question of whether the institution had improved and then immediately declined, or if earlier accounts ignored deficiencies.

In 1843, the *Huron Reflector* printed another damning article that condemned state officials for failing to provide a chaplain and consistent religious instruction for convicts. "The design of punishment is not revenge," the paper emphatically stated, "A higher and holier purpose exists . . . the preservation of society, and the reform of the offender."[12] The Ohio Penitentiary met none of those goals in its current state. Even though penitentiaries generated increasing scrutiny throughout the 1840s and 1850s, there was disconnect between rhetoric demanding reform and steps taken to fix growing and persistent problems. Reformers' arguments for improvements made them look good, but in reality the middle and upper classes cared little for inmates, who were the dregs from foreign lands and/or the lower classes.

During the late 1830s and early 1840s, a growing percentage of poor immigrants crowded state penitentiaries causing white middle-class civilians to lose interest in improving conditions.[13] Put simply, it was much cheaper to let penitentiaries get crowded. By midcentury, the silent system and solitary confinement vanished and discipline eroded at penitentiaries on both the Auburn and Pennsylvania models.[14] Regardless of the failure of the reform program, civilians evaluated imprisonment and state officials and reformers based inspection reports on the penitentiary program's founding ideals throughout the century.

Evaluating Penitentiaries and Military Prisons

During the Civil War, Union and Confederate officials and Northern and Southern civilians and prisoners evaluated military prisons based on penitentiary ideals. Concerns like sanitation, prisoner mortality, and just punishment became pronounced in the antebellum period and persisted into the war years. Two important sources reflect the main concerns of antebellum reformers that, perhaps unbeknownst to them, would linger beyond 1860: the annual reports of the Board of Managers of the Boston Prison Discipline Society and the writings of Francis Lieber, who vehemently defended the penitentiary program.

The Boston Prison Discipline Society published its first annual report in 1826. These reports provide a window into how antebellum reformers defined concerns that dominated discussions about imprisonment during the Civil War. The Reports of the Boston Prison Discipline Society are especially significant because they analyzed confinement across institutional types and national borders. Annual reports included findings on prisons in Europe, and on insane asylums, local and county jails, and juvenile houses of refuge in the United States. The Twenty-Third Annual Report published in 1848 even included a report on military imprisonment in Great Britain.[15] The comprehensive report reveals that nineteenth-century contemporaries applied common assumptions about the operation, management, internal conditions, and the experience of inmates to all carceral institutions, which transcended state— and even national—borders. Consequently, society members contended that the way localities, states, and nations treated inmates revealed their people's true character.

The society's reports outlined standards that prisons should meet. With regard to prison construction, they asserted that there should be "particular regard to *Security, Solitary Confinement at night, Inspection, Ventilation, Light, Cleanliness, Instruction and Sickness.*" Additionally, the society stressed that prisons should be orderly and outlined rules and regulations for the institutions' cleanliness, classification of inmates, prisoners' clothing, their diet, their employment, the mode of punishment, and the governance of prisons.[16] Two other major concerns that the society consistently emphasized were religious instruction and, more significantly, the rate of inmate mortality.

Concern about good ventilation, mild punishment, inmate mortality, and cleanliness remained constant throughout the nineteenth century in all carceral institutions. Members of the Boston Prison Discipline Society expressed angst over these deficiencies in their evaluation of penitentiaries and asserted that penitentiary oversight committees should improve treatment of lowly criminals. It is therefore not surprising that cries of injustice became louder during the Civil War, when citizen-soldiers, especially those of the middle and upper classes, suffered incarceration. The cries of the latter group, however, were louder and more abundant, and were recorded by literate male and female inmates, and not merely by select groups of reformers.

One difference between antebellum penitentiary inmates and wartime prisoners was that the former group left a scant written record, which shed little firsthand light on captivity, while literate middle and upper-class prisoners of war wrote copious letters home and countless diary entries that chronicled confinement. Penitentiary reports by wardens, physicians, and chaplains, if one was present, offered factual but often biased accounts of prison administration and imprisonment's impact on prisoners, forcing one to read between the lines for insight into inmates' lives.[17] Reform society reports offered the closest interpretation of incarceration as inmates might have seen it. Their accounts were replete with chronicles of imprisonment's problems and cries for change, which, in many cases, went unheeded.

Boston Prison Discipline Society members demanded that all should "be done to prevent suffering and sickness" among inmates and argued that sufficient ventilation and good water supply were absolute necessities. Polite society assumed that criminals should work to pay for their own confinement, but penitentiary officials bore responsibility for providing basic necessities and reasonable comfort, resorting to physical punishment only if necessary. The Boston reformers directed that inmates should receive "wholesome food in sufficient quantities" to preserve life and health and commanded that guards refrain from imprudent and cruel punishments. In the same breath, however, reformers condoned punishments such as stripes (whipping), chains, and solitary confinement on reduced diet, indicating that these were acceptable, even beneficial, punishments.[18] Penitentiary officials and certainly army officers, did not view these reprimands as torturous, but rather as an appropriate price to pay for disobedience.

Reformers condoned physical punishment, but they had no tolerance for high mortality rates in penitentiaries. It did not take long for Boston Prison Discipline Society members to signal this great concern that later dominated public discussion of Civil War military prisons. In their second report, the reformers noted that the mortality rate in penitentiaries in New York City and Philadelphia was 6 percent, a sharp contrast to those in Maine, New Hampshire, Vermont, Massachusetts, and at the state penitentiary at Auburn (New York), where it amounted to 2 percent. Society members demanded action and contended that this alarming difference necessitated immediate investigation. "THERE SHOULD BE NO SHRINK-

ING FROM SUCH AN INVESTIGATION," they screamed in 1827, "THE FACTS DEMAND IT." During this year, the population in the prisons under question ranged anywhere from one hundred to six hundred inmates, small totals when compared to Civil War military prisons.[19] Nonetheless, subsequent reports reveal that inmate mortality, even if only a small percentage, was a well-established concern before the Civil War. The reformers decried unacceptable mortality rates in their reports for the years 1828, 1833, 1837, 1841, 1842, 1845, 1850, and 1851. If a small percentage of criminals who died was enough to elicit impassioned concern, thousands of dying citizen-soldiers constituted outrage.

Punishment and the Lieber Code

Penitentiary reformers in both England and the United States criticized the breakdown of the solitary and silent systems and the rate of inmate mortality, and questioned wardens' ability to oversee a motley crew of inmates. Reform-minded political thinkers on both sides of the Atlantic, however, defended the penitentiary program, insisting that, despite its flaws, penitentiary discipline benefited both society at large and individual inmates. In 1843, English reformer Joseph Adshead commented on how the press generated widespread public discussion regarding the proper treatment of criminals. Adshead and Francis Lieber defended the American penitentiary program, especially the Pennsylvania (solitary) system, to counter unfavorable assessments printed in the London *Times*. Lieber's thoughts on the treatment of inmates, and his insights into where responsibility for punishing criminals rested, influenced penology and criminal law in the antebellum period just as the 1863 code that bears his name shaped military law.[20] Lieber's antebellum writings illuminated concerns about the mode of penitentiary punishment, and the Lieber Code echoed antebellum thoughts on the humane treatment of inmates, imprisonment's purpose, and civilians' relationship to the state. Lieber's antebellum and wartime writing provide another good example of how civil and military punishment were intertwined and would later influence assumptions about imprisonment during the Civil War.

Lieber's antebellum writings, particularly his *Popular Essay on Subjects of Penal Law and on Uninterrupted Solitary Confinement at Labor* and his 1839 letter to Governor Noble of South Carolina, highlight the function of imprisonment, illustrate the role of the state in administering punishment, and ultimately foreshadow problems with imprisonment that carried over from the antebellum period into the Civil War. Lieber's passion for this subject is palpable since he formed his thoughts on punishment and imprisonment through firsthand experience. Lieber suffered as a political prisoner at Kopenick in the early 1820s for his alleged role in a plot between German and French secret societies to overthrow their respective governments. In 1841 he sought pardon, and in 1842 the King of Prussia granted it, but imprisonment scarred Lieber permanently. Lieber lamented from Kopenick in September 1824 that he was permitted to laugh when he felt like weeping. "Oh! The misery of a prisoner's life," he moaned, "how one longs for the pure sweet meadows beyond these narrow walls!" These lines are among the few that exist from Lieber's captivity and indicate that his experience as a prisoner molded his views on punishment. Nothing could be worse than being blind and deaf to the outside world, deprived of mobility, and left alone with haunting thoughts of carefree childhood days.[21] Leiber believed that the state, to deter bad behavior, had to communicate that this fate awaited civilians if they erred.

According to Lieber, certainty—not severity—of punishment mattered most. He asserted that strong governments should adopt mild modes of punishment that reflected the state's paternal relationship to offenders. Lieber posited that the state was composed of moral beings, and that criminals declared war on society thereby forfeiting their rights. Imprisonment was the most acceptable punishment since it offered the possibility of political and/or moral reform and punished offenders according to class—psychologically for the middle and upper classes and practically for the lower classes. Incarceration, according to Lieber, was effective since "the shame necessarily attached to imprisonment" would be more "acute and give additional severity" when inflicted upon "a well educated man of the wealthier classes." Imprisonment equated high-ranking men with the lowly and leveled class distinctions.

On the other hand, Lieber contended that imprisonment caused "a greater loss" to offenders belonging to the "classes which necessarily live from hand to mouth" since it deprived them of freedom and their families of livelihood.[22] Lieber understood that the memory and stigma of imprisonment would forever haunt emancipated inmates regardless of socioeconomic status and believed that that memory would deter them from future malfeasance.

Imprisonment, as Lieber suggested, was a leveling experience—all that mattered to prisoners was their confinement. During the Civil War, incarcerated citizen-soldiers denounced imprisonment as Lieber had predicted and focused on personal shame and suffering in their diaries. Even lower-class conscripts reacted as Lieber anticipated since both prisoners and their families, who lived "from hand to mouth," suffered due to imprisonment—a complaint that dominated inmates' petitions for release.

Lieber's writings illustrate that the civil and military sectors shared many fundamental ideas regarding imprisonment and punishment. His assertion that imprisonment alone afforded the chance of "political or moral" reform signals another parallel between penitentiaries and military prisons. While the former intended to reform convicts into productive members of society, Northern and Southern military prisons, through their use of incentives for enemy captives to take the oath of allegiance, intended to change adversaries into adherents to their respective causes.[23]

When Lincoln tasked Lieber with drafting military laws, including those that would govern prisoners of war, antebellum concerns about punishment and imprisonment resounded in his work. General Orders No. 100 emphasized the familiar values of humanity and justice that guided the treatment of penitentiary inmates.[24] The Lieber Code parroted the concerns of the Boston Discipline Society and echoed Lieber's own antebellum writings. During wartime, the state employs military law, which, according to Lieber, should be "strictly guided by the principles of justice, honor, and humanity." These guidelines echoed the idea that the state is a moral entity and that strong states should employ moderate, humane punishment. The Lieber Code dictated that treatment of captives may "be varied . . . according to the demands of safety," but cautioned that the state should subject prisoners to "no other intentional suffering or indignity." This dictate parallels Lieber's antebellum thoughts on punishment, which directed that the state, operating on just principles, could punish offenders for its own self-defense or preservation. Finally, Lieber, like the members of the Boston Prison Discipline Society, directed that prisoners of war "be fed upon plain and wholesome food" and treated with humanity, noting that they "may be required to work for the benefit of the captor's government" according to rank and condition.[25] This last directive reflected the idea that all prisoners, regardless of distinction, should mitigate the cost of their detention.

The Civil War, its crisis of imprisonment, and the issues surrounding the treatment of prisoners fit squarely within the context of antebellum penal developments. The Civil War generated a crisis of imprisonment never before seen in America, and Northerners and Southerners interpreted this crisis, formulated policies to govern it, and made practical decisions about imprisonment and the treatment of inmates by drawing on established practices. Even punishments, such as whipping, bucking and gagging, branding, the shower bath, and solitary confinement, about which wartime prisoners of war complained, were common in civil and military punishment and, while perhaps offensive to citizen-soldiers, were not considered torturous by the day's standards.[26]

A combination of factors moved the Union and Confederate governments to hastily consolidate power over imprisonment, contradicting, at least in the view of inmates and the public, Lieber's claim that large states with strong governments should engage in slower, milder forms of punishment. Northern and Southern officials could not keep up with the influx of prisoners. The parole system waxed and waned, the exchange system broke down in 1863, and existing jails and penitentiaries filled with soldiers and treason suspects, as did military prisons that Northern and Southern officials constructed or commandeered out of necessity. The public and the press screamed that military prison inmates withstood harsh punishments and suffered from want of proper clothing, food, and space. But these were relatively familiar challenges. The population of military prisons far exceeded that of penitentiaries, but penitentiary officials also failed to mitigate problems caused when solitary cells housed upwards of four or six inmates. Penitentiaries provided the only standard available to Americans for evaluating imprisonment since military prisons did not exist under ordinary circumstances, but military prisons crammed with citizen-soldiers drew more attention.

The outcry of wartime inmates intensified since, if not for the war, the men who enthusiastically answered the call for volunteers as citizen-soldiers would have had little, if any, familiarity with military discipline, or the civilian system of punishment that it inspired. Citizen-soldiers chafed under military authority since Federal officials and elites who became Regular Army officers used the same disciplinary system on volunteers that both informed penitentiary punishments and compelled unruly army recruits to obedience.[27]

The Regular Army and Military Discipline

Understanding the status of the Regular Army in nineteenth-century America, the military law that governed it, and how military law informed the penitentiary program is also essential for comprehending the full context for wartime imprisonment. The American Revolution inspired reverence for citizen-soldiers in the militia ranks, but the patriots' experience with the British Army and the British Crown from 1763 to 1783 inspired deep suspicion and resentment of a standing army. Thomas Jefferson set the tone for nineteenth-century military policy by contending that a standing army was incompatible with democracy and a drain on the treasury. Consequently, both the American public and politicians thought negatively, if at all, of the army and navy.[28] The number of regular soldiers was insignificant, hovering around, but usually under 10,000 from 1815 to 1860, peaking at 16,024 in June 1860.[29]

Officers, who belonged to the middle or upper classes, were supposed to recruit sober, industrious Americans or faithful foreigners, but they often took men from city streets and prisons to fill quotas.[30] As Edward Coffman has noted, approximately 42 percent of enlisted men were illiterate prior to 1820.[31] The collection of foreigners, drunkards, reprobates, and incompetents elicited scorn from workers in the developing market economy. Workers viewed regular soldiers as cop-outs who intentionally avoided economic boom-and-bust cycles and thereby voluntarily relinquished rights that civilians enjoyed. In short, the American public at once despised and feared the army even though drudge work dominated the lives of regulars on the frontier.[32]

Enlisted men performed endless unenviable tasks. Before the Civil War, their main job was building and maintaining forts on the western frontier, an isolating occupation that encouraged drunkenness and desertion.[33] Soldiers received low pay, inadequate training, poor rations, and constant threat of disease in return for rough work.[34] Officers thought strict discipline was necessary to control unruly recruits, but punishments varied according to commanders' whims. Drunks, deserters, thieves, or mutinous soldiers suffered any of the following reprimands: death by hanging or firing squad, flogging (up to the legal maximum of one hundred lashes), branding, running a gauntlet, and doing extra duty with a log chained to one's leg.[35]

During both the Mexican and Civil wars, the citizen-soldiers who flooded the ranks were appalled at the possibility that they could face the same "brutal" corporal punishments that were routine for lowly regulars.[36] The Civil War exposed the main problem of Americans' aversion to a standing army: anytime volunteers answered the summons to defend their state and, by extension, their country, strict military discipline restrained individualism and was incompatible with the lofty motivations for enlistment. The fact that penitentiary officials inflicted the same punishments on criminals added insult to injury for the volunteers.

Army punishments were bedrocks of the penitentiary program, and courts-martial often sentenced military offenders to penitentiaries. Founders of the penitentiary program drew on military experience when they conceived of civil punishment. Elam Lynds, founder of the Auburn (congregate) system of penitentiary discipline, formed his outlook on discipline through military service. Military discipline informed inmates' daily routine and their movements: inmates rose and slept by the bell, answered dutifully at roll call, assembled in companies in the prison yard after work, and marched everywhere in lockstep. Lynds envisioned an army of captive workers who would live in solitary confinement at night and labor in congregate shops by day to manufacture shoes, nails, clothing, and saddles, among other items, for profit.[37]

Other facets of penitentiary life reflected military influence. Dario Melossi and Massimo Pavarini have noted that the Auburn system was structured "along military-hierarchical lines" and that many administrators, in addition to Lynds, had served in the army or navy, allowing them to adjust to their quasi-military life overseeing prisons. Superintendents and commandants wore uniforms, assembled inmates at specific times, changed the guard, and were expected to behave in a "gentlemanly manner, as if they were officers"— all facets reminiscent of military discipline. Penitentiary officials also maintained a detached relationship with prison guards and inmates, similar to the relationships between officers, noncommissioned officers, and enlisted men.[38] And like army commanders, the personal whims of prison commandants and superintendents influenced punishment in both penitentiaries and military prisons.

Blurred Lines: Military and Civil Justice

Throughout the nineteenth century, military law sanctioned many of the disciplinary practices used in penitentiaries, so it is not surprising that military officials drew on the penitentiary program to govern Civil War military prisons. The military and civil sectors utilized common practices to manage soldiers and prisoners. Courts-martial routinely sentenced enlisted men to penitentiary punishments. In 1806, Congress determined that courts-martial could sentence soldiers to hard labor for up to one month, and U.S.

Army regulations approved common penitentiary punishments for soldiers sentenced by courts-martial—offenders could be punished with death, confinement on a bread-and-water diet, solitary confinement, hard labor, and ball and chain. All of these practices continued during the Civil War.

The lines between civil and military prisoners blurred since the Federal Government incarcerated military prisoners alongside criminals, but not everyone agreed with this practice. Citizens' objections predated the formation of both the United States and penitentiaries. During the American Revolution, prisoners of war were often confined in local jails, which typically held debtors or individuals awaiting trial. This practice immediately conflated military and civil justice, and the overlap continued throughout the nineteenth century. The objections of angry Philadelphians captured George Washington's attention, but the practice continued since Americans had no separate system or accommodations to detain prisoners of war.[39]

After Americans won independence and established penitentiaries, federal officials continued housing military prisoners in penitentiaries. The new republic was fortunate to spend most of its early years isolated from wars that wreaked havoc on Europe, but those that permeated the American mainland laid bare problems with both the Regular Army and the new government's inexperience in dealing with military adversaries.

The United States government, on the eve of the War of 1812, lacked any system for dealing with military prisoners and consequently relied on civilian institutions. Officials understood that the crisis began with war's declaration and would end when the guns fell silent. American politicians and military officials had no reason to contemplate a system for dealing with prisoners of war because of the Constitution's ban on standing armies, the Regular Army's isolation on the frontier, and the fact that volunteer militias mustered only when needed.

Military officials used penitentiaries to solve the prisoner-of-war crisis during the War of 1812, just as they had turned to jails during the Revolution. The Auburn system required convicts to labor all day, but state officials, like those in Virginia, were unsure of what do to with the British prisoners. Virginia Penitentiary officials ultimately decided against compelling prisoners of war to work, and their counterparts followed suit during the Civil War, exempting some incarcerated soldiers from penitentiary labor.[40] But this decision caused disciplinary problems in penitentiaries during both the War of 1812 and the Civil War.

Housing military prisoners and British prisoners of war alongside criminals compounded overcrowding and created resentment between both categories of inmates at the Virginia Penitentiary. In 1813, penitentiary officials complained about the additional burden of keeping prisoners of war, particularly because of rampant disease. Virginian James Greenhow demanded that officials immediately remove the British prisoners since they worsened overcrowding in August, the "most sickly period of the year." The Brits, he complained, increased both the number and the malignancy of diseases.[41]

Disease-spreading prisoners of war also eroded discipline. Civilian prisoners and prisoners of war often engaged in different activities, and this bred animosity among the different categories of inmates. While criminals labored during the day, prisoners of war sat idle, since officials excluded them from hard labor. Overworked criminals likely wanted time to rest, while prisoners of war coveted any opportunity for physical activity, however repetitious.[42]

The Virginia Board of Inspectors was sensitive to and anxious about inmates' complaints. They fretted that the "entire idleness" of prisoners of war, when contrasted with the "rigid discipline" exercised over convicts, excited "dissatisfaction among the convicts." Officials could not keep prisoners of war and convicts entirely separate and prisoners' interaction exacerbated tensions since convicts labored where prisoners of war were held. Penitentiary officials devoted most of their attention to the laboring convicts, neglecting prisoners of war and jeopardizing security. Board members concurred with Greenhow that officers should remove the prisoners of war, but for a different reason: poor supervision necessitated it.[43]

The Ohio and D.C. penitentiaries also held members of the U.S. Army and Navy in the antebellum period and continued to do so during the Civil War. These cases illuminated concerns surrounding inmate classification, an ongoing problem throughout the nineteenth century. In 1840, the moral instructor of the Ohio Penitentiary noted that seventy-one of the 488 convicts were in the army and that fifty-two were former sailors, creating at least a theoretical distinction between convicts and military men.[44] But distinctions blurred toward midcentury.

By 1860, many penitentiaries held soldiers convicted of crimes in addition to prisoners of war, raising the question of whether or not soldiers could be classified as criminals. Scholars of the antebellum and Civil War years have overlooked both this question and how penitentiary officials disciplined incarcerated soldiers, either prisoners of war or men who violated military law. By the 1850s, penitentiaries were custodial and their purpose was punishment, so military officials, not surprisingly, used them to detain prisoners of war.[45]

The U.S. government depended on penitentiaries for punishment of federal offenders in the antebellum period and the U.S. Supreme Court's ruling in *Dynes vs. Hoover* (1857) formally sanctioned the Federal Government's ability to punish soldiers with penitentiary sentences. A court-martial found navy seaman Frank Dynes guilty of attempted desertion and sentenced him to six months' hard labor in the D.C. Penitentiary. Dynes contended that the military court lacked jurisdiction to try and sentence him, but the Supreme Court upheld the court-martial's sentence.[46]

The *Dynes* case formally sanctioned the extant practice of using penitentiaries to punish soldiers, a decision that further blurred the lines between military and civil punishment. The decision had an immediate impact on sentencing. In April 1860, a court-martial found Pvt. John Ryan, stationed at Fort Brown, Texas, guilty of violating the Ninth Article of War for firing a loaded rifle at his company's corporal with the intent to kill. In December 1860, another military court convicted navy seamen John Stevens, Edward Jones, and James Nicholson of revolt on the high seas off the Florida coast. The court sentenced each man to eighteen months' hard labor in the D.C. Penitentiary, which was a common sentence for civilians convicted of comparable civil-sector crimes.[47]

The Federal Government's power over criminal and military offenders was most directly felt through its operation of the D.C. Penitentiary, and the *Dynes* case set precedent for federal control over punishment of men in the armed forces. But federal offenders in state penitentiaries were largely beyond the Federal Government's reach. After federal offenders were lodged in state penitentiaries, state authorities could use federal inmates in the state prison labor system, reinforcing the notion that state officials were primarily responsible for state penitentiaries and their inmates.[48] State and federal officials were accustomed to this structure by the Civil War's outbreak. Both believed the mixing of federal and state prisoners was normal, and state officials were accustomed to monitoring all prisoners in state penitentiaries.

Since federal law mandated that state prisons detain individuals convicted of federal crimes, state officials exercised direct oversight of federal offenders.[49] There were few federal crimes in the antebellum period; some were ordinary crimes in a federal setting, which usually pertained to the army or navy (e.g., murder on the high seas). Others included forgery, perjury in a federal court, immigration offenses, customs violations, and smuggling. Americans preferred that state governments guided imprisonment. They gave scant consideration to the fact that state officials oversaw federal offenders since criminal justice was overwhelmingly the business of the states, not the Federal Government, in the antebellum years.[50] But during the Civil War, courts-martial sentenced soldiers to military prisons like Johnson's Island, Camp Chase, Old Capitol Prison, Castle Thunder, and Salisbury, among others, mimicking the precedent set in the *Dynes* case and expanding federal control over imprisonment. During wartime, the Federal Government influenced imprisonment in the D.C. Penitentiary, in newly established military prisons, and in extant state penitentiaries.

Lessons that Guided the Civil War's Crisis of Imprisonment

The U.S. and Confederate governments' wartime establishment and operation of military prisons was, like the establishment of penitentiaries and the criminal justice system, a work in progress. Union and Confederate military and political officials learned lessons from penitentiary operation and from the American Revolution, the War of 1812, and the Mexican War that informed their approach to the Civil War's crisis of imprisonment. Officials on both sides of the conflict during each war were not prepared to deal with a large influx of prisoners. Indeed, why would they have been? Before the Revolution, the British Crown assumed that colonists were part of the body politic, and military conflicts in North America were rare. When the Seven Years War broke out, colonial militia units aided the British Army as dutiful British subjects who enjoyed protection from the Royal Army without being subject to universal conscription. The American Revolution, however, forced British officials to make decisions about internal enemies that would later guide decisions that Union officials made during the Civil War.

The first problem was how to classify the American patriots who formed their own, in the British view, illegal and illegitimate government and mustered an army comprised of citizen-soldiers. Since the British fought members of their own empire, British military officials needed to decide whether to judge the patriots by international laws, which would grant them bel-

ligerent status and arguably political recognition, or by civil law, a decision
that equated rebellion with treason and left open the possibility of trying
participants for this capital crime.[51] The British did not formally recognize
the American cause, but did incarcerate patriots who fell into their hands.

Civil War contemporaries learned two other important lessons from the
Revolution. First, the British were unprepared for occupation of the American colonies and for housing thousands of prisoners since wars in the colonies were infrequent and the Crown did not anticipate fighting its own subjects.[52] The implications of this were significant—lack of preparedness in
holding prisoners during wartime was a common problem, even for empires
like Britain, which wielded significant military might. Why, then, should
we assume that Americans, living in a country whose Constitution forbade
a standing army, would have anything close to a system for dealing with a
crisis of imprisonment during the Civil War, or that an effective system could
be created expediently? The British and the patriots during the Revolution,
and Union and Confederate officials during the Civil War, solved this crisis by
housing enemy combatants or sympathizers in hulks (ships used as prisons),
in jails and dungeons, or in hastily constructed makeshift holding pens.[53]

The second lesson from the Revolution centered on the treatment of inmates. George Washington insisted that inmates receive humane treatment
and that commissaries be established to care for Americans in British hands
so that they could rejoin the patriot ranks upon release. Union and Confederate officials later grappled with the same issue as they demanded that packages from home be delivered to prisoners in enemy hands and debated allowing sutlers to supplement prison supplies by selling necessities and food.[54]

Finally, the Revolution taught contemporaries, and later generations, that
the treatment of prisoners was a matter beyond the control of political and
military officials. Rather, it depended on the culture and temper of the surrounding population and, perhaps more importantly, the season, geography,
and even temperature of the regions in which prisons were established.[55]

During the War of 1812, the Americans and the British again improvised
to deal with the prisoner-of-war crisis. Both sides agreed to an exchange
cartel in 1812, which established formulas for the exchange of enlisted men
and officers, stated that enemy combatants would receive humane treatment, authorized release of noncombatants such as chaplains and surgeons, prohibited whipping prisoners of war, and dictated that prisoners
of war receive the same rations as enlisted men in the field—all measures
echoed during the Civil War.

Perhaps more importantly, however, the War of 1812 set practical precedents for holding enemy combatants that the Union and Confederacy later enacted. Again, both sides utilized existing jails, prison hulks, and makeshift jails since they were convenient, readily available holding facilities. Federal officials also ordered the states to mitigate the mounting number of enemy prisoners. During the War of 1812, U.S. authorities commanded that Massachusetts, Kentucky, and Ohio hold British prisoners in state penitentiaries. Other states like Pennsylvania and Virginia followed suit and, in each case, blurred the lines between state and federal authority over imprisonment and inmates well before the *Dynes* decision was handed down. Finally, both the United States and Britain retaliated against their foe—especially through hostage taking. This was not surprising since, as previously stated, the laws of war sanctioned retaliation, but it nonetheless remained abrasive to a civilian population mustered to address a national military crisis.[56]

The United States and Britain in the War of 1812, and the United States in the Mexican War, used a parole system to alleviate overcrowding in prisons and uphold humanitarian principles. In this system, captors released enemy prisoners to their homes contingent upon a pledge never to take up arms against their captors.[57] This practice spared the Federal Government the expense and headache of ensuring humane treatment, while theoretically depriving the enemy of manpower. But this system did not fully absolve captors from responsibility for enemy prisoners—if men refused parole, the government had to guarantee them humane imprisonment.

All of these findings have important implications for understanding imprisonment in the Civil War Era. Penitentiary and military prison officials were, like other officials in the de facto criminal justice sector, without experience and professional training since there was no formal organized criminal justice system. Rather, criminal justice was developing and its counterparts, the police and the penitentiary, were new social inventions that, according to Lawrence Friedman, arose "out of a painful awareness that the pathologies of a mobile society demanded new techniques of control" and remained in state and local hands.[58] National authorities on the eve of the Civil War were therefore accustomed to turning to states to discipline offenders and followed the practices used in previous wars to address the prisoner-of-war crisis. The U.S. and Confederate governments logically implemented penitentiary practices in military prisons at the moment when national authorities, for the first time, bore great responsibility for prisoners.

National officials, North and South, learned important, albeit haunting, lessons from penitentiary operation. First, that overcrowding occurred rapidly, left officials scrambling for solutions, or forced them to wring their hands in despair since they could not enlarge existing institutions rapidly enough to accommodate an influx of prisoners. Second, that physical shortcomings and overcrowding in both penitentiaries and military prisons made it difficult for officials to ensure humane treatment, good ventilation, adequate provisions, and physical activities that would offset costs, fend off doldrums, and deter prisoners from misbehavior. And third, that state and federal prisoners—either civilians or prisoners of war—intermingled both in penitentiaries and military prisons during the Civil War as they had in previous wars.

The Civil War represented the greatest crisis of imprisonment ever witnessed on American soil, and interpreting it in the broader context of the development of nineteenth-century penitentiary development, military discipline, and previous military crises is not intended to detract from the suffering and loss of life generated by military prisons. Rather, it invites consideration of penitentiaries—long-standing institutions that were touched by war but remain on the sidelines of scholarly discussions of wartime imprisonment—and offers insight into how both military prison inmates and officials formed their identities and interpreted the institutions. The development of penitentiaries occurred relatively quickly at the turn of the century, but slowly compared to the speed at which the Union and Confederate governments established military prisons. This aptly describes how political officials, military officers, and conscripts experienced preparations for the Civil War. As Union private and former Andersonville inmate Nathaniel Shepard Armstrong Price confessed, the evolution from civilian to soldier was "more rapid than thorough" when the war broke out, and so was the method by which Union and Confederate officials established and operated military prisons.[59]

Penitentiaries and Military Prisons

Built on Common Ground

Penitentiaries in the United States garnered international attention, inspiring Alexis de Tocqueville and Gustave Beaumont, two curious and renowned Frenchmen, to cross the Atlantic and study the democratic republic and its prisons. By the time of their 1831 visit, penitentiaries, on either the Pennsylvania or Auburn systems, existed in nine of the Union's twenty-four states, and each experienced dramatic population increases between 1790 and 1830.[1] Penitentiaries fascinated the Frenchmen, but elicited criticism. Beaumont and de Tocqueville contended that imprisonment illuminated contradictions within a nation that prided itself on freedom. The travelers ridiculed the American penitentiary system, which included "prisons of all kinds, state and other," as "severe." This assessment both belied penitentiary founders' lofty goals and, like the Boston Prison Discipline Society reports, signaled that nineteenth-century contemporaries equated different types of carceral institutions and judged them by the same standards.[2]

American reformers, mostly belonging to the middle and upper classes, raised a ruckus about the ills of imprisonment. But the average American in the antebellum period—even in the 1840s, when reformers' cries reached a crescendo—knew little about day-to-day penitentiary operations.[3] By 1860, state penitentiaries faced severe disciplinary problems, stagnation, and repression so that, by the Civil War's outbreak, reform fell by the wayside and the only function that prisons performed was custodial.[4] Public outrage heightened during the Civil War since penitentiaries and military prisons detained civilians and citizen-soldiers. Americans demanded that penitentiaries and military prisons follow reformer Dorothea Dix's 1845 prescription that "the duty of the government to offenders, and the obligation of man to man, requires that all prisons should be established on just, and on Christian principles."[5]

Politicians in Virginia, Georgia, Ohio, and Washington, D.C., had lofty ambitions when they authorized penitentiary construction, and Union and Confederate officials in 1861 did not think that the war would last long enough for military prisons to become problematic. The ability of penitentiary and military prison officials to uphold Dix's prescription proved nearly impossible during the antebellum and Civil War years, but the initial expectations for penitentiaries continuously shaped assumptions about imprisonment during peacetime and wartime. Penitentiary and military prison officials believed that the institutions would correct the problems of crime and disloyalty and that inmates should mitigate costs through labor.

The Establishment and Purpose of Penitentiaries

State politicians believed penitentiaries could only improve society by tailoring punishments to fit crimes and sequestering riffraff. Visitors to Richmond, Virginia, in the late 1780s and early 1790s complained of gambling, tavern brawls, and street fighting, which included the gouging of eyes and biting of noses and ears. In the 1790s, a grand jury pondered how to restrain the vagrants, beggars, free blacks, and runaway slaves who infested Richmond's streets and plundered its residents.[6] Virginia's political leaders looked north for a punitive model and advocated penitentiary construction, arguing that the institution would reform inmates and obviate public corporal punishment.[7] Penitentiary construction commenced in 1796, and the prison opened in 1800, ushering in a new era of criminal justice, curiosity, and conviction about the penitentiary's place in society and politics.

The penitentiary immediately received mixed reviews, however. State politicians and many civilians demanded a penitentiary, but did not want to reside anywhere near it. Fear that the prison would depreciate land values discouraged civilians from settling in close proximity, and residential

The State Penitentiary, Richmond, Virginia, April 1865 (Library of Congress)

development consequently stalled along the James River near the penitentiary. Civilians nonetheless remained curious about what went on behind its imposing walls.[8]

Penitentiary architecture was impressive. The Virginia Penitentiary was an elegant three-story, symmetrical horseshoe with arched windows and ceilings. It contained 168 sleeping cells, which was its intended capacity. Each cell was twelve feet long and six-and-a-half feet wide with arched ceilings nine feet high. Fourteen basement cells were reserved for solitary confinement of refractory inmates. The penitentiary was primarily for men— architects reserved only six cells on the first floor for female convicts. This was not unusual. Female inmates, white and black, were an afterthought in the antebellum period since white female criminals fell from grace, and notions of proper womanhood did not apply to black women.[9]

The Virginia Penitentiary lacked more than provisions for female inmates in its early years. Perimeter security, consisting of a mere wooden wall, was also inadequate. Administrators demanded improvements to prevent escape, and eventually a brick wall was completed in 1824.[10] The improved penitentiary afforded Virginians a sense of security and an air of moral superiority since penitentiary sentences were more humane than short-term jail sentences and public punishment.

Residents and politicians in Washington, D.C., also thought that a penitentiary would be a better solution for crime. The city jail exceeded capacity in the early 1820s, and the U.S. House of Representatives quickly authorized construction of a federal penitentiary. The structure opened in 1831, eased overcrowding in the jail and, ostensibly, encouraged inmates to reform.[11]

The D.C. Penitentiary was imposing, like its counterpart in Virginia. A twenty-foot-high wall, containing two guard towers, separated criminals from lawful civilians. The prison contained 150 cells for male prisoners and 64 for females, rendering the intended capacity at 214. Cells sat back-to-back in a continued range four stories high. Each cell measured seven feet eleven inches long, three feet four inches wide, and seven feet nine inches high. Convicts glimpsed the outside world through windows that measured twelve feet three inches wide. But these portals also taunted inmates, reminding them that freedom was just out of reach.[12]

Like politicians in Virginia and Washington, D.C., Georgia lawmakers decided that a penitentiary could enhance the state's reputation. Legislators first proposed a penitentiary in 1803, but construction did not commence until 1812. Lawmakers and the press praised the idea of a penitentiary before it opened in the capital, Milledgeville, in 1817. Legislators believed that state laws should be humane, and the revised 1816 Penal Code reflected this ideal, at least rhetorically. The code announced that "cruel punishments" were suited to "despotic and arbitrary government," not republican government, which should be lenient. On the contrary, penitentiary punishment, according to the code, was "most moral, efficacious and merciful."[13] A wall, twenty feet high and two-and-one-half feet thick, detained inmates. Guards who gazed from one of four corner sentry boxes oversaw the prison's inner workings.[14]

Like other penitentiaries, Georgia's impressed residents. In November 1816, the *Georgia Journal* hailed the architectural feat—the prison stood three stories high and contained large halls, twenty-three lodging rooms, and four cells for refractory inmates. In 1816, the surrounding wall and workshops were yet incomplete, but the *Journal* was sure they would be awe-inspiring, standing two stories high and measuring 150 feet long with ornate porticoes and balconies. This original construction was solely for male offenders, but the paper proclaimed that the female department, once started, would be "precisely like the male." All told, the penitentiary would occupy one acre, and the *Journal* praised it as a "proud monument of the wisdom, public spirit, and humane policy of our state."[15]

Ohio politicians likewise sought a humane form of punishment after the state entered the Union in 1803. State politicians shifted the location of the

Ohio State Penitentiary (Courtesy of the Ohio History Connection, AL07752)

capital from Chillicothe to Columbus the following decade, but crime in Columbus concerned state politicians even before the legislature occupied the new capital in 1816. The Ohio State legislature sanctioned imprisonment for state offenses on January 27, 1815, and the state's first penitentiary opened that year.[16] The penitentiary soon became overcrowded as crime increased with population growth. In 1831, the Ohio General Assembly investigated the penitentiary, concluded that it served no "valuable purpose," and had become "a serious evil" that required "immediate remedy."[17]

The state assembly quickly authorized a new penitentiary predicated on the Auburn system. Construction, undertaken by prisoners, commenced in March 1833, and prisoners moved into their new, self-constructed quarters in October 1834.[18] A solid stone wall, thirty feet high and complete with sentry turrets, kept hundreds of inmates from the outside world. The penitentiary's original capacity was five hundred, but it later expanded to seven hundred, with sleeping cells arranged in two wings, each containing 350 cells. Cells measured seven feet long, three-and-a-half feet wide, and seven feet high. The women's wing of the prison consisted of a detached building in the prison's rear, two stories high, with twenty-four cells.[19]

The Virginia, D.C., Georgia, and Ohio penitentiaries occupied isolated yet prominent locations. The Virginia Penitentiary sat ominously on a hill on the banks of the James River, surrounded by two ravines; the D.C. Penitentiary occupied a promontory on the Potomac River, south of the Federal District; the Georgia Penitentiary was in a district on the north side of Milledgeville known as Penitentiary Square, christened in 1807 because of plans for penitentiary construction.[20] Finally, the Ohio Penitentiary stood on the east bank of the Scioto River, three squares west of High Street, a main thoroughfare.[21] The isolation of the prisons was practical from a disciplinary standpoint, but also daunted residents as they gazed upon the massive structures while going about their daily tasks.

The populations of the Virginia, Georgia, D.C., and Ohio penitentiaries grew steadily, with few exceptions, during the antebellum period. In 1817, the Virginia Penitentiary held 158 convicts. Just over twenty years later, the prison held 179 offenders; this increased to 211 in 1847, 313 in 1857, and 389 in 1860. The Georgia Penitentiary's population fluctuated slightly. It held 98 convicts in March 1831, 160 in November 1839, 155 in September 1840, and 179 in December 1855. The population decreased in June 1859 to 113 inmates. The D.C. Penitentiary's population increased steadily with time, but lagged behind others. In 1833, it held 42 convicts, ten years later it held 84. By 1853, the penitentiary's population totaled 106, and in 1860 it reached 169. The Ohio Penitentiary witnessed the most significant population increase and was the most crowded penitentiary under study. In 1832, it held 215 convicts, which increased to 461 in 1842. By 1852, the population reached 503, and by 1860 it totaled 932, well above the intended capacity of 700.[22]

Politicians and reformers in Virginia, Ohio, Georgia, Washington, D.C., and North Carolina envisioned the penitentiary as a reflection of a well-ordered society that offered offenders the possibility of reform and promoted citizens' faith in newfound state governments.[23] The dream, however, fell short of reality. State and national inspectors ventured behind penitentiary walls to chronicle ills, but seldom initiated improvements—an unfortunate foreshadowing of dialogue surrounding Civil War military prisons.

On his 1835 tour of penitentiaries, reformer William Crawford laid bare how overcrowding created a disconnect between vision and reality in the Ohio Penitentiary. He noted that the building's construction failed to prevent communication among inmates since at least four inmates slept in cells designed for one. Furthermore, Crawford complained that penitentiary officials "entirely neglected" inmates' moral and religious welfare, betraying the penitentiary's original purpose. He summarized conditions at the Ohio

Penitentiary by quoting an 1831 report to the Ohio legislature, which contended that "a more perfect system for the dissemination of vice could not be devised than is to be found within the walls of the Ohio prison."[24]

When state politicians authorized expansion of the Ohio Penitentiary in the 1830s, they foreshadowed an "improvement" tactic that both penitentiary and military prison officials used to mitigate overcrowding. Expansion, however, failed to improve inmates' conditions. Prison directors reported to Ohio's governor in 1838 that penitentiary officials could not control conditions since the state struggled with cholera, and the hot, dry summer exacerbated inmate mortality. The perplexed directors concluded that "it cannot be expected that there ever will be among the inmates of a prison, especially where a large number are congregated, the same degree of good health as among a like number of citizens at large." In essence, the directors admitted defeat and proclaimed maintenance of healthy conditions futile. Epidemics trumped the good intentions of reformers and politicians since disease ravaged the crowded prison, but remained "scarcely perceived by the citizen population of the surrounding country."[25]

Human error also contributed to and compounded failure. In 1856, the Ohio Penitentiary's directors complained that vermin infested the penitentiary, that it was in a "dilapidated and ruinous condition," and that food supplies spoiled due to improper attention.[26] Prison officials had little incentive, let alone energy, to initiate improvements or implement a reform program since they worked long, monotonous hours and became increasingly overburdened by overcrowding. In 1860, the Ohio Penitentiary's directors griped that overcrowding rendered regular Sabbath worship impossible since officials used the chapel to accommodate inmates and needed to erect an addition. The directors optimistically projected that the chapel's expansion would be complete and regular Sunday services and Sabbath school would resume by January 1, 1861.[27] But the penitentiary's population climbed steadily throughout 1860, forcing the state legislature in May 1860 to authorize convict labor for another enlargement. Additional construction, however, could not keep pace with the influx of prisoners. By January 1861, the population reached one thousand, and frustrated officials halted reform.[28]

What lessons can we draw from the Ohio Penitentiary's lackluster operation? Cynically, that calls for improvements of internal conditions amounted to nothing more than lip service. State officials and reformers championed solitary confinement, wholesome rations, and religious instruction. Prison officers, however, could not compensate for overwhelmed guards, epidemics, deteriorating infrastructure, and overcrowding. The Ohio Penitentiary's directors verified the ugly truth that by midcentury the penitentiary's sole purpose was punishment.[29] Despite good intentions, penitentiaries were ultimately punitive holding pens, as were wartime military prisons.

North Carolina's state legislators paid close attention to the Virginia, Georgia, and Ohio penitentiaries as they debated the pros and cons of erecting their own penitentiary. In December 1815, the General Assembly appointed commissioners to determine a possible location, the cost of construction, the appropriate size, and the materials required to build a penitentiary.[30] Their assessments reveal disagreement over the effectiveness of the reform program, the internal conditions of penitentiaries, and the cost to law-abiding civilians—all concerns that persisted into the Civil War.

Some North Carolina politicians reflected the optimism of penitentiary architects in Virginia, Georgia, Ohio, and Washington, D.C., and believed that the penitentiary would ensure humane punishment and reflect democratic and, perhaps more importantly, Christian values.[31] In 1846, Gov. Edward B. Dudley asserted that without a penitentiary, punishment was imperfect and arbitrary since it inspired costly appeals and was subject to the whims of individual judges. He believed that a penitentiary would tailor punishment to fit crime, minimize the likelihood of petition, render offenders useful to the state and, most importantly, put North Carolina on par with other Christian countries and states that established penitentiaries.[32]

Dudley's opinions indicate that state-controlled penitentiaries had the lofty task of maintaining order, or at least the semblance of it, in the new nation. Passionate arguments both for and against a penitentiary in North Carolina dominated the 1840s while the moral reform movement swept the North. In October 1842, the *North Carolina Star* contended that arguments in favor of the penitentiary outweighed those opposed, which were "few and feeble." The *Mecklenburg Jeffersonian* and the *Raleigh Register* captured the rival sides. The *Jeffersonian*'s writers condemned costly penitentiaries in the reviled "Yankee States" and denounced the prison labor system. In New England—the site of original penitentiary development—officials "put a man in the penitentiary for every trivial offence," which enabled the state to "make money by the *misfortunes* and the *crimes* of its citizens" through prison labor. The *Jeffersonian* contended that the penitentiary did not reduce crime since labor encouraged a massive hunt for criminals, who became cogs in a machine. Journalists instead favored corporal punishment, like whipping and branding, since these encouraged criminals to reform. Penitentiaries, on the contrary, sapped a man's free spirit, and made him "the slave of a keeper . . . for years immured in a dungeon and made to drag a clog like a beast under the lash to and from his daily toil."[33]

The *Raleigh Register,* on the contrary, favored penitentiaries. Journalists denounced state-sanctioned corporal punishment and lauded the potential of the penitentiary program. The paper believed that whipping, cropping, and branding precluded reform, and were "uncongenial to the spirit of the age, and revolting of humanity," while penitentiary punishment was wholly positive. Penitentiary committee members maintained that "Solitary confinement induces a communion with conscience," and "active employment gives a healthy action and beneficial direction to the mind." Benefits increased with time, and encouraged convicts to acquire "a habit of sober industry," a profitable trade and consequently the ability to resist temptations to crime.[34]

Antebellum North Carolinians remained divided over penitentiary construction—some endorsed it as a physical manifestation of civil government, while others prayed that "patriotism forbid there *ever* should be one established to burthen the tax payers."[35] North Carolina did not erect a penitentiary prior to the Civil War, but arguments about the merits and evils of imprisonment continued into the war years in and beyond North Carolina. Civilians, overall, remained skeptical of wartime prison construction, numerous Northerners and Southerners bemoaned their cost, and many decried the physical punishment and suffering of incarcerated criminals, political prisoners, and prisoners of war.

Military Prison Establishment

Ironically, North Carolina, stalled on antebellum penitentiary construction, but established one of the first Confederate military prisons, or "penitentiaries," as contemporaries called it.[36] The state governor played a major role in determining the location, securing land, and mustering guards for the prison, just as he would have done had the state sanctioned a penitentiary. Salisbury, the state's fifth largest town, was selected for the military prison since rail lines linked it with other Southern cities and facilitated the flow of prisoners to and from the depot.[37]

State and national politicians were concerned about the cost of Salisbury Prison, echoing a concern of antebellum penitentiary planners. Gov. Henry T. Clark believed the Salisbury site was a bargain. On June 10, 1861, he reported to the Confederate secretary of war that, unlike Hillsborough and Greensboro, Salisbury had a building ideal for a prison—an old cotton factory situated on sixteen acres. The structure could secure fifteen hundred to two thousand prisoners and the surrounding land allowed for increased capacity, upwards of ten thousand. The Confederate government could purchase the site for $15,000 and Clark predicted a postwar sale price of anywhere from $30,000 to $50,000, rendering it a wise investment.[38]

The bargain that North Carolina officials offered the Confederate government had added benefits. State and national officials were optimistic that they could sustain thousands of inmates inexpensively, a bonus since Southerners were reluctant to spend money on enemy prisoners, just as law-abiding civilians sneered at spending money on criminals. Officials contended that the surrounding countryside routinely yielded an agricultural boon that would feed inmates at minimal cost. R. H. Riddick, assistant adjutant general of North Carolina, boasted to Adjutant and Inspector General Samuel Cooper on August 3, 1861, that Salisbury was in the "most productive" region of the state. Riddick was confident that the commissary general of subsistence could contract with local producers who were left with an overabundance of fruits, vegetables, wheat, and meat since nearly a thousand men were at the front. This, Riddick was sure, would cost much less than the usual army ration. Confederate officials could not refuse the benefits and purchased Salisbury with Confederate bonds for the quoted price.[39]

Salisbury's financial outlook seemed bright, but prison life was bleak since it, like penitentiaries, fell short of lofty expectations. The realities of prison operations and lackluster internal conditions quickly tarnished the optimism that surrounded penitentiary establishment, and Salisbury reflected this trend as the hopes of state and national officials turned to consternation. Confederate officials ordered Governor Clark to raise a guard force, and he immediately cautioned Secretary of War L. P. Walker on July 27, 1861, that securing an adequate, reliable guard would be at best difficult and at worst impossible. "I shall meet with great difficulty in providing a suitable guard, as volunteers for the war entertain the greatest repugnance

Bird's-eye view of Confederate Prison Pen at Salisbury, North Carolina, taken in 1864 (Library of Congress)

to such a confinement themselves," Clark warned. His admonition high-lighted the familiar idea that many politicians and civilians thought prisons a good idea, but wanted nothing to do with them once they opened. Guard duty was undesirable since strict rules governed guards and they were exposed to the dismal internal conditions of prisons. In closing, Clark requested that Walker relieve him from the obligation of mustering a guard.[40] Benjamin refused the request, and Clark again complained in early November that he had no success in mustering a permanent guard force and requested a temporary guard for the "unpopular service."[41]

Salisbury remained poorly guarded and structurally incomplete when Confederate officials proposed sending inmates to it in late November 1861.[42] Nonetheless, the first federal prisoners—120 captives from the first Battle of Manassas—arrived on December 12, 1861.[43] From then on, Salisbury held a diverse mix of inmates from military convicts, to Union and Confederate deserters, hostages, political prisoners, Unionists, Union prisoners of war, and, later in the war, Union draft dodgers.[44] Inmates inhabited the old cotton factory, a four-story brick building approximately 120 by 45 feet. A palisade made of logs, fifteen feet long and rammed three feet into the ground, created a wall twelve feet high. Prisoners knew to avoid the "dead line," a trench, three feet wide and two feet deep, located about six feet inside of the wall and surrounding the entire enclosure, lest guards shoot.[45]

Officials in North Carolina were not the only people concerned about war-related prisoners. Washington, D.C., Ohio, and Virginia also established military prisons to preserve order amid the war's political and social upheaval. Federal officials in Washington initially held prisoners of war and criminals in existing prisons, but those quickly exceeded capacity. Union officials improvised by transforming the Old Capitol building, on the corner of First and A streets, into a makeshift prison. The structure, erected in 1800 as a tavern and boardinghouse, was in disrepair, with creaky stairs, decaying walls, and wooden slats covering windows, all of which created poor internal conditions akin to those in penitentiaries.[46]

The Old Capitol Prison held mostly political prisoners throughout the war, but also confined Confederate prisoners of war, suspected spies, and Union deserters.[47] Civilians from almost every state in the divided nation and from all walks of life, including highly educated men, merchants, and upper-class women, occupied the prison.[48] The building had a capacity of five hundred, but in 1862 federal officials commandeered a row of houses near the Old Capitol, which became known as Carroll Prison, increasing capacity to fifteen hundred.[49]

State penitentiaries punished civilians from their home states, but military prisons punished individuals from beyond state or district lines and redefined citizens' relationship to the national government. On August 14, 1862, Judge Advocate L. C. Turner directed Stephen D. Reed, U.S. marshal in Oswego, New York, that "all persons arrested for disloyal practices against the United States" should be sent to Old Capitol Prison "with charges and proofs against them to be tried before a military commission."[50] Old Capitol Prison's reach extended to distant areas like New York and caused concern among civilians in its immediate vicinity as well as among those in more remote localities. Civilians likewise grew leery of Camp Chase.

Union authorities had no intention of using Camp Chase as a military prison since they believed that the war would be short, but the camp became

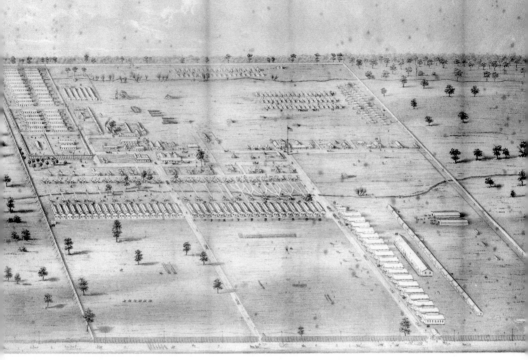

Camp Chase in 1861 (Courtesy of the Ohio History Connection, AL04216)

a wartime fixture in Columbus, Ohio. Following the Confederate bombardment of Fort Sumter in April 1861, both federal and state officials hastily raised and trained troops. Thousands of Ohio volunteers converged on Columbus in response to Lincoln's April 15, 1861, call for 75,000 volunteers. New recruits organized at Camp Jackson, four miles west of the state capitol. On June 20, 1861, state officials changed the post's name to Camp Chase to honor Salmon P. Chase, Lincoln's secretary of the treasury and former Ohio governor.[51]

Camp Chase served four functions throughout the war: as a training camp for Union recruits, a detention site for paroled Union soldiers, a mustering-out location for Northern troops, and a military prison that held political prisoners and prisoners of war.[52] The first prisoners, mostly political captives from western Virginia, Ohio, and Kentucky, arrived on July 5, 1861, just weeks after Camp Chase's establishment.[53] Political prisoners constituted the bulk of the prison's population from August 1861 through mid-1863. At that point, Union officials, for the sake of discipline, transferred most political prisoners and Confederate officers to Johnson's Island Prison in Sandusky Bay, Ohio, leaving mostly enlisted men at Camp Chase.[54]

Military prison officials, like their penitentiary counterparts, emphasized constant surveillance and severed inmates' connection with the outside world. An imposing plank wall, complete with guardhouses and parapet, surrounded Camp Chase's 160 acres. Prisoners knew to steer clear of the "dead line," a small ditch eight feet from the outer wall that surrounded the barracks.[55] Authorities organized the camp by creating three separate prisons. Prison No. 1 consisted of an acre while Prison No. 2 and Prison No. 3 were larger, approximately five acres each. Camp Chase's capacity ranged between 3,500 and 4,000, but it often held from 5,000 to 6,000 prisoners. Constant solitary confinement was impractical, but in 1863, federal inspectors recommended the construction of "eight strong cells" for "disobedient or violent prisoners" and the purchase of six pairs of handcuffs for special punishment. Overall, Camp Chase was a site of public fascination, albeit one that civilians wanted to avoid.[56]

Civilians understood that crimes like larceny, burglary, felony, and homicide warranted penitentiary sentences, but became only vaguely familiar with wartime crimes, despite the Federal Government's publication of offenses.[57] Vague directives frustrated civilians since, from the Revolutionary era, Americans expected laws to be fair, open, and easy to understand.[58] The list of offenses that warranted imprisonment at Camp Chase confused many individuals. On April 30, 1862, Maj. Gen. John Frémont, commander of the Mountain Department in Wheeling, Virginia, decreed that Camp Chase would hold treason suspects from Ohio, Virginia, and Kentucky. His circular warned that Union officials would detain any disloyal person accused of "having served under the rebel Government whether in the military, judicial, executive, or legislative departments." Persons "taken with arms in their hands" or engaged as guerrillas were also subject to detention and further orders from the War Department.[59]

The February battles of forts Henry and Donelson brought an influx of prisoners of war to Camp Chase, but federal and state officials decided even before this inundation that the prison could not accommodate all prisoners. In October 1861 Col. William Hoffman, the newly appointed commissary general of prisoners, looked for a location suitable for a second military prison. He considered two islands in Sandusky Bay on the seasonally frigid shores of Lake Erie. The first, Kelley's Island, seemed viable, save for its large vineyard. Hoffman nixed the location, echoing the antebellum idea that alcohol tempted men—even ostensibly responsible prison guards—to misbehavior. He instead selected the second island, Johnson's Island, for its proximity to Sandusky, which would discourage escape attempts since civilians would be on alert for Confederate fugitives. Close proximity to Sandusky would also eliminate the need for storage houses and save the government money. Hoffman directed the state governor to muster a guard of 100 to 150 men to oversee approximately 1,000 prisoners. Quartermaster General Montgomery C. Meigs approved Hoffman's plans and echoed the antebellum emphasis on humane treatment by exhorting Hoffman to establish the prison with the "strictest economy consistent with security and proper welfare of the prisoners." Meigs also reflected the belief that incarceration equated criminality by denouncing future captives as "erring men," a familiar phrase that middle-class reformers used to describe criminals.[60] Johnson's Island received overflow prisoners from Camp Chase and other prisoners who challenged the Federal Government either as enemy soldiers or through subversion on the home front.

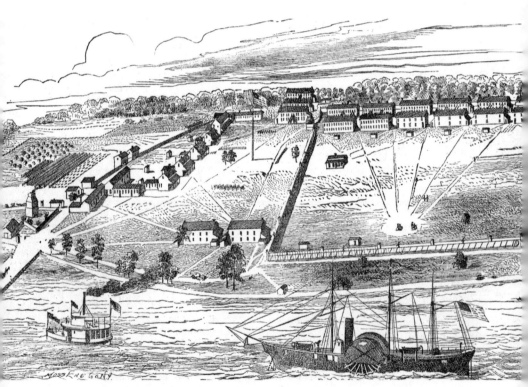

Johnson's Island (Courtesy of the Ohio History Connection, AL04257)

Prison officials throughout the nineteenth century kept records of prisoners, but the Civil War complicated this task. Hoffman directed military prison officials to keep registers of all prisoners, as did their penitentiary counterparts. In July 1862, the commissary general blurred distinctions between prisoners when he advised Maj. W. S. Pierson, commanding Johnson's Island, that all captives were considered prisoners of war, "some military and some civilians." When enemy soldiers arrived at the prison, officials recorded rank, regiment, and either company or town from whence they came. When officials received civilians, they substituted these categories with the offender's hometown, county, and state.[61]

Hoffman's request for this identifying information is revealing. First, it parallels intake registers from the antebellum period in which penitentiary officials recorded offenders' names, ages, places of residence, and crimes to familiarize themselves with prisoners before confining them with countless others whose identities mattered only at twice-daily roll calls. Second, it indicates that the classification scheme for prisoners of war and civilian offenders, who could be termed state or political prisoners, was a work in progress and, despite rhetorical distinctions, actually made military prisoners feel like, and compare themselves to, criminals.

Confederate authorities in Richmond also struggled with prisoner classification since they used Castle Thunder Prison to punish offenders from all over the Confederacy and mixed enemy combatants with civilian offenders. The Castle, after all, became, in the words of Commandant George Alexander, "the only penitentiary" in the Confederacy after its establishment in 1862.[62] In that year, Confederate authorities commandeered Gleanor's Tobacco Factory, Whitlock's Warehouse, and Palmer's Factory to create Castle Thunder. The Castle, like Salisbury, housed political prisoners, Union and Confederate deserters, and criminals from all over the Confederacy and it elicited criticism from the press.[63] For example, in January 1863 the *Raleigh Weekly Standard* lambasted the Confederate government's pursuit of subversives and condemned its curtailment of liberties. "God pity the poor creature who . . . is thrust on mere suspicion into Castle Thunder or the Bastille at Salisbury," the paper moaned, "and God save the State from the counsels and the control of the Destructive leaders."

This criticism pointed specifically at Confederate President Jefferson Davis's declaration of martial law in Richmond on March 1, 1862, and his suspension of civil jurisdiction and the writ of habeas corpus, which created antagonism between government officials and the public. The *Weekly Standard* decried Confederate officials' pronunciation of North Carolina as "a d—d nest of traitors."[64] Political prisoners streamed into Richmond given officials' suspicion. Castle Thunder consequently became a melting pot that detained black and white men and women of all classes.[65] Confederate deserters and political prisoners occupied the Gleanor building, which had an estimated capacity of 650. Whitlock's Warehouse, with a capacity of 350, confined black male and female prisoners and white women. Deserters and, later, Union prisoners of war occupied Palmer's Factory, with an estimated capacity of 400. Confederate officials detained persons on suspicion, so Castle Thunder quickly exceeded its capacity of 1,400.[66]

Many Northern and Southern military prisons became overcrowded, as did antebellum penitentiaries. During wartime, however, the stockades, makeshift holding pens, and commandeered buildings filled more rapidly than did antebellum penitentiaries, especially after the cessation of prisoner exchanges in the summer of 1863. Confederate authorities planned what became the

Castle Thunder Prison, Petersburg (Richmond), April 1865; photograph by Andrew J. Russell (Library of Congress)

war's most notorious prison amid these circumstances. Battlefield conflict in both the Eastern and Western theaters strained Richmond's prisons throughout 1863. Confederate authorities followed Secretary of War James Seddon's lead and called for the establishment of a military prison in Georgia and, as in Ohio, national officials consulted with state politicians. Seddon directed assistant adjutant general, Capt. William S. Winder, to visit Milledgeville while en route to Americus to get input from Georgia Governor Joseph Brown regarding the prison's location.[67] After this meeting, however, Brown largely disappeared from the historical record and Confederate officials, primarily Adjutant and Inspector General Samuel Cooper; Maj. Gen. H. Cobb, stationed at Atlanta; Assistant Quartermaster Richard B. Winder; and John Winder, Richmond's provost marshal (who later became Confederate commissary general of prisoners on November 23, 1864), established Andersonville.

These men faced the daunting, if not virtually impossible, tasks of constructing, staffing, supplying, and transporting prisoners to the new prison under significant economic duress. Assistant Quartermaster Richard B. Winder repeatedly petitioned other national authorities for food in late 1863 and early 1864. He reasoned that he could obtain corn and meal for enemy inmates from the nearest commissary, but lacked meat, flour, sugar, molasses, rice, soap, and candles. Andersonville's officials thus confronted an immediate supply deficit in early February, just weeks prior to the arrival of the first prisoners.[68]

While Winder was preoccupied with inadequate supplies, Gen. Samuel Cooper concerned himself with the prison's physical space. Cooper estimated that Andersonville's capacity would range from ten thousand to twelve thousand. Confederate authorities impressed slave labor from local planters, anxiously clamored for the construction of mills to grind grain for prisoners, worried about how to procure beef from Florida, and fretted about the construction of prisoners' quarters, storehouses, and hospital buildings right up to the day—February 20, 1864—on which inmates were scheduled to arrive.[69]

Confederate officials were immediately concerned about the institution's viability and practical oversight given this improvisation. General Cooper was also acutely aware that appointing an outsider to command could cause Georgians to be wary about the new military prison, an issue that echoed antebellum Southerners' suspicion both of prisons and centralized authority. He therefore advised Maj. Gen. Howell Cobb on February 7, 1864, that "it is due to Georgia" that the new commander hail from the state to "allay any sectional prejudices which might be anticipated."[70] While logical, this directive also foreshadowed a potential crossover in the lines of power between state and national authorities.

A few weeks later, on February 26, Seddon appointed Col. A. W. Persons commandant of Andersonville and granted him power over the prison guard. The directive seemed straightforward, but confusion ensued. On March 12, 1864, John Winder complained to General Cooper that his order directed Persons to "take command without designating to whom he shall report."[71] Winder's complaint underscored the fact that the Confederacy lacked a system for operating military prisons. Since national authorities were novices in prison operation, they had to work out kinks in communication between military, national, and state officials and learn how to manage prisons and prisoners haphazardly as the war progressed. The task became more difficult in 1864 as the prisoner population mounted and the South's monetary and material resources and lines of communication faced increasing strain. Nonetheless, inmates and civilians North and South clung to the antebellum belief that inmates should receive humane treatment while not posing a significant financial burden.

Labor and the Goal of Institutional Self-Sufficiency

Andersonville and other military prisons were established in the shadow of penitentiaries. No matter how dire the circumstances, political officials and the public assumed that both military prisons and penitentiaries should not impose a major financial burden. The expectation that penitentiaries be self-sufficient became embedded in the antebellum period and shaped Union and Confederate officials' concerns regarding the cost of military prisons.

Penitentiary officials believed that criminals should pay for their own confinement since their offenses burdened law-abiding civilians. In 1836, the directors of the Ohio Penitentiary eagerly anticipated the day when "the virtuous portion of our community will cease to be taxed for the support and punishment of the criminal." Similarly, the committee appointed to inspect the Virginia Penitentiary in 1824 contended that "society must be entitled . . . to remuneration" from convict labor and held that convicts should support themselves since they broke the law.[72] Consistent self-sufficiency and profits, however, were difficult to realize.

Cost-conscious penitentiary officials often used convict labor for internal improvements and wartime officials at both penitentiaries and military prisons employed this tactic. Labor equated punishment for some prisoners and constituted reward for others. Either way, prison officials saved money when they used convict labor for penitentiary construction or improvements. Elam Lynds, mastermind of the Auburn system, exemplified the view of using convict labor as punishment when he, at gunpoint, forced prisoners from Auburn Penitentiary to construct Sing Sing Penitentiary.[73]

Ohio officials used psychological, rather than physical, coercion. When the Ohio state legislature authorized enlargement of the penitentiary in 1833, officials selected inmates nearing the end of their sentences to complete the project and promised them that if they worked faithfully and did not attempt to escape, they would be released upon the job's completion. Frugal Ohio officials also used convict labor to save money. In 1837, Ohio Penitentiary officials ordered convicts to build a separate building for female prisoners and saved $78,428, or 7.5 cents a day per convict, compared to the rates of outside contractors. Wartime officials also thought that prison labor was logical. In 1864, the Ohio Penitentiary warden noted a separate building for insane convicts was completed "wholly by convict labor."[74]

Officials prized cost effectiveness and outsiders rejoiced when penitentiaries yielded profits. Journalists extolled the revenue that the Ohio Penitentiary generated in the antebellum period. In 1837, the *Alton Telegraph* reported that, for the first time, the penitentiary would be "sustained from its own resources." Two years later, in 1839, the New Orleans *Times Picayune* commented with an air of sarcasm that "they are getting to be profitable establishments, these state prisons." The inspiration for this assessment was, as both the *Picayune* and the *Huron Reflector* reported, a positive balance of between $19,000 and $20,000. Profits increased in 1840 when the Baltimore *Sun* reported that the penitentiary generated $25,000 in revenue. Newspapers reported similar profits throughout 1845, but the tone changed in the 1850s. In 1856, the *Elyria Independent Democrat* contended that emphasis on profit masked a dark reality. The paper complained that, according to the penitentiary's directors and warden, buildings were dilapidated and prisoners' quarters infested with vermin. The paper urged readers to question glowing reports and concluded that, since its establishment, the penitentiary "has been a constant tax upon the State" since profits never covered repair costs.[75]

Newspapers that covered the Virginia Penitentiary also reported profits early on, but then deflected attention from short revenue by focusing on items produced by prison labor that were sold on the local market. In 1811, the *Raleigh Register* boasted that the total profit generated since the penitentiary's establishment was $43,333.73, but did not offer a year-by-year assessment. More importantly, the paper claimed that convicts were "clothed by their own hands and fed by the products of their own labor." Twenty-seven years later, in 1838, the Philadelphia *Public Ledger* proclaimed that the profits generated by prisoners amounted to $19,313.37.

All seemed to be going relatively well until 1854, when the Raleigh *Southern Weekly Post* and the Milwaukee *Weekly Wisconsin* reported that a fire destroyed all penitentiary workshops, a catastrophe from which the institution took months to recover. Nonetheless, in 1856, the New Orleans *Times Picayune* announced that the penitentiary's manufactures for the fiscal year 1855 amounted to $66,324.67, a total greater than any previous year, except 1854, just prior to the fire.[76] From then on, the Richmond *Dispatch* routinely carried advertisements for items manufactured by prison labor and available on the local market. These wagons, boots, shoes, cart harnesses, drays, and wheelbarrows for sale represented penitentiary officials' desire to ensure the institution's profitability in the aftermath of catastrophe.[77]

The Virginia Penitentiary was not the only institution that fire devastated physically and financially. In 1843, the Georgia Penitentiary's workshops went up in flames. Newspapers estimated the total loss at anywhere from $20,000 to $50,000. Prior to that, the penitentiary generated profit and pleased journalists, civilians, and politicians. In 1829, the *Raleigh Register* and the New York *Evening Post* reported that the penitentiary was self-sufficient and required no money from the state treasury. Profits, however, were modest, totaling only $1,263. Journalists made it seem like the penitentiary recovered quickly after the 1843 fire. The *Raleigh Register* reported on November 21, 1845, that the prison "for the last two years" generated profits of $9,430.79. This total was likely consolidated to paint the penitentiary in a positive light. Profits remained comparatively meager and below those of the Ohio and Virginia penitentiaries—the *Raleigh Register* quoted 1847 profits at $10,000, while the Baltimore *Sun* scored them at $15,315.[78] The incongruent reports highlight journalists' inability to obtain accurate information about the penitentiary, but the positive balance met expectations.

Like journalists, inspectors rejoiced when penitentiaries generated profits, but lamented them as burdensome when labor fell short. In the 1840s and 1850s, D.C. Penitentiary inspectors and wardens John Dade and Thomas Fitnam bemoaned the deficit. Ironically, they attributed the financial shortcoming to the paucity of inmates and short sentences, raising questions about officials' commitment to the reform program. In 1841, a deficit year, the inspectors emphasized that the prison held only seventy-nine inmates and argued that sentences were too short for inmates to learn a trade. Warden Thomas Thornley likewise griped that convicts were the most "reckless in society" and therefore "unacquainted with the use of tools" upon entering prison, so officials devoted long, wasteful hours training them to be productive. Since inmates learned slowly and served brief sentences, Thornley argued that release came precisely "when their labor becomes valuable." New, inexperienced inmates, according to Thornley, lent themselves "to anything but the prosperity of the institution."[79] Antebellum officials' expectation that prison labor should be profitable created false hope, which persisted into wartime.

Wartime penitentiary officials expected prisoners' work to generate revenue, committed more fully to contract labor, and focused on producing products for military consumption.[80] Self-sufficiency, however, remained a difficult, if not impossible, goal and prison labor often could not overcome war's economic strains.[81] Officials blamed inadequate supplies or lazy inmates for the lack of profit, arguments reminiscent of Thornley's antebellum complaints.

War ravaged the South as battlefield conflict devastated towns, rampant inflation increased prices of necessary provisions, and the buying power of both civilians and institutions suffered.[82] Penitentiaries consequently faced supply shortages for two reasons. First, war demanded that states send most supplies to soldiers in the field. Second, despite the goal of self-sufficiency, penitentiary profits decreased during wartime and curtailed purchasing power. In 1862, the Virginia Penitentiary's surgeon lamented that rations were short due to the "exorbitant prices of meat, vegetables, medicines, soap, vinegar, and bedding," some of which were completely unavailable. He also complained that "the troubles of the times" left the prison full of idle inmates. Supt. Colin Bass confirmed in an 1863 report that convicts were sedentary for one-third of their sentences since "fabulous prices" precluded the purchase of supplies for the shops. The penitentiary therefore placed "a heavy burden upon the treasury," which unnerved officials since the war effort required extensive monetary and material support.[83]

In Georgia, initial optimism about the penitentiary's economic outlook turned to cynicism about inmates' ability and desire to work. In 1861, Col. James A. Green, principal keeper of the Georgia Penitentiary, boasted that the penitentiary had paid all debts from the fiscal year 1860, and the Committee on the Penitentiary noted that scheduled improvements were complete. These included a new brick building complete with hospital, chapel, and eating room; additional cell rooms; and brick workshops that, in conjunction with the original workshops, would enhance the "health both of convicts and officers."[84]

Officials wanted convicts who labored in the new workshops to produce supplies for Confederate troops. Colonel Green bragged that every department produced military equipment, and he was confident that that the inmates' labor would prove an "important auxiliary in securing our independence" if the conflict was protracted. Green concluded that penitentiary labor would help defeat "the criminal invaders of Southern soil."[85] Ironically, Green viewed penitentiary inmates positively as productive Southerners, and thought Union soldiers were the real felons.

Green's rosy outlook on both the prison's economic prospects and its inhabitants tarnished in 1862. The Georgia General Assembly's view of the prison contradicted that of a special military commission appointed to inspect how convict labor aided Confederate troops. Assemblymen credited Colonel Green's "faithful management" for the fact that the penitentiary paid $10,000 into the state treasury and fulfilled antebellum expectations about penitentiary profits. But this praise masked a deep-seated problem with convict labor that directly echoed the antebellum concerns of D.C. Penitentiary Keeper Thornley.

In the war's second year, Governor Brown ordered that an armory be established at the penitentiary and employed Mr. Peter Jones, who had long-standing connections to the manufacture of U.S. arms, as superintendent. This seemed like a logical step that would fuel the Confederate war effort, but the military committee appointed to inspect the manufacture of guns denounced convict labor as inefficient. Arms manufacturing was a skilled task that convicts had to learn as apprentices. Even after training, the inspectors complained that inmates took "no pride or interest in their work" since it was an "enforced routine," and they cared little whether the job was "well done or spoiled." Negligent prisoners wasted money and supplies, and armory overseers engaged in an endless cycle of training since convicts' terms expired just when they became "experienced and useful." The patriotic fervor that inspired penitentiary officials to praise convicts as loyal, productive Southerners faded by 1862, leading the military committee to recommend the establishment of another armory staffed by wage laborers who had monetary incentive to work carefully and efficiently.[86]

War's circumstances left penitentiary officials in a catch-22 situation. Convict labor and institutional self-sufficiency were expected, but the war complicated yet another common antebellum practice—the hiring out of convicts. As previously noted, officials' focus on profits increased their desire to increase commitment to contract labor.[87] But contracts often failed to materialize. For example, in 1861, the warden of the Ohio Penitentiary complained that the "unsettled state of the country" made it impossible to "induce manufacturers to take contracts for convict labor," leaving the prison short on profits.[88]

To make matters worse, multiple fires that same year prevented Ohio Penitentiary inmates from working much, if at all. In 1861, the prison burned four times and destroyed shops that produced saddles, cavalry equipment, and bullets for the Union Army. The penitentiary's bottom line consequently suffered and disciplinary problems escalated since idle inmates sat in overcrowded cells. According to one observer, penitentiary officials could barely monitor the 965 convicts, many of whom were accustomed to daytime labor.[89] Overcrowding fostered communication among inmates, and guards worried about potential rebellion. Guards were usually suspicious of inmates, even if they were working, but their regular suspicion stemmed from their belief that inmates could never be fully productive, another assumption that carried over from the antebellum period.

In the antebellum period, middle-class Americans looked down upon criminals and compared them unfavorably to law-abiding citizens who were committed to success in the market economy and prided themselves on individual achievement, mobility, and the accumulation of wealth.[90] Antebellum assumptions that criminals were idle, lazy, and dissipated persisted into wartime and provided penitentiary officials with a scapegoat for the prison's lack of self-sufficiency. [91] Self-sufficiency at the D.C. Penitentiary was never achieved in the antebellum period, nor was it realized during the war. As noted earlier, antebellum officials blamed the low prison population for the institution's lack of profit, and the penitentiary remained unprofitable in wartime despite the growing population. After Warden Hiram King assumed his post on April 12, 1861, he blamed the penitentiary's lack of self-sufficiency on "the stupid and inept Negro convicts" who had "predetermination to do as little as possible."[92]

Virginia Penitentiary officials also blamed the prison's financial woes on convicts' character. In 1863, Supt. Colin Bass noted that convict labor was not profitable since convicts were "worthless, diseased, depraved, and lazy characters, fished up . . . from the worse form of society." Authorities also griped that many male convicts entered prison "old and decrepit" or "deranged," rendering work impossible. Most female prisoners were likewise incapable of working, since many were "old and infirm" and lived in "cramped apartments" where they could not "be worked to any profit."[93]

Even if female inmates worked, the tasks assigned to them were not profitable. Captive women bore responsibility for the upkeep of the penitentiary "home" through sewing, ironing, binding shoes, spinning, and doing laundry for male inmates. Ohio Penitentiary officials enlisted female inmates to produce men's drawers, white shirts, and muslin for Union troops.[94] Soldiers in the field appreciated their efforts, but they did nothing for the penitentiary's bottom line.

Military Prison Labor

Many nineteenth-century civilians believed that all prisoners, military and criminal, should work. Reformer Frederick Wines contended that war occurred in courts and on battlefields and asserted that the "condition of a prisoner of war to that of a slave is but a step." Wines likened prisoners of war to criminals and concluded that compulsory labor was "a natural sequel of the condition of servitude, whether military or penal."[95] Military prison officials agreed and used prisoners to ease financial burden. The laws of war upheld this practice by stating that captors could compel prisoners of war to work as long as it did not directly harm their state of origin.[96]

The belief that imprisonment should not pose a financial burden transferred to Civil War military prisons. The public was well aware of imprisonment's cost. In 1862, the Richmond *Daily Dispatch* rejoiced when 3,300

Yankee prisoners left Castle Thunder since the Confederate government would henceforth save "$4,000 per day," the average cost of feeding its prisoners.[97] Since military prison officers faced increased financial strain as the war progressed, they, like penitentiary officials, often used prison labor to complete improvements both in and outside of prisons. Confederate officials emphasized the necessity of prison labor throughout 1863 and 1864. In July 1863, Maj. Isaac Carrington urged Capt. W. S. Winder to employ Castle Thunder prisoners serving long sentences to "materially lessen the expense of their keeping." Later in the year, Carrington contended that Union deserters, most of whom were "foreigners" and "common laborers," should work.[98] They built fortifications and performed other manual labor for the Confederate Army to defray the cost of clothing, food, and housing.

Southern civilians were accustomed to inmates working to mitigate costs, either in prison or on the public works, and the Richmond *Daily Dispatch* celebrated wartime prison labor. In February 1864, the paper praised the departure of forty-three Yankees to work in the North Carolina coal mines, making them "useful to the Confederacy."[99] Two years earlier, the *Dispatch* reported that Castle Thunder officials sent fifty men confined for "light offenses" under guard to "rebuild the bridge over the Rapidan River destroyed by the Yankees."[100] These jobs saved Confederate authorities money as the war sapped financial resources and manpower.

Assistant Adjutant General Garnett Andrews's 1864 inspection of Salisbury Prison also reflected the antebellum idea that prisons should be self-sufficient. He evaluated the prisoners and concluded that there were many "skillful mechanics, blacksmiths, gunsmiths, carpenters, shoemakers, joiners, harness makers, and tailors" among the Yankee deserters and convicts. He therefore believed that, with a supply of tools and materials, the prison "could be made not only self-sustaining, but of considerable value to the Government." Andrews recommended that the quartermaster procure items for the workshops so that the prison would at best be an asset and, at worst, not an expense.[101] Wartime officials also reflected the antebellum expectation that inmates find gainful employment upon release. In 1863, Insp. Isaac Carrington commented that Salisbury's prisoners should "earn their bread" during their captivity and then "go at large and seek employment" upon release.[102]

Richmond and Salisbury were not the only cities where officials required that inmates defray costs through work. Authorities in Washington used labor on public works to relieve overcrowding and expenses at Old Capitol Prison. In March 1863, General-in-Chief Henry Halleck noted that one hundred prisoners were sentenced to hard labor on public works and rejoiced that "the number is daily increasing." Halleck praised prison labor since it alleviated costs and eased officials' supervisory burden since the prison was "already too much crowded."[103]

Camp Chase officials also used prison labor to save money on internal improvements. In July and December 1862, Camp Chase's officials ordered inmates to dig vaults, whitewash buildings, drain standing water, and construct roads. Insp. H. M. Lazelle demanded that all work at Camp Chase "designed to in any manner benefit the prisoner" or "for their own comfort or improved condition" be performed "by prisoners so far as it is practical." Lazelle's position was consistent with the antebellum ideas that first, inmate labor saved money and second, that all prisoners, regardless of offense, benefited from work.[104] Penitentiary officials believed that the prison labor program taught inmates skills and increased industriousness, and Camp Chase's officials maintained this attitude. They ordered prisoners to improve cooking ranges, mend shoes, construct new buildings, build parapets, and dig wells and sinks.[105]

Camp Chase officials necessitated prison labor for improvements, but other military prison officials tied work to incentives, as did Ohio Penitentiary officials in the 1830s. During the Civil War, some Union prison officials used the prospect of labor to compel renewed loyalty to the United States. Camp Chase inmate William Duff recalled how many inmates, himself included, worked to strengthen prison walls and dig drainage ditches. Union officials rewarded the workers with "full rations," but Duff griped that officers demanded that inmates "take the oath of allegiance" to continue working—he and others refused.[106] In August 1864, Camp Chase officials permitted prisoners of war who took the oath of allegiance to construct a fence around the camp and often required inmates who took the oath to wear a badge signifying loyalty. The badge may have ostracized inmates, but those who pledged fealty thought labor a good reward, judging from Commandant William Richardson's November 1864 comments. Richardson requested that Hoffman permit prisoners who took the oath to construct buildings inside Camp Chase. The commandant knew that this was an effective tactic and declared that prisoners waiting to take the oath "expressed a desire" and were "anxious" to work.[107]

The story was different at Johnson's Island, where imprisoned Confederate officers refused work. Many of these men were accustomed to having slaves and believed manual labor—especially in prison—beneath them. Prison commander Lt. Col. William Pierson, however, expected that inmates police their own quarters. A frustrated Pierson reported subpar conditions in October 1863. He complained that "As to the fault of the prisoners themselves in not policing, it is my experience that prisoners (officers) will as a general thing do no more than they are compelled to do."[108] Union officials refused to compensate for inmates' shortcomings in cleanliness and let them mire in their own filth.

Inmates' refusal to work frustrated U.S. officers, but officers nonetheless expected that they work. In June 1864, Col. Charles W. Hill, commanding the post, commented that the policing of quarters improved, but lamented that it was "not quite what it should be." Since the prisoners were all officers, Hill sarcastically commented that it was "somewhat difficult to obtain the necessary amount of dirty work from them to keep their quarters, mess rooms, and kitchens in perfect order."[109] Two months later, Hill and other officials deemed the construction of gravel floors in the prison necessary and hired some outside carpenters. But, in an attempt to save money, officers also solicited carpenters and laborers from among the inmates to work for nominal compensation. The inmates, however, refused; Hill sarcastically surmised it was a "pure matter of dignity," and he equated the once high-standing enemies with lowly criminals. The prisoners, he satirized, "can beg clothing and food from the government, but can't labor even for their own convenience."[110] Hill ironically pointed out that the once independent men were dependent on the U.S. government for subsistence but, to save money, that same government relied upon the prisoners' willingness to work.

The situation was even more dire for Confederate officials in charge of Andersonville. Prisoners of war rapidly filled the stockade in February and March 1864, but infrastructure was lacking. On March 9, 1864, Col. Alexander W. Persons, commanding the post, detailed prisoners to work on different buildings.[111] This authorization came after Assistant Quartermaster Richard B. Winder informed Maj. A. M. Allen, commissary of subsistence at Andersonville, that Yankee prisoners detailed to work were to receive double rations as per directives from Richmond.[112] The central authorities in the Confederate capital thus seemed out of touch since there were no extra rations.

In August, Winder necessitated that Yankee prisoners of war provide for themselves to combat necessity. Winder wrote to Quartermaster Major F. W. Dillard, headquartered at Columbus, Georgia, and proposed to establish a shoe shop. "I can furnish from 500 to 1,000 shoemakers at once (prisoners of war)," Winder begged, exhorting Dillard to take over the shop since he oversaw the leather department and inmates needed shoes.[113] Whether or not Dillard assented is unclear, but further directives for work came on September 3, 1864. Assistant Adjutant General John Withers encouraged Maj. Gen. J. F. Gilmer, chief of the Engineer Bureau, to either impress or encourage prisoners to volunteer to drain the marsh within Andersonville's stockade.[114]

The circumstances that led penitentiary and military prison officials to employ prison labor to either improve prison space or to provide for themselves were similar in the antebellum and Civil War years. In the former period, overcrowding strained penitentiaries and prompted officials to focus on making prison labor profitable or use convict labor for prison improvements. During the Civil War, the steady influx of prisoners of war quickly strained military prisons, both at planned prisons like Johnson's Island and at hastily constructed facilities like Andersonville. While military prison officials did not aim to generate revenue in the same way as penitentiary officials, they assumed that inmates should work to offset the cost of detention whether on work details, in tasks to improve quarters, or to produce supplies for consumption.

The transition from peace to war did not usher in a new set of expectations for prison operation. Antebellum penitentiary architects and military officers were often one and the same and adhered to similar ideals. Elam Lynds, military man and architect of the Auburn system of penitentiary discipline, structured penitentiary administration along the military's hierarchical lines. Prisoners, the public, and prison officers believed that inmates should receive humane treatment and insisted that guards conduct themselves in a gentlemanly manner.[115] The pioneers of the penitentiary program envisioned self-sustaining, if not profitable, institutions based on prison labor and these assumptions influenced military prisons.

As in the antebellum period, wartime prisons garnered international attention. The thousands of Americans taken captive during the sectional crisis horrified London observers. In March 1864, the *London Times* offered the following summary, stating, "The whole land groans with dungeons and bastilles—in the North 34,000 Confederates, in the South nearly 20,000

Federals languish in imprisonment—in both sections an unknown number of suspected and often unoffending civilians and women pay the penalty of imputed opinion." High prison populations shocked civilians on both sides of the Atlantic and the *Times* noted that institutions, including Camp Chase, Johnson's Island, Castle Thunder, and Andersonville, were "words of terror known throughout the civilized globe," not just in the United States. "Where it may well be asked, will it end?" asked the *Times,* advancing a pointed question.[116] A question of equal importance, however, was how did these institutions earn this reputation and how did the men who operated them garner such power? The next chapter answers these questions.

Regulating Operation

Penitentiary and Military Prison
Officials' Quest for Order

Union and Confederate political and military officials, like antebellum penitentiary reformers, believed that prisons should safeguard peaceable civilians and afford inmates humane treatment. In 1863, the Confederate House of Representatives equated Castle Thunder Prison's purpose to that of penitentiaries, describing it as "the protection of society by the confinement of persons dangerous to its peace."[1] That same year, U.S. Commissary General William Hoffman condemned Richmond's military prisons as so filthy and crowded that it would shock humanity to confine in them "even the most abandoned criminals." Hoffman also denounced Union guards' treatment of Confederate prisoners at Camp Chase as "wholly unauthorized," and reaffirmed the U.S. government's desire to treat enemy captives with "all the kindness which a proper humane feeling prompts and which is consistent with their position."[2]

Achieving this objective, however, was difficult. Both penitentiary and military prison officials struggled given their inexperience in prison management and because of rampant overcrowding, a pressing concern throughout the century. National officials, North and South, learned about prison administration from state officials, who became accustomed to penitentiary oversight prior to the war.

During the Civil War, Union and Confederate officials worked with state politicians to establish military prisons, but lines of authority often blurred since state governors were reluctant to relinquish, or even share, oversight of any prison within their states. There was no federal prison system in the antebellum period, nor was there any reason for permanent military prisons, so Northern and Southern political and military officials did not know how to manage large numbers of prisoners—a task reserved for state politicians. Wartime penitentiary and military prison operation, administration, and the daily experiences of officials, therefore, were modeled on antebellum practices. All prison officers were inexperienced, but were expected to behave as gentlemen; guards endured poor living and working conditions; and regulations encouraged humane punishment and mandated that officers keep distance from, but closely monitor, inmates' behavior and correspondence.

Michel Foucault demonstrated how prison establishment defined abnormal behavior, which in turn delineated normal behavior and marked the boundaries of criminality.[3] But Foucault's interpretation overlooked how imprisonment defined normal and abnormal behavior for wardens and guards. Auburn system architect Elam Lynds believed order was central to penitentiary discipline and wanted constant surveillance for both inmates and guards.[4] Beginning in the antebellum period and continuing throughout the century, penitentiary officials were appointed based on the qualities that they possessed as men, distinguishing them from jailers. Reformers condemned jailers as crude and merciless, so penitentiary guards had to demonstrate good character through political and religious involvement.[5] The same held true for wartime military prison officials. But once on the job, strict rules, long hours, and residence in close proximity to prisons quashed individuality and often tarnished guards' character. The penitentiary was the product of elites' desire for an ordered society, but elites seldom influenced daily prison operation. Prison officials were respectable men, but far from elite themselves—pay was adequate for life's necessities but not for its comforts, and modestly paid guards did more to shape the practical aspects of nineteenth-century imprisonment than reformers and politicians.[6]

Administration and Guards—Managing the Institutions

In the antebellum period, state legislatures and governors appointed penitentiary officers, many of whom were political cronies with little, if any, experience with imprisonment. In the federal case, the U.S. Congress authorized the construction of the D.C. Penitentiary and appointed officials with similar "credentials"—or lack thereof. Inexperienced men overseeing matters of criminal justice was nothing new.[7] The practice dated back to the co-lonial period, persisted into wartime, and was adopted by military prisons.

Antebellum appointees at the Virginia, District of Columbia, Georgia, and Ohio penitentiaries commanded respect, but were novices in prison administration. Men seeking positions as penitentiary guards, keepers, or wardens in the Virginia, D.C., Georgia, and Ohio penitentiaries had to be honest, industrious, moral, and temperate—qualities that substituted for practical experience.[8] Ironically, as noted earlier, guards and wardens had to model impeccable behavior and participate in political and religious ac-tivities to procure a rather undesirable job.[9] Potential appointees for these and positions like deputy warden, physician, or clerk had to be respect-able gentlemen with reputable social connections. When the Civil War be-gan, Americans still expected prison officials to possess these traits, follow Christian principles, and treat inmates humanely.[10]

Commandants at the Virginia Penitentiary and Castle Thunder received appointments based on personal qualities, not practical experience. Martin Mims, appointed the first keeper of the Virginia Penitentiary in 1801, was described as an honest man, but his experience with imprisonment was limited to his position as the state's brick contractor during penitentiary construction.[11] George W. Alexander, whom Richmond's Provost Marshal John Winder appointed commandant of Castle Thunder on October 27, 1862, also lacked administrative experience. Ironically, the only prison ex-perience that Alexander had was as a prisoner of war.[12]

Commandants and guards were expected to behave as gentlemen, but once they assumed their posts, the standards of judgment often shifted. Penitentiary officers were expected to model positive qualities for inmates and ensure humane discipline. Keepers, however, could be exempt from this while guards remained accountable. For example, in Georgia, as in other states, the governor appointed keepers, who were often political hacks with no experience in penology. If the keeper's character slipped, outsiders judged his success on the cost of prison operation and profits from con-vict labor.[13] Guards, however, remained culpable. The 1816 Georgia Penal Code stipulated that any guard "guilty of willful inhumanity or oppression" would be removed, fined up to $100, and imprisoned with hard labor or in solitary confinement.[14] The double standard that was lenient toward com-mandants, but strict for guards perhaps stemmed from reformers' fears that guards could become "tools of the convicts" and cause trouble.[15]

Some guards may have colluded with inmates, but the biggest challenges that guards faced were boredom and disorganization. Good order was of the utmost importance to prison officials, but it required guards, who were easily distracted and desirous of social interaction, to be on heightened alert for extended periods of time. This was especially difficult at night and posed disciplinary concerns for both penitentiary and military prison guards. Darkness masked inmates' communication, and weary guards preferred sleep rather than duty.

The Virginia Penitentiary illustrates the challenges of guarding inmates after dark, especially since the prison had no permanent guard. From the institution's founding until 1846, a specially organized militia unit, the Public Guard, was on night patrol. The night watch changed posts frequently to encourage alertness, but rotation actually created disorder. The two-hour rotation schedule created windows for inmates to misbehave and/or attempt escape. Officials eventually scrapped this system and suggested that an Interior Guard assume regular night duty.[16] Preventing disorder, however, ultimately depended on the guards' vigilance and ability to monitor numerous inmates crowded into cells designed for solitary confinement.[17]

Long hours also undermined guards' attentiveness at the D.C. and Ohio penitentiaries. The public knew that guards worked long hours for low pay and considered their lack of motivation a risk. On May 5, 1854, one civilian, under the pseudonym "Justice," wrote a passionate letter to the editor of the Washington *Evening Star*. "Justice" criticized the conditions under which D.C. Penitentiary guards worked and contended that better pay would increase security. Guards were required to be at their posts by sunrise to escort inmates to work and supervise them until sunset. They remained on duty alternatively every third night, did not see their families for over thirty-six consecutive hours, and were on call the remaining four nights. "Justice" closed by scolding Congress for forcing penitentiary guards to remain "poor" since salaries of the "private artisan" had increased, but the "necessities" of penitentiary guards remained "entirely overlooked by those holding the remedial measures in their hands."[18] Inadequate pay and poor conditions rendered guard duty undesirable, but these were not the only problems.

In Ohio, journalists argued that the appointment system for penitentiary officers bred corruption, apathy, and lack of accountability. On August 25, 1858, the *Coshocton Democrat* complained that penitentiary directors received appointment from the governor; that directors then appointed the warden; and the warden, with consent of the directors, appointed subordi-nates. "This machinery is too complicated," the paper complained, "there are too many conflicting interests, influences, and opinions. Full responsibility rests nowhere, yet the subordinates are often saddled with the faults of the directors which are useless appendages."[19] The penitentiary remained under state supervision, but power vacuums continued. In March 1860, the Ohio legislature passed an officer accountability bill that fixed guards' compensa-tion, prescribed their duties, and determined the industries in which inmates would work, Nonetheless, confusion magnified during the Civil War. Confed-erate cavalry general John Hunt Morgan's November 1863 escape forced the legislature in March 1864 to increase the guards' pay to make the posts more appealing.[20]

The monotony of guard duty paralleled the industrial and market revolu-tions' deskilling of the American labor force. Prison regulations, like factory labor, forced the sacrifice of freedom, control of time, and political engage-ment.[21] In 1854, D.C. Penitentiary Warden Thomas Thornley maintained that "few persons employed by the government have more arduous and responsible duties to discharge than the guards."[22] Guard duty was physi-cally and mentally taxing and required constant attention and rigidness. Ohio Penitentiary rules prohibited guards from having any type of conver-sation. Guards had to maintain a constant presence, prevent communica-tion between convicts, and "refrain from singing, whistling . . . immoderate laughter, boisterous conversation, and exciting discussions upon politics, religion or other subjects . . . [which may] disturb the harmony and good order of the prison."[23]

Guard regulations transformed the independent character that men developed in civilian life. Violation of rules resulted in dismissal and dis-grace. Prison guards could be removed for intoxication, sleeping on their posts, failure to "maintain a character of sobriety and honesty," swearing or "other indecent language," and "inhumanity to the prisoners."[24] Guard duty was boring and isolating and the men longed to break the rigid routine.

Wardens therefore had to discipline both guards and inmates. In 1860, D.C. Penitentiary Warden C. P. Sengstack reprimanded guard Daniel Mc-Given for "refusal to comply with the general routine of prison discipline." The argumentative McGiven frequently disputed with other officers and re-fused to remain on duty in the absence of other guards. One Sunday morn-ing, McGiven preferred breakfast to the deputy warden's orders to open the prison. Sengstack consequently dismissed McGiven for "stubbornness and insubordination."[25]

Guards' poor behavior undermined penitentiary discipline and it plagued military prisons. In 1863, the behavior of Castle Thunder's guards reflected two major antebellum fears: collusion with inmates and negligence. In March, guard Michael Jordan conspired with inmates who wanted to escape and consequently faced court-martial. The Richmond press reported that Jordan faced "very severe" penalty, but gave no details.[26] Jordan's misbehavior occurred during a year when Castle Thunder's guards were generally apathetic toward their duties. On December 5, 1863, Lieutenant Colonel Elliott complained about guards' laxity and insubordination in General Orders No. 3. Military prison guards, like penitentiary counterparts, were expected to behave as gentlemen, and Elliot exhorted them to model behavior "above reproach as both soldiers and men" since "all eyes" were upon them. He noted that the command could only be vindicated if it could "point triumphantly to the fact that no single member of it has been arraigned for delinquency" since guards reflected the government's power.[27]

Officers closely monitored guards at both Union and Confederate prisons. As in penitentiaries, Camp Chase commandant William Richardson forbade guards on duty from talking with each other and with inmates. In 1862 Gov. David Tod permitted individuals "detailed for duty" in the prison to speak to prisoners, but Richardson remanded that order.[28] On April 1, 1864, he decreed that guards were "in no case" permitted to speak to prisoners, except "when the discharge of their duty compels them" to do so.[29]

These dictates were difficult to enforce, but common—they also governed guards at Castle Thunder and Andersonville. Castle Thunder's rules dictated that inmates could not leave quarters without "proper guard," so guards could approach prisoners only at that time. Military prison guards did not march prisoners in lockstep, but they ensured that prisoners moved outside of quarters in an orderly fashion.[30] At Andersonville, orders limited guards' communication with prisoner work details to official business, restricted all other communication with laborers, and authorized the arrest of anyone who violated this order. Orders also established procedures for guards returning to duty after approved absences. These stipulated that guards could not congregate on the depot platform upon arrival or departure from the prison.[31]

Guard duty at both penitentiaries and military prisons was grunt work. This, perhaps, was even truer during wartime since guarding military prisons was not romanticized like soldiering. As a result, young boys, old men, or members of the despised Regular Army often assumed these posts.[32] Most military prison guards were comprised of army units, but many, like the Public Guard at the Virginia Penitentiary, were not permanent. In Camp Chase's early months, guard duty fell to a number of "three months" men. This short term created administrative concerns and prompted Governor Tod to urge Colonel Hoffman to "raise a special corps for guard duty" to remedy inconsistencies just as antebellum Virginia officials had done.[33]

It took a few months, however, for authorities to establish a permanent guard at Camp Chase. In May 1862, a prison official noted that there was no guard "except a few citizens" to face a "threatened insurrection of prisoners."[34] Similar shortages were evident in July 1862. Capt. H. M. Lazelle's inspection found that one side of the prison was completely unguarded and had "no sentry except at night."[35] Prison officials temporarily remedied the shortage in August 1862, when the guard consisted of approximately one regiment charged with the oversight of 1,600 prisoners.[36] Hoffman's comments a month later reveal that the guard was still not permanent, however, and he argued that the only solution was to appoint a permanent commander and guard.[37] Hoffman had a legitimate complaint. In mid-October 1862, one inspector noted that only 101 men were available to guard anywhere from 723 to 1,600 prisoners.[38] To maximize the guards' effectiveness, Assistant Commissary General of Prisoners H. W. Freedley noted that seventeen sentinels occupied parapets so that "the whole camp might be overlooked." Two sentinels patrolled each gate and thirteen others formed a complete chain around the camp's exterior independent of those on the parapet.[39] This arrangement provided temporary relief, but inspectors kept pressing for, and eventually received, a permanent guard.

The 88th Ohio Volunteer Infantry, also known as the 1st Battalion, Governor's Guards, assumed control of Camp Chase on October 27, 1862, and held this post for the majority of its service.[40] Like the Virginia public guard, the 88th Ohio had a positive impact on discipline, although this took time to realize. In September 1864, one inspector noted that the regiment "changed the camp from a detestable mud hole to a fine, healthy, and well-organized" prison.[41]

Johnson's Island had better immediate organization than Camp Chase, but escape plots and inadequate guard strength nonetheless plagued officials. Commissary General Hoffman accepted Governor Tod's appointment of Col. W. S. Pierson as commandant in December 1861 and charged him with the "organization, discipline, and instruction" of guard companies. The 128th Ohio, also known as Hoffman's Battalion, became the camp's permanent guard in the spring of 1862, but rumors of a mass escape plot orchestrated from Canada put both Hoffman and Tod on edge. The 128th did not allay fears. Hoffman told Pierson that guard strength was adequate, but warned that "kindness alone will not keep prisoners in subjection," and sanctioned "severe measures" to discourage misbehavior. Tod, however, went further and ordered the naval steamer *Michigan* to Sandusky Bay. Escape threats persisted into late 1863 and Hoffman recommended adding three guard companies to the existing four prior to the bay freezing.[42]

Concerns about guard strength and prison security surfaced elsewhere as the war dragged on. In late May 1864, Maj. Thomas P. Turner and Andersonville Commandant Henry Wirz both complained about inadequate guard strength and ambiguous authority over the prison. Turner contended that the Yankee prisoners, especially officers, numbering between eighteen thousand and twenty thousand, were educated, courageous, desperate, and posed realistic escape threats. Turner had no confidence in the two thousand to three thousand "raw recruits" who guarded the camp since they were "without officers, undisciplined, and totally disorganized." Both Turner and Captain Wirz complained that Wirz was overworked and powerless. He served as commandant, adjutant, clerk, and warden, but ironically wielded no authority since other officers of equal rank refused to obey him.[43]

Guard strength remained inadequate, but the prisoner population increased in the summer of 1864. In June, prisoners totaled 24,000 and measles and whooping cough plagued guards. Andersonville's population peaked in July at 29,201 and Brig. Gen. John Winder requested more guards to police the stockade, hospitals, and work parties. Confederate officials were unable to address the situation until January 1865, when they formed a distinct command structure that encompassed prisons in Georgia, Alabama, and Mississippi. Andersonville's guard strength finally surpassed necessary levels just as authorities moved inmates elsewhere, consequently leaving posts in South Carolina and Augusta understaffed.[44]

Old Capitol Prison's guard force was also thin in early 1865, so it rotated frequently to ensure vigilance. In February 1865, Old Capitol Prison's population totaled 296 with only nineteen guards available for duty.[45] The guard consisted of three reliefs, each working two two-hour shifts.[46]

Prison officials were always outnumbered and had to choose between force and restraint to maintain order. In 1852, Ohio Penitentiary Chaplain William Roberts exhorted prison officials to be kind and firm, and avoid cultivating a "sense of injustice" among inmates with heavy-handed discipline. Guards shaped their masculinity through their jobs, and Roberts noted that guards could cultivate either noble or tyrannical qualities.[47] Some nineteenth-century contemporaries celebrated force, aggression, and risk as masculine virtues, but many reformers, including Roberts, believed guards should exercise self-restraint.[48] Circumstances changed during wartime as Castle Thunder's commandant George Alexander illustrates.

Castle Thunder earned a reputation for brutality soon after Alexander assumed command, substantiating the antebellum fear that power over prisoners could lead to abuse of authority. His tenure inspired the Confederate House of Representatives to investigate the prison.[49] Both Alexander and the committee believed that to "make a good officer a man must be a gentleman," but the committee preferred force to restraint and approved corporal punishments that invited earlier scrutiny from men like Roberts. Members sanctioned disciplinary tactics, which included bucking and gagging, whipping, isolating refractory prisoners in solitary confinement on a bread-and-water diet, and tying up prisoners by the thumbs. The committee concluded that Alexander's treatment of prisoners was "as humane as the circumstances would allow" and dismissed charges of cruelty.[50] Alexander's exoneration paved the way for his successor, Capt. William Richardson, to continue corporal punishment. The Richmond *Examiner* noted that Richardson exercised the "most rigid discipline," keeping prisoners secure and "in subjection" with corporal punishments common in penitentiaries.[51]

The Central Government and the States: Shifting Control

When Federal, Confederate, and state officials scrutinized punishments administered in military prisons, they continued a tradition of outside involvement in prison affairs established with antebellum penitentiaries. National officials on both sides of the Mason Dixon Line learned about prison management from state authorities, and the Federal Government's new involvement in imprisonment created confusion over whether state or federal officials had ultimate authority over military prisons. This was most evident at Camp Chase, where a contest for power ensued between federal officials and Ohio's governor.

Throughout 1861, Camp Chase primarily confined Confederate sympathizers from Ohio, Kentucky, and western Virginia, according to federal directives, but some captives were outliers. In August, Gov. William Dennison reported three prisoners guilty of common crimes, murder, and rape, while an unspecified number were charged with treasonous behavior. Dennison believed himself responsible for these inmates, and his correspondence with Secretary of War Simon Cameron illustrates how the war blurred civil and military authority. Dennison asked Cameron if he should hand the murder and rape suspects over to civil authorities for trial, or subject them to court-martial. He also wondered whether to classify the treason suspects as prisoners of war, or hand them over to federal courts for trial.[52] Dennison was accustomed to overseeing Camp Chase, but acknowledged that the war altered inmate classification and invited federal oversight of prisons.

Conversely, David Tod, Dennison's successor, was reluctant to subordinate himself to federal officials. From July 1861 until February 1862, Camp Chase housed mostly political prisoners and William Hoffman, as newly appointed commissary general of prisoners, struggled to assert authority. The Confederate sympathizers from Ohio, Kentucky, and western Virginia detained at Camp Chase were federal prisoners, but Tod believed that he had full jurisdiction over the prison since most inmates hailed from Ohio and the military prison was, like the penitentiary, in Columbus.[53] U.S. officials could have asserted control in April 1862 following the influx of Confederate prisoners of war from the Battle of Fort Donelson since these were federal captives. But Tod jealously controlled the camp, kept tabs on its commandant, and signed correspondence with federal officials as "Governor and Commander in Chief."[54]

Tod's craving for power over Camp Chase comes through clearly in his correspondence with federal officials regarding prison population, inspection, and improvements. In October 1861, January 1862, and February 1862, respectively, Tod directed state officials to investigate the cause of detention of numerous inmates, complained that he needed instructions regarding the "duties expected" of him regarding political prisoners sent to Camp Chase, and exhorted federal officials to discharge inmates to relieve overcrowding.[55] He even nagged General-in-Chief Henry Halleck in late March and early April 1862 to send 250 prisoners of war and at least 200 of the "most dangerous" Camp Chase prisoners to Johnson's Island. Halleck assented and permitted Tod to make provision for guarding inmates.[56] Tod likely relished the fact that federal officials fulfilled his wishes, not thinking that he was actually responding to federal directives.

Tod believed himself in charge of Camp Chase. In February 1862, C. P. Buckingham, adjutant general of Ohio, reified Tod's conviction: Buckingham limited visitation privileges to Camp Chase to the governor, the adjutant general, and quartermaster and surgeon generals, but stipulated that Tod could grant special authorization to other visitors. The next month, as the prison's population rose, Tod himself issued orders that paralleled those that governed the intake of penitentiary inmates to Commandant Granville Moody and the state militia, who guarded the camp. Tod, acting as "Governor and Commander in Chief" as he preferred, ordered the state guards to confiscate enemy weapons for return upon release; commanded them to record prisoners' names, ages, residences, and ranks, where taken, and where received; instructed that they divide inmates into messes and issue rations comparable to those given troops in the field; mandated that guards alone interact with inmates and supervise visitors; and ordered that guards screen letters to and from prisoners. Tod issued similar orders three times at Camp Chase.[57]

Correspondence indicates that Tod took orders from federal officials, but he believed, given antebellum practice, that state officials had power over imprisonment. Civilians were accustomed to state officials managing prisons and it was unclear to them whether state or federal officials wielded ultimate power over Camp Chase. Confusion escalated in April 1862, when Moody granted Confederate officers liberal paroles around Columbus. Pastor N. A. Reed, on behalf of numerous Columbus civilians, petitioned President Lincoln for redress in terms that confirmed Civil War contemporaries judged military prisons and inmates by penitentiary standards. Reed denounced Rebel soldiers as criminals and believed that they should be "treated with humanity, as we treat convicts in the penitentiary." But this was a difficult task, Reed contended, since it seemed to "be a mixed question as to who has authority at Columbus over the prisoners."[58] Reed wanted either state or federal officials to assert ultimate authority over the military prison, but that demand was not immediately met.

Camp Chase's lax discipline and unclear lines of authority stemmed, as they did at penitentiaries, from the appointment of inexperienced officials.

Camp Chase's first commandants, Col. Granville Moody and Col. W. B. Allison, provide good examples. Tod appointed Moody in March 1862. Moody, like penitentiary commanders, had modest experience with imprisonment. Tod appointed Moody based on that fact that Moody, a Methodist minister, visited Ohio Penitentiary inmates during the antebellum period.[59]

Prison ministry was different from prison management, however, and Moody elicited sharp criticism from federal inspectors and the public for leniency that bordered on negligence. Throughout April 1862, Columbus civilians griped that Moody allowed Confederate inmates to keep their slaves in prison and granted liberal paroles to Southern officers during which they, complete with side arms, roamed city streets.[60] Compassion was a good trait if used to help convicts find God, but not if it freed enemy combatants to, as Secretary of War Edwin Stanton complained, indulge in "treasonous railings" against the government in the state capital. Stanton's criticism, however, did not faze Tod. He defended Moody as "a strong anti-slavery Republican" who performed his duties "faithfully and discretely," a curt response that illustrated how Tod chafed when federal officials questioned his judgment. Despite Tod's defense, many federal officials and local residents hoped that Moody would resign and join his regiment on the battlefront. Much to their satisfaction, Moody's tenure ended in July 1862.[61]

Moody's successor, however, was not any better. Colonel Allison also possessed personal pedigree and political connections that secured him an appointment as commandant. Tod selected Allison, a lawyer and the son-in-law of Ohio's lieutenant governor, and supervised Allison just as he would have guided the state penitentiary's commander. But Allison, like Tod, irked federal officials.[62]

Allison's ties to state government did not help him in prison administration. He was a thorn in the side of Col. H. M. Lazelle, whom Hoffman directed to inspect Camp Chase after repeated charges of poor discipline. In his July 13, 1862, report, Lazelle complained that Allison was "not in any degree a soldier," was "entirely without experience," remained "utterly ignorant of his duties," and was "surrounded by the same class of people." Lazelle wanted to convince Tod that Allison was incompetent. This was not easy, however, since even Lazelle remained unsure of the authority that he had to instruct the governor in prison affairs, a good example of the unclear lines between state and federal power. Lazelle met with Tod before the inspection to try to establish federal authority over Camp Chase. But the inspector surprisingly noted that he "did not deem [himself] at all justified" in suggesting to Tod "in more than the most general terms" that Hoffman "had entire control of all matters concerning prisoners." Lazelle's message was weak, so Tod still believed himself in control.[63] Tod's influence continued until April 1863, when Brig. Gen. John S. Mason of the U.S. Volunteers, a professional military man, assumed command of the prison and solidified federal oversight.[64]

Federal officials might have taken over, but they discovered that appointing competent administrators was not easy. Appointees quickly learned that military prison duty was not glorious, unlike idealized battlefield conflict. Commanders' lack of motivation shaped prison discipline as it did at antebellum penitentiaries. In May 1864, an inspector general complained that Camp Chase's commanding officer, Col. William P. Richardson of the 25th Ohio Volunteers, was "an officer of intelligence, but not very active or diligent in the discharge of his duties." The inspector complained that poor policing, neglected sinks, and disheveled guards indicated "a want of proper military instruction."[65] Federal control failed to solve Camp Chase's problems, and did not help in other states.

As the war progressed, both Union and Confederate authorities increased control over military prisons, while state officials learned to relinquish or at least share power.[66] The relationship between Tod and federal officials highlighted the crossover between state and federal officials who administered military prisons in states accustomed to penitentiary oversight. But state and national officials also clashed over Salisbury, North Carolina's first major prison, even though they did not establish a penitentiary before the war. Ideas about the establishment and operation of penitentiaries influenced Salisbury's establishment and operation, but uncertainty over the locus of power hamstrung state and national officials throughout the war.

North Carolinians refused a penitentiary in the antebellum period so civilians first had to overcome aversion to prison establishment. Gov. Henry T. Clark admitted to Secretary of War Judah P. Benjamin in January 1862 that "local prejudice" against a military prison existed in Salisbury. But after the prison opened, Clark noted the "prejudice has been entirely removed." He and like-minded civilians believed that holding enemy captives reflected state power, and Clark eagerly waited to see how many prisoners Salisbury "may be blessed with."[67]

Clark was positive about the prison in 1862, but state officials had little control over it. State officials wanted to bolster prison security early in the war, especially since the war strained resources and civilians feared for their well-being. State officials recognized their subordination to the Confederate government and petitioned for redress. The first petitioner was Braxton Craven, whom Governor Clark appointed as Salisbury's commandant. Craven, like other nineteenth-century prison commandants, had no prior experience in prison administration and in December 1861, he confusedly asked Secretary Benjamin to confirm his authority. Craven questioned whether Benjamin would recognize him as commandant since Clark appointed him, inquired if he should report to the secretary of war, and requested that his rank be upgraded to command respect from subordinates. The penitentiary program undoubtedly influenced Craven's final request: He begged for the Confederate government to pay the salary of a prison chaplain since he believed he had a moral obligation to inmates.[68]

Benjamin, however, left the commandant in a lurch. The secretary of war's response likely confounded Craven and undermined his authority over Salisbury: Benjamin wrote that Governor Clark raised volunteers for the prison guard according to an act of the Confederate Congress, rendering them agents of the national, not the state, government from which Craven received his appointment. Benjamin then reluctantly concluded that if Clark deemed Craven the "best person to assume command," he could oversee the guard. Benjamin assented to Craven's request for a chaplain, but specified that Craven had no authority over the Confederate quartermaster stationed at Salisbury. The reply left Craven wondering what authority he could actually wield since, judging from the letter's salutation, Craven's rank remained unchanged.[69]

The situation worsened in April and May 1862. Clark, like other state governors, wanted to control the prisoners, but this put him at odds with George W. Randolph, Benjamin's successor as secretary of war. As Salisbury's population rose, Clark urged Randolph to take the moral high ground and parole a greater number of inmates than did Lincoln's government. Rhetorically, this move would have been a testament to the South's moral character, as when antebellum reformers called for improved penitentiary conditions. Realistically, however, it was a practical necessity. Clark noted that local civilians suffered because of the prison population, which made consumers "more numerous than the producers." Randolph, however, failed to act and Clark believed inaction compounded the crisis.

Residents also suffered since Governor Clark lacked power over Salisbury's guard. In another letter to Randolph, Clark noted that Benjamin, prior to leaving his post, put Confederate Major Gibbs in charge of the prison guard. But Gibbs simultaneously received permission to raise a regiment for the war, which he filled with guard companies. Salisbury's residents consequently panicked since three untrained artillery companies guarded prisoners. Clark relayed residents' demand for increased security, complained that he lacked jurisdiction over the camp, and lamented that even if he had power, he had no candidates from which to muster additional guards. Clark, at the War Department's mercy, begged Randolph to prohibit Gibbs from taking guards to the front until well-armed replacements arrived. "There is much apprehension and a feeling of insecurity in Salisbury on this subject which I think is entitled to consideration," Clark concluded.[70] Apprehension, however, remained throughout the war.

In November 1864, Salisbury Prison's population exceeded ten thousand and sent the townspeople into hysterics. Crowding contributed to poor health, inmates frequently escaped and, contrary to what state and national officials originally believed, the surrounding countryside failed to provide for enemy captives. Mayor John I. Shaver, head of the town commission, complained to Secretary of War James A. Seddon that local residents bore a disproportionate burden supporting inmates since Salisbury was the only prison in North Carolina, while at least three existed in Virginia, South Carolina, Alabama, and Georgia. Petitioners demanded that other Confederate towns ship supplies to Salisbury, and that the War Department transfer at least one half of Salisbury's inmates elsewhere. These complaints, however, were in vain. Seddon may have been unsympathetic, but realistically he could not change the Confederacy's dire circumstances in late 1864. He replied that the Confederate government had no other place for the captives, regretted that Salisbury's residents experienced "inconvenience or hardship," and shamefully admitted that the War Department could not provide relief.[71]

In Salisbury's case, state and local officials petitioned national authorities to alleviate conditions at an institution where founders' best-laid plans failed. Andersonville, on the other hand, faced challenges even before it opened, leaving prison officers to overcome both poor planning and the national government's inability to meet material challenges. According to Chief Surgeon Isaiah White, Andersonville was situated in barren country, its officers lacked necessary implements for finishing the prison, and prisoners arrived prior to its completion. Confederate officials in Richmond got wind of the nightmare, inspected the prison, and proposed remedies, but these, like reformers' reports of penitentiaries, did not translate into improved conditions.

On April 29, 1864, Assistant Adjutant General John Withers dispatched Capt. Walter Bowie to inspect Andersonville's management and internal conditions. This and subsequent inspection reports repeated the same complaints: population was too high, guard strength was too low, guards were disorganized and confused, inmates lacked provisions and adequate shelter, and the prison was disorderly. These problems haunted Assistant Adjutant and Inspector General R. H. Chilton, who was well aware of the nineteenth-century tendency to judge a people's moral character by its prisons. In November 1864, he predicted that Andersonville's shocking conditions were "calculated to bring reproach upon our government" since even Yankee inmates deserved the extension of "that treatment due from a Christian people."[72] During wartime, the population of enemy captives surpassed that of criminals, but the expectation that prisons reflect Christian principles and that prisoners receive humane treatment remained entrenched.

Controlling Inmates: Regulations and Punishment

The penitentiary program was designed to ensure just punishment and military prison officials replicated numerous penitentiary rules, regulations, and punishments. Inmate screening procedures established in penitentiaries persisted at many military prisons. Upon arrival, penitentiary officials subjected inmates to a process of calculated humiliation designed to strip them of pride and self-respect, reducing many to tears.[73] Officials scrutinized inmates, introduced them to prison rules, confiscated personal belongings, and served commitment papers detailing length of sentence. Guards then marched inmates to the penitentiary hospital for a general exam and noted any life-threatening conditions. Chaplains or other officials also questioned inmates about their religious outlook, drinking habits, education, and family circumstances. All of these measures communicated loss of independence to inmates.

Penitentiary officials—guards, wardens, and physicians—paid close attention to new inmates during inspection to familiarize themselves with a convict's habits and appearance so they could identify troublemakers if need be. The Ohio Penitentiary exemplified this process. In 1840, the moral instructor chronicled inmates' reading, writing, and education level, and praised "habitual readers of the Bible" and those who regularly observed the Sabbath. The instructor condemned criminals' association with "lewd women" and emphasized the dangers of intemperance, noting disgustedly that many inmates were drunk when convicted of killing or of intent to kill.[74] After questioning, officials required all inmates to shave their heads and faces and wear identical striped uniforms.[75] Officers' initial questioning of inmates was contradictory: they got to know each inmate, and then stripped inmates of any individuality.

Initial questioning of inmates was, ideally, their last prolonged verbal exchange. Rules demanded silence, but prisoners interacted in overcrowded cells and while at work since the whir of machines masked conversation.[76] Nonetheless, rules suppressed inmates' personality since they forbade discussion of ordinary topics or politics, and prohibited inmates from exchanging looks, laughing, quarreling, dancing, whistling, singing, running, or jumping. Inmates could complain to officials or the board of directors individually and only after the warden granted permission. Prisoners depended on officials to conduct interpersonal relationships both in and outside of prison, a dynamic evident in both penitentiaries and military prisons. Penitentiary and military prison officials inspected all correspondence to and from inmates and outsiders, and prisoners were prohibited from looking at or speaking with visitors.[77]

As in penitentiaries, captives—both prisoners of war and civilians—at Old Capitol Prison, Camp Chase, Johnson's Island, Castle Thunder, Salisbury, and Andersonville surrendered all arms, personal items, and valuables, such as watches and jewelry. Even amid dire circumstances in July 1864, Andersonville Commandant Henry Wirz confiscated Yankee prisoners' valuables, mostly silver watches, and Assistant Quartermaster R. B. Winder catalogued them by serial number and prisoners' name. All prison officials were supposed to return money and valuables to prisoners upon release, but wartime prisoners' money often got lost in administrative mix-ups. This occurred when Confederate authorities transferred federal prisoners from Richmond to Macon and then to Andersonville in July 1864, and when U.S. officials exchanged civilian inmates from the Old Capitol in March 1863. In the former case, Provost Marshall Isaac Carrington instructed the quartermaster to keep inmates' money in separate parcels for return. This, however, was nearly impossible since many inmates had died and authorities were unsure of the exact whereabouts of the living. In the latter case, the civilian captives' money did not materialize as planned at the point of exchange.[78]

After confiscating possessions, military prison officials, like penitentiary counterparts, questioned inmates about their backgrounds. The prison clerk recorded inmates' names, ages, residences, ranks, regiments, and companies, but keeping accurate records of military prison inmates was a challenge throughout the Civil War. In July 1862, as previously noted, Commissary General Hoffman directed Johnson's Island officials to keep ledgers that reflected the POW's rank, regiment, and company, and civilian ledgers that chronicled the offender's hometown, county, and state. But even this was too complicated. The next year, Hoffman reserved Johnson's Island for Rebel officers and "perhaps some few citizens," and directed Camp Chase officials to transfer inmates accordingly to control population at both camps and simplify officers' clerical duties.[79]

Classification and record keeping plagued officers at other military prisons. In April 1863, Hoffman requested that William Wood, commandant of Old Capitol Prison, furnish a list of inmates confined for disloyalty. Wood denied responsibility for recording prisoners' place of residence, date and location of arrest, charges, and arresting authority. "I am but the custodian of the prisoners and am unable to furnish you with the authority for the arrest," Wood wrote to Hoffman, "My duties are to receive the prisoner when committed by proper authority and hold him until released by proper authority." Wood knew that record keeping was common in prisons, but believed it was the purview of officials at the point of detention.

Confederate officials mirrored this protocol at Andersonville. In March 1864, the secretary of war tasked Gen. P. G. T. Beauregard and Gen. George Pickett with keeping record of prisoners to be sent to Andersonville. The generals were to have subordinates document the number of prisoners received, and each captive's name, company, regiment, state, and location of death, sickness, or escape. Subordinates submitted reports to Richmond immediately after transfer, ostensibly to cross-check receipts from Andersonville. This turned out to be a wise directive on behalf of the secretary of war since Confederate officials discovered in June 1864 that Andersonville lacked books "for the necessary records of the prisons."[80]

Once penitentiary and military prison officials registered captives' information, they tried to separate prisoners, either through solitary confinement, by gender, or by offense. The antebellum period established the precedent that inmate classification facilitated order, but overcrowding and the rapid influx of wartime prisoners rendered this difficult in both penitentiaries and military prisons. Penitentiary inmates were supposed to inhabit solitary cells, but in reality, they were seldom alone since penitentiary populations rose throughout the century. Military prison inmates also shared quarters since the makeshift or commandeered sites lacked solitary cells, but officials nonetheless categorized inmates. At Camp Chase, officers divided inmates into "conveniently sized messes" and parted "officers from the [enlisted] men as far as practicable," suggesting imperfections in the classification process.[81]

Officials at Castle Thunder and Old Capitol Prison used different buildings to classify inmates. Castle Thunder guards separated inmates as follows: Confederate deserters and political prisoners occupied the Gleanor's building; blacks and female prisoners were confined in Whitlock's Warehouse; and federal deserters and, later, federal prisoners of war were detained in Palmer's Factory.[82] At the Old Capitol, one room on the main floor confined Virginia citizens who refused the U.S. oath of allegiance. Another held federal officers, many of whom remained unaware of their offenses or were confined by order of the provost marshal. The floor above contained five rooms for solitary confinement, which mostly held female offenders, and federal officials confined prisoners of war in five Sibley tents in the prison yard.[83] Officials classified inmates to both punish and control them, but this "punishment" also enabled inmates to bond. Bonding often led to disobedience, which officers at both penitentiaries and military prisons addressed with corporal and/or lethal punishments.

State authorities concealed punishment from civilians behind penitentiary walls since public punishments could arouse sympathy for criminals.[84] Public whippings, humiliation, or hangings occurred inside penitentiaries, and military prison officials utilized these same punishments. Officials at both types of institutions also used solitary confinement, whipping, or the ball and chain. These military prison punishments were not, as scholars have contended, uniquely brutal since corporal, and sometimes lethal, punishments were condoned throughout the century. Penitentiaries and military prisons channeled the violent power of authorities in acceptable ways within a culture where corporal punishment was normal.[85] Corporal punishment did, however, elicit debate during the antebellum period and reached a crescendo during the Civil War since the sectional conflict broadened the demographics of inmates.

Perhaps the most controversial punishment in both penitentiaries and military prisons was whipping. Antebellum penitentiary administrators believed that whipping kept the balance of power in their favor. Penitentiary and military officials debated the efficacy of whipping, and official sanctioning of it fluctuated throughout the antebellum period.[86] In 1806, U.S. military laws limited whipping sentences by courts-martial to fifty lashes. This act was repealed in 1812, and whipping was entirely banned. In 1833, however, the repeal itself was repealed for deserters. Military law abolished all whipping in 1861 and this applied to Northern military prisons.[87]

The use and prohibition of whipping in penitentiaries coincided with its use and prohibition in the army since the civil and military sectors overlapped. Military law and penitentiary officials permitted whipping, with proper approval, from roughly the 1830s through the 1850s. The principal keeper of the Georgia Penitentiary boasted in 1824 that corporal punishment was "attended with good effects." Eight years later, the "cow-skin" and "slue-paddle" were permitted, and officers could supplement it with the wooden horse and the dungeon. Likewise, in his 1835 report on penitentiaries William Crawford called whipping the "most usual course" of punishment at the Virginia Penitentiary.[88] In the 1850s, the Ohio Penitentiary's rules and regulations also condoned whipping in "cases of a flagrant character" or of "a repetition of offenses." Regulations, however, required approval from the board of directors for whipping and set a maximum of ten stripes in one sitting or for the same offense.[89]

D.C. Penitentiary regulations also prohibited whipping without congressional authority, but in 1833 Warden Isaac Clarke argued for greater leeway to use the lash.[90] Clarke denounced Congress's restraint on whipping and maintained that discipline was ineffective without it. He begged the board of inspectors to petition Congress to grant liberal use of the whip. In 1836, however, the inspectors stood by the stance articulated in 1830 that held that "mildness and certainty of punishment" were more efficient than "*severity.*"[91]

Clarke consequently lobbied more adamantly for whipping, contending that its absence led to recidivism. He argued that former inmates desired recommitment since prison rules were mild and the fare good. Clarke believed that frequent whipping would "prevent *very often* infractions of the rules, *create* a proper subordination to their officers and *reduce* the frequency of *punishments.*" Inspectors again rebuffed Clarke in 1839. They instead supported "rigid" discipline, meaning that the warden should have a cell for every man. Clarke, somewhat suddenly, recanted in 1841, and his successors generally agreed with the inspectors' view.[92]

The controversy about whipping at the D.C. Penitentiary reveals that Congress controlled the practice both in the federal penitentiary and in the army, where officers used it to punish deserters. Whipping persisted in other state penitentiaries throughout the 1830s and part of the 1840s, the same time that it was permitted in the army. During those years, many penitentiary and military officials shared reformer Dorothea Dix's thoughts about whipping. Dix could never restrain her "instinctive horror and disgust of punishment by the lash," but conceded that "it may be sometimes *the only* mode . . . by which an insurrectionary spirit can be conquered."[93]

Penitentiary officials, however, changed their minds about whipping toward midcentury, just before military laws banned the practice. Throughout the 1840s and 1850s, Ohio Penitentiary officers preferred surveillance to corporal punishment to distance the penitentiary from the whipping controversy. In 1844, Warden John Patterson stated that the best way to enforce "strict obedience" was to "use the *lash* as sparingly as possible." Alternately, Patterson used the shower bath, a stream of cold water running over the offender's head, but believed that "vigilance" most effectively prevented infractions.[94] Likewise, in 1846, Chaplain James Finley, an antislavery advocate, contended that whipping had "a deteriorating influence on all those who engage in it," prisoners and officials alike. Finley opposed slavery and rejected whipping since he knew that Southern masters commonly whipped slaves.[95]

In 1856, the Ohio Penitentiary board of directors echoed Finley's belief that corporal punishment jeopardized the character of both administrators and victims. The directors instead favored solitary confinement since isolation "protects the convict from the outbursts of brutal passion" and ensured "wholesome discipline."[96] Finally, in 1858, Warden L. G. Van Slyke touted penitentiary discipline as "the pride of Ohio" since corporal punishment had been absent for almost three years. Van Slyke preferred solitary confinement for the "most refractory" prisoners. In 1858, Chaplain L. Warner seconded Van Slyke and championed moral control. He contended that if officers used force, the inmate's "animal nature and carnal passions will be developed—he will be *brutalized*," but if humane punishment persisted, the inmate's "moral nature will be developed—he will be *humanized*."[97] The ban on whipping at the Ohio Penitentiary in the late 1850s foreshadowed its 1861 prohibition in the military.

The Confederate Congress demonstrated in its 1863 investigation of Castle Thunder that Southern politicians shared the same interest as the Federal Government in monitoring whipping. This investigation revealed multiple instances where officials inflicted anywhere from twelve to fifty lashes on the Castle's inmates for fighting, stealing, and desertion, or as part of a court-martial sentence. It also underscored officials' belief that whipping was an effective disciplinary measure. Stephen Childrey, the prison's commissary, told the House committee that whipping "had an excellent effect" on inmates despite the fact that the Confederate Congress abolished whipping in the army.[98] This approval, however, was nuanced. The first minority report on the management of Castle Thunder called whipping "inhumane and inconsistent with our system of government," but simultaneously defended it since officers used it only "on persons of abandoned character" for "stealing, fighting, and abusing more helpless fellow-prisoners." Moreover, the committee concluded that whipping was "common in military prisons" and therefore should continue.[99]

Whipping was not the only corporal punishment available to penitentiary and military prison officials. Prison officials could also shoot inmates. Ohio Penitentiary officers fired on inmates for assault and rebellion. In 1861 and 1862, guards shot and killed one inmate in the act of attacking a foreman and shot another in the act of "murderous assault" on an officer.[100] Officers justified shooting by arguing that their lives were in danger and that guns pacified inmates "unaccustomed to obedience."[101] Similar conditions existed in military prisons.

The actions of Ohio Penitentiary guards foreshadowed the 1863 Lieber Code's guidelines for the punishment of military prisoners. The code allowed military prison guards to shoot escapees in the act and to inflict capital punishment on prisoners who plotted rebellion.[102] Commandants usually exonerated guards if they killed or wounded aberrant inmates since guards protected public security. For example, in 1862, one of Old Capitol Prison's guards, charged with shooting an escapee, was confined at Washington's Central Guard house, but a federal investigation concluded that the guard obeyed orders and praised his vigilance.[103]

Military prison officials believed that heavily armed guards would quash threats. Officials at Camp Chase and Johnson's Island supplied outnumbered guards with more firepower to discourage escape and revolt. Camp Chase's population was high in November and December 1863, totaling 2,145 on November 7 and 2,448 on December 7.[104] Consequently, Colonel Hoffman directed that guards "in part" be armed with revolvers since "a sentinel on post with his musket can only give one shot in case of an attack upon him," but revolvers gave "the strength of two or three men without such arms." Rumors of an escape plot swirled at Johnsons' Island in late 1863, and Governor Tod pushed Secretary Stanton to increase the guard to a full regiment. In response, the War Department honored Tod's afore-mentioned request for the steamer *Michigan* and Hoffman ordered 400 revolvers and 25,000 rounds of ammunition to Johnson's Island and other posts to assuage security concerns.[105] Bullets compensated for the lack of manpower and commandants supported guards' decisions to fire.

In late 1863, Camp Chase's guards shot and killed five inmates amid rumors that sympathizers of Peace Democrat Clement Vallandigham were plotting to release Confederate prisoners of war in Ohio.[106] Assistant Com-mandant A. H. Poten condoned guards' shooting of Confederate inmate Henry Hupman, who burned a candle after dark in violation of orders. Po-ten knew that the Lieber Code authorized the shooting of conspirators and believed that shooting Hupman reasserted order. Poten admitted dismay over the wounding of "a perhaps an innocent man, by a soldier who obeys his orders," but believed the incident was a good lesson since inmates fre-quently disobeyed guards. The prisoners, according to Poten, "have since changed their minds and obey."[107]

Commissary General Hoffman also supported guards' actions, contend-ing that escape rumors justified "more than usual severity" in the execution of orders. Hoffman concluded that three of the fatal cases had "sufficient justification," but noted that, in two cases, where sentinels fired into the barracks in "consequence of a light in the stove," the circumstances failed to "justify such harsh measures" though the sentinels seemed "only to have obeyed their orders."[108] Regardless, Camp Chase's prisoners learned that guards would meet escape plots with bullets.

Military prison officials dreaded mass conspiracies since inmates shared quarters and communicated freely. Memories of rumored escape plots were fresh in Colonel Richardson's mind in April 1864, when he ordered Camp Chase's guards to prevent loitering "around the outside of the prisons" and prohibit outsiders from approaching the prison "except at the gates," espe-cially at night. Any rush toward the prison fence would justify guards "firing upon the prisoners making the attempt." Prisoners always outnumbered guards, so officers instructed sentinels to work as a team to ensure that "nobody trespasses on the post of the sentinel next to him while his back is turned, and that nothing improper occurs along the line."[109] Sentinels had full authorization to fire if necessary.

The use of firepower was accepted in Ohio, at both Camp Chase and the penitentiary, during the Civil War. The Virginia Penitentiary's record regarding shooting and corporal punishment, however, is less clear. Virginia Penitentiary officials said little about the types of punishments administered during wartime, but it is likely that they used corporal punishment because of overcrowding and as a result of their assessment of inmates' character. Supt. Colin Bass's 1863 anxiety-laden annual report stated that the prison was crowded with convicts "of a class far worse . . . than has ever been in any one prison on the American continent." Bass vaguely described punishments, saying that it was "painful and embarrassing" to administer "inflexible" yet "humane" discipline.[110] Bass's ambiguous statement leaves his definition of humane punishment open to question, but suggests that he downplayed the necessity of corporal punishment to restrain inmates.

Punishments employed at the Virginia Penitentiary were unclear, but punishments in the D.C. Penitentiary were well documented in 1861 and 1862 and resembled those used before the war, including whipping. Inmates were sentenced to the dungeon, put in chains for up to twelve days, whipped with the cat-o'-nine-tails up to twenty-five times, whipped with the lash five to twelve times, and tied up by the thumbs for a half hour or an hour.[111] Suspension by the thumbs was also a common military punishment used in military prisons like Camp Chase, Andersonville, and Castle Thunder. Nineteenth-century contemporaries viewed these punishments not as brutal but as an effective means of ensuring obedience.[112]

Punishments, and offenses that warranted them, remained consistent from the antebellum period to wartime. The offenses of D.C. Penitentiary inmates ranged from feigning illness, to attempting escape, to communicating with prisoners of the opposite sex, to accidentally cutting fellow inmates, disobeying orders, using profane language, singing, laughing, and neglecting or damaging work.[113] Some of these offenses were minor, but punishment was swift and officers used familiar practices to control the rising prison population, which introduced both criminals and prisoners of war into the penitentiary.[114]

Examination of the *Official Records* reveals that military prison inmates committed many of the same offenses as penitentiary inmates. Inmates at Camp Chase, Johnson's Island, Old Capitol Prison, Castle Thunder, and

Andersonville insulted guards, devised escape plots, fought with or stole from each other, and demonstrated general disobedience. Officers punished inmates with bread-and-water diets, forced offenders to wear irons or a ball and chain, kept them in close confinement, implemented bucking and gagging, confined inmates in the dungeon, shot escapees, and whipped inmates.[115]

Corporal punishments were both common and controversial during the Civil War, but many individuals also thought that penitentiary sentences were inappropriate for volunteer soldiers since they primarily punished common criminals. Penitentiary inmates faced hard labor, solitary confinement on a bread-and-water diet, and confinement in leg irons or with a ball and chain.[116] These punishments did not fit the heroic image of the citizen-soldier, who had been viewed as the epitome of masculinity and honor since the American Revolution.[117] Nonetheless, wartime penitentiary officials continued the antebellum trend of administering penitentiary punishments to aberrant soldiers, emphasizing their fall from grace.[118] Some volunteers hailed from the middle and upper classes, but, like penitentiary inmates throughout the century, many soldiers incarcerated in military prisons and penitentiaries were also lower-class conscripts.[119]

Whether volunteers or conscripts, members of the Union and Confederate armies were unaccustomed to military life and to obeying orders from superiors. The spirit of individualism and independence that characterized the mid-nineteenth century often got soldiers into trouble and earned them terms in the D.C. Penitentiary.[120] Such was the case with Pvt. William Fahey of the 25th New York Volunteers. Fahey believed he "enlisted for a soldier, not for a laborer," and refused his captain's order to get wood, labeling him a "damn scoundrel." Fahey, like many other volunteers, believed himself to be above performing menial duties, but a military court sentenced Fahey to forfeiture of pay, dishonorable discharge, and three years' imprisonment in the D.C. Penitentiary with lowly criminals and a thirty-two-pound ball and chain on his leg.[121]

Federal officials routinely humiliated soldiers with sentences in the D.C. Penitentiary. Fahey was one of many Union soldiers who refused orders. Courts-martial found other soldiers guilty of desertion, insubordination, mutiny, absence without leave, "conduct prejudicial to good order," "conduct unbecoming of an officer and gentleman," drunkenness or sleeping on post, and using foul language toward or striking officers. Military courts sometimes ensured that the stigma of imprisonment followed deserters for the rest of their lives and branded them with the letter *D* upon the expiration of sentences. Deserters usually received this branding on their hip, so the pain of their offense remained even though the mark was invisible to many.[122]

Civil War soldiers were thus not immune from disciplinary tactics common in penitentiaries. Upon entering the D.C. Penitentiary, rules stipulated that the hair of convicts "be cut close." Courts-martial likewise ordered the heads of men convicted of mutiny or disobedience to be either fully or half shaven, equating them with convicts.[123]

Military offenders were not the only soldiers sentenced to penitentiaries; both the Ohio and Virginia penitentiaries also held prisoners of war and officials subjected them to penitentiary discipline. Prisoners of war were present in penitentiaries throughout the war, but became even more common as prison populations increased following the cessation of prisoner exchanges and the Battle of Gettysburg.[124] Northern and Southern officials sometimes used penitentiary punishments as retaliation, as per the Lieber Code. For example, in February 1863, the Richmond *Daily Dispatch* reported that over one dozen Yankee prisoners of war were sentenced to hard labor in the Virginia Penitentiary in return for Lincoln's incarceration of two Confederate officers in the D.C. Penitentiary on a "trumped" charge of robbing the mails.[125] Southerners disapproved of Northerners confining their soldiers in penitentiaries, but supported the Confederate government's use of penitentiaries to punish enemies. Northern civilians undoubtedly felt the same about penitentiary sentences—especially regarding Confederate cavalry general John Hunt Morgan's incarceration in the Ohio Penitentiary.

In July 1863, Morgan and his men raided Ohio and cost the state nearly $1 million. Union officials sentenced Morgan and his officers to the penitentiary as common horse thieves, conferring criminal status upon them and guaranteeing, at least ostensibly, tight supervision. Ohio Governor David Tod ordered Morgan and thirty of his fellow officers to the penitentiary since it was a "secure place." Upon entry, Morgan and his men were searched, stripped of valuables, separated from other convicts, and placed under military guard, but remained subject to penitentiary rules.[126] Southerners vehemently objected to the incarceration of the famed cavalrymen as common horse thieves.

Southerners abhorred the fact that penitentiary officials shaved the raiders' heads, which was standard practice for new convicts. The Richmond press argued that this "indignity" violated the laws of war since U.S. officials treated Morgan and his men "like convicts." Southerners believed such treatment unfit for soldiers, especially officers, and asserted that the shaving was a "petty exhibition of malice" on the part of Union officials.[127] Even Morgan's admission in a public letter to his wife that he was "kindly treated" failed to quell Southerners' displeasure. Their indignation intensified when, in January 1864, one of Morgan's men, Col. R. S. Cluke, a "distinguished officer," died in a dungeon in close confinement, a punishment commonly used to rectify convicts' misbehavior.[128] There was no mention of Cluke's offense.

Penitentiaries and military prisons shared more in common than punishments throughout the nineteenth century. Authorities at both institutions lacked experience; state and national authorities squabbled for control over prisons during wartime since the former were accustomed to prison oversight; penitentiary and military prison officers subjected prisoners to many of the same rules; and each institution held the same type of inmates. Penitentiary and military prison inmates also shared similar experiences. They faced poor physical conditions in prison, were stigmatized by imprisonment, and tried to pass the time of confinement through religious activities, bonding with other inmates, and work. Morgan and his men felt like convicts idling in the penitentiary, but these feelings were not reserved solely for penitentiary inmates. Many military prison inmates also confessed to feeling like criminals and compared themselves to felons. Captives' letters, diaries, and memoirs provide a window into how prisoners in both penitentiaries and military prisons viewed themselves and their circumstances, and this is the subject of the next chapter.

The Internal World
of the Prison

Inmates' Identity and Disobedience

On April 3, 1863, the *Liberator* reprinted a chronicle of "The Rebel Barbarities" from a Washington paper. The article directly compared prisoners of war to common criminals. It reported that men of the 22nd Ohio, captured after the Battle of Corinth while detailed to destroy a Georgia rail line, escaped from Rebel hands where they were "treated as felons were before prisons were reformed." The escapees suffered from leg irons, starvation, and scant light and air, but lived to tell the tale.[1] Military prison inmates commonly compared themselves to penitentiary inmates when they described their experiences of confinement. Prisoners' self-descriptions and journalists' depictions of them reveal that wartime prisoners found it difficult, if not impossible, to shake the association of imprisonment with criminality, which became entrenched with the establishment of penitentiaries.

Histories of penitentiaries focus on the rhetoric of reformers, prison officers, or boards of inspectors since their records are plentiful. Mary Gibson has noted that scholars of American penitentiaries have only recently begun to focus on "history from below" to capture the daily experiences of penitentiary inmates, who left few records.[2] Military prison inmates, on the other hand, left numerous diaries and letters, though outside correspondence was often biased since prison officials inspected every word. Regardless, prisoners' letters and diaries paint a vivid picture of how military prison inmates interpreted incarceration.

Military prison inmates internalized the criminal stigma and compared their experience to that of penitentiary inmates since Americans interpreted imprisonment through their understanding of the penitentiary program. Criminals and military prisoners were often housed in different physical structures, but significant parallels marked captives' lives in both institutions. Penitentiary and military prison inmates both engaged in religious exercises, craved education, experienced reform to varying degrees, withstood similar punishments, and undertook labor as punishment or reward. Prisoners also intermingled as criminals landed in military prisons and prisoners of war found themselves in penitentiaries.

The Stigma of Imprisonment and Prisoners' Identity

Incarceration robbed penitentiary and military prison inmates of freedom and sequestered them from free society. Pvt. William Duff, a Confederate prisoner of war at Camp Chase, contended that imprisonment was a leveling experience regardless of the holding facility. "Let that prison life be what it is," Duff wrote, "it may be of war or criminal or by quarantine or detention in some way . . . but being deprived of liberty and freedom is a terror and a horror to anyone." Duff contended that confinement tortured the mind and body so that inmates were "not themselves."[3] Penitentiary and military prison inmates felt despondence, anger, and helplessness, and the latter frequently compared themselves to the former.

Other prisoners of war echoed Duff's sentiments and resented feeling like convicts. "I'm doomed a felon's place to fill," an Old Capitol inmate scrawled on a prison wall.[4] Likewise, following his escape from Camp Chase in 1861, political prisoner A. J. Morey recalled that "men of every class and grade" were huddled in tight quarters and "treated as felons." Morey described how prison officials prohibited fires to warm the "half naked and shivering prisoners"; how shoddily constructed shanties leaked, soaking inmates and their belongings; and how the prisoners worried that they would "perish from the effects of cold and damp." Morey concluded his tirade with an indictment of the prison's officers and guards. "This treatment of human beings by those calling themselves Christians," he wrote, was "unparalled [sic]."[5] Similarly, upon learning of the plight of his men in Castle Thunder, Capt. E. C. Sanders of the 1st North Carolina Union Volunteers complained that they were "treated as felons of the deepest dye," not prisoners of war.[6] Penitentiary punishment provided the only lens through which soldiers interpreted imprisonment since penitentiaries became fixtures in American society while military prisons were temporarily bound to war.

Imprisonment, its social function, and its operating standards were defined in the context of penitentiary development. Consequently, Civil War military prisoners judged military prisons by standards used to evaluate penitentiaries. Antebellum reformers demanded that criminals receive humane treatment in penitentiaries and this expectation carried over into the Civil War. In 1863, Camp Chase inmate T. J. Churchill complained about poor conditions to Commissary General Hoffman and demanded that Union officials afford inmates "kind and humane treatment."[7] Similarly, Confederate prisoner of war Joseph Barbiere, who spent time at Johnson's Island and Camp Chase, disgustedly noted that Union authorities refused to allow a mother to visit a prisoner of war who was on his deathbed. Barbiere noted that visitation was a privilege that even "the vilest of criminals" pending execution received.[8]

Civil War contemporaries believed that imprisonment should change inmates since the penitentiary program emphasized reform, and they expected military prisons to do the same. In June 1863, the Washington, D.C., *National Republican* printed a letter from a loyal Baltimore Unionist to his turncoat brother, who became an inmate at the Old Capitol after being caught serving in the Rebel army. The loyal Union man approved of his brother's incarceration and believed that it would reform him. Imprisonment, according to the Yankee, would encourage his wayward brother to take the oath of allegiance to "atone" for the "sins" he committed against the United States and his "sins" against "God, who commanded [him] to obey the laws of [his] country."[9]

Journalists spoke of prisoners of war in moral terms and rejoiced when imprisonment reformed them. In March 1864, the *New York Times* printed an article entitled "Reformed Rebels," which noted that U.S. authorities released eighty-six Rebel deserters who took the oath of allegiance from Old Capitol Prison. Officials furnished the prodigal sons with transportation to New York City, where they ostensibly would again be productive members of society just as criminals were to be after their sentences.[10]

Commentators in the above cases expected military prisons to transform inmates' loyalty like penitentiaries were to reform convicts. Penitentiary punishment was supposed to be trying but humane, and this knowledge prompted Northern journalists to complain that Union authorities treated some enemy prisoners better than criminals. In April 1862, the *Cincinnati Commercial* complained that Confederate officers held at Camp Chase retained their slaves. The *Commercial,* like many Unionists, believed that the rebellion was unlawful, that slavery should end, and that Southerners should be treated as felons. "The question is, whether the criminals who have been taken with arms in their hands, shall be treated as prisoners guilty of high misdemeanors," the paper opined, "or fondled . . . as spoiled children." The *Commercial's* stance on Rebel inmates was clear—Confederate soldiers committed treason, the highest possible crime, were therefore akin to felons, and should be treated accordingly.[11]

While the *Commercial* contended that Camp Chase's officers should treat Southern prisoners as criminals, the *Vicksburg Whig* evoked images of cramped penitentiary cells and complained that Union authorities did in fact treat Confederate prisoners of war as "felons" in Northern "dungeons."[12] These competing depictions reflect how both Northerners and Southerners conflated the function of military prisons with that of penitentiaries. Civilians believed that enemy soldiers should be treated as criminals in military prisons, but they demanded distinction between criminals and prisoners of war when it came to their own POWs.

Civilians equated the two types of prisons throughout the war, and Northern and Southern journalists repeatedly referred to military prisons as penitentiaries, even in the war's later years. For example, On September 5, 1864, the *Richmond Dispatch* noted that sixty of Castle Thunder's inmates would be "sent off this morning to the Confederate States penitentiary at Salisbury, North Carolina," where they would remain until the "expiration of the sentence found against them." The paper did not specify whether the transferred inmates were common criminals, prisoners of war, or inmates under sentence of court-martial, but the direct comparison was clear. Northerners also referred to Salisbury as a penitentiary. On February 25, 1865, the *Zanesville Daily Courier* (Ohio) noted in its description of North Carolina's geography, that "the Confederate penitentiary" was located in Salisbury.[13] These late war descriptions indicate that Civil War contemporaries thought military prisons and penitentiaries analogous, a testimony to the ideological power of the penitentiary program. Americans, both in and outside of prison, believed that the stigma of imprisonment transcended institutional type.

The development of the penitentiary program shaped civilians' attitudes toward prisoners. James Finley, chaplain of Ohio Penitentiary, summarized a common nineteenth-century belief about penitentiary inmates, describing them as "far below the average of their race in mental character [and] moral condition."[14] Finley suggested that inmates were morally deficient, lacked personal character, and became further disgraced by imprisonment. This stigma shamed prisoners of war, impacted their personal identity, and shaped their outlook.

Andersonville prisoner William T. Peabody confessed to his diary how imprisonment humiliated him. Peabody's daily chronicle began in May 1864 and sadly ended with his death at Andersonville that September. He wrote in his diary as if writing to his wife, Hannah, who lived in Massachusetts, and shamefully confessed that "I have not written for I don't wish you to know that I am a prisoner." Peabody, like other inmates, detested the "prisoner's life" and considered Andersonville a "damnable place for a dog."[15]

The stigma of imprisonment embarrassed Peabody and caused him to keep his incarceration from his wife, but other inmates explicitly condemned how imprisonment equated them with criminals. Such was the case with Andersonville inmate George W. Pennington. Shortly after arriving at Andersonville, Pennington protested in his diary on May 28, 1864, that he and fellow inmates were "shut off from the rest of the world and can not hear half as much news as a murderer nor are we treated half as well." Pennington likened himself and his comrades to arguably the most heinous criminals and resented that convicts were treated better than prisoners at Andersonville.

Imprisonment angered Pennington and drove others to despair. Johnson's Island inmates, many of whom held rank in the Confederate Army, were often utterly despondent. For example, imprisonment tormented Capt. Robert Bingham and Capt. E. D. Dixon, respectively of the 44th and 55th North Carolina regiments, since they were accustomed to the independence and esteem inherent in Southern honor.[16] Bingham was incarcerated throughout 1863 and 1864, first at Norfolk, Virginia, then at Fort Delaware, and finally at Johnson's Island. He remained in denial of his captive status and confessed from Sandusky on Sunday, January 17, 1864, that he had "been much depressed often—not having a clear view of my acceptance" as a prisoner. On the Sabbath, Bingham acknowledged and took responsibility for his consequent spiritual depravity, stating, "Perhaps it is my fault that I am not more spiritual—indeed I know it is." Under ordinary circumstances,

Bingham could have regained his hope in God, but imprisonment negated his ability to do so. Bingham confessed that his depression and lack of faith were "in great part" his own fault, but he could not help "crying out in bitterness of spirit Oh Lord how long" as he pined for release.[17] Incarceration crushed Bingham's spirits as it did many criminals and inflicted a lasting psychological wound.

Captain Dixon, in postwar reflections, agreed that imprisonment was unbearable. Candid despair, as Bingham expressed, faded with time, but the negative experience of imprisonment remained with Dixon. He recalled prison life as "irksome, dull, and to those who are of a despondent nature, almost unbearable." Dixon did not mention whether or not he fit the latter category, but his reminiscences highlighted another commonality that penitentiaries and military prisons shared. Overcrowded penitentiaries facilitated communication among inmates and often bred toxic internal dynamics. Military prisons were almost always crowded and, as Dixon indicated, disorderly. "We had in prison almost every variety of character—the devout Christian, the Jew, the infidel, and the nondescript," he recalled, suggesting both the proliferation of religious sentiment and the ignorance of it, which encouraged misbehavior, a theme upon which numerous other military prisoners and penitentiary reformers commented.[18]

Expectation vs. Reality: Internal Discord, Reform, and the Role of Religion

Overcrowding exacerbated disorder in penitentiaries and validated the fears of prison administrators and reformers that the close association of criminals bred vice. The Ohio Penitentiary was near maximum capacity in July 1858 with 699 of the prison's 700 cells filled and the last occupied by August.[19] It was no coincidence that inmates acted up that month. Newspapers reported that the court of common pleas sentenced inmate Albert Meyer to hang for murdering fellow prisoner Bartlett Neville. Penitentiary authorities carried out the sentence on December 21, 1858, in the prison yard as a lesson for other convicts. Commitments, however, continued to increase and by March 1859 penitentiary authorities had to house three convicts in each solitary cell, use the hospital for additional living space, and hope that the threat of corporal punishment would keep convicts in line.[20]

Virginia Penitentiary inmates also turned on each other as the population climbed through the 1850s. On April 30, 1853, the Baltimore *Sun* reported that tensions simmered in crowded cells and precipitated a fray that led a "colored convict" to fatally stab another inmate named Smith.[21] Convicts' unruly behavior increased as the penitentiary's population rose. In 1857, the population reached 313 and each cell held two or three inmates. Supt. Charles Morgan contended that this made it "impossible to prevent the better class of prisoners from being corrupted, or at least brought under the corrupting influence of the more hardened in crime." He lamented that "the hope of moral improvement, in such condition, can hardly fail to be disappointed," and proposed isolating "obstinate and refractory prisoners" as a remedy.[22] Morgan appreciated the efforts of volunteers and chaplains who tried to inspire inmates to reform, but concluded that vice outweighed virtue amid rampant overcrowding. The next year brought much of the same. In March 1858, the New Orleans *Times Picayune* reported that the penitentiary population was greater than ever. "The cells are closely filled, there being from 2 to 4 in each cell," the paper complained, denouncing overpopulation as "a sad commentary on the morality of the times," both outside and inside of prison.[23]

Civil War contemporaries often made the same arguments. Military prison inmates frequently commented on how prison life and overcrowding encouraged bad behavior and eroded morality. Andersonville inmate John Duff lamented on October 2, 1864, the Sabbath, that he longed to be home and at church since prisoners lived "among sin and wickedness all the time." Sporadic preaching failed to quell misbehavior and Duff was fed up and fearful. His prior accounts from May 1864 were replete with instances of inmates engaging in unruly behavior. In late May, Duff recalled that three prisoners were caught stealing and that fellow inmates punished them by shaving the side of one man's head, shaving one side of another man's head and face, and bucking the third after cutting his hair close. Fellow inmate William Tritt recorded other penitentiary-style reprimands in late May and early July, when prisoners shaved thieves' heads and paraded them through the prison streets.[24]

Methodist Chaplain A. W. Mangum likewise noted that boredom and despair encouraged bad behavior that officers met with penitentiary punishments at Salisbury. He recalled that inmates sometimes fought and were "chained and closeted for it." Judging from the accounts from Andersonville

Bird's-eye view of Andersonville Prison from the southeast (Library of Congress)

and Salisbury, it is not surprising that Andersonville prisoner Nathaniel Shepard Armstrong Price wondered when he and his comrades would "get out of 'jail.'"[25] The internal dynamics of military prisons were eerily similar to those of penitentiaries despite the different physical spaces. Overcrowding and idle time bred trouble in military prisons and offenders suffered shaved heads, bucking, and solitary confinement in chains—all penitentiary punishments that had become ingrained in the minds of Civil War contemporaries.

Nineteenth-century contemporaries, both in and outside of prison, also believed that incarceration could reform inmates through education and religious instruction. Penitentiary inmates were supposed to have access to a state-appointed chaplain and wholesome reading material. These expectations spilled over to military prisons.

Some ministers themselves faced confinement and consequently had an opportunity to minister to inmates. Many Americans, before and during the Civil War, were incensed when ministers wound up incarcerated. The imprisonment of Protestant missionaries Elizur Butler, Samuel Worcester, and two others whom Georgia authorities sent to the state penitentiary ignited fierce controversy. Georgia authorities apprehended the ministers for violating a state law that required every person residing among Indians to take an oath of allegiance to the state. On October 15, 1831, the *Liberator* complained that these "Missionaries [were] confined in a Georgia Penitentiary with felons" for Christianizing and teaching the Natives to read, write, and cultivate the soil. But Dr. Butler contended that the clergymen continued their mission in prison. In June 1832, Butler and his peers organized a Christian class for inmates to encourage conversion. The class was a resounding success—nearly one-third of the convicts enrolled, proving, according to Butler, that "The Lord can bring good out of evil, light out of darkness, make the wrath of man praise him, and restrain the remainder."[26]

Religious instruction was one of the pillars on which the penitentiary program was founded, but religious influence in the Georgia Penitentiary was limited to the time that the missionaries spent in prison. State officials often had difficulty finding willing souls for these demanding positions. The rules and regulations for the Ohio and D.C. penitentiaries dictated that chaplains visit convicts' cells daily, preach on Sundays, operate the Sunday school, keep note of inmates' moral character and education, record punishments, and converse with convicts regarding their "reformation and spiritual welfare."[27]

Judging from penitentiary regulations, chaplains were supposed to play an active role in inmates' lives, but this seldom happened. In 1838 the Ohio Penitentiary's board of directors praised Chaplain Charles Fitch and noted that the convicts embraced the chance to benefit from his instruction. But Fitch's appointment expired two years later and a new group of directors dispensed with the chaplain's services despite his positive impact. The directors claimed that they could not replace Fitch since the state legislature was "adverse to the employment of any individual" as chaplain.[28] Chaplains were present sporadically in the 1840s and 1850s, but the state legislature did not appropriate funds for a regular chaplain and an assistant teacher until 1860 and the first quarter of 1861.[29]

A chaplain's presence at the D.C. and Virginia penitentiaries was likewise sporadic. Reformer Dorothea Dix noted that the D.C. Penitentiary had an appointed chaplain in the early 1840s at the height of the reform movement, but earlier inspection reports reveal no regular chaplain.[30] Chaplain John J.

Ungerer noted in 1837 that he had only "visited the institution . . . about five months," but believed that if inmates "are provided with a faithful and prudent chaplain, the happiest results may be anticipated."[31] Ungerer insisted that a regular chaplain was key to reformation, but consistency was lacking. This seems odd since the original penitentiary rules outlined the chaplain's duties and the penitentiary program was predicated on reform.[32]

The absence of a penitentiary chaplain was the norm by midcentury. Over a decade after Dix toured prisons, the Virginia Penitentiary still had no regular chaplain and, in 1857, Superintendent Morgan noted that volunteers oversaw moral instruction to compensate. According to Morgan, several ministers "voluntarily attended on Sabbath day" and held religious services "through the year" in the male department, while "a committee of ladies" with "commendable zeal" read scripture to the females when convenient.[33] Morgan's words foreshadowed a trend that continued during the Civil War: a chaplain's presence was expected at both penitentiaries and military prisons, but regular chaplains were absent. Instead, outside volunteers or prisoners themselves often orchestrated religious instruction in military prisons.

Wartime penitentiaries, like their antebellum counterparts, often did not have a regular chaplain despite penitentiary guidelines. The 1862 rules and regulations for the Ohio Penitentiary dictated that a chaplain be available to convicts, furnish Bibles, preach on Sundays, care for the sick and dying, speak only of religious matters, and refrain from teaching sectarian doctrines. Overcrowding interfered with the chaplain's ability to attend to convicts individually, but his presence was nonetheless expected.[34]

Penitentiaries established the expectation that the state should provide a chaplain and this expectation carried over to military prisons. Chaplains were often not assigned to military prisons, but many clergymen sought entry into military prisons as their forebears did at penitentiaries. For example, L. Molon, a local Catholic priest and chaplain of the 123rd Ohio Regiment, recognized the spiritual deficiencies of Confederate prisoners of war at Johnson's Island. Molon requested permission from federal authorities to enter the prison by using the antebellum argument that he could inspire positive change. "These poor misguided men would bear with resignation their well-deserved punishment if they only were allowed the consolation of a priest," Molon pleaded to Secretary of War Edwin Stanton in 1862. Molon argued that spiritual guidance should complement the provisions that Union authorities supplied for prisoners' physical needs. "Couldn't the same comfort be granted to their souls?" Molon implored, since he knew that clergymen were supposed to be present in nineteenth-century prisons. He continued, "It cannot be I am sure the intention of the Government which is now fighting for liberty to enslave the conscience of anybody." Molon's petition was especially significant since it contended that *Catholic* religious instruction could emancipate souls.[35]

Federal officials honored Molon's request. On September 8, 1862, Commissary General Hoffman directed Maj. W. S. Pierson, commander of Johnson's Island, to allow Molon to preach on Sundays and visit sick inmates, at special request, on other days.[36] Molon was not the only Catholic priest who reached out to Confederate prisoners. Rev. R. A. Sidley, who became Molon's successor, also petitioned to minister at Johnson's Island. Hoffman granted permission for Sidley to visit the prison under "proper restrictions" if inmates desired his services and provided that Sidley took the oath of allegiance.[37]

Johnson's Island prisoners had some preaching, but military prison inmates, like penitentiary counterparts, often went without regular religious instruction or visits from chaplains. Nonetheless, prisoners of war vividly recalled the impact of faith on their lives in prison and sometimes initiated their own religious exercises, as did Worcester and Butler in the Georgia Penitentiary. Religious devotion inspired many military prison inmates to reform, just as it did convicts. Many prisoners of war were accustomed to celebrating the Sabbath in their hometown, and the absence of formal services solidified the reality of imprisonment for several.[38]

Preaching and divine service in military prisons were newsworthy, as were stories of criminals' reformation. For example, the *Columbus Statesman* reported on October 4, 1862, that Rev. S. T. Griswold would preach at Camp Chase on October 5, weather permitting. The article was perhaps an invitation to interested Columbus civilians to attend alongside prisoners since visitors frequently toured the camp that year.[39] The religious exercises could be lengthy—the *Statesman* advertised that they would commence at 3 P.M. and continue until further notice.[40] Some prisoners had the privilege of hearing from ministers, but others improvised by reading scripture and initiating individual or small group reflection.

Religious instruction was supposed to encourage spiritual reform among captives, and this trend continued in military prisons either with help from chaplains or from inmates who sought individual guidance from the Bible. Religious conversion was common, though not without challenge, in military prisons such as Johnson's Island and Andersonville, two prisons whose conditions could not have been more disparate. Johnson's Island prisoners, mostly from the upper classes of Southern society, enjoyed better internal conditions, and had better provisions than did the thousands of men of every class crammed into the Georgia stockade.[41] Regardless of conditions, the memories of prisoners at both locations were strikingly similar to each other and to the scenarios that played out in penitentiaries.

Johnson's Island prisoners J. S. Joyner, Virgil S. Murphey, and Robert Bingham exemplified inmates' desire to observe the Sabbath, clung to their religious conviction, and highlighted how incarceration altered their spirits. Each man wrote in 1863 and 1864, a time when massive religious revivals swept both the Union and Confederate armies.[42] This phenomenon undoubtedly impacted inmates' thirst for religion but, as in penitentiaries, incarceration also inspired reform and appreciation of God's Word. On October 20, 1863, Joyner wrote to his mother about the long, weary months of confinement, but said that he enjoyed hearing sermons "on the Sabbath and quite often during the week" since "several of the officers are ministers." Joyner noted that ministers were relatively common at Johnson's Island even though five or six had "been sent away." He did not specify whether Union authorities released the men, or refused them entry.

Religious preaching and, more importantly, its impact continued throughout 1864. Joyner recalled widespread interest in religion and proclaimed that "several have joined the church." Inmates continued daily prayer meetings through the summer, and aid from chaplains and religious organizations persisted that fall. Joyner noted that the Young Men's Christian Association established a library—a goal originally set for penitentiaries—that included "about 500 volumes." Joyner recalled that inmates could read books at will, and they could fend off the doldrums working as librarian or assistant librarian as he did that September.[43]

Virgil Murphey shared Joyner's intellectual curiosity, but his affinity for the divine was flagging. Murphey read either secular or sacred texts. He perused legal tracts, Shakespeare, the Bible, and a Catholic work by Cardinal Wiseman entitled *The Church and the Catacombs*. Murphey was interested in God's Word and in the Catholic Church, but struggled with faith during captivity. Nonetheless, he read the Bible at his wife's request. On January

22, 1864, Murphey confessed to his diary that he read the last five chapters of the Second Book of Samuel to honor the "kind thoughtful admonition" of his "gentle wife," who urged him to "read daily several chapters of Scripture." Murphey admitted that the scriptures inspired him to behave in a manner "pleasing in His sight and in conformity with His laws." But Murphey's struggle with faith led him to give primary credit to his wife for his transformation. Murphey claimed that his wife, more so than Christ, made him "a more perfect human and truthful man than all the teachings of the world or the principle of the wise and virtuous."[44] Like Murphey, many prisoners felt ambivalent about religion amid the harsh prison environment.

Some inmates, like Robert Bingham, subordinated themselves to God's will, reluctantly accepted imprisonment, and tried to focus on their blessings. Bingham's entries from Johnson's Island in October 1863 recount how he used idle time for intellectual and spiritual improvement as he "caught up with the light literature of the day" and counted the good friends he had made. Bingham's positive tone compensated for the fact that he struggled both with imprisonment and with the idea that it was part of God's will. He noted that a religious revival in November 1863 revealed two sides to God. "God sent his spirit and comforted some and convicted others," Bingham sardonically commented, but immediately confessed that he faithfully read the Bible to ease his own suffering. Bingham painstakingly chronicled the day, November 29, 1863, that he finished the Book of Job and commented that while he may have been a casual Christian prior to the war, he would certainly "know how to appreciate a home Sabbath" if he ever got home.[45]

The late 1863 religious revival moved Bingham and others. On December 27, three prisoners tearfully professed faith in Christ, and on December 31, Bingham marveled at God's power since He converted men least likely to change—including himself. Bingham recalled that God chose the "most careless and outbreaking . . . to convince His people of His power" and commented that more good could result if the prison had a chapel. Bingham's full conversion came on January 1, 1864, as he, amid preaching and religious fervor in prison, made a New Year's resolution inspired by God's presence. "I feel deeply sensible of my own failures in duty," Bingham penned. He vowed that, "by God's help I will this year be more earnest in the service of my Lord and Master."[46]

Andersonville inmate William T. Peabody also turned to God through prayer meetings, scripture, and exposure to vice. Like Bingham, Peabody compared the Sabbath in prison to that at home. On June 5, 1864, Peabody wrote that Sundays in Andersonville were not like those he knew in New England. Rather, they were "more like Hell and a tough one too." The following day, two Catholic priests erroneously said the prisoners would soon be released, but Peabody remained optimistic. As time wore on, it became more difficult for Peabody to stay positive, but he concentrated on the words of spiritualists who visited camp, attended prayer meetings, and proclaimed God's goodness. This focus, coupled with Andersonville's dire circumstances and the fact that it was "a great place for swearing and all kinds of wickedness," inspired Peabody to reform. He promised his wife, in his diary, that if he returned home he would be "a different man, I hope better." He also swore that imprisonment taught him to be grateful, and pledged that if he survived, he would "never find fault with anything again."

Peabody's reformation and commitment to Christ strengthened with time. He vowed that if God spared his life, he would "devote the rest of [his] days to the Christian religion." Peabody did not need a chaplain to cultivate faith—Andersonville's vices inspired him to take refuge in Christ as a countercultural deterrent. He confessed that he "never thought so much of the Christian religion as I do since I came into this wicked place."[47]

Andersonville inmate John L. Hoster likewise clung to faith to withstand imprisonment, cherished Sunday preaching despite pining for home, and professed conversion. Throughout June and July 1864, Hoster noted frequent attendance at prayer meetings and long hours spent reading the Testament, especially on the Sabbath, to retain some sense of normalcy on the Lord's Day. Even though Hoster found comfort in God's Word, he could not ignore the void that imprisonment caused, commenting, "How pleasant would it be if with friends we could go to the house of worship." Nonetheless, Hoster carefully noted the exact text of the Bible on which fellow inmates preached, and recorded a strong wave of religious devotion during the week preceding July 17, 1864, the Sabbath. "Preachings and prayer meetings have been held during the past week and I learn that several have committed their souls to God," Hoster wrote in his diary, concluding with amazement that "God's Holy Spirit can find the heart of the persistent even in this loathsome place."[48] Other inmates, like James Vance, also claimed God as their only hope. Vance professed on June 17, 1864, that "All a man can do is to trust in God and keep clean" to withstand an abominable place like Andersonville.[49] Faith could at least distract thoughts from negative circumstances and inmates gravitated toward chaplains when they visited prison, but chaplains were also susceptible to human weakness.

Chaplain A. W. Mangum, like the flock he tended in Salisbury Prison, struggled with faith during his ministry. The Confederate government recognized the importance of a chaplain's presence in prison and dispatched Mangum to Salisbury. Mangum, however, sometimes denounced his assignment. He complained on March 14, 1862, about his pay, which was likely late judging from his characterization of the $75 that he received as "the only pay I have rec'd yet as Chaplain."

Mangum understood the importance of his office, but battled human weakness. He seemed generally pleased on one visit to Salisbury in January 1862, noting that inmates "were in a perfect bustle all the time here," that they liked the prison and its commander, and that they appreciated ministers since they were the only persons permitted to visit the camp. But Mangum's tone changed in April 1862. He noted that he traveled from Hillsboro to Salisbury, arrived at the prison at 4 A.M. and "then was forced to preach two long sermons," a seemingly odd complaint from an ordained minister. A few lines later, Mangum corrected his gripe, stating, "I am quite contented in laboring hard for the fulfillment of my duties. We cannot be poor when we have such a religion and such a Father such a peace—such promise and such a home before us," hinting at the heavenly reward that awaited believers upon death. Mangum's demeanor frequently shifted, but these thoughts sustained his ministry.[50]

Americans believed that the penitentiary program would change misfits into productive civilians, while military prisons would inspire inmates to adopt their captors' cause. Military prisons could even influence ministers who preferred spouting political rhetoric to preaching God's Word. Such was the case for Reverend Doctor Ross, of Huntsville, Alabama, who used the Bible to justify slavery and preached "secession and treason" under the watchful eyes of General Rousseau, a Kentuckian and a Unionist, who oversaw the city. Union authorities believed that imprisonment would change Ross and sent him to Camp Chase as authorities would have sent a criminal to a penitentiary "for the improvement of his health and morals."[51]

Both penitentiary and military prison inmates contended that imprisonment was transformative and inspired transformation, whether secular or sacred. The penitentiary program inspired change through regulations, silence, hard labor, and isolation, and these dynamics shaped the detention of military prison inmates.[52]

Prison Labor: A Tool for Reform, Reward, or Punishment

Nineteenth-century contemporaries believed that penitentiary labor, while punitive, would encourage inmates to reform, stave off boredom, and counter the ill effects of idleness. In the antebellum period, inmates at the Georgia Penitentiary worked on a strict, seasonal schedule. Unless they were sick, in solitary confinement, or resting on the Sabbath, inmates worked eight hours a day in November, December, and January; nine hours daily in February and October; and ten hours daily the rest of the year. In the antebellum period, inmates worked as blacksmiths, wagon makers, and carriage makers, and they produced supplies for the Confederate Army during the Civil War. Georgia Penitentiary inmates foreshadowed work that military prison authorities often required of prisoners of war—convicts "worked on their cells" for repair and maintenance.[53] The penitentiary program established the expectation that inmates were partially responsible for internal prison conditions, and military prison authorities believed the same.

Newspaper articles about the Virginia Penitentiary reflect Americans' belief that labor could transform inmates, that inmates should work in prison or on public works, and that administrators should exploit the trades that inmates brought with them into prison to facilitate reform. On June 7, 1817, the *Carolina Federal Republican* dismissed criticism of penitentiaries and contended that penitentiary discipline—which included inmates working in the boot and shoemaking industries, in tailoring, in thread and rope spinning, in carpentry, as wheelwrights, as coopers, as harness makers, as painters, and as carriage makers, button makers, and blacksmiths—brought convicts "back to a sense of duty and correct mode of thinking and acting."[54]

Nineteenth-century civilians fretted when penitentiary inmates were idle and frequently contended that they should work, under supervision, outside of prison to provide for themselves. Military prison officials later adopted—and adapted—this practice as they recruited prisoners of war to work on various details to procure their own provisions and avoid hiring outside labor to complete undesirable jobs, like burials.

State politicians set precedent for this grunt work through their authorization of convict labor. For example, in July 1845, the Ohio state legislature permitted penitentiary officials to contract out convicts to procure stone for public buildings and other public works. Penitentiary officials could reauthorize contracts upon expiration to "defray the expenses of the institution," provided that convict labor did not interfere with free labor. The *Cincinnati Chronicle* reported that penitentiary officials sanctioned convict labor in the quarry, which was about three miles from Columbus, expressly to prevent convict labor from being "brought into injurious competition with that of the free citizen."[55] Two years later, in 1858, the state legislature authorized the penitentiary warden and directors to use convict labor to complete the new state house as long as the convicts could "be advantageously employed" and "advantageously spared from the ordinary work of the prison."[56] In other words, the convicts performed tasks that penitentiary authorities deemed cost effective and law-abiding civilians found undesirable.

Virginia authorities in the 1850s often based the contracting out of convicts on race. On June 5, 1858, the state legislature passed an act that resulted in "73 negro convicts" being taken out of the penitentiary under "suitable guards" to complete the North River Canal and alleviate crowding. Of these 73 convicts, 68 were male and 5 were female; the latter cooked and washed for the men. The *Richmond Dispatch,* which published the story, concluded that this kind of labor "can be made more profitable" than any other and contended that convicts were "kept just as securely as if confined in the penitentiary."[57] State authorities fretted about the penitentiary's bottom line and, during the Civil War, this concern included provisioning inmates.

The Virginia Penitentiary's population remained high in 1862 and local civilians thought that criminals' work should provision the Confederate Army and alleviate shortages on the home front. On June 3, 1861, the *New York Times* published intelligence from Alexandria, Virginia, that inmates made gun carriages, wagons, axes, picks, flannel shirts, cloth for uniforms, army shoes, tents, wheelbarrows, and litters for the wounded, which saved the Confederate government money.[58] Over a year later, on September 4, 1862, the *Richmond Dispatch* reported that one local court docket had sixty-one cases awaiting trial and was likely to add at least twenty more. The paper estimated that at least two-thirds would be found guilty thereby necessitating expansion of the penitentiary to "accommodate the rapidly increasing number of inmates." The paper denounced the fact that many inmates sat idle and suggested that it would be "good policy" for the legislature to authorize their employment in raising coal from the Chesterfield pits since coal "bids fair to be high and scarce this winter."[59] The public had little tolerance for unproductive penitentiary inmates and felt the same about military prisoners.

Civilians expected that military prison officials treat their captives as penitentiary officials treated convicts. In November 1861, an unnamed Northern man complained to the New York Times that the prisoners held at Camp Chase were a "decided embarrassment" to Union authorities and exhorted them to run Camp Chase like a penitentiary. The man demanded that prisoners of war work and likened them to criminals, stating, "I am opposed to releasing prisoners, but I would put them all to work where they can earn their own living—a service to their country, which I fear most of them have never performed."[60] Work would teach prisoners, both civilians and prisoners of war, industriousness and serve as penance for their offense.

These attitudes remained as the war progressed. In November 1863, a disgruntled New York Times reader complained to the editor that Johnson's Island prisoners were treated too well: they lived in costly barracks, had plenty of food, received money from friends, and consumed valuable foodstuffs that should have been reserved for Sandusky civilians. The man demanded rectification through labor. "I do not wish unchristian retaliation, but could not these fellows work for their board upon the public works as well as be pampered in idleness?" he questioned. The man knew that inmates often worked outside of prison under close supervision, and was likely glad to know that military prison authorities often put prisoners to work.[61]

Military prison officials' employment of prisoners of war on wood, water, and burial details paralleled penitentiary labor—it spared the expense of provision and rendered captives useful. Water, wood, latrine, and burial details were menial jobs, but prisoners of war often preferred them to being idle all day, judging from Castle Thunder inmate Rev. John Hussey's complaint. He griped that inmates rarely moved about, except when the prison floors were scrubbed every three weeks and inmates were permitted into the prison yard for fresh air and exercise.[62] He, like many military prison inmates, would have welcomed work and those who had the opportunity grumbled when it was denied.

Prison labor at Andersonville, as at the Virginia Penitentiary, was sometimes racially motivated and caused resentment among Union captives. Andersonville's population was over thirty thousand in September 1864, and white prisoners objected that they languished in crowded quarters while black captives were seldom in the stockade. Prison authorities "distributed [black inmates] among the citizens, or employed [them] on Government works." Union inmates' complaints that black captives were "worked no harder than they are accustomed to be" verified that this amounted to slavery, but they nonetheless viewed labor as a privilege.[63]

Prisoners of war despised inactivity, but convicts sometimes inflicted physical harm upon themselves to shirk the burden of labor. For example, in 1854, a disgruntled burglar in the Ohio Penitentiary viewed work as degrading and chopped off his hand to avoid it.[64] Prisoners of war, however, craved the activity inherent in labor. Johnson's Island inmate James B. Mitchell complained of idleness in May and June 1864, and told his parents that he forced himself to take "at least a small amount" of exercise every day, which consisted of pacing. Otherwise, Mitchell spent most of his day reading, but became so despondent from "want of exercise" that he could not focus.[65] Mitchell would have relished the opportunity to work. Many of his comrades at Johnson's Island and other prisons also welcomed labor if they were physically able.

Confederate authorities lacked provisions for prisoners of war at Andersonville and often employed prisoners of war under guard to gather necessities, a practice that paralleled the contracting out of convicts since it mitigated the prison's expenses. Inmates desperately wanted to get out of the filthy stockade, but frailty often precluded their ability to perform manual labor. Prisoners knew that they had to muster enough strength to work so that they could have basic supplies, like wood and water. Inmate John J. Sherman recalled that wood was especially scant. Confederate authorities required two men per one hundred, in a "weakened condition," to carry sticks, eight feet long, on their backs and then split the wood for burning. The group of one hundred received only what laborers could carry. Nathaniel Price and Lyle Adair summarized the wood-gathering process: Captain Wirz allowed prisoners to volunteer at the stockade's south gate for wood detail. Three inmates at a time went under guard into the adjacent woods to gather wood and pine knots for fuel. This process seemed innocuous, but Adair's account from January 1865 told otherwise. Inmates had to carry heavy lumber on their shoulders from one-and-a-half to two miles once every two weeks and gather enough for that period. This, Price admitted, "relieved to some extent the fuel famine," but did not alleviate the shortage of vessels available to prepare food.[66]

Andersonville inmates had to construct their own shelters and feed themselves. Prisoner W. W. Day recalled that prisoners used the wood that work details procured to build shelters by sinking poles into the ground and fastening them with strips of bark, creating a space that was certainly smaller than a penitentiary cell. The work of survival did not stop there. Day also recalled that inmates tried to remedy the water shortage by digging wells with canteen halves.[67] Confederate authorities did not necessarily order this work, and they may well have mistaken it for tunneling to escape. But authorities could not provision so many inmates, and their labor mitigated the Southern government's burden of supply.

Union prisoners were aware that Confederate authorities ordered some tasks that challenged the U.S. cause, and some carefully distinguished between jobs that honored the oath that they took upon enlistment and those that ran afoul of it. Price recalled that Rebel authorities took a number of prisoners out of the stockade and supervised their work in the cookshops and bakeries or on burial details. Price approved, stating that these jobs were "not looked upon by the prisoners as being inconsistent with their duty as soldiers in the Union Army." But he and other loyal inmates denounced other jobs for which inmates volunteered. He noted that "there was not much hesitancy" in condemning men who accepted clerkships in Confederate offices and headquarters, the commissary, or positions on a driving team. These positions paralleled contract labor and Price admitted that the temptation to take parole for one of them enticed many prisoners since it got them out of the stockade "within prescribed limits." However, he and others considered such workers to "be giving aid to the cause of the Southern Confederacy" and bending to Southern overtures for changed loyalty.[68]

Andersonville's authorities frequently enticed prisoners to engage in the equivalent of contract work either to provision inmates or aid the Confederate cause. Inmate M. J. Umstead noted that some prisoners rejected Confederate propositions. He recalled on October 10, 1864, that prison officers entered the stockade "trying to enlist prisoners to work for the Confederacy," suggesting that inmates were reluctant to comply. Two weeks later, on October 26, Umstead revealed the source of prisoners' hesitancy. He recalled that Rebel authorities used labor to entice reform, meaning loyalty to the Confederacy. Officials paroled fifty men outside the stockade to work as mechanics, shoemakers, and boat makers, and Umstead screamed that fourteen of the laborers "took the oath of allegiance to the G-D—Confederacy."[69] Authorities' bribes were unrelenting. Other inmates recalled that authorities routinely sought carpenters, woodchoppers, blacksmiths, and molders from the inmates, and advertised that volunteers could go to Macon to make shoes for Confederate troops.[70]

Even if inmates refused work outside of Andersonville, Confederate authorities required that inmates police their own quarters. Captain Wirz and the guards divided inmates into detachments that elected their own sergeants. Sergeants were responsible for ensuring that inmates formed police details to clean their quarters. Inmates who refused to comply suffered punishment by ball and chain for the remainder of the day.[71]

Confederate authorities were not the only ones who demanded that inmates maintain their quarters and supply themselves. Union authorities at Johnson's Island either permitted or required inmates to work to ease economic burden and improve prison conditions. Prisoner Joseph Hubbard Saunders described the prison as a world in and of itself since inmates undertook every profession from shoemaking to dentistry.[72] On one level, these tasks represented privileges that Union authorities conferred upon prisoners, but they also enabled the government to "provide" humane treatment without cost.

Saunders enjoyed the prison economy, but other prisoners either openly disdained or begrudgingly undertook labor. Inmates' disdain for work was not surprising since many on Johnson's Island hailed from the upper classes. Capt. Robert Bingham repeatedly griped about performing various tasks, especially dirty work. In one instance, Bingham noted that he was part of a scouring detail and worked hard while "some of the detailed worked none." The job fatigued Bingham so much that he "had to go to sleep before dinner," something he had not done in quite some time. The following day, Bingham was at work again on a water detail, brought in eight buckets, and then emptied the chamber pot that he shared with his messmate. "I little tho't I'd ever do any such thing for anybody," Saunders disgustedly admitted. But the work did not end there. Later in his imprisonment he had to "split the mud" to procure eleven buckets of water on water detail, saw wood, clean spitboxes, and sweep the floor of his quarters.

Despite complaints, labor reformed Bingham as it did some penitentiary inmates. "I am of a rather agreeable temper any how and take things easy,"

Bingham wrote, "But this captivity almost overwhelms me sometimes, even tho' I know from whom it comes." He asked for God's grace to bear his trials and admitted that he had to change his attitude and accept work to survive imprisonment since Union authorities mandated it.[73] An unnamed exchanged comrade told the *Memphis Daily Appeal* that Union authorities "required" all the "labor of the prison, police duty, scavenger work, digging of sinks, etc.," to "be performed by the prisoners" and demanded "respect and implicit obedience to all their orders."[74]

While military prison officers frequently required labor from inmates, courts-martial sentenced other civilians and/or soldiers to hard labor in military prisons or penitentiaries for war-related offenses or common crimes committed in uniform. Courts-martial stirred controversy when they sentenced soldiers to penitentiaries, but the order in which courts-martial dictated punishments clearly communicated that soldier-criminals disgraced their office. The court-martial that found Charles Sprague of the 6th Wisconsin guilty of fraud chastised him, saying, "How much more the crime when committed by one in whom the duty of being a good soldier is added to that of the high obligation of being a good citizen." In another case, a court-martial found Pvt. John Nugent of the same regiment guilty of fraud and sentenced him to six months' imprisonment in the D.C. Penitentiary and subsequent dishonorable discharge. The court later stipulated that Nugent's discharge would precede his confinement in the D.C. Penitentiary since "no man who has the honorable position of a soldier should be at the same time a felon," an ironic statement since many incarcerated soldiers assumed that stigma.[75]

Soldiers like Sprague and Nugent were guilty of crime, but individuals held without probable cause elicited anger. In 1862, eight of the sixty-nine service men imprisoned at the D.C. Penitentiary were held with "no charges stated in the papers," and Massachusetts Sen. Henry Wilson complained that these men were "degraded as felons" since their punishment lacked justification.[76] Imprisonment in penitentiaries clearly equated soldiers with criminals, regardless of whether they were guilty, or merely suspected, of crime.

Union and Confederate officials conferred the same punitive function on military prisons when they sentenced offenders to Johnson's Island, Camp Chase, and Castle Thunder, among other locations. The main difference, despite some overlap, was that military prisons punished mostly war-inspired political offenses while penitentiaries mostly punished regular crimes. For example, men sentenced to hard labor at Johnson's Island included the following: in July 1862, a court-martial sentenced civilian Richard Eggleston of Covington, Kentucky, to sixty days of hard labor for "hurrahing for Jeff Davis." Almost one year later in May 1863, Gen. Ambrose Burnside ordered eight civilians to Johnson's Island to do hard labor during the war for "aiding and abetting those in arms against the United States Government." In February 1864, a court-martial sentenced Confederate military recruiters William Waller, Schultz Lesch, and two unnamed Kentuckians to hang for forming a Confederate military company, but later commuted the punishment to hard labor with ball and chain at Johnson's Island for the duration of the war. In retaliation, Confederate authorities sentenced Captain Ives of the 10th Massachusetts and Capt. R. C. G. Reed of the 3rd Ohio Cavalry to hard labor at Salisbury Prison for the war's duration.[77]

Courts-martial sometimes sentenced civilians to hard labor at military prisons for questionable loyalty, but they also sentenced civilians for common crimes, or soldiers for military offenses, to military prisons. For example, in May 1862, Henry Kuhl, Hamilton W. Wondon, and Canad Kuhl, three citizens of western Virginia, killed a Union soldier in "cold blood." Gen. John C. Frémont, commander of the Mountain Department, consequently sentenced the former two offenders to hang and the latter to hard labor at Camp Chase.[78]

Confederate authorities likewise carried out penitentiary sentences at Castle Thunder when they reprimanded soldiers for desertion. One imprisoned war correspondent from the *New York Herald* recalled that Confederate authorities frequently branded Rebel deserters, shot hundreds, and sentenced others "to hard labor and the chain gang" on prison grounds. The *Herald* journalist published this account to highlight Confederate authorities' "barbarous" treatment of inmates, including native sons who abandoned the Southern cause.[79]

In other instances, Union and Confederate authorities sentenced offenders to death, but later commuted the sentences. Commutation and, in some cases, the experience of imprisonment itself, inspired some prisoners to reject imprisonment's negative stigma. For example, Union authorities sentenced S. Boyer Davis, a spy, to hang at Johnson's Island, but commuted the sentence to imprisonment during the war. Prior to receiving word that the federal officials had commuted the sentence, Davis urged his wife to convey the following message to his friends at home: "Tell them, I died a man, a soldier, with a clear conscience, a firm trust in God and ashamed of nothing

I have done." Davis refused to let imprisonment disgrace him, at least rhetorically. His words represent how inmates could control the messages about themselves and their circumstances that they conveyed to loved ones. The poetic words that James B. Mitchell wrote to his mother from Johnson's Island also communicated this idea. "For though these walls our bodies may keep, they cannot confine our thoughts in sleep," he penned, dreaming of exchange and home. Mitchell's words raise the question of how inmates communicated with the outside world, which will be the subject of the next chapter.[80]

Life Out There

Inmates' Communications with the Outside World

The Fourth of July was a spirited day in civilian life, but a somber affair in prison. Thoughts of home haunted prisoners during the celebration of freedom. Instead of lauding independence, prisoners pondered detention amid recitations of the Declaration of Independence, patriotic speeches, and the musical strains of "Do They Miss Me at Home," which inmates sang with "particular feeling" given their circumstances. The *Philadelphia Journal*'s description of this Independence Day celebration seemed appropriate for prisoners of war commemorating their chosen side's version of America. This ceremony, however, occurred in 1859 at the D.C. Penitentiary and was held not by civilian-soldiers turned prisoners, but by incarcerated criminals. The convicts remained patriotic and just as tied to home as Union and Confederate prisoners of war, and both groups pined for home.[1]

Penitentiary and military prison inmates and those at home relied on prison officials to maintain relationships since officials screened written correspondence and monitored visits. Prison officials seemingly had ultimate control over prisoners' interpersonal relationships, but penitentiary and military prisoners' families and friends asserted their right to communicate with prisoners and expected that officials permit contact.[2] Correspondence between prisoners and outsiders was often superficial. Guards screened all letters, and inmates and outsiders often limited their writing to safe topics like life at home. The superficial knowledge about incarceration that prisoners offered undoubtedly caused consternation for relatives and friends, who worried about prisoners' well-being.

Family members encouraged prisoners to patiently bear confinement's hardships by seeking God's grace, and prisoners tried to reassure relatives that they were not suffering. Penitentiary and military prison inmates longed for home, begged the help of prominent relatives and acquaintances to secure release, and emphasized masculine duty, feminine submissiveness, or familial obligation in petitions. Inmates' letters to and from home portrayed the experience of imprisonment positively to assuage loved ones' fears and appease inspectors. In so doing, prisoners often validated the penitentiary program's key tenets of religious instruction, reformation, and education. Nonetheless, correspondence clearly reveals the agony of separation, the anxiety of not knowing when release would come, the challenges of prison life, and how prisoners redefined personal relationships while in captivity.

The Meaning of Written Correspondence

Throughout the century, outsiders communicated with penitentiary and military prison inmates through censored letters and contacted prison officials regarding confined relatives. Imprisonment forced all prisoners to redefine their personal relationships under the constraint of prison rules, which made inmates feel helpless and confused their associates.

Antebellum penitentiary inmates and their families left few records, and their thoughts are mostly accessible only through newspapers and the records of penitentiary officials. Many penitentiary inmates were immigrants and as three newspapers—the *Asheville News,* the *Brooklyn Daily Eagle,* and the *Ohio Statesman*—noted, recent immigrants often had no one in the United States to address. In 1856, these three papers printed a poem that an Ohio Penitentiary convict penned to his mother. The prisoner-poet wrote that his mother's heart would "bleed" if she heard that "her darling boy" was an "inmate of a prison in a foreign land." The convict pined for his mother and apologized for straying from her and his homeland. He confessed that friends deserted him when he was drunk, and lamented that he ended up in prison not knowing if his mother was yet alive, but hoping to meet her in heaven.[3] The man was sure that his mother loved him regardless, as many convicts' family members did despite the disgrace of incarceration.

Ohio Penitentiary Chaplain James B. Finley admired the unbroken bonds between inmates and relatives since letters constantly passed between inmates and kin despite the "afflicting event that separates them." He recalled another heart-wrenching letter to an inmate from his wife that professed her undying love. The woman's husband accidentally killed a child while drunk, but she nonetheless vowed to *"love [him] forever"* even though he caused their "poverty" and "wretchedness."[4] Unconditional love could sustain antebellum and wartime prisoners through captivity, or help inspire them to reform.

Many relatives hoped that their incarcerated loved ones would reform. After visiting her brother George Montgomery in the D.C. Penitentiary, Sarah Donnelly penned him a desperate letter. She told Montgomery that his imprisonment tore apart her family and plagued his "old and feeble" mother. Regardless, Donnelly assured her brother that even if he felt like he "had not one friend on Earth," she "had not forgot" him. Donnelly was sure that imprisonment, the equivalent of hell, would teach a needed lesson. She exhorted Montgomery to renounce crime and turn to Jesus since faith alone gave her peace.[5] John Shreene, whose son was in the D.C. Penitentiary, also encouraged moral reform. Shreene instructed his son to "be a good boy," to "mind and obey" keepers, and to "read the Bible and good books."[6] These letters reflected the penitentiary's purpose and met inspectors' approval, but strict regulations often caused prisoners to lose sight of acquaintances' affection.

Wartime penitentiary and military prison officials allowed only short letters on acceptable topics to and from home, and inmates and their family members agonized over the limitations imposed on their relationships. Samuel Burks Taylor and Thomas W. Bullitt, Confederate cavalrymen held at the Ohio Penitentiary, provide good examples. Taylor repeatedly reminded his sister that his communication was limited to immediate family members, that he could write only one page, and that he could receive only two pages at a time. Bullitt likewise told his sister that general correspondence was "restricted to two letters per week." Bullitt likely worried his sister when he emphasized that "penitentiary walls afford very little of that spice of life: 'variety,'" and confessed to feeling homesick as he reminisced about the "affections of . . . childhood." Taylor likewise left his sister feeling helpless when he wrote that there was nothing she could do for him since he enjoyed good health.[7] Taylor offered that sentiment to comfort his sister, but she and Bullitt's sister wanted to aid their brothers and likely disregarded rules governing correspondence since Bullitt and Taylor repeatedly reminded them of letter length.

Throughout the century, restrictions colored prisoners' interpretations of confinement. Prisoners could not write anything negative about prisons or officers due to censorship, and penitentiary and military prison officials closely monitored incoming communication since they wanted inmates to have little, if any, knowledge of outside events. The restrictions that military prison officials imposed on correspondence mirrored those that governed penitentiary inmates' writing. For example, officials at Camp Chase required all letters to and from prisoners to be examined, restricted the content of correspondence to matters "strictly of a private nature," and, as in penitentiaries, dictated that letters not "exceed one page of common letter paper each."[8]

Johnson's Island inmates faced similar scrutiny, which irked the captives since many were upper-class Southern officers who had commanded Confederate troops. These literate, educated prisoners resented how imprisonment negated privilege and rendered them subordinate to enemy officers, who determined when, on what topics, and how often inmates could write home. Independent Southern men were not accustomed to others dictating their personal lives, and they tried desperately to direct their own communication. Prisoner James B. Mitchell grew anxious since it took weeks for letters from the South to reach Johnson's Island. To assert a semblance of control, he advised his father that the quickest way to send a letter was to give it to a friend in Richmond, who could mail it from the capital. Inefficient mail was not Mitchell's sole concern—he also worried that his father's letters failed to reach him due to inappropriate length. "Take care not to write more than one page of *ordinary sized letter paper,*" Mitchell instructed since the silence from home was unbearable.[9]

Other prisoners at Johnson's Island also fretted that Union inspectors would confiscate letters based on content. Alfred E. Bell shared Mitchell's concern about length and admonished his wife to limit letters to one page of "perfectly plain and legible" text. He emphasized restrictions to ensure his wife's comprehension. "You surely understand the limits of our writing well enough not to write counterban [sic]," he penned. Bell wanted to hear from his wife and children as often as possible, but feared that some messages may be in Union hands.[10]

Johnson's Island inmate J. S. Joyner was frustrated that regulations impinged on family bonds. He, like Bell, directed relatives that letters should include only "subjects not contraband" so that he could hear from home more often. Restrictions crushed Joyner as he indicated in a September 1864 letter to his uncle. Joyner commented that he had received several letters from home, but lamented that he could not answer them all since prison rules permitted inmates to write only two letters per week. Restrictions were a constant reminder of the power that Union officials exercised over Confederate inmates' lives since they could not communicate freely with family and friends. Officials imposed limits on length for the sake of both security and expediency since inspection was burdensome, and these limitations demoralized the prisoners, who were once independent men. Letter writing was a privilege, but it left inmates like Joseph Hubbard Saunders unfulfilled. His simple wish to write his sister "a long letter" underscored how his present life differed from what it was in antebellum days.[11] Letters from home were unspeakably important. Prisoners obsessed over the seemingly endless time that it took correspondence to reach them, counted each time they heard from home, and despaired whenever the mail lagged.

Numerous factors impacted the delivery of prisoners' letters to and from home, from the operation of flag-of-truce boats to deliberations over prisoner exchanges and the temperament of inspectors. Military prisoners depended on words from home to mitigate loneliness and despair even though relatives and friends did not fully understand their predicament and many prisoners were ashamed since imprisonment made them feel like criminals. Political prisoner Charles Barrington Simrall commented to Belle Price, a casual acquaintance, in June 1863 that her letters were a "source of great pleasure" to him, an inmate at "the Bastille of Camp Chase." Simrall, enveloped in self-pity, later surmised that if "sympathy for a poor prisoner" inspired Price to write him a short note, then he surely could expect longer letters when friendship rather than sympathy drove correspondence.[12] Simrall nonetheless feared that the stigma of imprisonment would deter Price from writing. But like the family members of penitentiary inmates, she instead consoled Simrall through his dark hours.

Johnson's Island inmate Alfred E. Bell felt similar shame, but wanted to ensure that his letters reached home. He dolefully noted that he had "nothing of interest" to write to his wife since prison life was monotonous. But the seemingly blasé Bell had ulterior motives: He knew that mundane letters always passed inspection. He insisted upon regular correspondence with his wife despite banal content, and fretted when he heard nothing back. Bell and other prisoners at Johnson's Island tried to reassert control over their intimate relationships during long periods of silence. Bell began letters with this familiar refrain: "My Dear Wife, having become very anxious to hear from you I conclude to write you again it being some weeks since I received a letter from you." He continued by admonishing her that "you [k] now not the anxiety that I await a letter from you." Bell evoked the image of a desperate man helplessly awaiting a reply from home when he began three letters this way in May and June 1864.[13]

James B. Mitchell experienced similar doldrums at Johnson's Island and his correspondence—or lack thereof—with family members aroused either despair or elation. On February 9, 1865, Mitchell chastised his brother for failing to write. "I fear you have forgotten my existence," Mitchell cried. He then stated that if his brother only knew how much he thought about home and kin, he would "write at every opportunity." Despondency, common among prisoners, dominated this letter, but receipt of news from home had Mitchell walking on air. On February 17, 1865, eight days after complaining to his brother, Mitchell received a letter from his mother dated Christmas Day 1864. He proclaimed that news from home was "like a Christmas present" that brought more pleasure than a child "investigating the contents of his stocking."[14]

Mitchell received sporadic correspondence from home, sometimes going as long as three or five months without any word, but other times he received multiple letters in one day. Mitchell battled despair during each lag, and despair ironically led him to perpetuate the gap. On August 1, 1864, Mitchell wrote to his father that he rejoiced at the receipt of a couple of letters after "a long interval of suspense and anxiety." But in the next line, Mitchell confessed that he had not written as often as possible since "a prisoner has so little to write that it gives but little pleasure."[15] Mitchell's correspondence with family members clearly demonstrates how his identity as a prisoner provided the lens through which he interpreted messages. The stigma of imprisonment caused Mitchell to fear being forgotten, fueled his despondency, perpetuated his belief that he had nothing worthwhile to communicate, and caused him to overlook the fact that simple news from him would probably have sufficed for loved ones.

Other inmates experienced similar gaps in correspondence and consequent bouts of anxiety. Johnson's Island inmate J. S. Joyner was frustrated with unreliable mail delivery. He repeatedly wrote home, feared that many letters failed to reach family members, and implicitly questioned relatives' commitment to replying expediently. "I have written a great many letters home but have received but two," he complained on September 18, 1863, envious that fellow inmates received mail more frequently. "You must write oftener," he urged, since "some of the prisoners receive letters from home every week." Scarce news from home plagued Joyner through 1865. He complained on January 2 that he again wrote despite having "no letters to answer." The last letter from home reached him in late September.[16]

Prisoners feared that captors would not deliver letters due to censorship and/or the inefficiency of the wartime mail, and uncertainty heightened despair during periods without mail. Mail call aroused either joy or consternation, according to Johnson's Island inmate Joseph Hubbard Saunders. On April 28, 1864, Saunders, dismayed, complained that there was nothing for him in the Dixie mail. He griped to his mother that he once received letters regularly, but received only four that year to date. Two months later, Saunders noted that his mother's letters cheered his "low spirits" on his birthday, but despondency returned in 1865. Saunders last heard from home on October 11, 1864, and in January, he admitted that he had not written his mother since November 16, but had addressed other relatives and impatiently awaited replies. A note from his sister finally arrived on February 11, 1865. Saunders was elated, but wondered why he had previously received nothing from her since he had written her frequently.[17]

Letters from home often failed to reach prisoners elsewhere. Old Capitol inmate George Henry Clay Rowe wrote four times to his wife and heard nothing back. He lamented that thoughts of "her, and home, and children drive all idea of sleep away" since long, idle hours magnified his obsession with home and family.[18] Castle Thunder inmate John Johnson experienced similar frustration. Johnson, a Norwegian, penned letters home in his native language, but Richmond's provost marshal, John Winder, suspected subversive content and refused to send them. In July 1863, Johnson begged Winder to send his letters since he last heard from his family in December 1862. He assured Winder that the letters complied with regulations and discussed family matters—he merely wanted word from loved ones and to assure them of his health.[19] These common sentiments pervaded inmates' correspondence as they tried to reach family members.

Both prisoners and relatives craved knowledge about their beloveds' physical and mental state. Letters from relatives of Johnson's Island inmate James Metts demonstrate that concern about well-being went both ways.

On October 25, 1863, Metts's father rejoiced at a long-awaited letter from his son and stated that he made numerous attempts to get letters to Metts, but became "almost discouraged" from trying. Metts's father was anxious about his son, especially after learning that Metts had been wounded. He told James that he "suffered much" on his son's account and feared that his "cup already filled with trouble would be run over" if James died. James, meanwhile, solicited provisions from other family members to aid his healing. When Metts's Unionist uncle received James's letter, he noted that he pitied Metts's suffering, but had "no sympathy for the cause" for which he fought. James's uncle nonetheless furnished him with the requested clothing and money and likely relieved James's anxious father.[20]

Metts requested provisions, but other military prison inmates claimed they had plenty to eat and that their captors treated them well. These statements, likely influenced by censorship, differed markedly from postwar accounts of atrocities.[21] Many captives noted good health and spirits and exhorted loved ones to endure separation courageously. One Camp Chase inmate instructed his brother to "rest easy as to our treatment," since he had "plenty to eat, plenty to wear," and was "treated very kindly by all."[22] Similarly, Castle Thunder prisoner John Sullivan Healy assured his sister that he was "well" and had "very good treatment." Healy claimed that only knowledge of his family's condition could comfort him.[23]

Military prison inmates understood that it was difficult for family members to withstand both war's trials and their absence and emphasized that imprisonment could, as expected throughout the nineteenth century, inspire positive change. In so doing, prisoners of war acknowledged that military prisons, like penitentiaries, had a reformatory function. Camp Chase inmate W. C. Carnier urged his wife to patiently bear all trials and assured her that he would care for himself to "get home and take care" of her in the future. More significantly, he contended that confinement would make him a better husband. Prison was an all-male world, which sometimes inspired violence and rowdiness.[24] But imprisonment also necessitated self-control and required men to undertake traditional female roles for survival. Carnier claimed that men could carry these roles into domestic life upon release. He told his wife that he did a good deal of "cooking and washing and various other things about house keeping," but noted that this was a struggle since "men are bad home keepers." Nonetheless, Carnier believed that prison would make him a good cook so that he might be useful to his wife.[25]

Reform occurred as a result of military prisons officials' requirement that prisoners undertake domestic duties. Like Carnier, Old Capitol Prison inmate James J. Williamson noted that he and his roommates took turns each night in "the household work—cooking and cleaning up."[26] Carnier and Williamson offer a point of comparison between inmates' experiences at military prisons and penitentiaries. Work at penitentiaries ideally cultivated masculinity, shaping inmates into productive workers, but military prisons frequently "feminized" inmates, exposing them to women's work.[27]

Penitentiary and military prison inmates who reformed boasted to family members about their transformation. In late May 1846, Ohio Penitentiary's chaplain, James Finley, recalled a letter in which a prisoner admitted that he sinned against God and his "*good*" parents, but rejoiced that God's mercy turned him from errant ways.[28] Likewise, Camp Chase inmate Carter Louthan wrote to his sister that he had become "quite sober-sided" upon entering prison. Louthan commented that prison offered few opportunities for misbehavior and claimed that "those are good who have no particular temptation to do otherwise." He asserted that imprisonment helped him grow accustomed to good behavior, but asked his sister to judge his reformation and whether he was "not a better boy" when he returned to Virginia.[29] Louthan boasted of reform, but bemoaned the anguish of imprisonment. He experienced "the most painful solitude" since captivity cut him off from the pleasures of his sister's friendship.[30]

Solitary confinement was not necessary to make military prison inmates feel isolated. Both penitentiary and military prison inmates struggled to cope with feelings of isolation either on their own or with the help of family. In some cases, as Amy Murrell Taylor has noted, family members urged political conversion by taking an oath of allegiance to secure release.[31] In other cases, concerned family members encouraged inmates to keep up their spirits, to turn to God, and to remain positive for the sake of good health. Writing to her father in Camp Chase, one Kentucky woman acknowledged that war constituted "a time to try men's souls," and that incarceration exacerbated the pain. She assured her father that his family fervently prayed for his release. "Trust in God, be faithful and true and He will never forsake you," the woman wrote, urging him to "be cheerful and hopeful" to preserve his health and reminded him that God would judge his captors in the afterlife.[32] In these instances, family members emphasized the importance of religious instruction, a founding ideal of the penitentiary program. These exhortations met with inspectors' approval and provided at least temporary encouragement for prisoners. Written words, however, could not compare with face-to-face meetings.

Visitors and Visitation: Established Protocols

The guidelines that governed penitentiary visits and outside communication informed those that Union and Confederate officials implemented at military prisons. The 1816 Rules and Regulations for the Georgia penitentiary stipulated that the keeper had to approve all written communication, that no person could carry anything into or out of the institution for prisoners' use, that visits could occur only if both inmate and visitor exhibited good conduct, and that the keeper or an assistant supervise visits.[33] Similarly, Richmond authorities informed Maj. Mason Morfit, quartermaster of Salisbury, North Carolina, that "intercourse between prisoners and outsiders" was forbidden.[34] Northern instructions mirrored these mandates and those of the Georgia Penitentiary. Old Capitol Prison's keeper stopped conversations at the end of fifteen minutes, finished or not, and sent the visitor away. Union officials limited discussion to personal matters and required some visitors to take the oath of allegiance as a prerequisite to visitation.[35]

Civilians nonetheless believed that they had the right to contact officials about incarcerated relatives and visit prisoners. Numerous women throughout the century petitioned authority figures to connect with incarcerated husbands or sons. Mrs. Lamdin believed herself entitled to a visit with her husband, who was in the Virginia Penitentiary, and petitioned Virginia Governor Henry A. Wise three times in the late 1850s. Wise aided Lamdin each time. He wrote to Superintendent Morgan on October 25, 1856, December 4, 1856, and December 11, 1856, and asked permission for Lamdin to see her husband. Wise acted out of "pity" for Lamdin, stating that she had "come a long distance" for the visits.[36] Ann Bohlayer likewise contacted D.C. Penitentiary officials about her son's treatment. She claimed that federal officials erroneously convicted her son of assault since a "partial" jury ruled against him. Bohlayer, like other nineteenth-century contemporaries, viewed prison officials as paternalistic figures and urged Warden Sengstack to take "particular care" of, or exonerate, her son.[37]

Corresponding with prison officials was stressful, but seeing a family member in prison could be overwhelming. Both penitentiary and military prison inmates received visitors, but these encounters often evoked agony. The wife and child of one Old Capitol prisoner received a pass from Washington's provost marshal good for only one visit. The pass, which expired at sundown, created pressure to get to the Old Capitol in time. Once inside, the provost marshal dictated that a guard supervise the meeting and cut it off at fifteen minutes, hardly enough time for inmates and callers to get reacquainted or have any meaningful conversation.[38]

Some passes specifically limited the content of visitors' discussions. Catherine Best visited Old Capitol inmate William Carlisle on the conditions that the two converse "ON FAMILY MATTERS ONLY" under a guard's sight and for a maximum of fifteen minutes.[39] Officials sought to minimize the possibility that visits would threaten prison security, but time and content constraints unnerved visitors and prisoners. Civilians worried that their time would expire before they could use their passes as they navigated D.C.'s congested streets. They also feared that seeing loved ones in captivity would be too emotionally taxing.

Visits completely overwhelmed some prisoners. Old Capitol inmate George Henry Clay Rowe's wife visited twice during his imprisonment. After her second visit, Rowe watched through prison windows as she meandered through the city streets and became completely "exasperated" by his situation. His wife, he realized, was in a "strange city with no one . . . to take charge of her," and soon after she vanished from sight, Rowe yelled after her, completely "maddened." He violently shook the window bars and undoubtedly felt like a convict.[40]

Visitation, then, was both a blessing and a curse. Military prisoners wanted to see loved ones, but it was often too emotionally draining to see them in such a degraded state. Many captives, like Castle Thunder prisoner Junius H. Browne, could not get over feeling like a criminal. Browne contended that imprisonment rendered men unrecognizable. In a letter home, he declared that if his "best friend" were to see him, he would be unrecognizable. "Indeed," Browne concluded, "I do not know myself. I look like a felonious mendicant; and in France would be sent to the galleys on suspicion that I was an escaped convict."[41] Browne assumed the identity of a felon and wished to be spared the humiliation of seeing friends.

Inmates' friends and family members often shared these sentiments, and some chose not to visit at all. Passes granted to Old Capitol Prison visitors reveal that many individuals entered the prison only to bring provisions to inmates, most commonly clothing, all of which were subject to Superintendent Wood's inspection.[42] Bringing provisions to inmates solved the problem of painful visits, since friends and relatives supported prisoners while maintaining distance. Both Union and Confederate civilians could send packages to family members until February 1864, when Union authorities discovered that Confederate officials had sent packages intended for Union prisoners in Richmond to Gen. Robert E. Lee's army.[43]

Even if they found visits unbearable, both penitentiary and military prison inmates desperately wanted to communicate with the outside world, whether to beg for help, to check on acquaintances, or to get updates on the news. Sometimes this was as easy as talking with new inmates. New commitments to penitentiaries and military prisons knew of current events and inmates sought them out for stories. Old Capitol inmate John Marshal noted that when new prisoners arrived, many prisoners "gather[ed] round the stranger to learn the news" in what often became an "animated scene," especially if the newcomer was a prisoner of war with word from the front.[44]

Andersonville's prisoners also craved information about the battlefront and the prospects for release. Inmate David F. Weimer noted in June 1864 that new prisoners from the Western theater brought rumors of military success, but had "no encouragement for us poor prisoners." Other inmates, like Ira B. Sampson, knew that prospects for release were slim and focused solely on recent Union victories. He refused to believe Rebel guards when, on May 26, 1864, they reported that Confederate forces badly whipped Union troops at Atlanta.[45] Incoming captives were the best hope that Andersonville prisoners had for hearing outside intelligence. Visitors to other military prisons and penitentiaries were more frequent and their presence captivating.

Inmates' acquaintances visited prisoners to reunite, but curiosity drove other civilians to visit prisons. Ohio Penitentiary inmate Thomas Hines, one of Morgan's cavalrymen, stated that visitors had for the prison "a fascination equaled by no other in the State," and recalled the "great number of sight-seers who constantly stream through its iron doors." Visitation, according to Hines, remedied visitors' "faint conception" of actual penitentiary conditions.[46]

Public fascination with imprisonment was well entrenched prior to the Civil War and prison administrators recognized civilians' inquisitiveness as a potential source of revenue. In 1848, the Virginia Penitentiary Board of Directors suggested that a "small fee should be required of visitors" since "many other state prisons" imposed a charge. The directors noted that a considerable number of people visited "from idle curiosity alone," but complained that this could jeopardize discipline.[47] Civilians were equally fascinated with military prisons, which also became somewhat of a tourist attraction. On June 21, 1864, the *Cleveland Daily Leader* advertised a "Pleasure Excursion" that, for $1, would take passengers on the steamer *Morning Star* to Put-In-Bay Island "going in sight of Johnson's Island."[48]

Visitors caught the attention of both penitentiary and military prison inmates and heightened officials' concern for misbehavior. Some inmates tried to communicate with visitors, especially if they were important or could help secure release. In April 1834, D.C. Penitentiary inmate Dennis Larkin tried to solicit a visiting congressman. Larkin left his seat at work four times to approach the congressman, and penitentiary officials rewarded his efforts with four days in the dungeon.[49]

Larkin, like many other inmates, broke the rules governing interactions with visitors. Penitentiary inmates were not to look at visitors, but often cast them inappropriate glances. In January 1855, D.C. Penitentiary officials sentenced John Holley to one day in solitary confinement on bread and water for twice "gazing at visitors impudently." Officials somehow overlooked the more serious offense of inmate Joseph Cunningham until A. L. Stephens, the angry father of a female visitor, contacted the warden. Stephens complained that Cunningham insulted his daughter and her friend during their visit to the penitentiary by staring at the women "out of countenance," winking, making "other indecent signs" to the ladies, and "following them with his eyes up stairs and along the galleries looking at their feet and under their clothes as they walk along." Stephens fumed that Cunningham listened to the women's conversation while idling at his job cleaning lamps in the prison shop. Stephens told the warden that Cunningham ought to be removed from his position, replaced by some "decent" person, and taught a trade so that he could earn an honest living upon release.[50] The fate of this case is unknown, but it points to the disciplinary problems that could arise when visitors, especially young women, entered penitentiaries since male inmates were unaccustomed to having females in their midst.

Military prison officials also allowed visitors and outsiders, but remained cognizant that they could undermine discipline. Early in the war, military authorities prohibited all visitors to Camp Chase except for the governor, adjutant general, quartermaster general, surgeon general, the governor's private secretary, and people authorized by the governor.[51] But Ohio Governor David Tod routinely permitted curious citizens to tour the camp. The practice irritated military inspector Capt. H. M. Lazelle, who complained to Commissary General William Hoffman on July 13, 1862, that Tod allowed "for the benefit of all curious people . . . a regular line of omnibuses running daily from the capital to the camp, past the chain of outer sentinels to the commanding officer's quarters." Tod continued the antebellum practice of allowing tours to generate revenue, and Lazelle protested that anyone who paid twenty cents could visit the camp and go where they pleased except inside the barracks.[52] He, disgruntled, felt that Camp Chase was more effective as a public spectacle than as a site of military authority.

Lazelle argued that civilians should be prohibited for the sake of order. He complained that civilians' presence interfered with officers' sense of duty and encouraged arbitrary exhibitions of power as a public spectacle.[53] Governor Tod and Commandant Colonel C. W. B Allison allowed visitors despite Lazelle's critique. Lazelle protested that Tod and Allison's sole objective was to "make Camp Chase popular" rather than punish offenders. Camp Chase, however, was not the only prison that admitted spectators.[54]

Visitors' access to prisons was always a sensitive subject and many military prison and penitentiary officials monitored the practice closely. Castle Thunder's officials permitted visitors only during certain hours, supervised the whereabouts of outsiders, and restricted visits to Wednesdays and Saturdays.[55] Union officials also imposed restrictions. Late in the war, Commissary General Hoffman ordered that visitors could not enter military prisons without his approval, but granted short visits to "loyal" relatives of "seriously ill" prisoners.[56]

Outsiders wanted to visit inmates, especially if they were ill. In January 1862, the *Cincinnati Enquirer* questioned claims made in a letter to the editor that Governor Tod refused entry to the son of a critically ill political prisoner at Camp Chase. The author questioned the veracity of the story given that Tod routinely allowed visitors into the prison. The *Enquirer* hoped that Tod did not prohibit the son from visiting his sick father "simply because that father was a traitor" and argued that visitation was a universal humanitarian right.[57]

Sometimes prisoners received aid from well-intentioned strangers or Union and Confederate government agents. In August 1862, the Raleigh, North Carolina, *Weekly State Journal* summarized the account of Rev. A. J. Witherspoon, chaplain of the 21st Alabama. Union authorities captured Witherspoon on the second day of the Battle of Shiloh and held him at Camp Chase, among other prisons. The paper decried the punishment, but approved Witherspoon's recollection that the Yankees allowed "feeble and debilitated prisoners" to receive "delicacies and luxuries" from a local woman, Mrs. Judge Clark. Union authorities also extended humanitarian aid to U.S. prisoners of war at Andersonville. In November 1864, Union general William T. Sherman and Confederate general John Bell Hood permitted the Western Sanitary Commission to send supplies to Atlanta and, from there, to Americus. Sherman's maneuvers, however, impeded delivery and Confederate authorities informed the Commission that it needed to hand deliver the materials to Andersonville.[58] These limited supplies could not mitigate widespread suffering, but at least alleviated some sufferers. The same could be said for individual inmates who petitioned for and received pardons.

Pardon Petitions and their Outcomes

In both the antebellum and war years, state governors and national officials used pardons for both practical and humanitarian purposes—to relieve overcrowding, to reward good behavior, or to replenish dwindling army ranks. Penitentiary inmates knew that good behavior could secure timely—or even early—release, while misbehavior could prolong sentences.

Reporters scrutinized the pardoning power at both the state and national levels, even if mundane circumstances surrounded reprieve. On May 31, 1842, and August 8, 1857, respectively, the Baltimore *Sun* reported two pardons. In the first case, Ohio Governor Thomas Corwin pardoned Saunders Van Rensalaer, a former bank clerk being held for altering a check, from the Ohio Penitentiary. Second, President James Buchanan exonerated John M. Meeks, convicted of robbing the mails in Virginia, from the D.C. Penitentiary after serving half of his ten-year sentence. The *Sun* did not report on the motivations of Corwin or Buchanan—perhaps Van Rensalaer finished his sentence and Meeks exhibited good behavior, a common way to secure release. For example, D.C. Penitentiary inmate J. W. Morgan, imprisoned in 1853 on two counts of forgery, secured early release for good behavior. Morgan was supposed to serve six years, but in 1856 the New Orleans *Times Picayune* reported that the president pardoned him for "exemplary" conduct, which "greatly strengthened" his application."[59]

While some inmates gained pardon for good behavior, others earned release by pleading innocence or due to intense suffering. These pardons reinforced the humanitarianism of state officials who oversaw penitentiaries since they ensured justice and focused on inmates' well-being. On April 19, 1844, the Philadelphia *Public Ledger* noted that Georgia Governor George Crawford pardoned a "Celebrated Forger" named Thurston from the state penitentiary after seven years in confinement due to his "rapid decline with consumption." Crawford's decision prevented contagion among inmates and relieved Thurston's suffering, but ignored reports that, according to the *Ledger,* Thurston remained faithful to a larger band of forgers and had "abundant means at his command" to perpetuate crime.[60]

State governors pardoned other inmates who were innocent to rectify error. On April 7, 1858, the Coshocton, Ohio, *Progressive Age* reported the moving case of an "old Polish exile." Ohio Governor Salmon P. Chase heard that the man, who defended his country and then fled to the United States, was falsely accused of and imprisoned for burglary. The innocent convict never anticipated release, but Chase's eighteen-year-old daughter, upon hearing about her father's exoneration, personally delivered the old Pole his pardon. The man could scarcely find words to express gratitude, and the paper hailed the "fair and modest heroine" for orchestrating a "blessed scene" of vindication, which in turn reflected well upon her father.[61]

Wartime officials also issued pardons for good conduct or innocence, but prisoners often needed more support for their cases and courted prison wardens or guards to petition on their behalf. But sometimes even good behavior and officials' favor failed to secure release. In September 1861, Confederate President Jefferson Davis refused to pardon a young lawyer, Octavius Austin, who had served over six years in the Virginia Penitentiary for "the alleged offense of forging bounty land warrants." Austin believed that his detention was unjust and, judging from his occupation, had significant social standing. He and his sympathizers contended that a lawyer did not belong behind bars and sought pardon since his "continued duress" satisfied justice. Davis, however, rejected Austin's request despite "very meritorious conduct."[62]

Austin's case, and those of other wartime prisoners, verified Lieber's insights that imprisonment was particularly severe for educated men of the wealthier classes, and that the stigma of imprisonment left deep scars.[63] Many inmates sought pardon and became incensed when officials denied them. In 1861, the same year that Austin begged reprieve, many prisoners at the D.C. Penitentiary applied for, and were denied, pardons. The exasperated inmates protested through "mutinous conduct." Officials recognized that inmates' "disappointment" fueled misbehavior and grew leery of other discontented pardon seekers.[64]

Virginia Penitentiary officials judged the worthiness of pardon petitions on criteria that dated to the antebellum period. Antebellum officials pardoned inmates for good conduct, for spoiling mutinous plots, and for ill health and old age, since officials believed that it would be "inhumane" to detain enfeebled captives.[65] Many inmates who received pardons possessed a useful trade, were "very attentive to orders," or were "industrious, pious, and penitent," a testimony to the penitentiary's reformatory power.[66] B. P. Hussey was perhaps the best example of a reformed inmate whom officials pardoned. Hussey was twice convicted of felony, but practiced "uniform good conduct in prison" and acknowledged his fall from "the paths of rectitude and virtue and honor." Hussey contended that hard labor transformed him and he sought pardon since imprisonment left him friendless and isolated. Hussey promised Superintendent Morgan that, if released, he would "shun all that will intoxicate" since alcohol led him "into difficulties." Instead, Hussey would "live alone by the bread of honest industry and sobriety."[67] Morgan released Hussey in 1858.

Wartime governors continued the antebellum practice of pardoning inmates for good conduct and potential to contribute to society once released. Governors also alleviated overcrowding and, by extension, conserved the state's financial and material resources when they pardoned inmates for good behavior. In 1863, Virginia Governor John Letcher contended that he pardoned the most "meritorious" inmates to make room for "newcomers" and to "remedy or at least mitigate the evil" of overcrowding.[68] But Letcher had an ulterior motive for following the antebellum trend of releasing convicts who could contribute to society: He pardoned only inmates who would enter the Confederate Army.

Authorities frequently granted release to inmates who pledged future service or showed evidence of prior service in the Confederate Army. Many of the "meritorious" Virginia Penitentiary inmates who received pardons were once Confederate soldiers. Throughout the war, numerous soldiers sentenced for various crimes that ranged from larceny to murder of slaves, to manslaughter, to robbery were pardoned for their military service, for questions that surrounded arrest, for being drunk or in bad company when they committed crime, or for having committed crime accidentally—reasons that echo antebellum petitions. These pardoned men vowed to immediately reenlist.[69]

Officials pardoned other men and women since they had family members in the Southern army, a reward for sacrificing for the state. In 1863, Governor Letcher pardoned Charles Smith, sentenced to five years' imprisonment in the Virginia Penitentiary for forgery, because of good conduct and because his father and brother cared for "sick and wounded" Confederate soldiers. Similarly, Letcher pardoned Frances Marion since she had dependent children and because "her eldest son," not yet eighteen, had been in the army "since the war began," a very powerful plea.[70]

The main reasons for pardon at both penitentiaries and military prisons remained constant in the transition from peace to war. Officials pardoned prisoners if they were too young or too old, if they were ailing, if they demonstrated "good conduct" prior to their crime, if they had served most of their sentence thereby "vindicating" the law, if they were industrious and well-behaved in prison, if they could prove that they had dependents with no other source of protection, or if they benefited the state.[71]

If ill health or good behavior failed to win pardon, many penitentiary and military prison inmates petitioned family members, political officials, or wardens to intervene on their behalf. In the antebellum period, governors had no set criteria for judging cases and let personal acumen guide decisions.[72] Male and female penitentiary and military prison inmates therefore tugged on heartstrings, appealed to reason or emotion, or invoked family ties and/or social and political connections. L. Mara Dodge's study of female imprisonment notes that most women "represented their prison experience as a trying ordeal that tore them away from their loved ones, broke their hearts, and shattered their health."[73] But male prisoners, particularly those in military prisons, advanced the same arguments. The practice of appealing to emotion started in the antebellum period and continued during wartime.

Ohio Penitentiary Chaplain James Finley recounted how inmates' relatives emphasized family ties in emotional pleas for release. In July 1846, the mother of one inmate, William, informed him that she begged "through Heaven and [his] friends" that officials would release William to his "disconsolate and brokenhearted mother." William's mother also urged him to "lead a new life" and assured him of Jesus's saving power, hoping that reform would hasten his release. William's mother was not alone in encouraging good behavior—inmates spoke in self-deprecating terms about their crimes. Another Ohio Penitentiary inmate confessed in a letter home that he sinned against "God" and his "*good*" parents. The penitent thanked God for imprisonment and considered it "mild" compared with his "deserts," but asserted that only the presence for a mere hour of his "tender-hearted" mother could lift his spirits.[74] The convict's mea culpa was intentionally heartrending, but perhaps genuine, written in hopes of securing release thanks to a sympathetic inspector.

Military prisoners, like penitentiary inmates, exhorted family members, company commanders, or politicians to use social or political influence in desperate pleas for release. The outcome of most of these petitions is unknown, but prisoners' longing for freedom and outrage over incarceration are palpable in petitions as they urged acquaintances to help liberate them.

Many Camp Chase prisoners pleaded anxiously for assistance from relatives. In April 1862, inmate D. R. Fletcher complained of a "frightful" smallpox epidemic in camp and implored his mother to get his father to "do something to alleviate me from this prison." Similarly, prisoner John J. Guthrie urged his mother to "tell Pa to use all his influence to have me again returned to you."[75] What Fletcher and Guthrie's parents could have done is unclear since they resided far away, in Henryville, Alabama, and Memphis, Tennessee, respectively. At best, the men's confidence in their fathers' ability to help suggests that they had political or military connections. At worst, their pleas created false hope.

Johnson's Island prisoners issued more methodical directives about how to secure their release. J. S. Joyner wrote his uncle that he was unaware of the Confederate government's current stance on special exchanges, but knew that many had occurred. "I have been here 16 months and I think that I am as much entitled to that privilege as anyone who has not been in prison longer," he argued, adding that he repeatedly directed his uncle and other relatives to consult local judges and other influential men to get him released. Joyner demanded that his uncle persist and explained that he had written "fully" so his uncle "may take such steps as are deemed proper."[76]

Joyner's letter speaks volumes. His demands indicate that he was used to directing his own affairs and was determined to continue doing so—or at least feel as if he were doing so—from his relatively powerless position in prison.

Theodore P. Hamlin shared Joyner's desire for freedom and took it to the extreme. His letters home included repeated directions to family members on how to secure his release. On November 6, 1864, Hamlin informed his father that his time in the service expired on May 1 and emphasized that he would not reenlist. Imprisonment at Johnson's Island quashed whatever fealty Hamlin had to the Confederate cause and "reformed" Hamlin, as his desire to immediately "quit the servis" [sic] indicates. His father's efforts to secure Hamlin a parole or the U.S. oath of allegiance were simply too slow, however. Hamlin's father apparently questioned his son's sincerity, judging from Hamlin's repeated assertions that his father should not worry about him breaking parole under any circumstances. "I would rather have my head severed from my body than to be guilty of such an act," Hamlin pleaded.

That impassioned exchange occurred in January 1865, but Hamlin was still in prison in February. To make matters worse, Hamlin knew that he could get a special release with the help of friends as other prisoners had done. Hamlin directed his father to draft a petition on his behalf and employ "some influential Person" to take it to Washington and present his case to the commissary general of prisoners. This, too, failed, and Hamlin scolded his sister, in a letter dated March 16, 1865, for working "very slow." Hamlin, irate, watched many friends get out of prison after relatives worked only one month on their cases. "I have been here over four months and you all have promised me all this time to do all that you could," he cried, concluding, "I do not understand this . . . you know not how anxious I am to be released from here, if you did I am sure I would have been released before this."[77] Judging from his desperate letters, Hamlin's relatives were well aware of his desperation for freedom, but they apparently did not wield enough influence to fulfill his wish.

Other military prison inmates pleaded for help from political officials on the grounds of social prominence, ill health, exceedingly young or old age, or unjust imprisonment, as did penitentiary inmates. In April 1862, Camp Chase prisoner Frank W. Keyes drew on political connections and begged Honorable Judge Ortho Robards Singleton to "do all that can be done to effect an exchange" at the "earliest possible moment." Keyes contended that he was a "young member" of the army and a second lieutenant in a Mississippi regiment. Keyes felt that his rank rendered him above the trials of imprisonment and he was afraid of perishing from diseases that plagued the fourteen hundred prisoners at Camp Chase.[78]

Union prisoners of war employed similar strategies. Some directly addressed President Abraham Lincoln. In April 1862, A. N. Davis, captain of the 3rd Kentucky Cavalry, wrote Lincoln that the fifteen hundred prisoners at Salisbury were in a healthy location, but at risk of disease due to overcrowding. Davis's primary concern was the approximately one hundred political prisoners from Kentucky, many of whom were old, frail men who were "suddenly captured and taken from their helpless families." In closing, Davis played Lincoln off Jefferson Davis. He noted that some inmates had already addressed and received a reply from the Confederate president, and Davis hoped that Lincoln would "forthwith answer" him since many prisoners were destitute.[79]

As in North Carolina, prisoners at Andersonville determined that imprisoned officers should plead for exchange. Col. J. B. Dorr of the 8th Iowa Cavalry, Col. T. J. Harrison of the 8th Indiana Cavalry, and Maj. Gen. George Stoneman of the U.S. Volunteers informed Lincoln that inmates were starving, devoid of hope, and had become "utterly reckless of life." Many "crazed by their sufferings" wandered the prison in a "state of idiocy," while others deliberately crossed the dead line to die. At Andersonville, as at military prisons and penitentiaries, prisoners understood that promising to serve the state and appealing to humanitarianism were effective tactics in pardons. The officers pledged that, if released, they would "again do vigorous battle for our cause" and contended that the dictates of humanity required Lincoln to act.[80]

Southern civilians also begged President Jefferson Davis to have mercy on Andersonville's captives by employing familiar appeals to religion. Georgia's Rev. C. H. Stillwell petitioned on behalf of Andersonville's captives just as penitentiary chaplains pled for their charges. Stillwell exhorted Davis on September 7, 1864, to read the sixth chapter of the Second Book of Kings and emulate the King of Israel by sending the prisoners home on parole before winter's chill caused more harm than summer's heat. He understood that nations were judged on the treatment of prisoners, and contended that taking the moral high ground would "prove the greatest victory of the war" and would "do our cause more good than any three victories our noble troops have gained." Davis, according to Stillwell, should "exonerate" the suffering Union prisoners just as governors exonerated suffering convicts.[81]

Other penitentiary and military prison inmates and their kin employed family connections since they knew that officials had no set criteria to determine pardons.[82] In 1859, D.C. Penitentiary inmate George Hendricks assured his incarcerated brother, Pennel, that pardon was imminent. Hendricks contacted a prominent resident of their hometown, who then contacted U.S. Senator David Reid. Reid secured a recommendation from a local judge, which was "sufficient to procure a pardon" for Pennel.[83]

Absent direct political connections, prisoners and their relatives emphasized the social standing of inmates' families and underscored inmates' upstanding character. In 1859, O. L. Clarke, former clerk of courts in Marietta, Ohio, pleaded for the release of D.C. Penitentiary inmate John Williard. Clarke blamed Williard's crime of "passing spurious coin" and his intoxication on the bad company that he temporarily kept. He contended that Williard's offense was an aberration since he knew Williard was a reliable deputy sheriff and an honest collector for two business firms. Clarke also stressed that Williard's "aged mother," who lived alone, needed him at home.[84] Williard's fate is unknown, but Clarke's status probably enhanced his prospects for release since inmates often benefited from ties to influential citizens.[85]

Friends of military prison inmates also highlighted positive character traits like church membership, industriousness, and wealth in their petitions. R. Breckenridge, a citizen of Danville, Kentucky, pleaded on behalf of Camp Chase political prisoners Parker Todhunter and James Price. Breckenridge noted that Todhunter was a Baptist from "a very respectable family" whose members intermarried with other reputable families, while Price was from a devout Presbyterian family. Breckenridge contended that both men were of "good repute" and should not be punished as "criminals" for political offenses.[86]

Some prominent individuals also petitioned on behalf of African American inmates in Castle Thunder, and the petitioners emphasized inmates' honesty, good character, and religious disposition. In 1863, Confederate soldiers imprisoned Amos Barney and William Brown, along with six other free blacks, in Castle Thunder. Many "reliable citizens" from Richmond, like Rev. Dr. T. V. Moore, petitioned for the captives. He certified that Barney was "the husband of a member of my church" and stated that Barney and the other captives were "free negroes and noncombatants." Moore contended that Confederate authorities should release Barney and the others since they were "*free* colored Men and not Slaves" and had families in need.[87]

White inmates at Castle Thunder also sought help from religious figures. James Quinn, a political prisoner captured while working on one of Virginia's railroads, petitioned Rev. Bishop McGill, a prominent member of the community from which Quinn was detained. Quinn, a recent Irish immigrant, told the bishop that he had many religious connections in his homeland cognizant of his good character. Quinn stated that there were "no charges" against him, and that he had two brothers who were clergymen: One was chaplain to "his grace Rt. Rvd. Doctor Dixon arch Bishop of Armagh and Princebel of Old Ireland," and the other was "Right Revd. Terrance Joseph Quinn," who officiated under the "Bishop of the Diocese of Brisbane Queensland Australia."[88] Quinn hoped these direct ties to priests would inspire Bishop McGill to argue for his release.

If inmates lacked religious connections, their acquaintances invoked family obligations in petitions. In December 1862, Virginia Senator Robert Collier supported the case of Mrs. Charles Collins, wife of a political detainee at Salisbury. Collier's letter to Confederate Secretary of War James Seddon stated that Collins was a citizen of Prince George County, Virginia, when arrested, and he contended that Collins was innocent of disloyalty. More importantly, Collier claimed that Collins's wife, a poor refugee with three small children, had no means of financial support.[89] Collier urged Seddon to release Collins for the sake of humanity and his family.

Confederate prisoners and their relatives made similar arguments. Old Capitol political prisoner Thomas Jones noted that he had "an affectionate wife at home and eight young children all dependent upon me for protection and support." Kate Parr also begged for her father's release from Old Capitol Prison since he had a wife and young children dependent upon him for "support and protection." Kate contended that her family needed her father at home since the women "have been left exposed to outrage and want with no one to care for them." Dependents were at the mercy of Union occupants, and their helplessness haunted Southern men.[90]

Other political dissidents used this tactic to advance their cases. Old Capitol prisoner George Harbin—a Catholic and a Democrat—noted that he had several sisters depending on his labor for support, hoping that Secretary of State William Seward would grant him a long-awaited trial.[91] The friends and relatives of some Camp Chase prisoners also petitioned Seward on behalf of acquaintances, contending that inmates' families would suffer in their absence. Maysville, Kentucky, resident W. H. Wadsworth asked Seward for the release of six of his "constituents and townsmen" since their families were in "great distress." Wadsworth claimed that the men were innocent and posed no threat to the government since they were "slight, unimportant people" needed by their families.[92]

R. H. Hanson varied the plea that inmates should be released to care for their families. He sought discharge for his younger brother, Isaac, from Camp Chase since Isaac was a wayward youth. Hanson informed Samuel Galloway, judge advocate for Camp Chase, that "the malign influence and persuasions of older persons" manipulated the impressionable seventeen-year-old Isaac into joining the Confederate Army, which led Union authorities to arrest him. Hanson argued for Isaac's release so that he "may return to school" since his education was "sadly neglected." The Hansons were not of the criminal class, judging from Hanson's notation that he "went to school several sessions at Oxford" soon after Galloway graduated.[93] Hanson's words point to the importance of establishing personal or class connections with officials in petitions.

Many of Castle Thunder's dissident male inmates also appealed to Southern manhood, honor, and family obligation. Imprisonment emasculated men by stripping them of wives, children, property, and home, and Southern men contended that they could best serve the Confederacy at home.[94] In October 1863, political prisoners John Raden and William Lintz petitioned that they drew arms from the Federal government not to antagonize Confederate troops in East Tennessee, but to stop horse stealing. In December, Sam Milligan, a neighbor of Raden and Lintz, wrote to Confederate Secretary of War Seddon, insisting that his neighbors were innocent "worthy gentlemen" of "character and moral worth," and assured Seddon that their campaign against horse stealing "would be highly beneficial" at home.[95]

Requests that officials recognize upstanding character were common in the Confederacy. Castle Thunder inmate John W. Rider pleaded to Commandant William Richardson on January 18, 1864, after Confederate soldiers arrested him at his Virginia home for shirking military duty. Rider produced four discharges from physicians for "physical inability to serve in the C.S. army," and his captors promised him release, but it never came. Rider emphasized his masculine duty, stating, "I have a family of helpless little children at home who are motherless and can do the country far more

good at home on my farm than anywhere else." Rider contended that the
dictates of manhood necessitated his presence at home to fend off Yankee
invaders and that his family would starve without him.[96]

Desire to support family put Levi Bennett in a precarious situation. Bennett petitioned Gen. John Winder for release from Castle Thunder, stating
that Southern officials rejected his application for a position on a Confederate gunboat since he was "very deaf." Bennett, left with no way to support his dependents, became a Union Navy pilot in Virginia. Confederate
soldiers imprisoned Bennett for disloyalty, but Bennett told Winder that
"circumstances compelled [him] to accept the situation" to support his wife
and three small children. Bennett contended that, despite Union service, he
was a loyal Southerner and begged to return to his suffering family.[97]

The case of John Carper is similar. While camped with the Confederate
Army a short distance from his home, Private Carper left his post to nurse
his "severely" ill wife. Carper intended to return to duty afterwards, but Confederate soldiers arrested him on his way back to his regiment and locked
him in Castle Thunder. His petition to General Winder stressed his obligation to support his wife since "there was no one then to officiate or help" in
his absence, and this haunted Carper as he endured confinement.[98] Judging from Nina Silber's contention that Southerners were more likely than
Northerners to tie family concerns to the cause, petitioners who argued for
release based on family need may have been more successful in the South.[99]
Nonetheless, repeated petitions suggest that both Union and Confederate
authorities at least considered granting release based on family needs.

Union and Confederate inmates, both political prisoners and prisoners
of war, also argued that physical duress warranted release. Camp Chase inmates knew that military prison officials, like those at penitentiaries, were
concerned with humanitarianism and sympathetic to pleas that highlighted
maladies. In September 1861, fourteen prisoners of war from Virginia
pleaded for release since "seven were severely wounded" in battle, four were
"still very feeble" from wounds, and three were "just recovering from severe
spells of typhoid fever."[100] The outcome of this petition is unknown, but it is
possible that Federal authorities freed the men since they responded positively to other pleas of this nature. For example, Camp Chase political prisoner Jonathan Whistler, a Virginian unwillingly pressed into the Confederate Army, used sickness to his advantage. A prison inspector, B. F. Hoffman,
released Whistler since he was a "rheumatic man."[101] Likewise, Secretary of
War Edwin Stanton advocated the discharge of all "the invalid enlisted men"

who were prisoners at Camp Chase, while Union general Don Carlos Buell recommended the release of Confederate prisoner William Richardson, who was "wounded at Shiloh" and "captured while still disabled."

Federal authorities were sympathetic toward Rebel prisoners who languished in Northern prisons, and even more concerned for Northerners who suffered in Southern prisons. In October 1863, Old Capitol Prison's Supt. William Wood described to Federal exchange commissioner E. A. Hitchcock the poor conditions that Federal inmates faced at Castle Thunder. Wood highlighted a "number of Pennsylvanians" taken prisoner during Gen. Robert E. Lee's raid of that state, noted three members of the 1st Maryland Cavalry confined for over a year, and called attention to loyal Virginians, North Carolinians, and Tennesseans held for over fifteen months. The superintendent urged Hitchcock to release these men since they resided in "destitute and deplorable" conditions and winter was "fast approaching."[102] It is unclear whether men were released, but it is clear that the antebellum practice of advocating release for the infirm influenced Civil War contemporaries.

Many penitentiary and military prison inmates also questioned the fairness of the legal system, but bias was often difficult to prove. For example, in May 1860, D.C. Penitentiary inmate William Boyd complained of unjust imprisonment in a letter to his wife, contending that he was held "hostage" as a "prisoner of moral warfare." Boyd nevertheless believed in the "immutability of truth" and felt that when the truth prevailed, he would "be freed . . . and unlocked." Boyd's correspondence, however, does not indicate any petitions on his behalf, and the outcome of his case is unknown.[103]

Other penitentiary inmates who complained of unjust imprisonment had many supporters. In the early 1800s, 123 men signed a petition for the release of Virginia Penitentiary inmate William Nash. Nash was a sentinel at the local barracks and had shot a man while on duty. Petitioners contended that Nash "was absolutely without guilt or malice," and that the shooting, for which Nash was found guilty of second-degree murder, would "be a source of sorrow to him during the remainder of his life." Nash assumed guilt even though he fired according to orders and would have been punished if he had disobeyed, and his plea indicated his willingness to reform. The petitioners labeled Nash's trial unfair since the law forbade him from calling witnesses who would have proven that he was under orders from at least one superior.[104] Consequently, Nash was at the mercy of Virginia's governor for pardon.

James P. Couthouy, a U.S. Navy lieutenant commanding the steamer *Columbia*, made a similar statement in 1863. He petitioned Confederate officials for his parole and that of eleven other seamen because of unjust detention. Confederate authorities held Couthouy and his comrades as prisoners of war at Salisbury, but Couthouy questioned their punishment since they were apprehended after being shipwrecked and were unaware of President Davis's guidelines about U.S. officers appearing in arms on Southern soil. Couthouy contended that these dictates should not apply to seamen, but more forcefully claimed that "defenseless, shipwrecked mariners barely escaping with life" after an eighteen-hour swim to shore should be freed since the laws of war established a "claim upon the hospitality" of the enemy government. Luckily for Couthouy, Confederate officials agreed and granted parole.[105]

Many military prisoners believed their imprisonment was unjust, but unlike Couthouy's case, theirs indicate the chasm between how government officials and prisoners interpreted circumstances that led to confinement. Castle Thunder inmate Charles Dunham complained to Richmond's provost marshal, John Winder, that his papers revealed "nothing to impeach [his] loyalty or good intentions" toward the Confederate government. Dunham's file, however, shows that he attempted to go beyond Confederate lines without a pass. Nonetheless, Dunham repeatedly asserted that he never possessed any threatening information and swore he was a "friend of the [Confederate] government." Dunham was angry since Southern authorities denied him a trial and reserved the "right to expect to be treated as a friend" not "a foe, or a criminal."[106]

Castle Thunder political prisoner J. T. Kirby expressed similar outrage over the Confederate legal system and the suspension of habeas corpus. The circumstances surrounding Kirby's detention are unclear, but he adamantly and repeatedly demanded a "fair and impartial" hearing. Kirby wanted to disassociate his name from the criminal "stigma now resting upon it." He contended a trial would prove that Confederate authorities lacked evidence to convict him in either civil or military court, and demanded that he "should be tried within *reasonable time or discharged.*" He first implored prison authorities and then, over a year later and without success, petitioned General Winder, albeit to no avail.[107]

Kirby's petition suggests two things about civilians' opinions of both the Southern legal system and of imprisonment. First, it calls to mind Southerners' suspicion, born in the antebellum period, of both the legal system and prisons. Such misgivings, as Edward Ayers and Michael Hindus have demonstrated, slowed the establishment of penitentiaries in the South.[108] Second, Kirby's words indicate that Southerners' lack of faith in central authority ironically constituted the very reason why Confederate authorities arrested individuals on questionable evidence. During the war, national power expanded since political and military officials punished civilians of all classes on mere suspicion of threatening the Confederacy.[109] As the Confederate government orchestrated arrests and oversaw imprisonment, it shared, and often completely subsumed, functions that state officials controlled in the antebellum years.

Throughout the nineteenth century, civilians were interested in the well-being of their imprisoned loved ones, and visitors observed penitentiaries and military prisons from both near and far. Civilians remained fascinated with institutions of confinement throughout the century, but they feared escaped prisoners. Penitentiary and military prison inmates, however, craved human contact—whether positive or negative—and annoyed visitors, turned on each other, and challenged guards. Above all, prisoners craved freedom and used special privileges, friendships forged in prison, or individual ingenuity to challenge captors or flee confinement. The next chapter analyzes the orchestration and success of these often creative and sometimes desperate attempts at escape and disobedience.

Shifting Power Dynamics

Abused Privileges and Escape Attempts

Entryways at both penitentiaries and military prisons could be porous and inmates knew there was strength in numbers. In June 1843, seventy Georgia Penitentiary convicts agreed to a signal, rushed the guard, and broke open the gate. Eleven of the fugitives dispersed amid shots from guards— one was terribly wounded, six recaptured, and another died from wounds incurred during a fight with two "black fellows who arrested him." A similar scenario occurred twenty-one years later in July 1864. Confederate prisoners at Camp Chase plotted an Independence Day stampede, which they enacted as the sanitary cart exited the prison gate. At that signal, a gang of prisoners rushed and overpowered the sentinel. Thirty fled as the Ohio guards, like those in Georgia, quickly fired at the fugitives, wounding two. The others hid in nearby woods, but the foliage did not conceal them from members of the 88th Ohio Regiment. The guards recaptured all of the runaways and wounded two of them in the process—one man had to have his arm amputated, but the other was not seriously hurt.[1]

These two mass escape attempts indicate that penitentiary and military prison inmates resisted confinement and that guards responded in similar ways. Prisoners at both types of institutions disobeyed rules, challenged guards, or attempted escape out of desperation. Michael Meranze has noted that escapes increased among penitentiary inmates after 1815. Evidence from the penitentiaries under study supports this trend, and confirms officials' fears that overcrowding facilitated premeditated resistance. Some inmates acted alone, but many worked in pairs, in threes, or en masse.[2]

General disobedience and escape attempts continued during wartime in both penitentiaries and military prisons. Penitentiary and military prison inmates engaged in small-scale resistance, and devised elaborate plans for escape and/or revolt since officials could not restrict inmates' communication. The balance of power in prison may have, as Larry Goldsmith contended, favored guards, but inmates often disrupted that balance.[3]

Internal Dynamics: Prisoners' Actions and Guards' Reactions

Inmates shifted the prison's internal dynamics by communicating with each other, with visitors, and with guards either in accordance with or in violation of prison rules. Overcrowding at penitentiaries on the Auburn system encouraged inmates to disregard the rule of silence, and outnumbered guards could not possibly reprimand each offender.[4] Inmates' communication with each other undermined internal order despite officials' attempts to enforce silent labor. Similarly, military prison officials tried to prohibit inmates from congregating or talking after dark. Both tasks were challenging at best and impossible at worst. Penitentiary and military prison inmates' communication with guards, other captives, and visitors ranged from benign to confrontational, captured guards' attention, and forced guards to try to reinstate the status quo.

Penitentiary inmates rose early in the morning at the sound of a bell, labored in shops, and were otherwise confined in cells, with breaks only for meals and observance of the Sabbath.[5] Repetition, designed to instill discipline, often bred boredom and inmates' desire for negative attention. Convicts subtly broke the rule of silence by cursing, whistling, singing, or laughing. They disrupted labor by quarreling, striking other convicts, stealing items from the shops, spoiling or refusing to do their work, threatening to fight other convicts or guards, and being insolent. Instead of sitting quietly in chapel on Sundays, inmates took advantage of being in close proximity in the pews and often laughed or talked.[6] Inmates constantly faced the threat of punishment for insubordination, but they sometimes invited confrontation with guards and created a cyclical pattern of retaliation.

Ohio Penitentiary officials who punished inmates rather arbitrarily, for actual breaches of discipline or for failing to perform sufficient work in the shops, risked inspiring vengeance. In 1844 after enduring punishment, one prisoner murdered the guard and was subsequently hanged. Two years later, another prisoner, an Osage Indian, became violent following punishment. The Indian noted that guards "sometimes strike me" and that he "make[s] war" on them in response. Yet another inmate struck an officer with a billet of wood in retaliation for punishment.[7]

Disgruntled penitentiary inmates often attacked their captors and/or fellow inmates with tools. In December 1837, one frenzied Ohio Penitentiary prisoner attacked and wounded one guard and four or five other inmates with a knife before authorities overpowered him. In this instance, officials restored order, but in others, inmates actually defended officials, not their compatriots, since they knew that being suspected of collusion could bring death. In the early 1840s, individual inmates at both the Ohio and Virginia penitentiaries attacked officials with axes. In the former case, a convict named Clarke killed the guard in charge of the stone-cutting shop. Clarke bludgeoned Sells, the unsuspecting guard, on the head with a broad ax while the guard was washing up. Several convicts swarmed Clarke and held him until the warden appeared, but they were too late to save Sells. Clarke consequently faced the gallows. At the Virginia Penitentiary, an inmate named Winston assaulted a guard by the name of Ferguson with an ax, but two other convicts seized and disarmed Winston in time to save Ferguson's life. Winston faced "prompt" punishment, likely death, judging from the fate that other Virginia Penitentiary inmates met for similar offenses.[8]

Virginia Penitentiary officers inflicted lethal punishment on prisoners who affronted them, setting an example for other inmates. In 1845, officers executed prisoner Moses Johnson for "rebellion and the murder of an officer." That same year, inmate John Evans received an increased sentence for "rebellion and assault of an officer," ensuring that he would die in prison. Superintendent Morgan believed these punishments produced "a decided improvement in discipline and subordination" since they demonstrated the high price to be paid for threatening officials.[9] Inmates' disobedience, however, never fully subsided.

Penitentiary inmates often angered guards through overt or subtle communication. On August 2, 1860, a D.C. Penitentiary inmate by the name of Frank loudly cursed the guards, and earned one day in the dungeon in double irons. Officers reprimanded inmates who dared to communicate by putting them in solitary confinement on a bread-and-water diet, sometimes without a blanket or bed. Virginia officers often permitted inmates to keep a Bible and a slate with them to promote reflection and repentance, but punishment did not render inmates silent.[10]

Opportunities for interaction, either subtle or overt, abounded. Penitentiary inmates devised intricate communication methods through tapping, winking, whistling, or whispering in crowded cells and while at work.[11] Prisoners also creatively and mischievously communicated with guards and visitors, temporarily breaking the monotony of prison life at the risk of punishment. D.C. Penitentiary punishment registers reveal inmates' desperation for contact and detail officers' attempts to control prisoners' communication. Most offenders' names appear on the registers only once, indicating that the punishment inflicted—usually solitary confinement or whipping followed by solitary confinement—usually discouraged repeat offenses.[12]

Many prisoners intimidated officers through communication. In March 1832, D.C. Penitentiary inmate Washington Barker twice threatened the keeper's life and consequently spent seven days in the dungeon. That May another inmate, Ryan Barker, berated the guard, and received twelve days in solitary confinement. Ryan Barker learned not to irk the guards, but solitary confinement did not deter him from further misbehavior. In 1840, he spent a week in the dungeon for the forbidden practice of repeatedly attempting to feed other prisoners in their cells.

Other D.C. Penitentiary inmates engaged in more severe misbehavior. In December 1839, Addison Brown repeatedly assaulted an officer and consequently spent twenty days in solitary confinement.[13] Ten years later, in 1849, Warden Sengstack noted the case of an "incorrigible" black inmate who "had to be severely punished almost every week." Sengstack planned to whip the man and place him in the dungeon on a low diet for attacking the officers assigned to bring him to trial for a misdemeanor. Sengstack was about to administer the sentence when the prisoner, perhaps motivated by fear of physical punishment or solitary confinement, demonstrated a "conciliatory" disposition. Sengstack instead reproved him gently for his "obstinacy" and noted that the man became one of the most "docile and respectful" prisoners.[14]

Sengstack and other officials may have written their reports to enhance their reputation since records emphasized how punishments inspired reform. This trend continued into the 1850s. In December 1855, inmates Bill Woodward and John Barr threatened officers multiple times, but changed their ways following punishment. Woodward resisted a guard six times and officials sentenced him to four days in solitary confinement on bread and water. The following June, Barr struck an officer three times with a hammer. Prison officials handcuffed Barr, kept him standing for four hours, and then put him in a cell on bread and water for nine days. According to official reports, both Woodward and Barr "promised to do better" after punishment.[15] The reporting officers likely put words in the inmates' mouths, but punishments alerted inmates that challenging officers resulted in swift reprimand.

Other D.C. Penitentiary inmates turned on each other. In June 1860, a male convict named White used water as a weapon when he took a small drink from his cup and threw the remainder on another inmate. Officials sentenced White to be whipped for this seemingly minor offense. The punishment was never carried out, however, as White admitted his transgression and, according to officers, "made a solemn promise to do better," as had Woodward and Barr. These inmates allegedly changed, but officers punished recalcitrant inmates. In March 1861, officers punished a black inmate, A. Price, with fifteen lashes and solitary confinement for "occasionally" cutting a fellow prisoner, insolence, and threatening other inmates. Similarly, officers sentenced convict Binnin to fifteen lashes and four days in the dungeon for punching another inmate three times and knocking him down while walking in line.[16]

Some D.C. Penitentiary inmates communicated to cause trouble. Others simply wanted to engage in conversation, but broke rules nonetheless. According to officials, many talkative prisoners failed to learn from punishment, unlike inmates who assailed officers. Officials repeatedly reproved a prisoner named Drew for running across the yard to speak to another convict while at work. Warden Sengstack, however, halted further punishment since he considered Drew "a very ignorant man, not capable of discretion" and impervious to reform. Sengstack also noted the case of a white boy who, nearly every day, left his seat at the shoe shop to socialize. Sengstack reprimanded the boy, but he repeated the offense multiple times in the next hour. Officers consequently tied up the boy by the thumbs for two-hour periods or tied him up and whipped him, but the lad's determination to communicate remained.[17] Sengstack, fed up with the boy's insolence, wrote him off as an imbecile. Officials sometimes denigrated inmates' intelligence to justify punishments, and this could have applied in the boy's case.[18]

D.C. Penitentiary inmates also devised creative ways to communicate with members of the opposite sex. In May 1832, convicts Jane Byers and Isaac Brogdan plotted regular meeting times at the privy. Officials caught on to the scheme after the fourth time and sentenced Byers to five days in the dungeon, but did not record Brogdan's punishment. Officers may have spared Brogdan from punishment since nineteenth-century contemporaries normally viewed women as temptresses who led men astray, an outlook that explains Byers's punishment.[19] Byers and Brogdan were not the only inmates who interacted with members of the opposite sex. In May 1832, inmate Samuel Peoples twice tried to pick the lock to the women's ward, so officers sentenced him to the dungeon for an unspecified period of time. A black prisoner named Jackson withstood similar punishment for talking with women through a window.[20] Individual acts of disobedience irked officers, but punishment, or the threat of it, could restore the status quo. Collusion among inmates, however, was more difficult to squelch.

In August 1859, Ohio Penitentiary officers were on edge since they suspected that some inmates who were detailed to construct an addition to the penitentiary were plotting revolt. On August 5, the two ringleaders took advantage of guards' inattention and made a break for a nearby cornfield. Guards' first inclination was to give chase, but they noticed that the work detail, totaling about fifty men, stood ready to flee. The guards split—some pointed weapons at the horde set to run and others fired on the two escapees. Guards inflicted what was likely a fatal wound on one fugitive and serious injury on the other.[21] Opportunities for communication during work hours enabled penitentiary inmates to plot subversion. Military prison inmates likewise took advantage of crowded conditions and communication to plot revolt.

Prisoners at Camp Chase and Johnson's Island threatened guards in the same manner as did Ohio Penitentiary inmates. In May 1862, Camp Chase prisoners attempted a revolt and the resulting commotion enabled three prisoners to escape. Officials notified prisoners that any future attempts would result in fatalities, but prisoners remained undeterred.[22] In November 1863, Camp Chase inmates took advantage of paranoia about an outside plot intended to liberate prisoners. Inmates intended to rush the guard at the same time that Peace Democrats plotted to liberate the prisoners, but authorities thwarted the plan.[23] The next year, in December 1864, twenty-four inmates at Johnson's Island rushed the guard on the prison's northwest side and attempted to escape using hastily made scaling ladders. Guards immediately opened fire, killed two fugitives, and knocked down one, but five men climbed over the wall. Running to freedom on an island was difficult, however, and Union authorities soon recaptured the escapees.[24]

Military prison officials inflicted the same punishments on prisoners that penitentiary authorities used on unruly inmates. Some rebellious inmates at Castle Thunder were, in fact, criminals. In December 1862, the Richmond *Daily Dispatch* reported a plot to "assassinate the Castle's sentinels on Christmas night." The ringleader was Yankee David Weish, "a murderer by profession," whom authorities punished with "stripes" and then confined him in irons on a "bread and water diet." This devilish plan came just weeks after the *Dispatch* detailed a November 1862 plot to blow up the prison. Conspirators exploded "several pounds of powder," which caused alarm, shook the building, and shattered glass windows. One of the plot's masterminds was a Yankee inmate "to be tried for murder," whom authorities punished with "close confinement."[25]

Prisoners in both military prisons and penitentiaries sometimes threatened to start fires or used existing conflagrations to resist. When fires, either accidental or intentional, erupted in penitentiary shops, inmates took advantage of the consequent confusion to attempt escape. The Virginia Penitentiary burned a few times—first in August 1823. This fire cost the state $200,000, but no prisoners escaped. Fire raged again in the workshops in December 1854. One convict fled while officials secured the remainder and ordered them to extinguish the flames. It is unclear whether these fires were accidental or intentional, but inmates elsewhere intentionally started blazes.[26]

Georgia Penitentiary inmates, either alone or in collusion, made numerous attempts at arson. In April 1817, one prisoner started a fire as a diversion in hopes of masking his own escape. Five years later, a small group of inmates twice attempted to burn the workshops. Officers identified the perpetrators and had them whipped, placed in irons, and shaved half of each man's head. Arson attempts continued in subsequent years. In May 1831, inmates intentionally started a fire that completely destroyed the roof and necessitated that Milledgeville's residents stand guard to deter escapees. Seven years later, a copycat arsonist-inmate plotted a blaze, but authorities detected it in time to prevent damage.[27]

Prisoners throughout the century knew that starting fires was a relatively effective method of resistance and wartime captives continued the practice.

In July 1861, Virginia Penitentiary inmates, who manufactured goods for the Confederate Army, burned the workshops to stop goods from reaching Southern soldiers. They assumed that Confederate authorities could not replace the machinery and wanted to hurt the cause. A similar situation occurred at Salisbury in 1864. Prison officials suspected that incendiaries started a blaze that consumed several buildings, including those that housed leather and other supplies.[28] Targeting workshops and/or supplies caused physical and fiscal damage to the Confederacy and forced officials to confront the fact that workshops could undermine, rather than reinforce, order.

Penitentiary shops often facilitated interaction among inmates, which encouraged misbehavior instead of reformation. D.C. Penitentiary inmates occasionally organized mass resistance while at work. On April 16, 1856, forty inmates employed in the shoe shop gathered in the prison yard and refused to work for want of meat. Officers suspected that Lucas, the ringleader, and numerous followers possessed shoe knives. Lucas was indeed dangerous—and intelligent. The board of inspectors reasoned that Lucas's motivation stemmed from interaction with outsiders. Lucas "had been indulged in holding too free correspondence with his relatives" and was "furnished with books and other privileges," so officers punished Lucas and his motley crew with a bread-and-water diet for several days.[29] Both penitentiary and military prison officials failed to completely cut off inmates from the outside world, and interactions with outsiders often enabled prisoners in both types of institutions to cause trouble. Captives also earned officials' favor, secured privileged positions, and then used them to resist.

Trusted Inmates: Privileges, Escapes, and Whistleblowers

Throughout the century, seemingly trustworthy penitentiary and military prison inmates secured special jobs and some used the accompanying knowledge of the prison to plot escape. Prisoners tasked as cooks, bakers, and for other special jobs became familiar with the prison's layout and forged alliances with low-ranking staff members.[30] D.C. Penitentiary inmates who served as cooks and bakers frequently spoke with guards at mealtime. These interactions, according to the warden, alerted inmates to items "passing without the prison walls" and fostered "familiarity" with guards' personalities, which "by no means conduces to the security of the prison" since inmates could use these insights subversively.[31]

Inmates at the D.C., Ohio, and Virginia penitentiaries used special assignments to devise escapes. Prisoners Barrett and Jones, assigned as bakers, escaped from the D.C. Penitentiary in March 1861. Guards released Barrett and Jones from their cells at 3 A.M. to attend to the bakehouse, located in the prison yard. Negligent night guards did not notice Barrett and Jones scaling the walls with tools from the bakehouse, and they fled between 3 A.M. and 5 A.M. Barrett and Jones created intricate escape apparatuses with baking implements, forming a rope out of baking cloths and attaching S hooks from the pot rack to the end of the rope. The men got the rope to the top of the outer wall, which was twenty feet high, with a pole created by nailing together the handles of bread shovels. These audacious acts seemed too obvious to miss, so the warden dismissed the guards on duty and the officer in charge of the bakehouse for disobeying orders essential to the oversight of the bakers.[32]

A similar escape took place at the Ohio Penitentiary in August 1846. After prisoners were secured in sleeping cells, a guard walked through the penitentiary with an inmate detailed as a cook. The officer held a single candle that dimly lit the dark halls. When the men approached a window, the cook blew out the candle, jumped through the window, and scaled the palisades. The cook reached a nearby cornfield, shed his striped pants, donned a plain pair stolen from the prison, and fled. The warden offered a reward of $100 for the cook's recapture, but the search was futile. Chaplain Finley, perplexed, commented on the ease with which convicts used their positions to earn guards' trust and then violate rules instead of relying on good behavior to shorten sentences. Finley said the cook was a trusted inmate who behaved "so well" that he was sure to "have been pardoned" before his thirty-year term expired.[33] But the cook abhorred prison life and found the prospect of immediate freedom too tempting to wait.

Other convicts also viewed special tasks as a potential ticket to freedom rather than a means of reform. In 1854, two Virginia Penitentiary inmates who were detailed to use a handcart to remove debris from the workshops to an outer enclosure broke through the gate and fled in different directions. Penitentiary guards and local civilians recaptured the fugitives and guards denied them any further special assignments. D.C. Penitentiary convicts

Attwell and Fugitt likewise illustrated the risk that officials incurred when they tasked inmates with special duties. In early 1861, officials chose these men to empty straw into the prison yard. Officer William Maxwell accompanied Attwell and Fugitt outside, but the inmates headed for the outer wall as soon as he wandered away. Maxwell realized that something was amiss and called the convicts, but received no reply. He then hurried to where the men should have been, but it was too late—the convicts had escaped. Maxwell and a nearby soldier pursued the escapees through a brickyard, over a hill, and under a riverbank to the house of Fugitt's brother, a likely conspirator. The deputy warden soon arrived on horseback and detained the escapees.[34]

Penitentiary and military prison inmates also used prison resources to devise individual escape plots. In 1840, one clever Georgia Penitentiary convict procured an extra uniform and some straw with which he created a dummy. The convict duped the careless night inspectors by situating his doppelganger as if he were wistfully staring out his cell window. Meanwhile, the escapee concealed himself in an air chamber and later escaped over the outer wall. Unsuspecting authorities did not notice anything amiss until the next morning. When the keeper unlocked the fugitive's cell, he found a dummy that refused to assemble for roll call.[35]

In a similar vein, Camp Chase prisoner William Bramlet took advantage of other resources—the day laborers whom Union authorities admitted into the prison to dig ditches. Bramlet knew that guards could not restrict conversations between inmates and laborers, and quickly learned that the workers were Southern sympathizers. Bramlet convinced the workers to furnish him with clothing and tools and, at the end of one day, he walked out with his new friends and reached the Confederacy. Another day laborer helped a Camp Chase prisoner who was held in close confinement escape to Canada. Castle Thunder inmate Capt. C. W. Savage likewise tried to escape disguised as a washerwoman, but his attempt, unlike those at Camp Chase, failed.[36]

Military prison inmates, like those at penitentiaries, had to be wary of other prisoners who might side with officials and help them prevent or stop disorder. In June 1864, some Johnson's Island prisoners tried to take advantage of the fact that authorities ordered inmates to cook for themselves. Numerous men removed a plank from a cookhouse in the middle of one barracks and excavated a tunnel that opened beyond the prison wall. In their tunnel, the conspirators stored three roughly constructed ladders, three knives notched into saws, bed ticking tarred to be waterproof, a lantern made of an old fruit can, and three life preservers made of corked canteens. But before the connivers could utilize their handiwork, an inmate in the hospital tipped off the guards and authorities uncovered the plot. The conspirators, enraged at the hospital patient's disclosure, attempted to hang him, albeit in vain.[37]

Another inmate, writing under the pseudonym Xenophon, spied on fellow inmates for personal gain. In January 1865, he informed Maj. Edward A. Scovill, commanding the 128th Ohio overseeing Johnson's Island, that inmates in his block, Block One, were working on a tunnel through which some had escaped. Prison authorities reserved that block for prisoners who were either about to, or already had, taken the U.S. oath of allegiance, so Xenophon's alleged discoveries were all the more alarming. He made a quid pro quo proposition to Scovill—Xenophon refused to reveal his identity, or that of the excavators, unless Scovill accommodated his demands for improved conditions. The volunteer spy confided that he had been in the prison for only about two months, during which time he also witnessed an inmate in close confinement acquire a pair of Yankee blue pants in hopes of escaping. Xenophon stated that he would give the names of the escapees and potential fugitives if he could do so "without creating any suspicion" among his messmates. The self-ordained spy taunted Scovill with intelligence, but pledged to continue only if Scovill allowed him to build a separate room in the old mess hall, which would improve his lot and relieve him from taking the oath of allegiance, an act that, despite his "loyalty" to U.S. officials, he refused since he believed the war was almost over.[38]

Self-serving whistle-blowers at Andersonville also helped authorities foil escape plots. Numerous prisoners recalled how captives betrayed comrades' desperate quests for freedom to gain reward or to avoid punishment for implication in the plots. James Vance disgustedly stated that inmates disclosed tunnels to receive extra rations. Others, like John Hoster and Andrew G. White, noted that an inmate, in return for a plug of tobacco, alerted guards about tunneling efforts. The potential fugitives, White among them, shaved the whistle-blower's head and "pricked a large T" on his forehead with indelible ink. Prisoners soon determined that having the informer stand in the sun for two hours, turning continuously for all to see, while holding the word "Traitor" written on a page from White's memoranda book, was insufficient retaliation, so they tattooed the entire word on his forehead. Two days earlier, Alonzo Decker complained that another inmate informed Rebel authorities of a ten-foot tunnel dug about forty feet from his tent. Decker and his comrades discovered the snitch's identity, shaved his head, put a card reading "Traitor" on his back, and marched him around camp for all to see. The betrayed prisoners despised others who colluded with guards, and their chosen punishments demonstrate how the penitentiary program informed nineteenth-century discipline since they employed the same tactics, like shaming and head shaving, that penitentiary officials used to discipline convicts.

Confederate authorities appreciated tips, but could not halt every escape attempt. According to Decker, some other prisoners tunneled out in May 1864. Officers punished more than just offenders to discourage escape from Andersonville. Confederate authorities also reprimanded the sergeants of the "nineties," squads organized for ration distribution, and all members of a particular ninety that housed any offenders. Inmate David Weimer recalled that if an inmate from a ration squad escaped, Confederate authorities denied all members the entire day's rations. Rebel guards tried to coerce inmates into foiling escapes by ransoming rations, holding sergeants accountable for the behavior of their men, and forcing captured escapees to wear a ball and chain, a punishment with which penitentiary inmates were familiar.[39]

Confederate authorities also took precautionary measures to counter inmates' attempts at tunneling or using special duties to escape. In 1864, Salisbury officials posted a line of sentries about a hundred feet outside the prison wall and tasked a squad of fifteen guards to regularly inspect inmates' quarters for tunnels. This work commenced in November and guards discovered sixteen tunnels by the next month.

At Andersonville, authorities required inmates to participate in wood details. Prisoners on wood details used this job to attempt escape, just as penitentiary inmates had manipulated special tasks. In February 1864, inmate John C. Ely recalled how authorities recognized this danger. The "Johnnys are getting very much alarmed on our account," he mused, "fearing that we may break out" while on assignment. Confederate fears were well founded. Robert Kellogg noted that in early June 1864, six men on a wood detail overpowered the guard and escaped. But Kellogg was not so daring. He feared reprisal for escape and fretted that Confederate authorities would rescind prisoners' participation in wood details, which temporarily got them out of the stockade. Rebel authorities searched the men for weapons or other digging implements prior to letting them go out for wood, perhaps a step that penitentiary officials should have taken when they assigned special jobs to inmates.[40]

Escapes: Individual Attempts, En Masse Plots, and the Role of Guards

In the above instances, guards did their best to stop inmates from absconding, but plenty of inmates approached guards, tried to win their sympathy, and hoped that guards would collude in escape attempts. Like penitentiary inmates, military prison captives knew that they risked life and/or limb when they talked with captors. Extra supplies or successful escape could make the risk worthwhile, but plans often backfired at both types of institutions. In the late 1830s, Georgia Penitentiary inmates tried to bribe a guard to give them a duplicate set of keys. The loyal guard, however, informed the principal keeper, who advised the watchman to feign acceptance of the plot to catch the perpetrators. After the inmates opened their cells, the keeper and some other guards waited for them at the end of the hall and promptly returned them to quarters without opening fire or inflicting corporal punishment on them. This discouraged other would-be escapees. For example, in December 1826, guards shot and killed two armed Georgia Penitentiary fugitives who got beyond the walls and refused to surrender. In Ohio, the Penitentiary's Board of Directors, in December 1839, proclaimed that guards' decision to shoot an escapee in the act was "perfectly justifiable."[41]

Military prison inmates also tried to enlist guards' help with escape. In January 1864, four prisoners of war and one civilian prisoner at Johnson's Island attempted a plot nearly identical to that of the Georgia Penitentiary convicts, and officials foiled the attempt in exactly the same way. The schemers offered $200 to two guards, who agreed to turn a blind eye to their plot. Guards, however, knew that they could both get the money and punish the perpetrators. They took compensation of $150 and three gold watches, then informed the officer of the day, and allowed the tricksters to get a certain distance from the stockade. The duplicitous guards then detained the fugitives and marched them back to their old quarters, minus their riches.[42]

This punishment was mild compared to the fate that other escapees suffered. In September 1862, Castle Thunder's guards shot and killed inmate

Silas Richmond, who, according to authorities, possessed "signs of debility of mind." Richmond attempted to rush past the guard and out of prison, but a guard's bullet lacerated his bowels and he later died in the prison hospital. Gunfire also stopped other plots. In May 1864, Old Capitol Prison's guards fired on ten fleeing prisoners, shooting one in the hand, and enabling them to recapture each man.[43]

Some guards were vigilant, but military prison inmates sometimes escaped due to guards' laxity or complicity. In November 1864, an imprisoned Rebel spy/mail carrier escaped from Old Capitol Prison through the carelessness of a night sentinel—the inmate simply walked out undetected. Similarly, in November 1864, a North Carolina man apprehended four out of five Yankee inmates who fled Salisbury. The civilian concluded that guards' negligence or corruption facilitated their escape. He suspected guards of foul play since the escapees offered him a bribe to release them, which he refused. Instead, the man resolved to return them to the pen while the fugitives vowed to break out again.

Other Salisbury inmates owed their success to a specific guard who, unlike the double-dealing guards at the Georgia Penitentiary and at Johnson's Island, refused to betray fugitives. Political prisoners Junius H. Browne and Albert Richardson, both newspapermen, owed much of their success to Lieutenant Welborne, a prison guard and Unionist who defected from the Rebels. In December 1864, Welborne furnished the fugitives with instructions on how to reach Union lines, and sympathetic blacks guided the journalists as they meandered through Tennessee. Confederate authorities should have learned not to trust Welbourne and other war-weary guards in early 1865. Welborne facilitated the escape of several other inmates in January 1865, the same month that seven Union prisoners bribed another, likely war-weary, guard and made their exit. No harm befell any of these men from interacting with Rebel watchmen, who became prisoners' ticket to freedom.[44]

Military prisoners at other locations were more judicious about when and how they approached guards. Johnson's Island inmate Robert Bingham drew a distinction between battle-tested guards and the Hoffman Battalion, the regiment organized specifically for guarding the prison. Bingham respected one lieutenant commanding the guard since he was "an old soldier & very polite & really kind." Bingham often chatted with this man and learned that a "cordial hate" developed between veterans and the Hoffman guards, but did not indicate whether or not he or other prisoners gained anything more than camaraderie from this man. There was no befriending or even testing men in the Hoffman Battalion, however. Those guards never proved their gallantry under fire and, according to Bingham, became "quite bold" in January 1864, shooting at "everybody," even for simply visiting the latrine at night. This reaction was, perhaps, extreme, but inmates knew that motion after dark invited close scrutiny.[45]

As at Johnson's Island, guards at Andersonville sometimes fired on inmates to deter escape, and inmates weighed the pros and cons of interacting with their captors. Shortly after several escape attempts in June 1864, inmate Ira B. Sampson noted that a guard murdered a comrade from the 45th New York who was too near the prison walls. Some inmates who approached the dead line wanted to trade with guards for necessities, but inmate Nathaniel Shepard Armstrong Price recalled that talking to guards involved walking a fine line between life and death. Guards could either alleviate deficiencies through trade or kill inmates for attempting conversation. Price recalled that prisoners and guards were in close proximity in places like Richmond and Danville, but Andersonville's guards were perched on pigeon roosts situated at least twenty feet from the dead line. Prisoners, therefore, faced "a strong probability of getting shot" when they attempted to trade with guards. Nonetheless Price, on several occasions, risked death or injury to procure potatoes or wild onions from guards to fend off scurvy.[46] Price's risk paid off and he survived Andersonville, where death was so common.

The anecdotes from Johnson's Island and Andersonville suggest that guards' behavior was uneven, at least according to inmates. Guards in the above cases were hypervigilant, but other penitentiary and military prison guards were overwhelmed by overcrowding. Inmates took advantage of both dynamics to escape. In October 1860, officials noted that the D.C. Penitentiary was filled to its "utmost capacity" at 169 inmates. This emboldened four inmates to escape. The first fugitives, men by the names of Wilson and McDonald, evaded the oversight of overtaxed guards. Wilson first snuck into the clothes room and procured civilian clothes for himself and his coconspirator, and the two later returned to the closet when guards were preoccupied. They quickly pulled out a stowed ladder and scaled the prison wall completely undetected. Overcrowding necessitated that all guards patrol the inner halls, leaving the outer yard unguarded for several hours during which time the convicts disappeared.[47]

Prisoners Johnson and Small escaped from the D.C. Penitentiary that same month. Overcrowding forced the deputy warden to forego daily inspection of inmates' cells. The two cellmates, aware of the lapse, easily concealed a cache of hatchets, chisels, and knives, which they used to dig out of their cell. All four escapees remained at large, creating consternation for penitentiary officials and hope for other inmates that escape could be successful. Members of the Board of Inspectors denounced the escapes and called, albeit in vain, for the fugitives' speedy detention. Arrest and punishment, according to the Board, would reinstate discipline and reaffirm officials' ability to control inmates, but incidents like this continued in the 1860s. Ohio Penitentiary officials faced similar challenges during the Civil War.

Officials at the Ohio Penitentiary were concerned with two types of prisoners—common criminals and members of Gen. John Hunt Morgan's Confederate cavalry. Union cavalrymen captured Morgan and his men in late July 1863, and federal officials confined them in the Ohio Penitentiary, a place from which they thought "escape would be impossible."[48] Penitentiary officers treated Morgan and his men as common criminals and subjected them to the same process of calculated humiliation as convicts.[49] Officers stripped the men of possessions, shaved their heads, forbade communication with convicts and guards, and placed each in a solitary cell.[50] Morgan and his men followed the regular penitentiary routine: guards marched them to meals at 7:30 A.M. and at 3 P.M. At 4:45 P.M., guards ordered silence and locked them in their cells, and lights went out at 8 P.M.[51]

Imprisonment stripped the men of individuality, besmirched their personal honor, and represented a stark contrast to Confederate cavalry service where the soldiers rode freely in defense of the Confederacy.[52] Morgan and his men plotted escape to reclaim honor and defy U.S. authorities. In the process, they highlighted contradictions in developing U.S. military law. In 1863, General Orders No. 100 sanctioned escape as a "natural act" and the "patriotic duty" of imprisoned soldiers but, according to Union officials, this applied only to federal soldiers who fled Southern prisons. The Lieber Code also dictated that officers could punish participants in a general escape with death "as an extreme measure."[53] Both interpretations applied to Morgan's escape. In the aftermath, Southerners cheered Morgan's bravery, while Northerners condemned him and demanded punishment as outlined in the Lieber Code.

Penitentiary rules governed Morgan and his men, but penitentiary officials, who were state employees, were responsible for them for only a short time. Conflict arose between state and federal officials over Morgan and his men since the Union Army arrested them, but federal officials classified them as common criminals. Despite this classification, federal authorities exempted Morgan and his men from working in penitentiary shops. Warden Nathaniel Merion worried that idleness would breed problems since the Rebels were removed from the oversight of ward masters and many became ill from inactivity. Boredome and poor supervision allowed the men to network and devise a massive escape plot, which they enacted due to the negligence of military guards whom federal officials installed in November 1863. Merion objected to this decision—he ran the penitentiary with an iron fist and feared that the new military guard, which consisted of men largely unfamiliar with penitentiary routines, would not fulfill their supervisory duties. Merion's fears grew when U.S. authorities increased the number of Confederate prisoners they sent to the penitentiary from thirty to seventy.

Merion's concerns about the ability of federal troops to keep order were well founded. Federal guards quickly lost interest in their post, and Morgan's band took advantage of their inattention. The military guards ignored the guidelines that Merion required of penitentiary guards: federal guards stopped daily inspections of inmates' quarters and instead allowed the Confederates to sweep and clean their quarters without supervision, a common practice in military prisons. The unsupervised Confederates easily smuggled knives from the dining hall into their cells and started digging a tunnel in early November.[54]

Morgan and many of his men inhabited a range of cells on the prison's lower level and knew that an air chamber below their quarters could facilitate escape. After days of undetected digging, Morgan and six of his men fled on November 20. Outraged, Merion and the penitentiary directors contended that the men would not have escaped if they had "remained under civil authority."[55] State officials regarded themselves as superior disciplinarians since they gained years of experience in penitentiary administration before the war when the federal government's role in incarceration was minimal. Federal officials, according to the state, should have left decisions about penitentiary discipline up to them.

Morgan's feat influenced both Northern and Southern inmates proving, as Rebecca McLennan has argued, that escapes often had a widespread impact and could inspire efforts elsewhere.[56] Morgan, somewhat ironically, encouraged Union prisoners of war in Richmond to attempt a similar escape, and inspired the remainder of his men to try to flee from the Ohio Penitentiary. In February 1864 the rest of Morgan's men, whom penitentiary authorities held in solitary confinement for their collusion in the November escape, confiscated knives and planned to overpower the guard while on their way to breakfast. Prison officials, however, learned from experience, detected the plan, and marched the men to and from meals under double guard.[57]

Fascinated Southern newspapermen covered Morgan's escape and the extensive search for him while anticipating his arrival in Richmond. The press extolled Morgan's escape as twenty-three days of "unremitting labor" that achieved the goal of freedom and, in so doing, unwittingly informed Union inmates at Richmond's Libby Prison of the feat.[58] Morgan visited the prison soon after his arrival in Richmond on January 9 and the details that he provided to fellow Kentuckians held at Libby inspired a semisuccessful tunnel escape in early 1864. The Union escapees achieved only limited success, but the incident nonetheless demonstrated the danger of Morgan's visit and publicizing a successful escape.[59]

Prisoners who dug tunnels filled long, dull hours with seemingly productive work and hoped that their ditches would lead to freedom. Officials who found these passages quashed hope and ruined hours of hard labor undertaken by men in a depleted physical state, which added insult to the injury of punishment. Southern authorities, like those in the North, reprimanded tunnel architects either physically or psychologically. Andersonville inmate Andrew White recalled in July 1864 that he and his comrades nearly completed a tunnel, but the Rebel quartermaster discovered the project and ordered a gang of black laborers to fill it in. Commandant Wirz subsequently kept White and his compatriots under close surveillance and sent a guard to intimidate the excavators. One guard pointed a revolver in White's face and swore he would blow White's "D—— Yankee brains out." Ten days later, Wirz prohibited all prisoners from congregating near a line of poles recently placed near the stockade walls, lest Confederate artillery open fire. These physical threats, coupled with disease, devastated many inmates psychologically, White included. By September he confessed that all hope for escape vanished and claimed that his captivity would involve a "battle between my constitution and my strength to hold out" versus "starvation, brutality, and disease."[60]

Escape attempts increased as the population climbed through the summer and fall of 1864 despite steep odds and Andersonville's remote location hundreds of miles from federal lines.[61] Inmates frequently commented on tunnels, returned escapees, and authorities' attempts at halting escapes. Perhaps dwelling on escapes, even those that failed, kept hopes of freedom alive. Daring prisoners who attempted escape braved bloodhounds and threats of cannon fire, and their acts forced Confederate authorities to maximize limited manpower for surveillance.

Mother Nature nearly aided a mass escape on August 9, 1864, when torrential rains turned the stream running through the center of the prison into a river that washed away about thirty feet of the stockade. Guards and inmates had conflicting recollections of the incident. Guards recalled that they discouraged escape by assembling the militia and firing warning shots from their sixteen mounted cannons, which were trained on prisoners. Inmate Alonzo Tuttle Decker recalled the scene differently. He commented that Rebel authorities feared mass escape, ordered all guards to man their guns, and put a double guard at every post. Some inmates got away despite these precautions, however. Prisoner James Vance remembered that some men escaped by sawing out of the stockade amid the confusion, but later noted that the Rebels recaptured and punished some fugitives with ball and chain.[62]

Officers inflicted similar punishment on other penitentiary and military prison inmates who attempted escape or taunted guards. Prisoners who could not orchestrate mass escape attempts tried to abscond individually or in small groups, and these attempts heightened guards' sensitivity to activity near windows, doors, and walls. In March 1840, a D.C. Penitentiary inmate named Wright cut a hole through the wall of his cell, but as the Baltimore *Sun* reported, officials "happily detected" the hole before he could flee. Nine years earlier, in 1831, D.C. Penitentiary inmate John Taylor scaled the prison walls, but guards swiftly recaptured him and locked him in the local jail in Fredericktown, Maryland, where he died of cholera. The following year, John Laurence escaped the same way, but officials quickly apprehended Laurence and he finished his sentence in the Philadelphia Penitentiary. Escapes continued in 1833, when two white prisoners and one black prisoner fled the D.C. Penitentiary. Officials recaptured all three, and sentenced the former two to the Baltimore Penitentiary and the latter to the Philadelphia Penitentiary.[63] It is unclear whether D.C. Penitentiary officials placed fugitives in other penitentiaries by choice or by convenience, but they may have wanted to prevent successful escapees from inspiring copycats in familiar quarters. Whatever the case, officials detained fugitives from the D.C. Penitentiary without inflicting physical harm. This reprimand differed from those at the Ohio and Virginia penitentiaries, where guards fired on fugitives.

In August 1839, Lake, an Ohio Penitentiary prisoner, attempted to instigate an insurrection. He conspired with coworkers in the prison shop to flee during work hours but, when the time came, Lake was the only prisoner who ran. The officer in charge hailed Lake multiple times, but it looked as if he had a clear path to freedom. Another guard quickly fired on Lake, "aiming low," intending to "cripple rather than kill him," but the fact that Lake was "rapidly descending a hill" altered his position and resulted in death. Inmates were outraged, but penitentiary officials defended the shooting and contended that the officers "were strictly in the performance of their duties as prescribed by law."[64] Ohio Penitentiary guards readily fired to stop escapees since it was an effective deterrent. Another casualty from an escape attempt was not recorded until 1860, when the physician noted that one of the year's three deaths was due to "a gun-shot wound received while attempting to escape."[65] Otherwise, the threat of being shot was enough to prevent Ohio inmates from running.

Severe consequences, including extended sentences or death, seldom deterred Virginia Penitentiary inmates from attempting escape, however. Fugitives plagued prison officials in the antebellum period, especially when the prison lacked a perimeter wall. Inmate Jeremiah Whitson knew that there was no outer wall and he fled on August 30, 1800, by removing the window grating from his cell and walking off. Three years later, several prisoners tried to cut through the prison's brick wall, but guards detected the extensive ploy and shot one conspirator for using "insolent and menacing language." Instead of running to freedom, the severely wounded man and his compatriots languished in prison. Prison officials thought that constructing first a wooden wall and, in 1824, a brick wall would discourage future escape.[66]

The wall, however, did not deter inmates determined to break free. In 1841, Supt. Charles Morgan noted that the wall rendered the possibility of escape "remote," but complained that it did not prevent inmates' "many attempts to cut out of the cells." Inmates throughout the century understood that tunneling could be done inconspicuously and Virginia Penitentiary inmates knew that it was next to impossible for guards to hear them if they dug during rainstorms. Morgan reported that, in 1840, three inmates attempted escape—and one succeeded—by digging out, and he was sure that such attempts would be "continued by desperate fellows, who knew that freedom was within reach."[67]

Morgan's assumption proved correct. In 1851, he noted that two free blacks, Wingfield Butcher and Robert Evans, were "under prosecution for breaking up their cells" with intent to escape. Each man consequently received an additional year of imprisonment. This punishment, however, did not deter Butcher, who cut through his cell door in another attempt to flee. Other inmates also attempted to break jail. Morgan noted the effort of a white inmate, William Pogue, who broke out of his cell and tried "cutting through the front wall of the eastern wing," but to no avail. Pogue then got an accomplice, Charles Jones, and the two miscreants fled beyond state lines. Alarmed, the *Brooklyn Daily Eagle* alerted civilians to be on the lookout for two "desperate criminals" who escaped the Virginia Penitentiary "by the expert use of a saw."[68] Antebellum inmates generally acted alone or in groups of two to five, but higher prison populations during wartime encouraged coordinated plots at penitentiaries and military prisons.

High population posed disciplinary threats at the Georgia and Virginia penitentiaries. In 1861, the population of the Georgia Penitentiary eclipsed two hundred—nearly double its total in the late 1830s. Convicts took advantage of the high population in late July 1861 and many attempted to rush out. Guards opened fire, killed one fugitive instantly, wounded another who later died, and broke the back of a third, but they failed to prevent four convicts from absconding.[69] These fugitives worked in concert, as did those at the Virginia Penitentiary, where overcrowding also facilitated escape. The Virginia Penitentiary's population was high throughout the war, ranging anywhere from 318 to upwards of 360 convicts.[70] Officials were concerned since the prison's maximum capacity was 250, and the excess population forced three or four convicts to share cells designed for individual confinement. In December 1862, officials reported that inmates who obtained "false keys" tried to escape, attempted a "mutiny of a very serious character," and filled guards' pistols with beeswax to render them inoperable. Officers did not discover the plot until it was in action, but foiled it despite sabotaged weapons.[71]

Virginia inmates devised a similar "murderous assault" on one guard in March 1864, but another prisoner alerted officials of the plot since he feared consequences for failing to report the conspiracy.[72] Nothing ultimately came of the plot, but it nonetheless demonstrated how the penitentiary's internal power dynamics could shift in favor of prisoners when the population was high. Penitentiary inmates proved that they could threaten keepers either verbally or physically, thereby upsetting the normal power structure.[73] High population, therefore, concerned both penitentiary and military prison officials and guards anxiously watched for collusion among inmates.

Tension plagued Camp Chase officials throughout the fall of 1863 and early 1864. John Hunt Morgan's men were crowded into the prison, Morgan's actual escape from the Ohio Penitentiary rattled locals, and rumors of a Copperhead plot designed to release Confederate prisoners in Ohio abounded. Camp Chase's population hovered around 2,500 in September 1863, and some inmates took advantage of guards' inability to wield full control over the camp. In late September 1863, three Confederate inmates—Sgt. L. Potts, Pvt. G. Compton, and Sergeant Ross orchestrated a plot that liberated twelve prisoners, themselves included. The men tunneled under the outer wall and then scattered to elude guards. All safely reached the South. Incidents like this and Morgan's successful break inspired similar attempts. In March 1864, Gen. Basil Duke, one of Morgan's right-hand men, withdrew his parole, requested to be sent back to Camp Chase, and consequently aroused Union authorities' suspicion. Prison officials surveyed Duke closely, uncovered a plot to overpower the guard and rush the gates, and confiscated numerous short knives, files, and screwdrivers from potential participants.[74] Duke and his compatriots were not fortunate enough to follow in their leader's footsteps.

Guards at Johnson's Island also worried about potential escapes in late 1863 as rumors that Rebel sympathizers in Canada were conspiring to free the prison's four thousand inmates, attack and destroy Sandusky and Buffalo, and then flee to Canada. Union authorities consequently ordered the steamer *Michigan* to Sandusky Bay to bolster security, but prison officials remained uneasy. Prisoners knew that Union authorities were on edge as they hastily increased the prison's fortifications. Inmate Robert Bingham recalled on November 11 that the Yankees ordered five hundred additional guards to the prison and mocked their insecurity. "Nine-hundred men and a full gunboat to keep 2,000 unarmed men in a pen with a wall fifteen feet high around it and a sentinel every 50 yards," he quipped, "Brave men! But a heavy guard is all right—for we are ripe for any desperate effort." Increased defenses did not faze inmates. On November 13, one captain of a propeller boat policing the bay reported that inmates dug a three-hundred-foot-long tunnel and aimed to capture the *Michigan* and other propellers to raid Buffalo's shipping.[75]

The Canada plot ultimately turned out to be a humbug, but Johnson's Island inmates continued efforts to escape in January 1864. While some prisoners thought escape was the best way to achieve freedom, others like E. D. Dixon, Robert Bingham, and Virgil Murphey believed the risk not worth the reward, either due to the brutal Ohio winter or the threat of punishment. On New Year's Day, Dixon recorded that the temperature dropped from thirty-two degrees above zero at sunrise to twenty-seven below by 4 P.M., and opted to remain in enemy shelter. But the frigid air inspired fast runners. Dixon recalled how "notwithstanding this intense cold five prisoners scaled the enclosure and made for the mainland." Three successfully reached Canada and freedom, but Union authorities returned two cold, tired men to quarters.

Robert Bingham could have participated in a similar escape attempt in early January 1864. Comrades invited him to climb the fence with them, but he concluded that "it is too cold and the chances are too bad" and opted to stay in prison rather than brave the elements. Bingham had little faith that escape would succeed, though he did know that the previously mentioned men never returned to prison. He wanted nothing more than to get away from Johnson's Island, but hopelessly concluded that "any general plan will be discovered and any small plan would be overpowered," a conclusion that doesn't match Dixon's description of the punishment that the recaptured January fugitives received.

Recapture was the only punishment that Dixon remembered Union authorities administering to the New Year's Day escapees, and Virgil Murphey's diary entry from January 21 likewise noted mild punishment. Light reprisals temporarily emboldened prisoners. Murphey, on the 21st, recalled that the Yankees caught one Confederate inmate in the act of tunneling, pick in hand, and merely ordered him to his quarters without further punishment. "Indeed our right to escape is acknowledged by the prison authorities and an effort for its practical execution does not incur harsh penalties," Murphey concluded, impressed with guards' conformity with the Lieber Code's sanction of prisoners attempting escape. But the actions of Union authorities the following day forced Murphey to retract both his statement and his admiration. Murphey recalled on January 22 that Colonel Hill compelled an officer caught attempting escape to stand on a barrel for five hours. He and his comrades condemned this punishment as an "open and vindictive violation of a principle universally acknowledged" as a right to prisoners. These punishments perhaps explain why Bingham refused invitations to escape.[76]

Rebel guards likewise stood on the lookout for fugitive Yankee inmates, but recapturing all escapees was sometimes impossible. In March 1862, Confederate Army chaplain A. W. Mangum informed his sister that six Yankee prisoners escaped from Salisbury and only three were caught. Four months later, in July 1862, James Addison Lowry, a member of the 57th North Carolina Regiment standing guard at Salisbury, described the organized chaos that ensued when Union inmates made a dash. At midnight on July 17, between six and eight Yankees ran off, triggering the alarm—a beating drum—at which the guards rushed to the guardhouse on the double quick. Their haste did not guarantee 100 percent return, however. Confederate guards fired on the fugitives and wounded two, whom they recaptured. Guards did not apprehend the third until two days later and, according to Lowry, the rest remained at large.[77]

Some inmates preferred the anonymous cover of night to mask escape. Others directly confronted their captors. Castle Thunder inmates Ed Boon, Edward Carney, Tomas Cole, and John A. Chapman assaulted keepers as they attempted to break out. Pvt. Sutton Byrd of the 53rd North Carolina tried to apprehend the "desperate characters," but the offenders pulled a gun and killed him. The ensuing chaos enabled all three men to disappear.[78]

These men engaged guards on the spur of the moment in the midst of escape, but other prisoners methodically attacked their captors. On November 25, 1864, three Salisbury prisoners obtained weapons and attempted to overpower the relief guard, which consisted of nine men and a sergeant, as the detachments changed posts. Upwards of a thousand men joined the rush to escape, but Confederate authorities reported unprecedented loyalty of two imprisoned convicts and three Federal deserters, who sprang into action on behalf of officials. The perpetrators suffered thirteen killed, three mortally wounded, and sixty others wounded, while the guards suffered two killed, one mortally wounded, and eight or ten slightly wounded. Since much of the guard force was incapacitated, the two loyal convicts promptly avenged the murder of the sergeant of the guard by killing his assailant, and the Federal deserters killed one fugitive and wounded another.[79] It is not clear from the report whether the ringleaders were killed, or if they even intended to inspire more participants, but the escapees likely did not expect fellow inmates to side with their captors.

Guards feared mass disobedience throughout the war, but, like penitentiary officials, they were also constantly suspicious of the questionable behavior of even one or two inmates since it could breed larger problems. In November 1862, Maj. Peter Zinn, post commander, noted that Camp Chase's guards had "difficulty in having [lights] put out in messes four and five." Instead of obeying orders to extinguish the lights, inmates rushed into the open space outside their barracks and ignored guards' orders to return to quarters. The sentinel nearest to the affray opened fire since he feared that the prisoners were trying to break out and was duty bound to quell disobedience with firepower. The guard's bullet instantly took the life of inmate William Jones but, according to Zinn, the sentinel's action was justified.[80]

Two years later, Camp Chase's guards confronted other seemingly minor acts that portended potentially larger trouble. In 1864 guards shot and wounded Junius Cloyd for foul play as he repeatedly went to a forbidden side of the prison at roll call. Guards also shot and wounded Joseph Rutter and Malilon Hurst for throwing water into a forbidden side of the prison and using "abusive language toward the sentinel" when ordered to desist. Guards in these circumstances feared for their safety and dreaded escape attempts, as evidenced by Commandant William Richardson's assessment of the shootings. These incidents occurred soon after fears of the Copperhead conspiracy had subsided, and Richardson condoned the guards' actions since "a very insubordinate spirit" prevailed among prisoners for "four or five weeks, manifesting itself in resistance to prison rules and possible escape."[81]

Guards at Old Capitol Prison dealt with similar issues. They ordered political prisoner George Henry Clay Rowe away from prison windows after he stuck his head out a distance that defied orders. In retaliation, Rowe mustered the support of one companion to curse the sentinels and the guards threatened to fire. The guards' response is understandable since prison rules dictated close confinement for inmates who looked out of the windows. The threat of firepower seemed to check inmates' behavior, judging from how Rowe's roommates reacted every subsequent time he taunted guards. Rowe noted that his friends were in "terror of being shot" when he insulted the sentinels and they begged him to stop.[82]

Confederate military prison officials also faced these challenges. Some prisoners at Castle Thunder attempted escape by jumping out of windows or by digging. Desperation often motivated these attempts since many escapees were condemned to die. Inmate David Rogers, sentenced to be shot for desertion, successfully escaped by crawling out of his cell window and scaling down the side of the building. William Brander, sentenced to hang for murdering a Confederate soldier, also escaped. He crawled through a skylight, tied a long strip of blankets and clothing to a chimney, lowered himself to the ground, and ran to freedom. Capt. A. Webster, condemned to the gallows for violating parole, was not as lucky. Webster jumped from his third-story window, injuring himself and enabling guards to recapture him. They later placed him under double guard.[83]

Both penitentiary and military prison inmates faced the prospect of death if escape attempts went awry. But the threat of death or physical punishment did not stop many prisoners from plotting escapes since the potential for freedom outweighed the potential risks. Penitentiary and military prison guards combated threats of escape and disobedience from both individual captives and groups of inmates. Attempts at both types of institutions often stemmed from overcrowding and guards' inability to survey all inmates at all times. Inmates' disobedience and escapes altered the power dynamics of penitentiaries and military prisons, but such instances were risky and relatively rare. Escape attempts, inmates' disobedience, and officials' responses to these actions were very similar at penitentiaries and military prisons, and they illustrate the continuity of imprisonment in peace and war.

Male inmates were not alone in their efforts to shape identity, disrupt the internal dynamics of prisons, attempt to break free, and strive to maintain interpersonal relationships with those at home. Female inmates throughout the nineteenth century also shaped the internal dynamics of prisons. The presence of women in prison in the antebellum period was relatively insignificant and officials often overlooked them, but wartime increased the number of female commitments and officials could not ignore them.

Fallen from Grace

The Experience of Female Inmates

In late April 1864, the *Dayton Empire* reported that the "beneficent" U.S. government was preparing a house in Cincinnati for the reception of female prisoners. "This indicates a renewal of the war upon women," the journalist complained, and then wondered when someone would write a history of prisons like this and Camp Chase, where "many an innocent man and tender female have been shut within the foul and loathsome walls for months at a time, charged with no crime, conscious of no guilt, and discharged without trial."[1]

Nineteenth-century Americans were accustomed to men facing incarceration, but female inmates shocked them. Throughout the century, prison officials had a difficult time deciding how to treat female inmates whom many considered, as L. Mara Dodge has noted, "more hardened and depraved than male inmates" and "beyond the hope of redemption."[2] Female penitentiary inmates were a rarity before the Civil War, officials did not make special accommodations for them, and none of the nation's first penitentiaries had completely separate facilities for female convicts.[3] The number of incarcerated women was small in the antebellum period. Seldom could more than one or two women be found in a Southern penitentiary before the Civil War and, generally speaking, the number of female inmates in the antebellum years rarely constituted more than 10 percent of the total population of prisoners and was often much less.[4]

Circumstances changed during the Civil War. According to Edith Abbott, wartime criminal statistics are hard to come by, but in general, the number of female inmates in penitentiaries peaked in 1863 and 1864.[5] Military prisons also filled with female captives as war increased women's visibility in the public sphere. Castle Thunder, for example, detained approximately one hundred women throughout its existence.[6]

Officials' concern over female inmates heightened as the nineteenth century progressed. Wardens initially had sole oversight over female inmates, but by midcentury many penitentiaries employed a matron to provide special care for women. Officials segregated inmates by gender as best they could despite the absence of a female ward, and military prison officers followed suit. Wartime officials separated male and female inmates in newly established military prisons, and federal authorities established two female prisons, one in Louisville, Kentucky, and the other named Chestnut Street Prison, in St. Louis, Missouri, presaging the women-only prisons that sprang up after the Civil War.[7]

Regardless of where they were held, female inmates elicited public conversation about the morality of women and about the character of the authorities that detained them. Historians, however, have generally overlooked the fact that prisons are gendered institutions that reflect assumptions about proper male and female behavior.[8] Imprisoned women faced an even harsher stigma than men since incarceration equated an irredeemable fall from grace. Female inmates nonetheless faced many of the same challenges as their male counterparts—they struggled to assert their identity, challenged the authority of captors, sought freedom by attempting escape, and maintained relationships with those at home despite stringent supervision. The press and penitentiary officials generally disparaged female criminals, especially black women, both before and during the Civil War. But as the excerpt from the *Dayton Empire* suggests, wartime officials also elicited criticism for detaining so many members of the fairer sex.

When women, typically blacks and poor whites, committed crime in the antebellum period, prison officials assumed a paternal role and supervised them. However, prison officials and chaplains neglected female inmates and believed women incapable of reformation. Although female inmates participated in prison labor—most commonly spinning, weaving, sewing, or washing clothes for male inmates—officials did not believe that labor, or education, or religious instruction would reform women regardless of race. Black female criminals were considered promiscuous and permanently degraded, and whites were deemed irredeemable since they violated their moral nature.[9]

Women: Imprisoned and Neglected, but Sometimes Praised

Women were not considered equal members of the state and were excluded as voters and jurors. State officials treated women as subjects and reserved the right to punish them.[10] Women—black and white—constituted a small percentage of state penitentiary populations. The female population at the Ohio Penitentiary never exceeded 2 percent in the antebellum period; the number of black and white inmates was about the same. Even in 1860, when the penitentiary held 15 women, they made up only about 1.5 percent of the total population, which numbered 949. In Virginia, women never exceeded 6 percent of the total penitentiary population, and it was more common, though not necessarily typical, for black women to outnumber white women. The racial dynamics in Washington were similar to those of Virginia. The D.C. Penitentiary's female population hovered around 8 percent for most of the antebellum period, with the exception of 18 percent in 1850.[11]

The 1816 Georgia penal code mandated that male and female inmates be kept separate, leaving the impression that penitentiary officials would be prepared to receive female convicts. Anticipation of female prisoners did not, however, translate into practical steps to ensure separate quarters. The women's ward remained simply a good idea as the *Georgia Journal* reported in November 1816. The female department would be "precisely like the male," said the *Journal*, but immediately mentioned that it "has not yet been commenced."

Female inmates at the Georgia Penitentiary vexed administrators despite, or perhaps because of, their rare presence. Female convicts frustrated officials, so authorities released women, rather than take responsibility for them. The Baltimore *Sun* reflected the attitude of Georgia officials in December 1847, when it reported that only two of the penitentiary's 128 convicts were female. "We trust that these two will be discharged, and the law so altered as never to send another woman to this receptacle of thieves and robbers," the paper proclaimed, advancing a latent argument that women never belonged in prison and supporting officials' decision to discharge them. State law sanctioned imprisonment of women, but only about twenty females inhabited the penitentiary from 1817 to 1850. As the *Sun* presaged, the governor substantiated the notion that women were out of place in prison and eventually pardoned all but three of them to rid the penitentiary of its "bothersome convicts."[12]

Penitentiary architects and officials routinely failed to plan for and/or neglected female inmates since penitentiaries were designed to hold large numbers of men.[13] Southerners were more resistant than Northerners to the women's rights movement and to political, social, and economic expressions of female autonomy. Accordingly, Southern prisons were particularly ill-equipped to deal with women and officials were reluctant to interact with female inmates who challenged acceptable behavior.[14]

Women's living quarters at the Virginia Penitentiary were inferior to men's and their work conditions were also subpar.[15] In 1811, monthly visitors William Price and George Williamson noted that the male workshops were in good order, but lamented that the women's ward "was in a very bad condition owing to their neglect in not being more cleanly." Instead of blaming this shortcoming on the women, the visitors surprisingly faulted the keeper. Price and Williamson believed that the keeper neglected discipline and demanded that he compel obedience from the women.[16] This, however, was an ironic and seemingly impossible request since men believed that female criminals, regardless of race, were impervious to reform.

Journalists disregarded incarcerated black women, but repeatedly boasted of the paucity of white women in the state penitentiary as a marker of the superiority of white females, the state of Virginia, and the South. On March 1, 1833, the *Pittsburgh Gazette* praised the Virginia Penitentiary, noting that the total population was 150, of which only 8 were women. "To the honor of the state, be it said, there is not a single *white woman* amongst [the prisoners]," the paper bragged, touting the morality of Virginia's white women. Eighteen years later, the *Lynchburg Express* contended that the absence of white women in the Virginia Penitentiary indicated that the South was morally superior to the North. The paper proclaimed that the penitentiary held no white women in 1851 and asked, "Can our Northern contemporaries, who are wont to sneer at Southern morals say as much? Not one of them, we expect." The Richmond *Enquirer* also used the absence of white women in the penitentiary to laud the morality of the South in general and of Virginia's white women in particular. In October 1853, the *Enquirer* reported that there was not a single white female among the 264 inmates and contended that this reflected favorably on Virginia's white women since state laws applied to both men and women. The *Enquirer* concluded that women could "claim to be 264 times better than the males."

The paper did not stop heaping praise there. "We feel inclined to make a comparison to this and other states in the Union," it continued, "more particularly in reference to the Northern penitentiaries; but as comparisons are said to be odious, we will only remark that no other state out of the 31 can, we believe, make a similar boast."[17] This assessment at once placed Virginia's women on a pedestal and excoriated Northern authorities that incarcerated women as oppressive, an argument that resurfaced during the Civil War.

Southern states were not alone in flaunting the lack of incarcerated women. In Ohio, penitentiary directors and journalists used the penitentiary's white female population—or lack thereof—to claim bragging rights for their state and for white women generally. Ohioans refrained from pointing fingers at the South, however. In December 1839, the Board of Directors reported that the penitentiary held only two white women, neither of whom was an Ohio native. The directors consequently paid "a handsome and deserved compliment to the intelligence, virtue, and moral excellence of our country women." Three years later, in February 1842, the *Cincinnati Republican* reported that there were only three women among the Ohio Penitentiary's 481 convicts and concluded that this was "fine evidence of the freedom of the gentler sex from the contamination of crime."[18] Penitentiary officials made similar remarks on the penitentiary's gender dynamics in the next decade.

The Ohio Penitentiary directors simultaneously praised and criticized women by highlighting the gender ratio of inmates. Since the ratio of male to female inmates was skewed, they bragged that white women were above crime, but contended that some women were bad mothers who inspired crime. In 1855 the directors noted that there were 601 male and 5 female inmates in the penitentiary and commented that "the proportion of 120 males to one female in the prison" was of "curious and gratifying remark." These numbers, according to the directors, proved that the mother's example did much to "mould the character of the growing man," failing those who wound up in prison. But all was not lost. The directors also used the proportion of male to female inmates to pay "homage" to women and hoped that they would inspire men to behave.[19] Judging from these assessments, there existed two disparate interpretations of female offenders in the nineteenth century: Officials often denounced incarcerated women as an unspeakable disgrace, but the relative absence of women in prison was a source of public pride.

Female Prisoners and Misconduct

The behavior of female inmates, however, often lent credence to the belief that criminal women were unruly, and few penitentiary officials believed women capable of change. Chaplains seldom ministered to women since, as Ohio Penitentiary chaplain James Finley complained in April 1846, ministry in the women's ward detracted from time spent with male convicts. Finley was frustrated that his work among the women was fruitless. After reading part of Matthew's gospel to the women one Sunday in April, Finley noted that they were "as obdurate as rocks," since woman, "when really depraved and fallen, is not only the wickedest, but the most hard and unmanageable of beings."[20]

Finley labored unsuccessfully for months. He repeatedly complained that the women, who were predominantly white, "were much worse, in every respect, than the men," validating the idea that criminal women were beyond redemption and challenging the press's glowing assertions about white womanhood.[21] During the summer, however, the warden took the women into the prison yard for recreation, and Finley noted an immediate change in their demeanor. From that moment, Finley said the women were "subdued and softened" and that his work was "much lighter, more profitable . . . abundantly more acceptable," and facilitated some reform.[22]

Finley's experience may have been an anomaly. Penitentiary officials' neglect of female inmates encouraged misbehavior and eventually motivated officials to appoint a matron. Female prisoners in the D.C. and Ohio penitentiaries were often disruptive prior to the matron's appointment. In May 1840, D.C. Penitentiary inmate Lidia Green spent nine days in solitary confinement for scalding fellow inmate Mary Scott with hot water five times. Green was no stranger to punishment. That February, she spent twelve days in the dungeon for bringing food to a woman in her cell three times.[23]

Women at the Ohio Penitentiary caused similar stirs in the mid-1840s. The prison held only nine women, but one visitor claimed that they created more trouble than all five hundred male convicts since the women took out their anger on each other. Female inmates incessantly fought, scratched, pulled each other's hair, cursed, and yelled. They also cut one another with knives left in the women's ward. Officials removed the knives and stationed a male guard toting a horsewhip to restore order, but the unfazed women continued their improprieties.[24]

Other female inmates at the Ohio Penitentiary challenged prison officers. In September 1846, Chaplain Finley noted that one woman verbally and physically assaulted an officer at dinnertime. When the officer brought the woman dinner, she swore that "God never made man able to conquer her" and told the guard to "go and feed the devil." The officer replied that he would rather feed her, further incensing the woman. She quickly hurled a tin dipper at the guard's head, and then engaged him in a "pitched battle." The officer eventually detained the woman and locked her in her cell, where Finley heard her pray that God would send her "immediately to hell, which . . . was a better place than a penitentiary."[25] Female inmates, like this woman, who harmed one another or threatened guards validated the notion that criminal women were dangerous and primitive.[26] But punishment was only a temporary fix for disobedience. The following decade, officials determined that the appointment of a matron was necessary to assert order in the women's ward and keep female inmates from, as Dorothea Dix noted during her 1844 visit, exercising their "evil gifts on each other."[27]

The 1855 rules and regulations of the Ohio Penitentiary dictated that a matron teach female convicts to read and "administer such moral and religious advice" as "calculated to promote order, decorum, propriety of behavior, and reformation." Men were thus formally excused from the day-to-day oversight of women, but retained responsibility for punishing female inmates since all women, even those in positions of authority, were subordinate to men. The warden required the matron to report infractions to him so that he could administer punishment.[28] Male penitentiary officials had little interest in criminal women beyond chastisement since retaining the power to punish was a testimony to their overall authority.

D.C. Penitentiary officials likewise thought women were a negative distraction for male guards. In 1854, Warden Thomas Thornley excused male officers from duty in the female department and left the women without any oversight. Thornley justified the shift, stating that *"more important duties"* elsewhere demanded the guards' attention. For about a year, D.C. Penitentiary officials did not even need to budget for the care of female inmates since volunteer supervisors visited their ward. Thornley credited the good behavior of women to the chaplain and to many visitors, particularly one local woman who was "pre-eminent in her endeavors to instruct them in lessons of morality and scriptural truth."[29] But good order in the female department quickly deteriorated and officials appointed a matron on October 1, 1855.

In her first report, Matron C. F. Marceron called into question the rosy picture that Thornley painted the year before and noted that the female department was in "disorder." Marceron griped that the women refused to work unless forced and that "ill humor" prevailed among them. Marceron, however, retained hope that the women could change, an attitude that defied common male assumptions about female criminals. After encouraging industry and urging the women to develop a work ethic, Marceron found all inmates "respectful and obedient" and had no "cause to recommend punishment." Just as wardens hoped to exact reform from male inmates, Marceron hoped "with the help of God, to do some good" for the women.[30] Marceron's appointment offset male officers' neglect of the female department and enabled them to tend to duties that they deemed more important, trusting the seemingly impossible task of female reform to a matron. But provisions for the care of female inmates remained minimal and haphazard throughout the nineteenth century, and matrons often could not squelch bad behavior.[31]

Female inmates acted up since they knew that Matron Marceron had sole charge of them and could not control their every move. D.C. Penitentiary inmate Emily Bryant was quarrelsome immediately upon entering prison and encouraged others to misbehave. Many women refused to work since they knew that Marceron had to call on male officials to administer punishment, and they understood that this time-consuming process left time for misbehavior.[32] Inmates adeptly, albeit temporarily, used numerical superiority and nonviolent resistance in the female ward prior to the Civil War. Female commitments in both penitentiaries and military prisons during the war years, like females during the antebellum years, perplexed administrators.

Wartime military mobilization disrupted social relations and left both Northern and Southern women alone on the home front. Women assumed many traditional masculine roles, including crime. In the South, the crimes that women typically committed before the war—fornication, bastardy, and prostitution—declined, but property crimes such as larceny, forcible entry, and rioting increased from 1861 to 1866.[33] Women convicted of crime during the war were sentenced to male-dominated penitentiaries, but military prisons also held women whose presence forced administrators to confront the challenge of provisioning female inmates. Like their antebellum counterparts, wartime penitentiary and military prison officials could not ignore female inmates, either due to their numbers or their behavior.

Female commitments increased slightly during the Civil War, and wartime penitentiary administrators confronted a familiar antebellum problem.

Even though the percentage of female inmates remained low, the increase in the female population was often more than officials were prepared to handle. For example, the Virginia Penitentiary held anywhere from ten to twenty-five women, and the Ohio Penitentiary consistently held sixteen to eighteen women. These numbers exceeded antebellum totals, but the total percentage of incarcerated women hovered around 1–2 percent at both institutions, with the exception of 8 percent at the Virginia Penitentiary in 1863.[34] Female inmates plagued Virginia Penitentiary officials. The women often were idle since the prison's overcrowding and lack of supplies prohibited female inmates from working. In 1863 Supt. Colin Bass complained that the twenty-five women in prison could not "be worked to any profit for want of room" because the women were "huddled together in rooms so small that work cannot be done but by a very limited number."[35] Bass likely did not care that the women were idle since their prospects for reform were bleak, but he regretted that the penitentiary did not profit from the women's work.

Throughout the century, female prisoners undertook traditional house-keeping tasks. Georgia Penitentiary officials preferred to rid the institution of women, but failing this, they housed the few female inmates in a separate room on the second floor near the kitchen and ordered them to sew or complete other domestic chores.[36] Gendered expectations followed women into prison. Female criminals, whether lower or middle-class, betrayed the cult of domesticity when they committed crime, but domestic roles shaped the lives of female penitentiary inmates. They sewed, made clothes, ironed, bound shoes, spun, and washed for male inmates.[37] These duties rendered female inmates responsible for the upkeep of the prison "home" and reminded them of gender-appropriate behavior.

Wartime penitentiary administrators also subjected female prisoners to domestic work. But instead of having female inmates undertake chores for the prison "home," they recognized that women's work could benefit troops at the front. When war broke out, numerous female aid societies sprang up in the North and mobilized women to produce clothes for the Union Army. Ohio Penitentiary officials enlisted female inmates to aid these voluntary organizations, particularly the Soldiers' Aid Society and the Sisters of Charity in Columbus.[38] Penitentiary officials mandated that female inmates do patriotic work and ordered female criminals to sew men's drawers, white shirts, and muslin for the aid societies to donate to Union troops. Ohio Penitentiary officials might have believed criminal women incapable of reform, but patriotism was expected of both law-abiding and law-breaking women.

Patriotic work became a source of pride for the matron and female inmates. It taught the women proper domestic roles and, ironically, put criminals somewhat on par with civilian women who aided voluntary organizations as they supplied troops.[39]

Female Military Prison Inmates

Female inmates detained for war related offenses, like suspected treason or aiding the enemy, perplexed Union and Confederate officials just as they frustrated penitentiary administrators. Female military prison inmates faced circumstances similar to those apparent in antebellum and wartime penitentiaries. Public discussion about and criticism of female offenders magnified during wartime, but officials who oversaw the imprisonment of women during wartime also elicited scrutiny.

Women committed crime as they adjusted to war's circumstances or aided their respective causes. For example, examination of the *Official Records* and Richmond's newspapers reveals that Southern women committed crime out of financial necessity or political conviction when they sold liquor to the enemy, spied or otherwise supported the Union cause, passed counterfeit money, engaged in prostitution, acted as "suspicious character[s]" or "wanderer[s]," and donned male clothing to enlist in the Confederate Army.[40] Union authorities arrested women for similar offenses since the government was on high alert for suspicious activity. Data gleaned from the *Official Records* indicates that authorities detained women at Camp Chase and Old Capitol Prisons for spying, secessionist sentiments, aiding the enemy, prostitution, treason, and crossing enemy lines without proper authorization.[41]

War drew women into the political melee, inspired them to support their chosen cause, and sometimes led male authorities to use women as leverage. For example, during the 1863 Winchester campaign, the Richmond *Daily Dispatch* noted the arrival of six Yankee women at Castle Thunder. Union Secretary of War Edwin Stanton, unnerved at the prospect of Southern authorities holding these women, along with five others, urged federal authorities to "take [Southern] hostages for their safe return."[42]

Women acted politically more often than officials used them for political leverage, however. Authorities in and around Old Capitol Prison were sensitive to any hint of misbehavior that women might exhibit, especially if they threatened the prison's security. Passersby who even so much as looked toward the Old Capitol raised the suspicion of Union authorities. Authorities arrested numerous women who allegedly signaled to prisoners. In May 1862, U.S. officials arrested three ladies, two of whom were the wife and daughter of a prominent officer of the Senate. One of the ladies repeatedly and rapidly pressed a handkerchief over her mouth as she passed the prison, piquing a guard's interest. Authorities escorted the women to the guardroom and informed the ladies that they violated a public order prohibiting the waving of handkerchiefs or making any motion likely to be interpreted as a signal to the prisoners. The order obligated officers to arrest any suspicious person and raised the question of what one *could* do outside of the prison. The offender alleged that she was merely wiping the juice of a recently eaten orange from her face, but authorities were not convinced. They held the snacking woman, but released the senator's wife and daughter, who had political ties.[43]

The order governing the behavior of individuals outside of the Old Capitol was written broadly and led to other similar incidents. About a week later, the *New York Times* reported that authorities arrested two "tolerably good looking young females," reputedly strangers in D.C., for signaling to prisoners and sent them to Washington's Central Guard House. The paper noted that the women refused to give their names, which supported suspicions that they were up to no good. Union officials also sent three other women— Anna Brenaugh, Mary A. Cooper, and Fanny Brenaugh—to the Guard House in April 1863 for signaling to Old Capitol inmates.[44] Authorities suspected that these women could aid inmates' escape or incite rebellion and rapidly took them into custody. Officials' troubles with female inmates often magnified after detention, however. Military prison authorities, like penitentiary officials, stopped women's misbehavior in public, but were not sure how to handle them in prison.

Women's presence in military prisons posed administrative challenges just as it did at antebellum and wartime penitentiaries. Northern and Southern military prison authorities were unprepared to deal with women, and those who ended up in military prisons faced the same circumstances as male prisoners, a fact that unsettled polite society. In April 1863, Union authorities arrested Fannie Battle, the daughter of Confederate general Cullen A. Battle, in Nashville for acting as a Confederate spy, smuggling goods, and getting a forged pass. Battle denied the charges, but special commissioner for Camp Chase, Samuel Galloway, concluded that Battle was "affable and attractive and well qualified by manners and mind to be influential for evil to the loyal cause." Galloway believed that Battle's detention was justified, but the *Memphis Daily Appeal* fretted that she and her five or six accomplices would suffer in Camp Chase since their sentence was for the duration of the war. The paper concluded that only the Southern officers and men who had been captives at the "bastille" could "form a correct estimate of the horrible privations" that these ladies would face.[45]

Union authorities employed the antebellum practice of segregating inmates by gender and were reluctant to hold women at Camp Chase. On April 23, 1863, the prison's commander noted that there were "no suitable accommodations" for the women. These five female prisoners represented a number no greater than those held in penitentiaries and, as at the Georgia Penitentiary, the paucity of females in and of itself perplexed officials. Camp Chase had no readily available facilities for them and it made little sense to construct any. Camp Chase officials consequently adopted a blend of antebellum strategies. They removed the women, as in Georgia, and relocated them to a site with other female captives. Federal authorities mimicked the construction of women's wards in penitentiaries when they subjected them to prison regulations, sent the women to a house near the quartermaster, and placed the women "in the immediate charge of a loyal female," akin to a matron.[46]

Authorities at the Old Capitol Prison also made special accommodations for or removed female inmates to sites specifically designed for the detention of women, presaging the women's prisons that emerged in the postwar period. Union authorities detained two women, Mrs. Turner and Miss Buckner, of "first Virginia families," in late October 1862 for attempting to smuggle quinine south. Federal officials deemed Buckner, despite her youth, capable of serving her sentence at the Old Capitol, where she would join other women like Belle Boyd, Antonia Ford, and Rose Greenhow. Nonetheless, they instead held Turner with a cabinet minister "in consideration of her age," but also ostensibly to guarantee close supervision.[47]

Later in the war, federal authorities sent some women from the Old Capitol to the Fitchburg House of Correction (Massachusetts) since they, like antebellum penitentiary and Camp Chase's officials, believed that complete separation of male and female inmates was appropriate. In April 1864, federal authorities sent three women to the Old Capitol for attempting to convey letters and medicine to the Rebels, and then balanced the intake by sending Mary Johnson and Carrie Jones, alleged Rebel spies, to the Fitchburg prison for "safe keeping." In September that same year, federal authorities shifted

Old Capitol Prison, Washington, D.C., circa 1864 (Library of Congress)

two women, charged with aiding desertion by furnishing citizens' clothing to soldiers, from the Old Capitol to Fitchburg to be held with other women.[48] These examples echo the established practice of segregating inmates by gender and attempting to address the needs of female inmates.

Sometimes incarcerated women faced more severe circumstances than did men. Old Capitol Prison authorities had their hands full with notorious spies Rose O'Neal Greenhow and Belle Boyd. Due to the reputation of these women, prison officials regularly prescribed punishments that unruly male and female inmates received in penitentiaries. Upon entry, officials placed Greenhow and her accomplices under a "guard of six men," who were to keep them "in close confinement" and to permit "no communication with any one whatever."[49] Assistant Secretary of War C. P. Wolcott likewise directed prison officials to keep Boyd in "close custody," expressed consternation when officials disobeyed, and demanded a thorough investigation to determine why officials ignored the order.[50] Union authorities' treatment of Greenhow and her accomplices garnered significant public attention, especially since authorities confined male political prisoners in one room and let them talk with each other, albeit under the supervision of undercover detectives.

Federal authorities first held Greenhow in Washington's Sixteenth Street Prison and moved her and her friend, Mrs. Baxley, to the Old Capitol in early 1862. The press watched with great interest as Greenhow, according to the

New York Times of January 22, 1862, seized the opportunity to at once praise and patronize Union prison officials for her treatment. Residents gawked as a carriage arrived to transport the ladies to their new quarters. Greenhow reached out, thanked the guards for their courtesy, and then sarcastically wished that the guard might, in the future, "have a nobler employment than that of guarding defenseless women."[51]

This portrait of Greenhow contrasted with a depiction of her that appeared in an Ohio newspaper a few weeks earlier. The *Times* portrayed Greenhow having the upper hand morally as she criticized the individual guards who had charge of her and the federal government for incarcerating women. On the contrary, the January 10, 1862, edition of the *Zanesville Courier* printed a disparaging portrait of Greenhow's behavior in prison. When Greenhow lost her "cake" containing her escape plan, she violently rang the bell for more food. After a guard honored her request, she furiously threw the cake down some stairs. Imprisonment, in the *Courier*'s estimation, drove Greenhow mad and the paper concluded that authorities must have cut off Greenhow "from her allowance of a quart of wine a day."[52] The two news pieces capture the range of emotions that female imprisonment stirred up during the Civil War—some civilians sided with the women and criticized how male government officials assaulted womanhood with imprisonment. Others supported the government's detention of women, denounced their subversion of the Union cause, and embellished women's bad behavior to emphasize their fall from grace. Either way, military prison officers, through imprisonment, exercised paternal oversight of aberrant women since the war drew male relatives to the front.

Imprisonment as a Paternal Substitute

Women misbehaved in both civilian life and in prison during the antebellum period, but the context of war magnified the frequency and severity of women's bad behavior. The few antebellum female inmates frequently rebelled against the restrictiveness of incarceration and constant supervision, as did their male counterparts. Women, however, were more accustomed than men to constant oversight in day-to-day life given gender norms under which women were to be seen, but not heard, in the domestic sphere. Lower-class women could not conform to this middle-class ideal, and imprisoned women often forged their identity through disobedience. Middle- and upper-class women, like Greenhow, acted up in prison, but also criticized their confinement and the men responsible for it. Penitentiary and military prison authorities reasserted paternal authority and reminded women of appropriate gender behavior through imprisonment.

Penitentiary wardens who supervised matrons and punished female inmates in the antebellum period assumed the role of a patriarch in the lives of criminal women. Union and Confederate authorities also felt obligated to supervise aberrant women who lacked male oversight.[53] In January 1863, Camp Chase's authorities were shocked to find two women in the prison who adopted alter egos, donned soldiers' clothing, and tried to enlist in the Union Army. Prison authorities immediately entrusted them to a policeman, who escorted them home to Cleveland. Similarly, as territory in western Virginia became contested in May and June 1863, Union Provost Marshal B. S. Roberts ordered women and children out of their homes. The Richmond *Daily Dispatch* noted that federal authorities evicted sixty-three women and ordered sixty-two females without "natural protectors in the South" to Camp Chase.[54] Sarcasm of the Southern journalists aside, this anecdote indicates that Union authorities used prisons to watch independent or disorderly women.

Castle Thunder authorities routinely supervised abandoned Southern women who were tempted to crime. Mobilization left many women without white male protection, and officers at Castle Thunder took it upon themselves to ensure female virtue.[55] War trumped Victorian opposition to incarcerating women, and sentences at Castle Thunder punished illegitimate behavior, suppressed lustfulness, and protected female virtue to uphold the Southern cause and its male defenders.[56] In July 1864, the Richmond *Examiner* reported that Confederate authorities established a department at Castle Thunder dedicated exclusively to "the detention of a number of depraved and abandoned women," which paralleled the women's wards established at some penitentiaries. Confinement, according to journalists, would prevent the women from "following the army and contributing by their pestilential presence to the moral [decay] of the soldiers." The *Examiner* contended that the camp followers trailed the army "like carrion crows that snuff a field of slaughter," distracted Confederate soldiers from duty, and tested their moral composition. War forced these ladies to become public women, and Southern authorities believed that they needed close supervision.[57] Southern men—

including prison officials—had to protect the state, which was portrayed as feminine, and shield their daughters, sisters, and wives from Yankee invaders.[58] Ironically, as the camp followers demonstrated, Southern men also needed to defend the state and its soldiers from women by imprisoning those who betrayed domesticity.

Women who donned soldiers' trappings and enlisted violated gender norms by assuming masculine identity. Masquerading female soldiers often wound up in Castle Thunder. Prison officials reprimanded their challenge to gender norms, but Richmond's journalists sometimes approved of their actions, if not their charade. Journalists' assessments of female soldiers paralleled the antebellum press's discussion of the moral character— or lack thereof—of female prisoners.[59] Patriotic women were necessary, but male authorities closely monitored women's expression of patriotism.

Some women believed that they could overcome the "misfortune" of their sex by changing their clothes.[60] A case in point was Loretta Janeta Velazquez, also known as Lt. Harry T. Buford. Velazquez was no stranger to imprisonment by the time Confederate authorities detained her in Richmond in July 1863. Union officials first captured Velazquez in New Orleans shortly after the fall of Fort Donelson in early 1862 and charged her as a spy. Consequently, many Southerners knew of Velazquez's exploits and were on the lookout for her despite her defense of the South.[61] Velazquez traveled to Richmond after her release from prison in New Orleans and her reputation followed her. She "almost immediately" triggered General Winder's suspicion. She kept her male costume, but her "feminine ways" blew her cover. Winder believed that a woman in pants was up to no good and Confederate authorities again charged her with being a Federal spy and "a woman in disguise" and locked her in Castle Thunder.[62]

Velazquez's male disguise elicited conflicting interpretations from General Winder, Castle Thunder Commandant George Alexander, and the Richmond press. Velazquez noted that Alexander took interest in her since he believed that she intended to aid the Confederacy. Regardless, Alexander rejected Velazquez's masquerade and admonished her behavior. Alexander wanted Velazquez to work for Winder's secret service corps, but stressed that she first needed to "resume the proper costume" of her sex, a view with which Winder agreed.[63] Alexander released Velazquez and she worked for Winder, but ignored Alexander's warning. Clad in pants, Velazquez set out for North Carolina on a mission that Winder designed as a trap to punish her feigned masculinity.[64] Both men believed Velazquez could help the South, but they demanded that she did so within the confines of womanhood.

The press offered a different spin on Valezquez's case. Like Alexander and Winder, journalists condemned Velazquez's ruse, but nonetheless admired her patriotism. After Alexander released Velazquez, journalists commented not only on her dress, but also on her class, noting that she had long enjoyed significant privilege. The *Examiner* reported that Velazquez was "wealthy" before the war, boasting an annual income of $20,000. Control of such monetary assets indicated unusual power, especially since, as the paper noted, the money was hers, not her husband's. Velazquez never conformed to gender conventions, so it is not surprising, as the *Examiner* reported, that she spent her money "getting medicines for the Confederate government," and that she wielded a musket in "several battles."[65] While Winder and Alexander tried to force Velazquez to reclaim her femininity, journalists suggested that she never possessed it and was perhaps better suited for masculine endeavors.

Velazquez challenged the dictates of proper womanhood, but the press praised how she, in false persona, aided the Confederacy. As Velazquez headed south on July 17, 1863, the Richmond *Sentinel* announced that "Lieutenant Buford" would return to the fray following a sentence at Castle Thunder. The paper approved of Velazquez's ruse, although it acknowledged this and her impersonation of an officer as the cause of her imprisonment. Southern journalists considered female soldiers on a case-by-case basis and favored women who took up arms early in the war, followed lovers into battle, or, as in Velazquez's case, were wounded under fire.[66]

While the Richmond press embraced some women like Velazquez, it scorned others like Mary and Mollie Bell. In so doing, the journalists instructed women on how *not* to support the Confederacy. In October 1864, the Richmond *Whig* detailed the capture of the Bells, aliases Tom Parker and Bob Morgan, who served two years under Confederate general Jubal Early. The *Whig* commented that Mary "looked every inch a snug little soldier boy," but Mollie failed to make "such a favorable impression." The paper estimated that they killed "more than a dozen Yankees with their own guns," but echoed Winder's condemnation of Velazquez, concluding that the Bells deserved time in Castle Thunder for their chicanery. Female offenders thought incarceration was a harsh penalty for voluntary service, but Southern officials believed that soldiering was unacceptable for women, who should have encouraged *men* to fight.[67]

Southern journalists sometimes linked Yankee sympathizers' ability to undermine the Confederate cause with the offender's physical appearance—the ugliest women were the most dangerous.[68] One good example was Richmond resident Mrs. Patterson Allan. The Raleigh, North Carolina, *Register* condemned Mrs. Allan, a Yankee by birth and education, since she aided the Union. Richmond resident Sally Brock weighed in on Allan's case, noting how Allan, the wife of a "wealthy and respectable citizen," used her status to spy on the Confederacy. Allan transmitted sensitive information that she had gathered to Rev. Morgan Dix, whose son was Union general John A. Dix. The *Register* was incensed that Allan received a light sentence: confinement with the Sisters of Charity, instead of in Castle Thunder. Allan was a cunning spy, and the *Register* fumed that she should receive corporal punishment like a man. "Her sex ought not to protect her from just punishment," the journalist bellowed, concluding, "we hope to hear that she has been hung."[69] Wealth and influence, however, shielded Allan.[70]

In Allan's case, the press and Southern officials voiced opinions opposite of the case of Velazquez. The press demanded harsh condemnation, but Secretary of War James Seddon procured a light sentence: confinement with the nuns. Brock noted that this decision was offensive and unpopular, especially since Union officials inflicted "unwarrantable and lawless imprisonment" on suspected Southern spies, like Rose O'Neal Greenhow.[71] Brock and the *Register* demanded that Confederate officials retaliate for Greenhow's close confinement in the Old Capitol from January to May 1862, during which time U.S. authorities forbade her from communicating with anyone.[72] Confederate authorities' decision to afford Allan mild treatment perplexed Brock and Southern journalists, but they were likely pleased with the punishment of Dr. Mary Walker, a powerful figure whom the press judged as anything but feminine.

Journalists frequently targeted Walker, who assumed a masculine role and donned male clothing to aid Union soldiers.[73] Walker, an army physician, was doubly offensive since the South suffered from a shortage of female nurses. Many elite Southern women felt that nursing was incompatible with womanhood since it meant seeing death firsthand and risking disease.[74] Walker, on the contrary, stepped right into the fray—wearing pants—an appalling example of the dangers of Northern feminism. She lived in the male world of the army and routinely saw shattered limbs, gruesome wounds, and uncovered male bodies. Walker's service shocked the Richmond press and their coverage of her case sent clear messages about proper womanhood.

Confederate soldiers captured Walker in Georgia in April 1864, when she was an assistant surgeon in the Army of the Cumberland. Southern papers ridiculed Walker, who "was riding a man's saddle, with one foot in each stirrup" when arrested, as an anomaly.[75] Walker reached Richmond, still in male attire, and created quite a stir among local civilians. Both the *Sentinel* and *Whig* mocked Walker, reporting that she, dressed "in full male costume," was "quite ugly," and attracted hordes of "Negroes and boys" who formed her "volunteer escort to Castle Thunder." The *Whig*, perplexed by Walker's masculine appearance, stated that her gypsy hat was the only item that "might be construed as announcing her sex."[76] Journalists characterized Walker's gender as unrecognizable even before she reached prison, and her behavior in prison was worse than that of male inmates.

Walker's conduct can be interpreted in a few different ways. L. Mara Dodge has noted that female inmates knew, and deliberately exploited, the fact that their presence in prison was disruptive by antagonizing officials.[77] Walker recognized she had celebrity status in the Confederacy because of her role with the Union Army, so she could have intentionally irritated prison keepers. Even *Frank Leslie's Illustrated* of New York reported that she bore imprisonment "like a man," and instructed her mother not to grieve her. This editorial suggested that Walker could take care of herself, a task for which women were assumed incapable.[78] Walker's independence and her professional accomplishments clashed with domesticity and defied the Confederate cause, so she had to be stopped.

This leads to another interpretation of Walker's behavior in prison, which calls to mind the unruly behavior of female inmates at the D.C. and Ohio penitentiaries who mercilessly turned on each other in the antebellum period. Like her antebellum predecessors, Walker's unruly behavior negated her femininity, and Richmond's journalists derided her to discourage women from assuming masculine roles. Journalists delighted in Walker's demise as captivity drove her insane. The *Examiner* commented that imprisonment angered "Miss Doctress, Miscegenation, Philosophical Walker," and caused her to beat up fellow female inmates. Walker allegedly "pitched into several of her room-mates in long clothes, and tore out hand fulls of auburn hair from the head of one of them." Afterwards, Walker "proclaimed secession, and went into another apartment, where she is now lady and lioness of all she surveys."[79] The moral of the story was that, as in the antebellum period, wartime female prisoners were out of control. Walker's burst of violence, however, contrasted with the appeal to womanhood that she allegedly used in a plea for release.

Instead of withstanding imprisonment, Walker, according to Richmond papers, begged for early release.[80] The Richmond *Whig* reported that Walker detested confinement and sneered that "the disgusting production of Yankee land" repeatedly petitioned Provost Marshal Winder.[81] The *Enquirer* chimed in that she did not mind "if she sinks the Doc or [appears] in the woman" to get out of the Castle, indicating that imprisonment inspired reform—a feat that only male inmates were deemed capable of achieving. Walker appeared masculine enough to reform and reclaim her feminine identity, but this change was fleeting. The editorial's subsequent characterization of Walker as a "sensible female" because of her willingness to jettison her male costume in return for freedom marks the first instance where Richmond journalists described Walker as feminine.[82] A month later, however, Walker vacillated and the *Examiner* again degraded her. Journalists noted that she was willing to "waive all title and stand upon the dignity of her sex" to secure release, but asserted that Walker would "never, never give up pantalettes," opting to "die in prison first."[83] Walker never fully conformed to Southern expectations of feminine behavior—nor did she want to—and so the press mocked her out of disbelief and disgust. Ultimately, Richmond journalists were appalled that Walker used her talents to aid Union soldiers, challenging both the Confederate cause and traditional gender roles. But Walker's change in tone from masculine to feminine in her plea for release was a tactic that other women also employed.

Another high-profile inmate, Mrs. T. Webster, petitioned President Jefferson Davis for release, and appealed directly to womanhood as evidence of repentance. Mrs. T. Webster was, in reality, Hattie Lawton, posing as the wife of Timothy Webster, a Yankee spy. Confederate authorities detained Lawton and Mr. Webster in early 1862 when they were working as Pinkerton operatives stationed in Baltimore. After trial by court-martial, Webster became the first Union spy executed in the Confederacy on April 29, 1862, while Lawton served one year in Castle Thunder.[84] Lawton made a strong appeal to the South's accepted gender order for release. Lawton told Davis that she was a "poor, weak woman whose future looks, oh, so cheerless" and argued for freedom since she was "a South adoring woman." In a great, self-serving turn of events, Lawton directly invoked her conformity with Southern womanhood, pleading, "Does a mother harm her child, a child her mother? The South is my mother. I will not harm her. Her glory is my pride. I look to her like a bleeding bird for succor. I have suffered . . . let me go home where I may seek some spot, and unnoticed pass the remainder of my dreary, dreary days."[85] Lawton's plea reveals her transformation and willingness to conform—at least on the surface—with prescribed gender roles to appease Confederate authorities. Her emphasis on her powerlessness appealed to officials' gentlemanly obligation toward weak and dependent women, in this case one who had allegedly reformed. Lawton's tactic succeeded and authorities freed her about a year after her "husband's" hanging.[86]

Regardless of their class status or offenses that landed them in prison, female inmates, like their male counterparts, could not overcome the stigma of imprisonment. Even those in military prisons thought of incarceration in terms reminiscent of penitentiaries. Rebel spy Antonia Ford's writing from the Carroll Prison annex of the Old Capitol provides a good example. Authorities granted Ford special privileges, like the ability to send for her trunk of personal items. Ford sent to her mother, with this request, a collar and a poem, both constructed in prison. In the first stanza of her poem, Ford noted that she made the collar in her "prison cell" and confessed that imprisonment exacerbated loneliness and longing for her mother. Ford felt like a criminal and resented that she was "confined by iron bars, and locked in with a key." She wished to be at home with her mother, and the final stanza of her poem fantasized about the day that she would return home, "never more to roam"—certainly the wish of every prisoner regardless of institution.[87] War's end fulfilled this wish, albeit slowly, for many military prison inmates but made it seem like freedom would never come for others. The South's surrender resulted in imprisonment in penitentiaries and military prisons for Union adversaries and high-level Confederate officials.

War's Legacy

Closing Military Prisons and Rethinking Penitentiaries

Imprisonment was transformative—the experience either hardened inmates, strengthening their inclinations to vice, or broke inmates, causing them to bend to their captors' dictates and reform. Released penitentiary inmates either slipped down the path of recidivism or rose above crime and rejoined society. Likewise, military prison inmates, at the end of the Civil War, either accepted the United States government or remained unrepentant Rebels. The experience of captivity before, during, and after the Civil War left an indelible mark on prisoners, leaving many unable to shake the stigma of imprisonment. Even military prison inmates bore this scar as one man who was held at Salisbury, Libby Prison, and Castle Thunder contended. The ex-prisoner concluded that acquaintances would forever identify former captives "in accordance with the enormity of the crime committed."[1] It mattered little, if at all, whether individuals suffered incarceration in a military prison or in a penitentiary given the strong association of imprisonment with criminality. Imprisonment was a leveling experience prior to and during the war, and it remained such after the war.

Right after the Civil War, federal and state officials, in addition to civilian reform groups, continued the long-standing trend of inspecting and proposing remedies for the evils of imprisonment, which seldom resulted in meaningful change. State penitentiaries again elicited scrutiny in the late 1860s at the same time that the U.S. Congress investigated conditions in Southern military prisons. Military prisons coexisted with penitentiaries for a time after the war to help restore order and punish wartime offenders, many of whom held visible positions in the Confederacy or otherwise posed a significant threat to the Union. Interest in prisons remained elevated after the Civil War, but widespread concern for the plight of inmates again receded as citizen-soldiers-turned-prisoners went home and state officials, especially in the South, turned to convict leasing to control emancipated slaves.

Although public attention faded and interest in imprisonment again manifested itself in the formation of reform organizations, the inner workings of military prisons and penitentiaries in the postwar years remained static. Officers received appointments as favors; debates swirled around the use of corporal punishment; and inmates acted up, attempted escape, or professed reform to assert their identity. The often-shrill cries of incarceration's injustice focused on former prisoners of war who recorded their personal tales of suffering in enemy hands. Meanwhile, the plight of penitentiary inmates again made for good talking points for American and international reformers, but failed to generate significant change. Penitentiaries kept the public's attention for a while after the war since many Union and Confederate veterans remained in prison and civilians did not want those who sacrificed in the ranks to suffer incarceration.[2] North Carolina politicians authorized penitentiary construction within this context. Lofty rhetoric again masked internal decay by 1870, when the newly established, albeit unfinished, North Carolina Penitentiary received its first inmates.

Closing Military Prisons

The Civil War left the nation in chaos. Federal officials temporarily used military prisons to preserve order in both the North and the South before again relying solely on penitentiaries. During the war's final months, President Lincoln further blurred the lines between civil and military punishment by designating many Northern penitentiaries—including the Ohio Penitentiary—as military prisons.[3] Concurrent use and federal control of both penitentiaries and military prisons occurred in Columbus, and was vitally important to Richmond's postwar security because of the fall of the Confederate capital and the presence of federal soldiers who were empowered to arrest civilians.[4] In their final days, military prisons held some of the war's most egregious offenders and detained criminals, both civilians and soldiers, while federal officials discharged prisoners of war.

Execution of the conspirators (Library of Congress)

As the Civil War ended, federal officials released prisoners of war and closed military prisons, but discharging military prisoners was a slow process. Federal officials vacated Camp Chase by July 1865, but had greater difficulty shutting down Old Capitol Prison and Castle Thunder since they held many criminals and penitentiary space was at a premium in Washington and Richmond. Washington, in particular, needed cells. In 1862, federal authorities adjoined the D.C. Penitentiary to the city arsenal to equip troops and sent penitentiary inmates elsewhere. They shipped adult offenders to the state penitentiary at Auburn, New York, and juveniles to the Baltimore House of Correction. After the war, however, U.S. officials needed the penitentiary to hold the Lincoln conspirators immediately before their execution, and realized that they could not close the Old Capitol Prison as quickly as they had planned, although they began to shift inmates out of it a few weeks before the Confederate surrender.[5]

Federal officials began evacuating Rebel officers, enlisted men, and guerrillas from the Old Capitol in late March 1865, leaving mostly inmates awaiting court-martial. But this did not clear the Old Capitol of all prisoners of
war. On April 10, the *Cincinnati Enquirer* reported that over five hundred
Rebel officers of all grades remained in prison, prompting the question of
when to release them and the enlisted men they had led. Union authorities decided that prisoners who posed little or no risk to the reunified nation could go home first. In June 1865, Gen. Ulysses S. Grant initiated a
move that was part humanitarian and part practical when he discharged
all wounded Rebel prisoners who swore allegiance to the U.S. government.
By month's end, only two Southern inmates above the rank of captain remained in the prison. Many former Confederates went free, but federal
authorities determined that some U.S. soldiers who violated military law
necessitated oversight and moved them to different locations. For example,
in August 1865, federal officials transferred two New York soldiers from the
Old Capitol to New York's Sing Sing Penitentiary and Concord State Prison
to complete their sentences.[6]

The number of prisoners dwindled as the summer progressed, so federal
officials prepared to close the Old Capitol and relinquish its grounds. In late
June, the Supreme Court decreed the prison and its grounds available for
auction, but the sale was postponed and the prison remained open through
early fall. In November 1865, Secretary of War Edwin Stanton directed that
Old Capitol Prison "be immediately broken up" and that Union deserters
be moved to "some other suitable place." The "suitable" locations that U.S.
officials had in mind varied: they discharged some inmates, turned others
over to civil authorities in light of the restoration of the writ of habeas corpus, and planned to send the remainder to Fort Whipple, Virginia. Federal
officials finally closed Old Capitol Prison in early December 1865, and the
London *Times* reflected on the history of the "famous bastille" as an institution that once held an astonishing 1,004 prisoners, leaving only 11 "in
duress" when it closed.[7]

Prior to its closing, federal officials held high-ranking Confederate officials, such as Virginia Governor John Letcher, Georgia Governor Joseph
Brown, South Carolina Governor Andrew McGrath, North Carolina Governor Zebulon Vance, Andersonville commandant Henry Wirz, and Salisbury
commandant John Gee at the Old Capitol. Each man met a different fate:

Federal authorities sought information from Brown in the trial of Jefferson Davis, executed Wirz, and tried and exonerated Gee. President Andrew Johnson released Letcher upon receipt of his word that he would return immediately to and remain in Virginia. Letcher was repentant enough to secure freedom, but prison authorities had their hands full with Vance, who, upon detention, exhibited defiance and tried to scapegoat North Carolina's Unionists by claiming that they shared equal guilt.[8] These ex-Confederates witnessed federal power in the nation's capital, while others experienced its reach in the former Confederate capital.

When the Union Army recaptured Richmond, federal officials took over Castle Thunder and, through it, reasserted federal authority in the vanquished city. U.S. authorities detained one high-ranking Confederate, Col. Lucius B. Northrop, chief commissary to the Southern armies, at the Castle, but used the prison mostly to subjugate the Southern people.[9]

Flames that engulfed the city at war's end ironically spared both Libby Prison and Castle Thunder and U.S. officials quickly filled the prisons with miscreants. The Richmond *Daily Dispatch* noted that U.S. authorities, like their Confederate predecessors, confined "many hardened criminals" in the prison since the city's social order collapsed with the Confederate experiment. Federal authorities used the Castle for a range of inmates, including civilians, both white and black, and U.S. soldiers, mostly deserters. As during the war, federal authorities ordered prisoners to work to save money, revive the city, and improve inmates' morals. Castle Thunder authorities routinely assigned a portion of the prisoners to chain gangs for terms of either thirty-six or ninety days. Lieutenant Leare, Richmond's chief of police, supervised the offenders as they cleaned the streets and alleys of the defeated capital.[10]

Crime was so prevalent in Richmond that federal officials delayed Castle Thunder's closing. They originally ordered the prison to be vacated on December 12, 1865, but the continued influx of inmates rendered that impossible. Union authorities finally closed the Castle in January 1866, planned to transform the prison into storehouses, and transferred its remaining prisoners to Libby Prison.[11] But while the Castle remained open, space was at a premium. Federal officials continued the practice, begun during the war by Confederate authorities, of confining individuals accused of common offenses, like property crimes and crimes against people, at the Castle regardless of its designation as a military prison. From April 1865 until January 1866, Union officials held citizen prisoners and former Rebels in Castle

Thunder for criminal activity. Their offenses included vagrancy, drunkenness, habitual drunkenness, drunk and disorderly conduct, stealing, petty
larceny, horse stealing, wife beating, and assault and battery.[12] For example, between December 12 and 30, 1865, the Richmond *Daily Dispatch* reported that U.S. troops who policed the city sent individuals to the Castle
for stealing, drunk and disorderly conduct, roaming the city without proper
pass, selling liquor to soldiers, fighting in the street, shooting, assault, and
battery. The paper reported a total of seventy-seven commitments, including twenty-five U.S. soldiers and forty-four African Americans.[13]

Soldiers who oversaw martial law imprisoned blacks, but Richmond's
white residents nonetheless condemned military rule as "degrading to the
white race." One man complained to the New York *World* that soldiers
imprisoned whites for insulting freedmen, that black men could carry
sword-canes in the street without punishment, and that if whites failed to
apologize to blacks in the event of insult, authorities carted them to Castle
Thunder to "spend some days on bread and water."[14] This editorialist was
undoubtedly pleased when federal officials targeted U.S. soldiers in the city
for drunk and disorderly conduct, desertion, or for being in the city without
proper pass, but his focus remained on the overturned racial order and how
Union conquerors treated white Southerners like criminals.

Trying to Untangle the Lines of Civil and Military Authority

In the postwar years, as in years past, officials confined individuals convicted
of civil or military offenses in either military prisons or in penitentiaries.
Individuals in Ohio and Virginia committed familiar crimes, including attempted homicide, stealing, grand larceny, assault and battery, attempted
rape, horse stealing, pocket picking, larceny, forgery, burglary, murder, in-
cest, and stabbing.[15] Many offenders ended up in military prisons while they
were still open, while political prisoners ended up in penitentiaries. After the
war, however, many inmates, politicians, and civilians demanded a clear distinction between civil and military authority and resented authorities' use of
both types of prisons. Americans ideally wanted restoration of the primacy of
civil authority. At minimum, they demanded that military prison and penitentiary officials record and publicize the number of inmates sentenced by
civil or military courts.

Individuals accused of civil offenses who landed in military prisons and civilians subject to military law who ended up in penitentiaries routinely made headlines and challenged Lincoln's designation of penitentiaries as military prisons. Americans preferred civil over military law and wanted state officials to regain control over sentencing and imprisonment. Examples of the confusion and passion surrounding this issue surfaced at the Virginia, Georgia, and Ohio penitentiaries and at Castle Thunder, Camp Chase, Johnson's Island, and Old Capitol Prison, with the Ohio Penitentiary and Old Capitol Prison generating the most controversy.

White Southerners in Georgia challenged penitentiary sentences decided by courts-martial and criticized federal Reconstruction policy, specifically the Reconstruction Act of 1867, which put the South under martial law.[16] In November 1868, the *Augusta Chronicle* reported the case of W. J. Brennan, who contested the legality of his detention after trial by military tribunal. Civil authorities in the town of Bainbridge arrested Brennan for killing another man in a street fight and he appeared before the county's Superior Court, which granted him bail. Shortly after, Gen. George Meade, military commander of the post, rearrested Brennan and ordered a court-martial. The military court sent Brennan first to Fort Jefferson, a military prison in the Florida Keys, and then to the Georgia Penitentiary after Brennan's friends sued for a writ of habeas corpus. The Putnam County Court consequently heard Brennan's case. The judge sustained the writ and remanded Brennan to the Decatur County sheriff. Recalcitrant Georgians and the *Augusta Chronicle* denounced federal overreach and, in outrage, boasted that the court left open to question the constitutionality of the Reconstruction Act. They also praised the court's condemnation of Brennan's conviction as illegal *"because the right to a trial by jury was denied the prisoner."*[17] The Union may have won the war, but the battle over control of sentencing and imprisonment during Reconstruction had just begun.

In Virginia, both military and civil courts decided offenders' fates and issued penitentiary sentences. A military commission in Richmond sentenced a man to three years in the Virginia Penitentiary in February 1866 for assault and battery with intent to kill after he attacked a man at a Negro ball. Four months later, the Augusta Circuit Court sentenced Robert Lewis, a "colored" man, to three years in the penitentiary for grand larceny. Likewise, in May 1868, the Petersburg *Progress Index* reported on a man who could not stop stealing. During the Civil War, he deserted from the Union Army, thereby robbing the United States of manpower. After the war, the

Buckingham County court tried, convicted, and sentenced the man to the Virginia Penitentiary for five years for horse stealing.[18] Civilians likely felt that both of these sentences were just, but questioned the authority of military courts to issue penitentiary sentences.

In July 1868, the Petersburg *Progress Index* vividly described the poor conditions in which penitentiary inmates lived, advancing a latent argument that individuals under sentence of court-martial should not be subject to penitentiary sentences. The paper chronicled inmates' daily routine, conditions, demographics, and the sentencing authority responsible for their imprisonment. It noted that there were six citizens in the penitentiary imprisoned by order of military commission "without the benefit of a jury." One under a twelve-year sentence, three sentenced to ten years, one under a five-year sentence, and the last had a three-year term. The *Index* omitted each person's crime, but the paper's implicit criticism of courts-martial issuing penitentiary sentences leapt from the page.[19]

The Federal Government's use of penitentiaries to house military offenders was certainly not new. But after the Civil War, the practice of military courts sentencing individuals to penitentiaries aroused public anger reminiscent of that which surrounded the 1857 Supreme Court case of *Dynes vs. Hoover*, which ultimately sanctioned the practice at the D.C. Penitentiary. Federal use of that penitentiary halted during the war and was limited after since federal officials only temporarily revived the prison to hold the Lincoln Conspirators. Public dialogue, therefore, focused on other penitentiaries, especially the Ohio Penitentiary. Lawmakers and journalists who complained about the presence of military prisoners in the Ohio Penitentiary seldom referenced Lincoln's classification of that and other penitentiaries as military prisons. His order did not reach civilians, fell on deaf ears, or was deemed invalid after the war even though the war's end did not exonerate all wartime offenders. The return to peace also did not terminate the Federal Government's increased involvement with state penitentiaries.

In December 1865, a group of Ohio Penitentiary inmates serving under sentence of court-martial attempted mutiny. The *Raleigh Daily Standard* reported that the deputy warden summoned the men to his office to reprimand them for refusing orders. The prisoners spurned the call, challenged officials to take them by force, and armed themselves with clubs. The recalcitrant men started a melee when guards arrived, which caused the warden to break open one inmate's head with a cane while guards shot and severely wounded another. The ploy ultimately failed and officials sequestered the ringleaders in the guardhouse.[20] Outsiders probably would not have condoned violence, but many civilians and politicians shared inmates' concerns about housing military prisoners in the penitentiary.

Sympathetic lawmakers and journalists demanded accountability from penitentiary officials and often required them to report the number of military prisoners confined in penitentiaries. The issue gained significant attention in late December 1865 and early 1866, and journalists kept close tabs on the experience of military prisoners in the Ohio Penitentiary. On December 26, 1865, the *Adams Sentinel* reported that the War Department ordered the release of sixty-three military prisoners confined on sentences from courts-martial, leaving twenty imprisoned. A few weeks later, Ohio state legislators adopted a resolution that required the warden to report the number of military prisoners, their names and places of residence, date and place of sentence, length of sentence, and crime committed. The legislators concluded that when furnished, the report would show a "fearful record of wrong-doing—of men incarcerated without law as criminals by the petty tyranny of court-martial."[21]

The White House and the Supreme Court also had to confront the issue of civilians sentenced to penitentiaries by courts-martial. In April 1865, President Johnson was sympathetic toward numerous men whom courts-martial sentenced to death. The offenders were involved in the Sons of Liberty conspiracy that, in late 1863 and 1864, opposed U.S. conscription and plotted to release Confederate inmates from Northern military prisons. Johnson pardoned one of the men and commuted the sentence of another. The Supreme Court also weighed in on the jurisdiction of military commissions. Ultimately, Lambdin P. Milligan, one of the conspiracy's leaders whose death sentence Johnson commuted to life imprisonment at the Ohio Penitentiary, won his case. The Supreme Court, in *Ex Parte Milligan* (1866), voided Milligan's wartime conviction by military tribunal and decreed that the Federal Government could not establish and try noncombatant civilians in military courts where civil courts remained in operation.[22]

The Federal Government, however, could legally subject U.S. soldiers and former Confederates to military law for both military and common crimes, but the fact that courts-martial mandated penitentiary sentences remained controversial. Forty-six men under sentences from courts-martial for desertion, robbery, larceny, misdemeanors, and guerrilla activity entered the Ohio Penitentiary in July 1865 to serve terms ranging from one to ten years. Three months later, eighteen military prisoners sentenced by court-martial arrived at the Ohio Penitentiary from Little Rock, Arkansas. The military court found the offenders guilty of larceny, drunkenness, sleeping on post, desertion, embezzlement, selling side arms, and serving as Rebel guerrillas.[23] Penitentiary sentences illustrated the continued interconnection between the military and civil sectors of punishment, and showed soldiers that military law superseded civil law while they were in the service.

The jurisdiction of courts-martial extended into 1866, but federal officials began to see the wisdom of scaling back military power that year, likely in light of the controversy surrounding the *Milligan* case. In May 1866, a court-martial sentenced twenty-six regular army soldiers to the Ohio Penitentiary for desertion and insubordination.[24] Another court-martial sentenced Confederate army surgeon Dr. Payne to death, but federal officials commuted the sentence to life in the penitentiary. The War Department deemed it unwise and unjust to hold Payne and other military prisoners at the Ohio Penitentiary. In July 1866, they released Payne along with fifteen other military prisoners from confinement.[25]

Although these men went free, the Ohio Penitentiary held military prisoners throughout the decade. There were twenty-three inmates under sentence of court-martial in the penitentiary as of October 31, 1868, and in March 1869, lawmakers again required that the warden furnish captives' names, places of residence, dates and places of sentence, duration of sentences, and offenses. The *Cincinnati Enquirer* denounced the military's continued power in the aftermath of war, and publicized Senator Hutchinson's resolution that demanded statistics on military prisoners. The paper concluded that there was no better cause the assembly could champion than seeing if any constituents were "unjustly held in durance vile by the authority of an illegal tribunal." The *Enquirer* contended that the victims of military authority had been "forgotten" with no steps taken for their release, just like inmates at the French Bastille.

Judging from repeated demands from state legislators, interest in this issue ebbed and flowed throughout the 1860s, but the practice continued into the next decade. The Ohio Penitentiary's 1870 annual report reveals that penitentiary officials dispensed with classifying inmates by race in their recapitulation. Instead, they classified inmates by gender and noted whether they were sentenced to the penitentiary by state courts, U.S. civil courts, or U.S. military courts. The state legislature's demand for reporting was met, but confinement continued—a good example of how, throughout the century, outsiders' demands for changes in imprisonment often rang hollow. Release came slowly and on an individual basis. At least one man won reprieve in 1870. That March, the secretary of war directed that Ohio Penitentiary officials release John Hogs of Company E, 18th Illinois Infantry, who, in 1864, was sentenced to twenty-one years at the penitentiary for an unspecified crime.[26]

Civil War Veterans: Imprisoned or in Power

Enlisted men under sentence of court martial were not the only group of soldiers-turned-captives who sparked outrage. Veterans struggled to readjust to civilian life after the war and often ended up in penitentiaries, replicating a pattern from earlier in the century. Alexis de Tocqueville noted that the disbanding of armies encouraged criminal activity among veterans after the War of 1812 since they were temporarily deprived of employment. The incarceration of Civil War veterans in the postwar period likewise spiked.[27] Many Union and Confederate veterans filled Northern and Southern penitentiaries and, as military officials had done in previous years, postwar penitentiary administrators paid them special attention. Imprisonment conferred a negative stigma upon veterans that contradicted the image that they, as former soldiers, were expected to uphold.[28] Citizen-soldiers who sacrificed part of their lives in the ranks, willingly or not, brought their military skills into prison and sometimes used them to challenge prison officials and/or hamstring the prison industrial system by slowing production or misbehaving.[29]

Postwar penitentiary officials, like their predecessors, treated incarcerated veterans the same as criminals. At the Ohio and Virginia penitentiaries, administrators assessed soldiers' service records like they judged criminals' education and family backgrounds. Officials noted whether or not veterans received honorable or dishonorable discharges, and assumed that members of the latter group were more likely to cause trouble. In 1869, Ohio Penitentiary officials recorded 198 Union and 5 Confederate veterans, of whom 191 received honorable discharge and 7 deserted. That same year, Virginia Penitentiary officials noted 44 white Union veterans and 15 to 20 former Confederate servicemen, but omitted to record whether or not these men caused any problems.[30]

While some former soldiers suffered incarceration, other high-ranking Civil War veterans received administrative appointments in penitentiaries

as political favors. Well-connected appointees often lacked practical experience, continuing the trend that began in the antebellum period and persisted
during the war in both penitentiaries and military prisons. In the postwar
period, many Civil War veterans, particularly Southerners, experienced financial strain. As a remedy, Virginia state officials appointed veterans like
Henry R. Jones, former adjutant in the Confederate quartermaster's department, to penitentiary posts since they were "reduced to poverty" and had
sizable families to support.[31] Jones was appointed in 1870, when the federal garrison left Richmond and shifted political control back into Southern
hands. State appointments of cash-strapped Confederate veterans provided
income for needy men, ensured that penitentiary management was acceptable to Southerners, and constituted a move that was both practical and political since the U.S. government denied pensions to former Rebels.[32]

Military commanders and prisoners of war sometimes received appointments as prison commandants since state officials believed that military
leadership and/or incarceration was adequate preparation for prison management. Postwar appointees lacked practical experience in penology, as
had their predecessors who oversaw penitentiaries and military prisons.
Gen. C. C. Wolcott, whom the Northern press touted as "one of the most
brilliant officers in Sherman's Army," served as warden of the Ohio Penitentiary for over three years.[33] In Virginia, Gen. John Schofield, district
commander of Richmond during Reconstruction, appointed former prisoner of war Burnham Wardwell as warden of the Virginia Penitentiary in
1868, possibly as a reward for his wartime loyalty.[34] Wardwell, a devout
Unionist, ran an ice business in Richmond before and during the Civil War,
and Confederate authorities consequently arrested and held him in Castle
Thunder for much of the war.

Wardwell's experience as a prisoner made him sensitive to the penitentiary's internal conditions and he wanted to initiate positive changes. Like
previous wardens, Wardwell's intentions yielded few, if any, concrete results and stirred plenty of controversy. His experience with imprisonment
seemingly made him uncomfortable punishing inmates with the dungeon,
the whipping post, and gagging. However, Wardwell's solution to these
problems—reviving the contract lease program that began before the war—
proved to be equally, if not more, detrimental to convicts since it resulted in
numerous deaths. Convicts could be worked to the point of exhaustion and
were regularly exposed to disease.[35]

Postwar surgeons' reports reveal the brutality of the convict lease system. In 1871, surgeon M. M. Walker noted that thirty-one convicts died accidentally while working on the Covington and Ohio Railroad, but stated that contractors were not required to submit monthly reports of railroad laborers to penitentiary officials. Penitentiary conditions, while far from ideal, were not necessarily deadly by comparison. That same year, thirty-eight inmates died in the penitentiary, but annual reports noted that death resulted from disease or natural causes.[36] Even though convicts frequently died working on the Covington and Ohio Railroad, state officials and some former Confederate soldiers praised Wardwell for his reform efforts and his promotion of sectional healing, while others viewed him as the embodiment of Yankee intrusion.

During Reconstruction, sectional healing, industrial development, corporate malfeasance, and government corruption eventually overshadowed other controversial issues, especially the rights of freedmen, and the Virginia Penitentiary reemerged as a focal point.[37] Some Northern papers highlighted Wardwell's conciliatory nature and admirable management in the late 1860s, the very same year, 1869, that Congress released its report of Southern military prisons.[38] Northern papers, like the *Bangor Daily Whig and Courier,* lauded Wardwell and stressed the importance of the Union. In July 1868, Virginia State Guardsmen visited Wardwell at the penitentiary and thanked him for "raising upon the dome of this institution that starry flag we love so much, and against which many of us fought during the dark days of the rebellion." According to the Guard, Wardwell represented the long-awaited reestablishment of federal authority in the former Confederate capital, and hailed him as an "honor" to the prison. The men pledged loyalty to Wardwell, praised him for arranging soldiers' quarters "so comfortably and nicely," and noted that never before had a warden done "as much for the comfort and welfare of the prisoners."[39] The *Whig and Courier*'s report was likely exaggerated since the meeting coincided with the Fourth of July, which emphasized national unity.

Southern papers, on the other hand, decried Wardwell's leniency and proclaimed him a menace to the Southern racial order. Shortly after his appointment as keeper, Wardwell appointed three black and three white officers and one black doorkeeper, putting blacks—possibly freedmen—in powerful positions identical to those that whites held. The Petersburg *Progress Index* implied that the racial dynamics of the prison hierarchy

encouraged softening of rules and resulted in improved conditions for inmates, especially blacks. The paper reported on May 25, 1868, that two
black prisoners, one male and one female, each began three-year sentences
and concluded that they entered the pen at a "good time" since Wardwell
recently announced "more liberal fare for his boarders." In November, the
Index again mocked Wardwell as a "great philanthropist" who aimed to
pardon all convicts and abolish the death penalty.[40]

The paper clearly favored unrepentant Rebels, resented Wardwell's progressive racial attitudes, and loathed the fact that a Southern Unionist controlled the penitentiary. According to an article that the *Index* reprinted
from both the Richmond *Examiner* and *Enquirer,* other Virginians—even
penitentiary inmates—shared these views. In July 1868, the Richmond
papers described the scene in the penitentiary on the Fourth of July—the
same day about which the *Whig and Courier* had boasted. Wardwell allowed the inmates a day of rest and invited them to sing "Rally 'Round the
Flag" in celebration, after which he urged three cheers for the Stars and
Stripes. The inmates responded "feebly," but when an "impenitent rebel"
proposed three cheers for the Confederacy and its flag, they were "heartily
given." Wardwell, hamstrung since he allowed the inmates a day of rest,
was disgusted, but did not punish the Rebels.[41] Virginians continued fighting the Civil War in and through the penitentiary, and penitentiary conditions in Virginia and elsewhere remained bleak after the war.

Postwar Penitentiary Conditions and Convict Leasing in the South

The internal dynamics of the Virginia and other penitentiaries remained
dismal throughout the late 1860s. Emancipation destroyed the South's social and economic order and Southerners used the legal system to control
free blacks. Southerners used penitentiaries to punish whites during the
antebellum and war years, but emancipation shifted the demographics of
penitentiaries. White Southerners reestablished racial domination through
detention of blacks, and black prisoners quickly outnumbered whites.[42]
Reconstruction ended in Virginia when the federal garrison withdrew in
January 1870. Sources do not indicate the number of incarcerated blacks at
the Virginia Penitentiary from 1866 through 1869, but the total population
in 1866 was 299; in 1869 it increased to 600, and in 1871, one year after

the federal withdrawal, the population spiked to 828, of which 672 were black.[43] The black population alone in 1871 exceeded the penitentiary's total population in 1866 and 1869.

The Georgia Penitentiary witnessed similar racial dynamics, and debate over convict leasing swirled. As in Ohio, Georgia state legislators demanded accountability from penitentiary administrators, but during Reconstruction they were most concerned with documenting inmates' race rather than their military service. On July 29, 1868, the state Senate adopted a resolution that required the keeper to report the number of white and "colored" inmates. Almost one year later, in early June 1869, the *Atlanta Constitution* and *Milledgeville Recorder* reported that the penitentiary's population climbed as May progressed. The penitentiary held 409 inmates, of whom two-thirds were black and 364 worked on the railroads.[44]

Arguments for and against leasing convicts to railroad companies surfaced in the state legislature in early 1869 and, come May, the convict leasing system gained steam. The *Atlanta Constitution* reported that 50 convicts were sent from the penitentiary to work on the Macon and Brunswick Railroad during the first full week of the month. The paper marveled that convicts were "hired out as fast as they come in" at $10 a head per year, leaving only 49 inmates in the penitentiary. By August 1870, high population and leasing were the norm. The principal keeper reported a total of 384 convicts in the penitentiary, but did not disclose their race. He instead praised the 1869 legislative act that sanctioned the practice of contracting able-bodied convicts to Messrs. Grant, Alexander and Company. The system saved the state the expense of detaining convicts in the penitentiary and provided low-cost railroad construction.[45] Discussion of labor's reformatory impact vanished in the debates over convict leasing. At the end of the Civil War and throughout the latter half of the 1860s, brief examples of imprisonment's reformatory power emerged from military prisons and penitentiaries, but ultimately faded with the closing of military prisons and the passage of time.

Reform in the Postwar Period: The Oath, Education, and Religion

In the war's final months, and in the months following the Civil War, prisoners either remained recalcitrant or exhibited willingness to reform, two attitudes with which penitentiary officials were familiar. In military prisons, reform meant abandoning allegiance to the Confederacy. Some inmates will-ingly embraced the U.S. oath of allegiance, but others swallowed the eagle re-luctantly or remained unrepentant. The Confederacy's defeat inspired many to accept the U.S. oath since they understood that only the Federal Govern-ment could release them from confinement. But some individuals rejected the U.S. oath and preferred incarceration to acceptance of a government against which they had fought. Inmates at Camp Chase and Johnson's Island illustrate the sharp differences between those willing to come back into the national fold and those who denied the end of the Confederacy.

Union authorities used military prisons like Johnson's Island to recon-struct the polity when they administered the oath of allegiance to Confed-erate inmates. Southern prisoners remained divided just before and right at the war's end. Some claimed that the experience of imprisonment made them even "better rebels" and they openly defied the Yankee government. On the contrary, inmates who had taken the oath of allegiance were overjoyed at news of the Confederate surrender. Federal authorities shielded these prodigal sons from the rocks, snowballs, and threats on their lives that their staunch Confederate comrades hurled at them by removing oath takers to separate barracks. While reformed Southerners cheered the war's end and hoisted the Stars and Stripes, secessionist hardliners hissed the colors.[46]

Federal officials knew that accepting defeat would be difficult, if not im-possible, for many former Confederates. They simultaneously made provi-sions to prolong the detention of unreconstructed Rebels and encouraged other enemy prisoners to reclaim the U.S. government. In late May 1865, President Andrew Johnson offered former Confederates amnesty if they willingly swore to support the Constitution, accepted abolition, and pledged loyalty to the Union. Many former Rebels, including Confederate officers, were hesitant to betray the Confederacy despite defeat, and federal officials detained these unrepentant men at Johnson's Island since it was easily ac-cessible and was a difficult post from which to escape.

Camp Chase also housed inmates reluctant to reembrace the Union, and officials afforded them treatment similar to that which state officials granted penitentiary inmates upon release. When penitentiary officials re-leased criminals, they provided them with money from the prison fund for transportation home. Federal officials likewise furnished Camp Chase pris-oners who took the oath of allegiance with transportation home, but some inmates chose imprisonment over renewed loyalty to the United States.

The *Cincinnati Enquirer* praised the wisdom of 1,470 inmates who had been released upon taking the oath prior to May 27, 1865, and noted that of the 3,400 left, only 1 commissioned officer, 2 citizens, and 11 noncommissioned officers and privates declined the opportunity to take the oath. The paper denounced these men as "obstreperous "cusses" who "refuse to be comforted" and sarcastically opined that they would find good boarding at forts Delaware and Lafayette.[47]

The amount of time that it took military prison inmates to take the U.S. oath varied, but reclaiming the government they once spurned was the only logical option, according to some former Confederates since federal agents alone could release them. A few prisoners, like a former Rebel officer privy to education while imprisoned at Johnson's Island, immediately acknowledged the futility of defending the vanquished Confederate cause. On April 23, 1865, the *Boston Journal* printed a letter in which the prisoner urged former Confederates to, "without any scruples of conscience," give "adhesion to the new order of affairs," to quickly embrace the restoration of law and order, and to use the blood that had been shed to bind the nation's wounds. This attitude likely surprised U.S. authorities since they were suspicious of former Confederate leaders who possessed the education necessary to lead the rebellion. Federal officials accordingly released prisoners of war below the rank of colonel and captain in May and June 1865, but extended the captivity of higher-ranking officers who had mobilized and led troops.[48]

Changing allegiance was not the only way that wartime imprisonment transformed prisoners. Many military prisoners also experienced religious and/or intellectual reform as did penitentiary inmates. In the postwar period, the reformation of both penitentiary and military prison inmates made for good press. The penitentiary reform program continued to wane in the late 1860s, but newspapers highlighted instances of penitentiary inmates who found God or otherwise engaged in self-improvement. In July 1869, newspapers from Macon and Atlanta, Georgia, reported that the governor commuted the death sentence of Henrietta Greer, "a negress that murdered a child to get $3.20," to life in the Georgia Penitentiary since she confessed guilt and exhibited signs of "imbecility." The governor was sympathetic to Greer since testimony was circumstantial, her trial occurred amid significant public outrage, and her counsel was inexperienced. Pardon did not fully exculpate Greer, but the Macon papers boasted that she was "smart enough to learn to read and write during her incarceration," which challenged the antebellum idea that women, especially blacks, were incapable of reform.[49]

Other states attempted to revive the penitentiary reform program, albeit in vain. In the late 1860s, the Ohio state legislature appropriated $2,000 to the penitentiary warden and chaplain for the purchase of library books for the prisoners, but this move was purely symbolic. That same year, state officials removed Chaplain A. G. Byers from his post since he allegedly told inmates that state assemblymen deemed the convicts "outcasts of society" who were unworthy of Christ and of exposure to His teachings. Assembly-men punished Byers for alleged misrepresentation of state officials, but the press reported that reform persisted. The Elyria *Independent Democrat* announced in August 1870 that about one half of the penitentiary's one thousand inmates "experienced religion."[50]

Some inmates, however, relapsed rather than reformed. In Virginia, the Petersburg *Progress Index* covered the 1868 trial of recidivist Lew Valden, a white man sentenced for larceny. After learning that he had already served one term in the state penitentiary, the Petersburg circuit court added five years to his sentence "for the improvement of his morals," which obviously necessitated more time.[51]

Military prison inmates also repeated crimes or fell into old, bad hab-its upon release. On September 13, 1865, the Elyria *Independent Democrat* covered the execution of Camp Chase prisoners Hiram Oliver and John Wes-ley Hartup, Union soldiers and brothers-in-law, convicted by court-martial of murdering J. M. Cook, provost marshal of the 17th District of Ohio. The men led a life of crime and the paper described them as "hardened villains before they entered the army" who were about to meet a deserved fate. A similar story about a recidivist soldier, Edward F. Brown of Marion County, Ohio, surfaced two years later in September 1867. Brown joined the Union Army against his parents' wishes when the Civil War began. His parents got him out of the service, but he planned to enlist in the Rebel Army and again defied their wishes. The latter enlistment never happened since U.S. authorities arrested Brown for desertion while he was ill and before he had the chance to go south. Brown spent two years at Camp Chase and, upon release, returned to Marion County, where his "reckless disposition" led him into the company of "dissipated characters" with whom he continued mis-chief. He was indicted for robbery in Washington County, Ohio, and shot two men sent to detain him after he had been released on bail.[52] Old habits, in Brown's case, refused to die. Confinement at Camp Chase failed to teach him that he must abide by both civil and military laws, and he had the opportunity to compare life in a military prison with that in a penitentiary due to his postwar offenses.

Some military prisoners, however, seized idle time in confinement and, like some penitentiary inmates, used it for self-improvement to advance their social standing once released. Such was the case with William Bingham, who was imprisoned at Johnson's Island during the war. On June 13, 1866, the *Cincinnati Enquirer* reported news from the Presbytery of Tuscaloosa, Alabama, that Bingham had "prosecuted his theological studies carefully while a prisoner on Johnson's Island" and recently earned his license to preach. Prisoners like Bingham who recognized that imprisonment could—and ideally should—inspire reform were not alone.[53]

Closed Military Prisons: Funding Social Improvement

When federal officials closed military prisons, their disposal of prison grounds or funds raised from the sale of the sites reflected the idea that reform should be central to imprisonment. The belief that prisons should facilitate reform and encourage positive contributions to law-abiding society drove the decisions that U.S. officials made when they relinquished Camp Chase, Johnson's Island, Salisbury, and Castle Thunder. Federal officials acted on this impulse and allocated resources used to construct and operate Camp Chase to care for indigent Union veterans. In 1867, U.S. congressmen introduced a joint resolution "donating to the State of Ohio the buildings, sheds, furniture, lumber, and other property of Camp Chase" to be used in "the erection of the State Asylum for the Idiotic." Representatives later modified this order and directed that materials from Camp Chase be used for the benefit of the National Asylum for Disabled Soldiers. President Johnson approved the measure on March 21, 1867.[54] The use of prison materials for the benefit of the insane echoes reformers' desire to use prisons for both punishment and social improvement. But it also continued the trend of sequestering problematic individuals in institutions that inspired reformers to demand, but fail to implement, change.[55]

Similar scenarios emerged from the closing of Castle Thunder and the auction of the Salisbury Prison grounds. In May 1865, Castle Thunder's original key was sent to New York and auctioned off, ironically, for the benefit of the orphans of Union volunteers, offering them temporary assistance in the war's aftermath.[56] Throughout its existence, Castle Thunder housed, and officials seemingly provided paternal oversight for, dependent women who lacked male oversight.[57] Funds raised from the key's raffle enabled Castle Thunder to again afford dependents paternal guidance even after its doors closed.

Another group of dependents emerged in North Carolina and all across the South after the Civil War—the four million emancipated slaves who clamored for land, labor, education, and protection of civil rights. The Freedmen's Bureau, established by the U.S. Congress on July 16, 1866, needed funding to build and operate schools, redistribute land, establish health care facilities, oversee labor contracts, and register freedmen to vote. The Bureau had control of Salisbury Prison and offered its sixteen acres to the highest bidder to raise needed funds. The highest bidder, Mr. Hinton Helper, paid $1,600 cash for the site—a far cry from what Confederate officials projected the site would be worth at war's end. The money undoubtedly enabled the Freedmen's Bureau to do some good, but fell far short of initiating meaningful change, just like the Bureau itself and its ambitious goal of land redistribution.[58]

Federal officials intended for Camp Chase, Castle Thunder, and Salisbury to aid distressed individuals, but their intention for Johnson's Island was both practical and reflective. The island's owner proposed to use two-thirds of the lot for grape cultivation to feed and provide wine for the local population, and to establish summer homes on the remaining property. The Fort Wayne *Daily Gazette* praised the decision and reported that a portion of the island would be reserved for visitors who wished to reflect on the sectional conflict or visit the graves of deceased relatives or friends. The Federal Government would slowly remove the fortifications and ordinance department, but would keep the Confederate cemetery. The paper was sure that the burial grounds would "form an attractive feature for years to come" and inspire pilgrimages and conversation about the cost of war. The Johnson's Island cemetery provoked discussion in a more passive way than the 1867 congressional investigation of Southern military prisons. This report, published in 1869, dedicated much space to the horrors that occurred at Andersonville.

Investigation of Southern Military Prisons

In July 1867, the United States House of Representatives formed a committee to investigate the "treatment of prisoners of war and Union citizens held by Confederate authorities" during the war.[59] The comprehensive report took years to compile as former prisoners living in just about every state in the union addressed one of three correspondents. Recorders collected each former captive's name, branch of service, rank, names of Confederate officers in charge, and "full statement of all the facts known to the writer touching his own imprisonment or treatment, and that of others, either soldier or citizen," and "giving as far as possible, names, places, and dates, with names of Confederate officers in charge." Three thousand responses flowed in and the committee selected those "deemed most valuable" to compile a "faithful and true official history of the wrongs and sufferings endured by the national soldiers and loyal citizens at the hands of the Confederate authorities." The committee's methodology was thus both broadly construed and narrowly biased.

The gentlemen who initiated and approved the investigation wanted to hear from prisoners who suffered at enemy hands, and the report's emphasis on the extent to which Christian principles, humanity, and the laws of war guided imprisonment fit with the rhetoric surrounding the development of penitentiaries in the early nineteenth century. But the committee had another significant goal in mind—to exonerate the U.S. government for any responsibility for the suffering of their citizen-soldiers and conscripts in enemy bastilles. Members contended that the system of slavery trained Southern "devotees to acts of cruelty . . . which the civilized world now stands against," rendering slavery partially responsible for inmates' suffering in Southern military prisons. The committee vehemently rejected Southerners' claim that the breakdown of prisoner exchanges amounted to willful federal neglect of Union prisoners in enemy hands. They exonerated U.S. officials from any guilt associated with inmates' suffering and denounced Confederate prison officials, particularly Andersonville commandant Henry Wirz, as criminals.[60]

Congress's investigation of Southern military prisons reflected similar themes that the Boston Prison Discipline Society illuminated in its antebellum reports. Antebellum and postwar committee members focused on the general treatment of prisoners, quality of the food they received, shelter provided, punishments administered, death rate, and treatment when sick. But the parallels between reports went beyond specifics—the Congressional Committee and the Boston Prison Discipline Society brought overarching context to their reports. The latter included information about penitentiary formation in the United States and Europe, and it considered different institutions like county and local jails, military prisons, and penitentiaries in one report. The congressional report followed suit. Its early pages provided context for the treatment of prisoners of war in savage and half-civilized nations, in nations informed by Christian and humane principles and guided by the laws of war. It detailed the British treatment of prisoners during the American Revolution and, finally, it categorized Confederate prisons into two classes: the first included buildings and temporary prisons, which consisted of cotton and tobacco factories, courthouses, jails, and penitentiaries; and the second included makeshift stockades and enclosed camps. This comparative approach was not new judging from the comparative and comprehensive context in which the Boston Prison Discipline Society analyzed imprisonment and chronicled the different carceral institutions.[61]

Other themes from the congressional investigation aligned with the debates in which North Carolina residents and politicians engaged when they considered penitentiary construction in the late 1860s. Congressional committee members echoed antebellum refrains when they debated the social function of imprisonment, the power of captors over captives, the responsibilities captors had to prisoners according to the principles of Christianity and humanity, and whether captors could compel prisoners to work.

The North Carolina Penitentiary

As congressional representatives chronicled the horrors of military prisons, North Carolina politicians and journalists resumed the debate about penitentiary establishment that they began in the antebellum period. Rhetoric in support of and in opposition to the penitentiary parroted familiar refrains that centered around humane punishment, the overall effectiveness of imprisonment, the penitentiary's potential to generate profit, and the benefits of penitentiary establishment compared to corporal punishment, like whipping. General Assembly member L. S. Gash penned a letter to the editor of the Elizabeth City *Pioneer* in which he echoed Francis Lieber's argument that penitentiaries ensured the certainty and humanity of punishment. Gash denounced branding and whipping and argued that the penitentiary would guarantee that punishment was "better graded." He complained that the punishment for stealing a pocketknife and horse stealing, two disparate crimes, was identical—thirty-nine lashes on the bare back for each. Penitentiary sentences for the graver crime, horse stealing, he presumed, would be longer and sentences that included hard labor could punish crimes "more equitably, and more humanely, and generally with better results" than corporal punishment.[62]

In November 1866, the *Raleigh Sentinel* supported Gash's position, with some caveats. Even after the war, the *Sentinel* noted that some North Carolinians remained opposed to a penitentiary, but many slowly changed their minds, either due to a "change in social status," perhaps referencing the war-inspired increase in incarceration and the South's subsequent defeat, or because of the conviction that the state penal code was too "barbarous or too rigid for this *enlightened* age." The *Sentinel* departed from Gash, contended that the penitentiary was necessary to sequester criminals who were "rotten at the foundation," argued that imprisonment spared offenders from capital punishment, and offered the possibility, albeit remote, of reform at little cost and injury to the public since captivity removed offenders from both temptation and opportunity to commit crime.[63]

Disagreements over penitentiary construction simmered throughout the latter half of the decade. The *Charlotte Democrat* echoed the antebellum refrain that most people in the state opposed penitentiaries. Law-abiding civilians, according to the *Democrat,* would rather see criminals whipped or hanged than "pampered at State expense in a penitentiary." This was a seemingly strange argument since, until Wardwell's tenure at the Virginia Penitentiary, few ever equated imprisonment with pampering unless military prison or penitentiary officials were trying to protect their own reputations. Like others throughout the century, the *Democrat*'s writers believed that the stigma of imprisonment was impossible to overcome. At the conclusion of sentences, former inmates were "turned loose on society with a character already so damaged to destroy all pride and self-respect." The underlying grievance against penitentiary construction ultimately boiled down to resentment of Northerners. The paper concluded that many state legislators wanted a penitentiary "to allay the opposition of Northern public opinion to our present mode of [corporal] punishment," and concluded that if Northerners disapproved of North Carolina's ways, they should "stay out of the state."[64]

Despite opposition, the new state constitution, adopted in 1868, authorized penitentiary construction and many towns competed for the privilege of housing the penitentiary. Contenders, including the town of Salisbury, parroted the reasons that led Confederate authorities to choose Salisbury as the location for the state's military prison. The first location to vie for the penitentiary was Lockville, near the Deep River, which touted its natural resources. The *Wilmington Journal* noted that the Federal Government recognized the value of the region's mineral deposits prior to the Civil War and contemplated establishing an arsenal there. After the war, the paper used this point to smear the district's "carpetbagger" representative, who pushed for the penitentiary by accusing him of desiring to arm freedmen. Nonetheless, the paper contended that penitentiary construction at Lockville would lay the foundation for the region's future wealth. Another civilian, in a letter to the editor, denounced Raleigh, Lockville's competitor, since transporting coal there for steam power would be expensive. Lockville offered coal and iron in close proximity to where convicts would build the penitentiary.[65]

Raleigh was not Lockville's only rival. In August 1868, residents of Greensboro contended that the town offered abundant timber, the promise of becoming a railroad center, a healthy climate, a good water supply, a rock quarry, and abundant brick from which to build the penitentiary. These arguments mirrored those that Confederate officials advanced when they selected Salisbury as the site for the Confederate military prison.[66]

Salisbury's residents made their own arguments for becoming the home of the penitentiary. The mayor's office offered land in Salisbury to the state and boasted that the region was replete with granite from which the penitentiary could be built and other profits turned by manufacturing millstones, posts, windowsills, and steps. The town also had excellent rail connections, abundant springs, and plentiful timber. Proponents found it odd that legislators had "overlooked what nature itself points out as the place of all places in the State for the erection of a State Penitentiary."[67] The problems of supply that Salisbury Prison's officials faced during the war were forgotten and the town's residents again wanted to host prisoners, but state senators later deemed the location unhealthy.[68]

Ultimately, these towns lost their bids to Raleigh. Salisbury's residents were displeased, but understood the assembly's logic since it made sense for the penitentiary to be located near the seat of government for "convenience." According to the *Charlotte Democrat*, Raleigh's offer of ten acres and $10,000 was too good to pass up, but this story was farcical. The penitentiary committee actually purchased twenty-two acres in southwest Raleigh close to rail lines and a stone quarry. Construction commenced in late 1869.[69] State legislators and Raleigh's penitentiary proponents were satisfied, but the institution generated criticism since state officials awarded construction contracts to Northerners. The *Tarborough Southerner* screamed that the project was an "Ohio job" since the chief architect was an Ohioan and contractors from Ohio and Pennsylvania won bids for brickwork, stonework, cell doors, plastering, carpentry, and painting. The paper protested that the "carpet bag men" treated home mechanics with "perfect contempt," but construction commenced nonetheless. The contractors heeded lessons from years past and began constructing a female wing in November 1870. Laborers worked hastily on the penitentiary since hundreds of convicts strained crowded county jails that year.[70]

Inmates moved onto the penitentiary grounds on January 6, 1870, before the main building was finished, and their initial quarters bore haunting resemblance to Civil War military prisons. Officials held inmates in a temporary log building surrounded by a wooden stockade upon which guards paced in and out of pigeon roosts. As time passed and Reconstruction ended, familiar allegations of inhumane treatment abounded. In February 1872, the Raleigh *Tri-Weekly Era* blamed the "Ku-Klux Democracy" for starving inmates. The paper contended that criminals deserved lawful punishment, but held that "*starvation is not to be found on the statute book.*" Later that year, the Raleigh *Daily Era* complained that officials punched refractory inmates and gagged inmates with bayonets, which sometimes killed them. The lofty hopes of penitentiary proponents were, as in the antebellum period, dashed, albeit at a much quicker pace in North Carolina.[71] But this was not the only state penitentiary to come under fire. As penitentiary populations rose and internal conditions deteriorated, a new host of postwar reformers criticized penitentiary operation and again urged humane punishment, albeit with lackluster results.

Conclusion

In the late 1860s, reformer Enoch Wines organized the American Association of Prison Reformers. It met for the first time in 1870 and two years later convened an international prison congress in London.[1] Reformers called attention to the plight of criminals and shortcomings in prison operation, but the rhetoric of reform again yielded scant change. In its declaration of sentiments, the American Association of Prison Reformers held society responsible for criminals and asserted that prisons should reform inmates, repeating a familiar refrain that emerged in the antebellum period and continued during the Civil War.[2] Reformers once more described imprisonment's purpose in lofty terms, but prison officials confronted the same problems that plagued carceral institutions throughout the century: allegations of brutality, overcrowding, unsanitary conditions, and hardened inmates.

Former inmates who avoided recidivism agreed that imprisonment should inspire positive change. In 1871, former Ohio Penitentiary inmate James Trimble gave a speech at Cleveland's Temperance Hall No. 184, and stated that prisons "should be made reformatory institutions," instead of continuing "as heretofore, to be exclusively vengeance-wreaking, humanity crushing dens of guilt." Trimble also advocated religious instruction, urged officers to make inmates feel that they "have a market value," and contended that prisons should educate, not degrade, inmates.[3] These sentiments parroted the concerns of national and international reformers in the late nineteenth century.

Wines's International Congress on Prison Discipline also drew attention to the issue of punishment versus reform, a subject that he considered "one of the gravest social problems" and one that generated widespread interest throughout the century in both the United States and Europe. Many state governors and other politicians rallied to this cause and urged public education regarding imprisonment since it was "vitally important to the welfare of society" and was "intimately connected with the protection of life and property, social order, and social happiness, philanthropy and civilization."[4]

The words of the prison congress mirrored the opinions of late eighteenth- and early nineteenth-century reformers. They contended that prisons reflected a nation's level of civility, democracy, and benevolence. The initial founders of penitentiaries used these same arguments to prompt reconsideration of punishment after the American Revolution.[5] During the Civil War, both penitentiaries and military prisons tarnished the reputation of the United States as thousands of inmates died of disease, deprivation, or punishment. In the postwar period, reformers articulated lofty concerns about the importance of reforming criminals and improving prison conditions. But, as Trimble suggested, a disconnect between the intentions of reformers and actual prison conditions lingered, just as it did throughout the antebellum and Civil War years.

In 1897, Frederick Howard Wines reflected on the evolution of punishment from the medieval period through the nineteenth century and posed a central question: Does imprisonment attain maximum efficiency without degenerating into oppression?[6] Consideration of this question was evident to varying degrees throughout the antebellum period. It reemerged forcefully during and after the Civil War and guided reformers' and civilians' thoughts about imprisonment in the postwar period. As in Europe, wars in the United States inspired reevaluation of incarceration and elicited discussion on how to improve methods of punishment and imprisonment.[7] The Civil War followed suit and, as Eric Foner has noted, mobilized Northern reformers to act with "a renewed sense of purpose," albeit with scant concrete results when it came to imprisonment.[8] Reformers devoted significant attention to prisons, but often got lost in their own rhetoric.

Economic, political, ideological, and cultural trends influenced the nineteenth-century vision of punishment and led to the establishment of penitentiaries and military prisons.[9] The administration, operation, punishment, and experience of inmates and administrators at both types of institutions were strikingly similar throughout the century. Lines of civil and military authority crossed during the Civil War as state politicians were reluctant to relinquish or share power with federal authorities, and postwar civilians demanded that military power recede. In peacetime and in wartime, the men running prisons had negligible, if any, experience in penology. Superintendents, wardens, and commandants received political appointments from the time when penitentiaries first appeared in the early 1800s, and this trend continued through the 1860s. Prison officials were only required to possess "high qualities of the head and heart" to oversee civil and military prisoners.[10] Penitentiaries and military prisons often differed structurally, but they had much in common, including the types of inmates held. Both detained common criminals and military offenders, and the primary purpose of both was detention despite reformers' lofty goals and because wartime imprisonment kept captives from supporting the enemy's cause either in arms or on the home front.

The establishment of penitentiaries and the consequent association of imprisonment with criminality shaped the identity of both penitentiary and military prison inmates. Penitentiary inmates surrendered their independence because they committed a crime and lived forever with the stigma of imprisonment, often with the additional blemish of recidivism. Military prison inmates could not shake the idea that incarceration equated them with felons even though military law distinguished between criminals and prisoners of war. George F. Root's popular tune "Tramp! Tramp! Tramp! The Prisoner's Hope" reflected the ideological power of this stigma. Despite the thousands of prisoners of war held in open-air stockades like Andersonville, Root's song begins and ends with an unnamed prisoner sitting in a "prison cell" waiting for the day that liberators would open the "iron door." Root himself could not resist drawing parallels between military prisons and penitentiaries in the song, and many military prison inmates fully identified with this comparison since they felt like felons whose hope was diminished, name tarnished, and freedom restricted.[11]

Prison officials controlled the lives of all prisoners, and prisoners resisted to assert their identity. Captives clamored for release and many petitioned officials for freedom by emphasizing their changed behavior, appealing to captors' sympathy by highlighting ailments or needy family members, or invoking personal or family social standing. Others challenged the power structure through disobedience and escape attempts. Prison officials directed captives' personal relationships by closely monitoring written correspondence and visits. Both penitentiary and military prison inmates and their acquaintances chafed under this oversight, but wartime captives, especially citizen-soldiers, found supervision particularly abrasive.

Many nineteenth-century contemporaries—before, during, and after the Civil War—were uncomfortable with soldiers being held in penitentiaries, and civilian-soldiers rejected confinement in both penitentiaries and military prisons. When both types of institutions became more crowded and, consequently, more visible during the Civil War, individuals both in and outside of their walls heightened demands that they be humane, and became increasingly interested in the experience of prisoners.

After the Civil War, the public remained curious about what went on behind prison walls. Prisons became a point of general public interest and, in Ohio, even became a leisure activity. Throughout the summer of 1877, various railroad agencies offered excursions to Columbus, where passengers were conducted to the Ohio Penitentiary, were allowed to see the prison's wards and workshops, and could watch the institution's twelve hundred prisoners at dinner and at work.[12] Viewing opportunities like these, and those that took place in penitentiaries and military prisons both before and during the Civil War, hint that prisons will always inspire somewhat morbid curiosity. Civilians never wanted to become prisoners themselves, but they were curious about the circumstances in which inmates lived.

Reform organizations also remained interested in all types of institutions of confinement throughout the nineteenth century. In the 1870s, the International Penitentiary Congress of London thought it appropriate, as did the Boston Prison Discipline Society, to consider all types of prisons in one report, from state penitentiaries to local jails, since the differences between them were few and far between, aside from physical structure. If military prisons had existed in this decade they likely would have been included in this report. The conclusions that Congress made in 1873 aptly summarize the administrative state of military prisons and penitentiaries from 1800 to 1870. Regarding discipline, Congress concluded that "little is sought beyond the security of the prisoner and the convenience of the prison-keeper." In the area of reform, Congress stated that many prisoners of "all classes" left the prison "no better than they entered it." This assessment suggests that prisons perpetuated a criminal class and that prisoners, both criminals and even some Civil War veterans, once released, had a difficult time readjusting to society and often found themselves reincarcerated—a hauntingly familiar refrain in the modern day.[13]

Notes

Introduction

1. John Henry King, *Three Hundred Days in a Yankee Prison: Reminiscences of War Life, Captivity, Imprisonment at Camp Chase, Ohio* (Atlanta, Ga.: Jas. P. Daves, 1904), 83–84.

2. Blake McKelvey, *American Prisons: A History of Good Intentions* (Montclair, N.J.: Patterson Smith, 1977), 64, 66.

3. Lonnie Speer groups military prisons into seven classes: (1) existing jails and prisons; (2) coastal fortifications; (3) old buildings converted into prisons; (4) barracks enclosed by high fences; (5) clusters of tents enclosed by high fences; (6) barren stockades; and (7) barren ground. Lonnie R. Speer, *Portals to Hell: Military Prisons of the Civil War* (Mechanicsburg, Pa.: Stackpole Books, 1997), 9–10.

4. Mark E. Neely Jr., *The Fate of Liberty: Abraham Lincoln and Civil Liberties* (New York: Oxford Univ. Press, 1991), 45; Lawrence M. Friedman, *Crime and Punishment in American History* (New York: Basic Books, 1993), 66. The Confederate Constitution defined treason in the same way; see *Constitution of the Confederate States,* Mar. 11, 1861, http://avalon.law.yale.edu/19th_century/csa_csa.asp. The Confederacy had similar classifications and took numerous political prisoners. See Mark E. Neely Jr., *Southern Rights: Political Prisoners and the Myth of Confederate Constitutionalism* (Charlottesville: The Univ. Press of Virginia, 1999); Stephen C. Neff, *Justice in Blue and Gray: A Legal History of the Civil War* (Cambridge, Mass.: Harvard Univ. Press, 2010), 21–22, 215; Henry W. Halleck to George B. McClellan, Dec. 3, 1861; United States War Department, *The War of the Rebellion: A Compilation of the Official Records of the Union and Confederate Armies* (Washington, D.C.: Government Printing Office, 1880–1900), Series II (hereafter cited as O.R.), vol. 3, 150–51, http://ebooks.library.cornell.edu/m/moawar/waro.html.

5. This focus dominated the work of the following authors who questioned whether Union and Confederate officials intentionally maltreated enemy inmates and the extent to which prisoners suffered. William Hesseltine, *Civil War Prisons: A Study in War Psychology* (1930; repr., Columbus: The Ohio State Univ. Press,

1998); William Marvel, *Andersonville: The Last Depot* (Chapel Hill: The Univ. of North Carolina Press, 1994); Charles W. Sanders Jr., *While in the Hands of the Enemy: Military Prisons of the Civil War* (Baton Rouge: Louisiana State Univ. Press, 2005). Historian James Gillespie has noted that 23,436 of the 220,000 Confederates died in Northern prisons, a 12 percent mortality rate; and 22,576 of the 270,000 Union prisoners died in Southern pens, a mortality rate of 8.3 percent. James M. Gillispie, *Andersonvilles of the North: The Myths and Realities of Northern Treatment of Civil War Confederate Prisoners* (Denton: Univ. of North Texas Press, 2008), 33. Roger C. Pickenpaugh, *Captives in Gray: The Civil War Prisons of the Union* (Tuscaloosa: The Univ. of Alabama Press, 2009); Roger C. Pickenpaugh, *Captives in Blue: The Civil War Prisons of the Confederacy* (Tuscaloosa: The Univ. of Alabama Press, 2013); Benjamin G. Cloyd, *Haunted by Atrocity: Civil War Prisons in American Memory* (Baton Rouge: Louisiana State Univ. Press, 2010); John K. Derden, *The World's Largest Prison: The Story of Camp Lawton* (Macon: Mercer Univ. Press, 2012); Elizabeth C. Bangert, "The Press and the Prisons: Union and Confederate Newspaper Coverage of Civil War Prisons, 1861–1865" (MA thesis, William and Mary, 2001).

6. Francis Lieber, *General Orders No. 100*, articles 15, 56, 59, and 75, http://avalon.law.yale.edu/19th_century/lieber.asp#sec1; John Fabian Witt, *Lincoln's Code: The Laws of War in American History* (New York: Free Press, 2012), 39, 232–33.

7. Edward L. Ayers, *Vengeance and Justice: Crime and Punishment in the Nineteenth-Century American South* (New York: Oxford Univ. Press, 1984), 34; Matthew J. Clavin, "'The Floor Was Stained with the Blood of a Slave': Crime and Punishment in the Old South," in Tarter and Bell, *Buried Lives,* 265.

8. David J. Rothman, *The Discovery of the Asylum: Social Order and Disorder in the New Republic* (Boston: Little Brown, 1971).

9. Thomas L. Dumm, *Democracy and Punishment* (Madison: Univ. of Wisconsin Press, 1987), 126; Mark Colvin, *Penitentiaries, Reformatories, and Chain Gangs: Social Theory and the History of Punishment in Nineteenth-Century America* (New York: St. Martin's Press, 1997), 47; David J. Rothman, "Perfecting the Prison: The United States, 1789–1865," in *The Oxford History of the Prison: The Practice of Punishment in Western Society,* ed. Norval Morris and David J. Rothman (New York: Oxford Univ. Press, 1998), 111; Rothman, *Discovery of the Asylum,* xix, 240.

10. L. Mara Dodge, *Whores and Thieves of the Worse Kind: A Study of Women, Crime, and Prisons, 1835–2000* (Dekalb: Northern Illinois Univ. Press, 2002), 266; Michael Ignatieff, *A Just Measure of Pain: The Penitentiary in the Industrial Revolution, 1750–1850* (New York: Pantheon Books, 1978); David Garland, *Punishment and Modern Society: A Study in Social Theory* (Chicago: Univ. of Chicago Press, 1990); Erving Goffman, *Asylums: Essays on the Social Situation of Mental Patients and Other Inmates* (Garden City, N.Y.: Anchor Books, 1961); Mary Gibson, "Global Perspectives on the Birth of the Prison," *American Historical Review* 116, no. 4 (Oct. 2011): 1040–63.

11. Colvin, *Penitentiaries, Reformatories, and Chain Gangs,* 1–2; Goffman, *Asylums,* 4–5.

12. Garland, *Punishment and Modern Society,* 21.

13. James B. Jacobs, *Statesville: The Penitentiary in Mass Society* (Chicago: Univ. of Chicago Press, 1977), 6.

14. Elizabeth Dale, *Criminal Justice in the United States, 1789–1939* (New York: Cambridge Univ. Press, 2011), 1.

15. Ibid., 9–10, 83.

16. Neely Jr., *Southern Rights,* 9–10, 37. Neely notes that the Confederate Congress authorized suspension of the writ of habeas corpus for "about one third of the war's duration," while President Abraham Lincoln suspended the writ in some places within two weeks of Fort Sumter's fall in April 1861, and that the suspension lasted for about twice as long in the Union as it did in the Confederacy. Confederate President Jefferson Davis declared martial law in Richmond on March 1, 1862, also suspending civil jurisdiction and habeas corpus. For broader discussions of wartime Richmond and the imposition of martial law, see Arch Frederic Blakey, *General John H. Winder, C.S.A.* (Gainesville: Univ. of Florida Press, 1990); Frances H. Casstevens, *George W. Alexander and Castle Thunder: A Confederate Prison and Its Commandant* (Jefferson, N.C.: McFarland, 2004), 32–40.

17. Lawrence M. Friedman, *A History of American Law,* 3rd. ed. (New York: Simon & Schuster, 2005), 212, 214.

18. Ibid., 217.

19. In her study of imprisonment during the American Revolution, Judith Madera notes that prisoners' accounts clearly demonstrate that "imprisonment was a leveler" as it negated military rank. Similarly, Lawrence Friedman has commented on the nondiscriminatory nature of penitentiary punishment, noting that these institutions "treated all inmates alike." Judith I. Madera, "Floating Prisons: Dispossession, Ordering, and Colonial Atlantic 'States,' 1776–1783," in Tarter and Bell, *Buried Lives,* 195; Friedman, *History of American Law,* 454.

20. Nicole Hahn Rafter, *Partial Justice: Women, Prisons, and Social Control,* 2d ed. (New Brunswick, N.J.: Transaction Publishers, 1990), 64. Much scholarly focus rests on penitentiaries in New York, Pennsylvania, and Massachusetts, specifically. W. David Lewis, *From Newgate to Dannemora: The Rise of the Penitentiary in New York, 1796–1848* (Ithaca: Cornell Univ. Press, 1965), vii–viii; Rebecca M. McLennan, *The Crisis of Imprisonment: Protest, Politics, and the Making of the American Penal State, 1776–1941* (New York: Cambridge Univ. Press, 2008), 12; Michael Meranze, *Laboratories of Virtue: Punishment, Revolution, and Authority in Philadelphia* (Chapel Hill: The Univ. of North Carolina Press, 1996), 4.

21. Dario Melossi and Massimo Pavarini, *The Prison and the Factory: Origins of the Penitentiary System,* trans. Glynis Cousin (Totowa, N.J.: Barnes & Noble Books, 1981), 116.

22. Michael Stephen Hindus, *Prison and Plantation: Crime, Justice, and Authority in Massachusetts and South Carolina, 1767–1878* (Chapel Hill: Univ. of North Carolina Press, 1980), xxi.

23. William Francis Kuntz, *Criminal Sentencing in Three Nineteenth-Century Cities: A Social History of Punishment in New York, Boston, and Philadelphia,*

1830–1880 (New York: Garland, 1988), 142. In the postwar period, the shift to convict leasing, especially in the South, raised issues of race. In her study of imprisonment in Pennsylvania, particularly of Eastern State Penitentiary, Jen Manion notes that early reformers refused to acknowledge the role of race in punishment, that race as the basis for segregating male convicts emerged in the early 1800s, and that the organization of female offenders by race began in 1814, but did not mean that women were segregated along racial lines. Jen Manion, *Liberty's Prisoners: Carceral Culture in Early America* (Philadelphia: Univ. of Pennsylvania Press, 2015), 132, 139, 145.

24. All statistics from this and the preceding paragraph are from Speer, *Portals to Hell,* 323–40.

25. Larry Goldsmith, "History from the Inside Out: Prison Life in Nineteenth-Century Massachusetts," *Journal of Social History* 31, no. 1 (Autumn 1997): 111. Goldsmith notes that the prison's balance of power was uneven since guards had the upper hand, but he contends that inmates were nonetheless influential.

26. Ibid., 110.

1. Shared Theories

1. Report of Daniel Meeker, surgeon, U.S. Volunteers; O. Q. Herrick, surgeon, 34th Illinois Volunteers; Wm. M. Houston, surgeon, 122nd Ohio Volunteers; H. J. Herrick, surgeon, 17th Ohio Volunteers; J. Marcus Rice, surgeon, 25th Massachusetts Volunteers; John T. Luck, assistant surgeon, U.S. Navy; Augustine A. Mann, assistant surgeon, 1st Rhode Island Cavalry, Nov. 26, 1863, O.R., vol. 4, 390.

2. Leslie Patrick, "Afterword," in Tarter and Bell, *Buried Lives,* 283.

3. Scott Reynolds Nelson and Carol Sheriff, *A People at War: Civilians and Soldiers in America's Civil War, 1854–1877* (New York: Oxford Univ. Press, 2007), 155–56.

4. Meranze, *Laboratories of Virtue,* 4, 14.

5. Rebecca M. McLennan, *The Crisis of Imprisonment: Protest, Politics, and the Making of the American Penal State, 1776–1941* (New York: Cambridge Univ. Press, 2008), 19, 23; Meranze, *Laboratories of Virtue,* 4.

6. Susan O'Donovan, "Universities of Social and Political Change: Slaves in Jail in Antebellum America," in Tarter and Bell, *Buried Lives,* 125–27; Friedman, *Crime and Punishment in American History,* 49, 82.

7. Rothman, *The Discovery of the Asylum,* xiii, xviii–xix.

8. For an overview of the Auburn system and its origins, see Chapter 4 in Lewis, *From Newgate to Dannemora.* For an overview of the operation of and disciplinary tactics on the Pennsylvania system, see Meranze, *Laboratories of Virtue.*

9. *Weekly Raleigh (N.C.) Register,* Dec. 6, 1810, 3; "The Georgia Penitentiary," *Georgia Journal* repr. *The Raleigh (N.C.) Minerva,* Nov. 29, 1816, 3.

10. "Ohio Penitentiary," *Alton (Ill.) Telegraph,* Oct. 4, 1837, 1; "The District Pen," *Baltimore Sun,* Apr. 29, 1852, 4; "Penitentiary of the District of Columbia," *Baltimore Sun,* Feb. 15, 1853, 4; *New Orleans Times Picayune,* Apr. 10, 1846, 4.

11. "Georgia Penitentiary," *New York Evening Post,* Jan. 3, 1832, 2.

12. "From a Correspondent at Columbus," *Norwalk (Ohio) Huron Reflector,* Jan. 18, 1831, 3; "Ohio Penitentiary," *Norwalk (Ohio) Huron Reflector,* Feb. 21, 1843, 5.

13. Kuntz, *Criminal Sentencing in Three Nineteenth-Century Cities,* 142.

14. Friedman, *Crime and Punishment in American History,* 82, 155–56, 159; Dale, *Criminal Justice,* 34; Jennifer Lawrence Janofsky, "Hopelessly Hardened": The Complexities of Penitentiary Discipline at Philadelphia's Eastern State Penitentiary," in Tarter and Bell, *Buried Lives,* 110.

15. For a report on prisons in Europe, see *Twenty-Second Annual Report of the Board of Managers Prison Discipline Society, Boston, May 1847* (Boston: Damrell and Moore, stereotyped at the Boston Type and Stereotype Foundry, 1848); for a report on military imprisonment in Great Britain, see *Twenty-Third Annual Report of the Board of Managers Prison Discipline Society, Boston, May 1848* (Boston: T. R. Marvin, stereotyped at the Boston Type and Stereotype Foundry, 1848); for an example of reporting on other mentioned institutions, see *Twenty-Fourth Annual Report of the Board of Managers Prison Discipline Society, Boston, May 1849* (Boston: T. R. Marvin, stereotyped at the Boston Type and Stereotype Foundry, 1849).

16. *First Annual Report of the Board of Managers of the Prison Discipline Society, Boston, June 2, 1826* (Boston: T. R. Marvin, Congress Street, 1827), 7, 14–29; emphasis in the original.

17. Larry Goldsmith, "History from the Inside Out: Prison Life in Nineteenth-Century Massachusetts," *Journal of Social History,* 31, no. 1 (1997): 110.

18. *First Annual Report of the Board of Managers of the Prison Discipline Society,* 9, 10, 19, 25, 28.

19. *Second Annual Report of the Board of Managers of the Prison Discipline Society, Boston, June 1, 1827* (Boston: Perkins and Marvin, 1829), 69–70, 95–96; emphasis in the original.

20. Joseph Adshead, *Prisons and Prisoners* (London: Longman, Brown, 1845), 13, vi.

21. Frank Friedel, *Francis Lieber: Nineteenth-Century Liberal* (1947; repr., Clark, N.J.: The Lawbook Exchange, 2003), 42–43, 213.

22. Francis Lieber, *A Popular Essay on Subjects of Penal Law, and on Uninterrupted Solitary Confinement at Labor as Contradistinguished to Solitary Confinement at Night and Joint Labor by Day in a Letter to John Bacon, Esquire. President of the Philadelphia Society for Alleviating the Miseries of Public Prisons* (Philadelphia: Published by Order of the Society, 1838), 27, 38–39, http://books.google.com/books?id=-iHINIeYa9UC&pg=PP13&dq=lieber+popular+essay+on+subjects+of+penal+law&hl=en&sa=X&ei=CoQxVKr6NJTDggSMtIGICQ&ved=0CFAQ6AEwBg#v=onepage&q=lieber%20popular%20essay%20on%20subjects%20of%20penal%20law&f=false; Francis Lieber, "Letter to His Excellency P. Noble, Governor of South Carolina," in Lieber, *Popular Essay on Subjects of Penal Law,* 39, 40, 48–49.

23. Incentives included better rations and/or quarters and the ability to receive parole to work. Negatively, "incentives" could involve avoiding punishment. Angela

M. Zombek, "Citizenship—Compulsory or Convenient: Federal Officials, Confederate Prisoners, and the Oath of Allegiance," in *The Civil War and the Transformation of Citizenship,* ed. Paul J. Quigley (forthcoming).

24. Lieber, *General Orders No. 100,* Article 4 (Apr. 24, 1863), The Avalon Project, http://avalon.law.yale.edu/19th_century/lieber.asp.

25. Ibid., articles 4, 75, 76; Lieber, *A Popular Essay on Subjects of Penal Law,* 22, 24. Abraham Lincoln ordered that the Lieber Code, also known as General Orders No. 100, be delivered to every field commander in the Union and Confederate armies. Confederate commanders and politicians never formally accepted the order, but informally abided by it. Robert C. Doyle, *The Enemy in Our Hands: America's Treatment of Enemy Prisoners of War from the Revolution to the War on Terror* (Lexington: The Univ. Press of Kentucky, 2010), 92–93.

26. Mark Neely Jr. denounces the use of "torture" at Washington, D.C.'s, Central Guard House. According to Neely, these torturous methods of punishment included hanging by the wrists in handcuffs and the shower bath. Examination of imprisonment in the antebellum period reveals that these tactics were standard. See Neely Jr., *The Fate of Liberty,* 210–12. Opposition to whipping in both penitentiaries and in the army occurred almost simultaneously, starting in the 1830s.

27. For an excellent study of how class status, the organization of the volunteer units, and the relationship between officers and enlisted men, who hailed from the lower classes, impacted Union military discipline and Northern concepts of manhood, see Lorien Foote, *The Gentlemen and the Roughs: Manhood, Honor, and Violence in the Union Army* (New York: New York Univ. Press, 2010).

28. Clayton R. Newell and Charles R. Shrader, *Of Duty Well and Faithfully Done: A History of the Regular Army in the Civil War* (Lincoln: Univ. of Nebraska Press, 2011), 1.

29. Edward M. Coffman, *The Old Army: A Portrait of the American Army in Peacetime, 1784–1898* (New York: Oxford Univ. Press, 1986), 42–43; Newell and Shrader, *Of Duty Well and Faithfully Done,* 3.

30. Peter Guardino, "Gender, Soldiering, and Citizenship in the Mexican-American War of 1846–1848," *The American Historical Review* 119, no. 1 (Feb. 2014), 26; Coffman, *The Old Army,* 13, 14, 15, 138.

31. Coffman, *The Old Army,* 17.

32. Ibid., 137.

33. Ibid., 19, 22; Newell and Shrader, *Of Duty Well and Faithfully Done,* 145.

34. Newell and Shrader, *Of Duty Well and Faithfully Done,* 45.

35. Coffman, *The Old Army,* 23.

36. Guardino, "Gender, Soldiering, and Citizenship," 42.

37. McLennan, *The Crisis of Imprisonment,* 4, 58–59. For information on Elam Lynds, see Colvin, *Penitentiaries, Reformatories, and Chain Gangs,* 90; *Perrysburg (Ohio) Journal,* Mar. 5, 1857, 2.

38. Melossi and Pavarini, *The Prison and the Factory,* 158. For an excellent study on class divisions and discipline in the Union Army, see Foote, *The Gentlemen and the Roughs.*

39. William E. S. Flory, *Prisoners of War: A Study in the Development of International Law* (Washington, D.C.: American Council on Public Affairs, 1942), 55–56.

40. Federal officials housed Confederate general John Hunt Morgan and his cavalrymen in the Ohio Penitentiary following capture after their 1863 Ohio raid. Morgan and his men were not subject to labor.

41. James Greenhow the Governor, Aug. 31, 1831, *Calendar of Virginia State Papers,* 10:278, in Paul W. Keve, *The History of Corrections in Virginia* (Charlottesville: Univ. of Virginia Press, 1986), 40.

42. In his study of Elmira Prison, Michael Gray contends that inmates who engaged in prison labor led lives that "seemed less harsh compared to those without work." I believe that this applies to military prisoners in penitentiaries, especially since prison officials often punished misbehaving inmates by putting them in solitary confinement. Michael Gray, *The Business of Captivity: Elmira and Its Civil War Prison* (Kent, Ohio: The Kent State Univ. Press, 2001), 86.

43. "Proceedings of the Quarterly meeting of the Board of Visitors," Sept. 7, 1813, Virginia Penitentiary, *Penitentiary Papers, 1796–1865,* Subseries C, Library of Virginia (hereafter cited as LVA).

44. Ohio Penitentiary, *Annual Report of the Directors and Warden of the Ohio Penitentiary to the Governor of Ohio, 1840,* 14, Ohio Historical Society (hereafter cited as OHS).

45. Mary C. Thornton, *A Complete Guide to the History and Inmates of the U.S. Penitentiary District of Columbia, 1829–1862* (Bowie, Md.: Heritage Books, 2003), 37–38.

46. *Dynes v. Hoover,* 61 U.S. 65, 15 L. Ed. 838 (1857).

47. Case of John Ryan, Circuit Court, District of Columbia for the County of Washington, May 10, 1861; Case of John Stevens, Edward Jones, and Tom Johnson, U.S. District Court Southern District of Florida, Dec. 24, 1860, RG 48, Records of the Department of the Interior, Entry 473, Box 4, National Archives and Records Administration II (hereafter referred to as NARA II).

48. Linda Dailey Paulson, "Leavenworth Federal Penitentiary," in *Encyclopedia of Crime and Punishment,* vol. 3, ed. David Levinson (Thousand Oaks, Calif.: Sage Publications, 2002), 1008.

49. Dale, *Criminal Justice in the United States,* 9–10.

50. Friedman, *Crime and Punishment,* 261–62.

51. Doyle, *The Enemy in Our Hands,* 3; David Dzurec, "Prisoners of War and American Self-Image during the American Revolution," *War in History* 20, no. 4 (Nov. 2013): 431.

52. Witt, *Lincoln's Code,* 22.

53. Doyle, *The Enemy in Our Hands,* 12; Dzurec, "Prisoners of War and American Self-Image," 435.

54. Doyle, *The Enemy in Our Hands,* 12, 30.

55. Ibid.

56. The British also hauled some American prisoners to England and held them in the Dartmoor prison. Doyle, *The Enemy in Our Hands,* 12, 59–62, 64.

57. Ibid., 59, 71.

58. Friedman, *Crime and Punishment in American History*, 12–13.

59. Nathaniel Shepard Armstrong Price Papers, circa 1861 to circa 2010, Library of Congress, Washington, D.C. (hereafter cited as LOC).

2. Penitentiaries and Military Prisons

1. Dumm, *Democracy and Punishment*, 107.

2. Gustave de Beaumont and Alexis de Tocqueville, *On the Penitentiary System in the United States and Its Application in France* (Carbondale: Southern Illinois Univ. Press, 1964), 53.

3. Colvin, *Penitentiaries, Reformatories, and Chain Gangs*, 81; Lewis, *From Newgate to Dannemora*, 204.

4. McLennan, *The Crisis of Imprisonment*, 83; Colvin, *Penitentiaries, Reformatories, and Chain Gangs*, 107.

5. Dorothea Lynde Dix, *Remarks on Prisons and Prison Discipline in the United States*, with a new Introduction by Leonard D. Savitz (1845; repr., Montclair, N.J.: Patterson Smith, 1967), 68–69.

6. Virginius Dabney, *Richmond: The Story of a City*, rev. ed. (Charlottesville: Univ. Press of Virginia, 1990), 34, 48.

7. Keve, *The History of Corrections in Virginia*, 2, 23. Philadelphia's Walnut Street Jail heavily influenced Virginians' ideas regarding the erection and function of penitentiaries.

8. Dabney, *Richmond*, 48.

9. Dodge, *Whores and Thieves of the Worst Kind*, 13, 14, 27; Kali Gross, *Colored Amazons: Crime, Violence, and Black Women in the City of Brotherly Love, 1880–1910* (Durham: Duke Univ. Press, 2006), 35. Edward Ayers has noted that there were seldom more than one or two white women per year in Southern penitentiaries before the Civil War. Ayers, *Vengeance and Justice*, 62.

10. Keve, *History of Corrections in Virginia*, 24, 26–27; William Crawford, *Report on the Penitentiaries of the United States*, with a new introduction by Norman Johnston (1835; rept., Montclair, N.J.: Patterson Smith, 1969), 106.

11. Crawford, *Report on the Penitentiaries*, 91.

12. Ibid., 102; Dix, *Remarks on Prisons*, 47–48.

13. No. 380, "An Act to Reform the Penal Code of This State, and to Adapt the Same to the Penitentiary System," Penal Code 1816 in Lucius Q. C. Lamar, Esq., *A Compilation of the Laws of the State of Georgia, Passed by the Legislature Since the Year 1810 to the Year 1819, Inclusive* (Augusta: T. S. Hannon, 1821), 564. Mary Patricia Walden, "History of the Georgia Penitentiary at Milledgeville, 1817–1868" (MA thesis, Georgia State Univ., 1974), 29.

14. Walden, "History of the Georgia Penitentiary," 36.

15. Ibid., 3.

16. The Ohio state capital moved from Chillicothe to Columbus. Harry G. Simpson, "The Prisoners of the Ohio Penitentiary, 1883," Western Reserve Historical Society, Cleveland, Ohio (hereafter cited as WRHS), 10.

17. Ohio General Assembly, 1831–32, "Report of the Standing Committee on the Penitentiary, Mr. Kirtland from the Standing Committee on the Penitentiary," 1, Ohio Historical Society, Columbus, Ohio (hereafter cited as OHS).

18. Charles C. Cole Jr., *A Fragile Capital: Identity and the Early Years of Columbus, Ohio* (Columbus: Ohio State Univ. Press, 2001), 119–21.

19. Speer, *Portals to Hell: Military Prisons of the Civil War,* 149; *Norwalk (Ohio) Huron Reflector,* Jan. 18, 1831, 3; Crawford, *Report on the Penitentiaries,* 127; Capt. Thomas H. Hines, "Thrilling Narrative of the Escape of Gen. John H. Morgan from the Ohio Penitentiary," WHRS (Columbus: O. P. Print, 1887), 1–2; Dix, *Remarks on Prisons,* 48.

20. James C. Bonner, *Milledgeville: Georgia's Antebellum Capital* (Athens: The Univ. of Georgia Press, 1978), 24.

21. Crawford, *Report on the Penitentiaries,* 102, 106; Hines, "Thrilling Narrative," 1–2.

22. Population statistics for the Georgia Penitentiary gleaned from the following sources: Board of Inspectors Report, 1831, Board of Inspectors Reports 1820–73, Georgia Archives, Morrow, Atlanta, Georgia; "Criminal," *Baltimore Sun,* Nov. 14, 1839, 3; "Georgia Penitentiary," *Raleigh (N.C.) Register,* Dec. 17, 1841; *New Orleans Times Picayune,* Dec. 5, 1839, 1; "Well Filled," *Newbern (N.C.) Daily Progress,* June 21, 1859, 2; Angela M. Zombek, "Transcending Stereotypes: A Study of Civil War Military Prisons in the Context of Nineteenth-Century Penitentiaries and Penal Development at the Ohio, Virginia, and D.C. Penitentiaries and at Camp Chase, Castle Thunder, and Old Capitol Military Prisons" (PhD diss., Univ. of Florida, 2012), 224–29, http://ufdc.ufl.edu/UFE0044907/00001.

23. Anna Vemer Andrzejewski, *Building Power: Architecture and Surveillance in Victorian America* (Knoxville: Univ. of Tennessee Press, 2008), 40.

24. Crawford, *Report on the Penitentiaries,* 126–27.

25. "Director's Report," in Ohio Penitentiary, *Annual Report of the Directors and Warden . . . , 1838,* 5, OHS.

26. "Director's Report," in Ohio Penitentiary, *Annual Report of the Directors and Warden . . . , 1856,* 3, OHS.

27. "Director's Report," in Ohio Penitentiary, *Annual Report of the Directors and Warden . . . , 1860,* 4, OHS.

28. "Enlargement," *Portsmouth (Ohio) Daily Times,* May 12, 1860, 2; *Huntington Indiana Herald,* Nov. 7, 1860, 3; *Bloomsburg (Pa.) General Advertiser,* Jan. 26, 1861, 3.

29. "Director's Report," Ohio Penitentiary, *Annual Report of the Directors and Wardens . . . , 1856,* 3–4.

30. *Raleigh (N.C.) Register,* Dec. 22, 1815, 3.

31. Meranze, *Laboratories of Virtue,* 4, 14.

32. "Shall We Have a Penitentiary?" *Greensboro (N.C.) Patriot,* Feb. 14, 1846, 3.

33. "State Penitentiary," *Charlotte (N.C.) Mecklenburg Jeffersonian,* Nov. 22, 1842, 2.

34. *Raleigh (N.C.) Register,* Jan. 10, 1845, 2.

35. *Charlotte (N.C.) Mecklenburg Jeffersonian,* Dec. 13, 1842, 3.

36. "Sent to Salisbury," *Richmond (Va.) Dispatch,* Sept. 5, 1864, 2.

37. Louis A. Brown, *The Salisbury Prison: A Case Study of Confederate Military Prison* (Wendell, N.C.: Avera Press, Broadfoot's Bookmark, 1980), 15.

38. Clark was governor ex officio at this time. Henry T. Clark to Hon. L. P. Walker, June 10, 1861, O.R. II, vol. 3, 682; Wm. Johnston to Governor Clark, July 25, 1861, O.R. II, vol. 3, 693–94; A. C. Myers to Capt. H. McCoy, Nov. 14, 1861, O.R. II, vol. 3, 740–41.

39. R. H. Riddick to Gen. S. Cooper, Aug. 3, 1861, O.R. II, vol. 3, 699; Wm. Johnston to Hon. J. P. Benjamin, Nov. 2, 1861, O.R. II, vol. 3, 736.

40. Henry T. Clark to Hon. L. P. Walker, July 27, 1861, O.R. II, vol. 3, 693.

41. Henry T. Clark to Hon. J. P. Benjamin, Nov. 4, 1861, O.R. II, vol. 3, 738.

42. Burton Craige to Hon. J. P. Benjamin, Nov. 27, 1861, O.R. II, vol. 3, 748.

43. Speer, *Portals to Hell,* 31.

44. Brown, *The Salisbury Prison,* 59, 63–65.

45. Ibid., 29–30.

46. Lucille Griffith, ed., "Fredericksburg's Political Hostages: The Old Capitol Journal of George Henry Clay Rowe," *The Virginia Magazine of History and Biography* 72, no. 4 (1964): 398; Speer, *Portals to Hell,* 41.

47. Speer, *Portals to Hell,* 82.

48. James J. Williamson, *Prison Life in the Old Capitol and Reminiscences of the Civil War* (West Orange, N.J.: N.p., 1911), iii; John A. Marshall, *American Bastille: A History of the Illegal Arrests and Imprisonment of American Citizens during the Late Civil War* (Philadelphia: Thomas W. Hartley, 1869), 324.

49. Speer, *Portals to Hell,* 41.

50. L. C. Turner, judge advocate, to Stephen D. Reed, Aug. 14, 1862, O.R. II, vol. 4, 390.

51. Osman Castle Hooper, *History of the City of Columbus, Ohio: From the Founding of Franklinton in 1797, through the World War Period, to the Year 1920* (Columbus, Ohio: Memorial Publishing, 1920), 47.

52. Gilbert F. Dodds, *Camp Chase: The Story of a Civil War Post* (Columbus, Ohio: The Franklin County Historical Society, a Civil War Centennial Project, n.d.), 2–3.

53. Ibid., 2.

54. Speer, *Portals to Hell,* 137, 47.

55. R. M. Gray, *Civil War Reminiscences,* 48, Civil War Collection, Reel 2, OHS; Speer, *Portals to Hell,* 138.

56. According to Lonnie Speer, Camp Chase's all-time high in population was nine thousand in January 1865. Speer, *Portals to Hell,* 138; H. M. Lazelle to Col. W. Hoffman, July 13, 1862, O.R. II, vol. 4, 201.

57. Prison records for 1860 provide insight into the most common antebellum crimes. The Virginia, Georgia, Ohio, and D.C. penitentiaries punished mostly young men between the ages of twenty and thirty who committed property crimes. The most common crime in Virginia was grand larceny; in D.C., it was larceny; and in Ohio, it was burglary. The second and third most common crimes varied—in Ohio the second most common crime was larceny, and the third was a combination of the top two: burglary and larceny. In Washington, nothing came close to larceny. In 1860 the D.C. Penitentiary held ninety-two inmates for that crime, with the second most common offense being felony, with thirteen commitments. Finally, in Virginia, the second most prevalent crime was homicide, with second-degree murder coming in third. Virginia held more violent offenders than the Northern prisons, a phenomenon already recognized by scholars. Leonard Beeghley has noted how violent crime was more common in the South. Beeghley notes that homicide rates were "very high." For example, the homicide rate in South Carolina during the antebellum period was four times that in Massachusetts. Beeghley notes that slavery had a "corrosive effect on human relationships throughout the South" since it led whites to believe that they were above the law and free to act out against not only slaves, but other whites. Southerners commonly used violence to settle personal differences, which often resulted in death. Leonard Beeghley, *Homicide: A Sociological Explanation* (New York: Rowman & Littlefield, 2003), 52.

58. Friedman, *A History of American Law,* 215.

59. *Richmond Daily Dispatch,* May 14, 1862; Headquarters Mountain Department, Wheeling, Va., Apr. 30, 1862, http://imls.richmond.edu:80/d/ddr/.

60. W. Hoffman to Gen. M. C. Meigs, Oct. 22, 1861, O.R. II, vol. 3, 54–57; M. C. Meigs to William Hoffman, Oct. 26, 1861, O.R. II, vol. 3, 122–23.

61. W. Hoffman to Maj. W. S. Pierson, July 2, 1862, O.R. II, vol. 4, 117.

62. George Alexander's Defense, Apr. 13, 1863, O.R. II, vol. 5, 917.

63. "A General Military Depot," *Richmond Daily Enquirer,* Dec. 10, 1862, in Mike Gorman, ed., *Civil War Richmond,* www.mdgorman.com/Written_Accounts/Enquirer/1862/richmond_enquirer,_12_10_1862.htm.

64. Quotations in this and the above paragraph from "Wickedness of the Destructive Leaders," *Raleigh (N.C.) Weekly Standard,* Jan. 14, 1863, 1.

65. For information regarding Davis's declaration of martial law and suspension of habeas corpus, see Neely Jr., *Southern Rights,* 37. For broader discussions of wartime Richmond and the imposition of martial law, see Blakey, *General John H. Winder;* Casstevens, *George W. Alexander,* 32–40.

66. See Speer, *Portals to Hell,* 93, for all divisions of inmates and prison capacities.

67. J. W. Pegram to Capt. W. S. Winder, Nov. 24, 1863, O.R. II, vol. 6, 558.

68. R. B. Winder to Maj. A. M. Allen, Feb. 3, 1864, O.R. II, vol. 6, 914.

69. S. Cooper to Maj. Gen. H. Cobb, Feb. 7, 1864, O.R. II, vol. 6, 925; R. B. Winder to Gen. John H. Winder, Feb. 17, 1864, O.R. II, vol. 6, 965–66; R. B. Winder to Gen. J. H. Winder, Feb. 20, 1864, O.R. II, vol. 6, 976–77; R. B. Winder to Maj. J. P. White, Feb. 20, 1864, O.R. II, vol. 6, 977.

70. S. Cooper to Maj. Gen. H. Cobb, Feb. 7, 1864, O.R. II, vol. 6, 925.

71. Special Orders, No. 47, Adjutant and Inspector General's Office, Feb. 26, 1864, O.R. II, vol. 6, 993; Jno. H. Winder to Gen. S. Cooper, Mar. 12, 1864, O.R. II, vol. 6, 1041–42.

72. Ohio Penitentiary, *Annual Report of the Directors and Warden . . . , 1836*, 2, OHS; Virginia Penitentiary, *Penitentiary Papers 1796–1865*, Subseries E; Box 4, Folder 11, House of Delegates Penitentiary Committee Report, 1824, LVA; Virginia General Assembly, Joint Committee on the Penitentiary, *Report of the Joint Committee on the Penitentiary*, 1835, Virginia Historical Society (hereafter cited as VHS); Virginia General Assembly, Joint Committee on the Penitentiary, *Report of the Joint Committee to Examine the Penitentiary, 1840–1841*, VHS.

73. Sing Sing Penitentiary opened in New York in 1826 to relieve overcrowding at Auburn Penitentiary. David Levine, "Sing Sing Prison, Ossining, New York: A History of Hudson Valley's Jail up the River," *Hudson Valley Magazine,* Sept. 2011, www.hvmag .com/Hudson-Valley-Magazine/September-2011/Sing-Sing-Prison-Ossining-NY -A-History-of-Hudson-Valleys-Jail-Up-the-River/index.php?cparticle=1&siarticle =0#artanc.

74. Simpson, "The Prisoners of the Ohio Penitentiary," 11; Cole, *A Fragile Capital,* 121. Similarly, at New York's Elmira Prison, officials employed convict carpenters for half the cost of outside contractors. Gray, *The Business of Captivity,* 56–57; Ohio Penitentiary, *Annual Report of the Director and Warden . . . , 1864,* OHS, 550.

75. *New Orleans Times Picayune,* Jan. 6, 1839, 2; "Ohio Penitentiary," *Alton Telegraph,* 1; *Huron (Ohio) Reflector,* Dec. 10, 1839, 1–2; "Governor's Messages," *Baltimore Sun,* Dec. 17, 1840, 1; "The Ohio Penitentiary," *Elyria (Ohio) Independent Democrat,* Dec. 31, 1856, 1. Ohio Penitentiary profits for the 1840s, as reported in newspapers, were as follows: 1842: $18,000; 1843: $22,670.05; 1845: net gain reported $48,313. All totals from the *Alton Telegraph,* "Ohio Penitentiary," Feb. 5, 1842, 3; "Ohio Penitentiary," Mar. 4, 1843, 2; "Ohio Penitentiary," July 19, 1845, 2.

76. Citations from this and the preceding paragraph from "Worthy of Imitation," *Weekly Raleigh (N.C.) Register,* Mar. 14, 1811, 3; "Virginia Penitentiary," *Philadelphia Public Ledger,* Mar. 1, 1838, 4; "Virginia Penitentiary," *Raleigh Southern Weekly Post,* Dec. 16, 1854, 2; "Fire in the Virginia Penitentiary," *Milwaukee Weekly Wisconsin,* Dec. 20, 1854, 2; "Virginia Penitentiary," *New Orleans Times Picayune,* Oct. 11, 1856, 2.

77. In my survey of newspapers through the database Newspapers.com, such aggressive and repeated advertising did not appear until the summer of 1857. Examples of ads may be found in the *Richmond (Va.) Dispatch* on the following dates: July 9, 1857, 4; July 27, 1857, 4; Aug. 27, 1857, 4.

78. For costs incurred by fire, see "Penitentiary Burnt," *Baltimore Sun,* Nov. 14, 1843, 1; *New York Evening Post,* Nov. 15, 1843, 2; *Boston Liberator,* Nov. 24, 1843, 2; *Wellsboro (Pa.) Tioga Eagle,* Nov. 29, 1843, 2. Profits for 1829: *Weekly Raleigh (N.C.) Register,* Oct. 22, 1829, 1; *New York Evening Post,* Dec. 1, 1829, 2. 1845 profits: "Georgia Penitentiary," *Raleigh (N.C.) Register,* Nov. 21, 1845, 3. 1847 profits: "Georgia Penitentiary," *Raleigh Register,* Nov. 24, 1847, 2; "Georgia Penitentiary," *Baltimore Sun,* Dec. 22, 1847, 4.

79. Thornton, *A Complete Guide,* 26; "Message from the President of the United States transmitting the Annual Report of the Inspectors of the Penitentiary in the District of Columbia," H. Exec. Doc. No. 45, 33rd Cong., 1st sess. (Jan. 16, 1854), 3, New York Public Library (hereafter cited as NYPL).

80. McLennan, *The Crisis of Imprisonment,* 83.

81. Ibid., 84.

82. The relative purchasing power of Confederate notes in gold went from $1.05 on May 1, 1861, to $1,200 on May 1, 1865. "Confederate Inflation Chart," in Gorman, *Civil War Richmond.*

83. Doc. No. 6, *Annual Report of the Board of Directors of the Penitentiary Institution, Year Ending September 30, 1862,* 25, LVA. Doc. No. 7, *Report of the Superintendent of the Penitentiary, 1863,* 5, LVA.

84. Georgia, General Assembly, Senate, *Journal of the Senate of the State of Georgia, at the Annual Session of the General Assembly, begun and held in Milledgeville, the Seat of Government, in 1861* (Milledgeville, Ga.: Boughton, Nisbet & Barnes, State Printers, 1861), 29, 131–32.

85. Ibid., 132.

86. Georgia, General Assembly, Senate, *Journal of the Senate of the State of Georgia, at the Annual Session of the General Assembly, begun and held in Milledgeville, the Seat of Government, in 1862* (Milledgeville, Ga.: Boughton, Nisbet & Barnes, State Printers, 1862), 25, 13, 124–25.

87. McLennan, *The Crisis of Imprisonment,* 83.

88. Ohio Penitentiary, *Annual Report of the Directors and Warden . . . , 1861,* 8–9, OHS. Missing annual reports prevented me from knowing what happened after 1861.

89. "Destructive Fire," *Columbus (Ohio) Crisis,* Oct. 24, 1861; Ohio Penitentiary, *Annual Report of the Directors and Warden . . . , 1861,* 5, OHS.

90. Michael S. Kimmel, *Manhood in America: A Cultural History,* 2d ed. (New York: Oxford Univ. Press, 2006), 17.

91. Stephen Dalsheim, "The United States Penitentiary for the District of Columbia, 1826–1862," *Records of the Columbia Historical Society, Washington, D.C.,* vol. 53/56, The 42nd Separately Bound Book (Washington, D.C.: Columbia Historical Society, 1953–56), 135.

92. Thornton, *A Complete Guide,* 37.

93. Doc. No. 9, *Annual Report of the Board of Directors of the Penitentiary Institution, Year Ending September 30, 1863,* 7, LVA.

94. Jen Manion notes that women's work was vital to the maintenance of the prison. Manion, *Liberty's Prisoners,* 37. Ohio Penitentiary, *Annual Report of the Directors and Warden . . . , 1861, 1862,* and *1863,* OHS.

95. Labor in military prisons was common and deserves more scholarly attention. In his study of Elmira Prison, Michael Gray contends that inmates who engaged in prison labor led lives that "seemed less harsh compared to those without work." Gray, *The Business of Captivity,* 86. Frederick Howard Wines, *Punishment and Reformation: A Study of the Penitentiary System.* (1985; repr., Memphis, Tenn.: General Books, 2010), 39.

96. William E. S. Flory, *Punishment and Reformation: A Study of the Penitentiary System,* (1895; repr., Memphis: General Books, 2010), 74.

97. "Local Matters: Departure of Yankee Prisoners," *Richmond Daily Dispatch,* Sept. 15, 1862, http://dlxs.richmond.edu/d/ddr.

98. Isaac H. Carrington, Report of Com. July 31, 1863; Com. Carrington to Capt. W. S. Winder, AAG, Sept. 26, 1863; BR W Jr. to Ass. Sec., Sept. 26, 1863, Record Group 249, Entry 131, Box 1, NARA I.

99. "Off for the Coal Mines," *Richmond Daily Dispatch,* Feb. 23, 1864, Mar. 14, 2010, http://dlxs.richmond.edu/d/ddr.

100. "Local Matters: Current Items," *Richmond Daily Dispatch,* Sept. 8, 1862, http://dlxs.richmond.edu/d/ddr.

101. Garnett Andrews to Gen. W. M. Gardner, Aug. 12, 1864, O.R. II, vol. 7, 586–87.

102. Isaac H. Carrington, Report of Com. July 31, 1863; Com. Carrington to Capt. W. S. Winder, AAG, Sept. 26, 1863; BR W Jr. to Ass. Sec., Sept. 26, 1863, Record Group 249, Entry 131, Box 1, NARA I.

103. Montgomery Meigs to Henry Halleck, Mar. 23, 1863, O.R. II, vol. 5, 385.

104. H. M. Lazelle to William Hoffman, July 13, 1862, O.R. II, vol. 4, 201; H. M. Lazelle to William Hoffman, Dec. 31, 1862, O.R. II, vol. 5, 132–45.

105. F. S. Parker to W. P. Richardson, Sept. 4, 1864, O.R. II, vol. 7, 764–65; W. P. Richardson to William Hoffman, June 20, 1864, O.R. II, vol. 7, 382.

106. W. H. Duff, *Six Months of Prison Life at Camp Chase, Ohio,* 3rd ed. (Clearwater, S.C.: Eastern Digital Resources, 2004), 31.

107. Michael Gray notes that inmates who took the oath at Elmira also wore "a red badge as an outward sign of their new allegiance as they performed their chores." Gray, *Business of Captivity,* 85; William Hoffman to William Richardson, Aug. 14, 1864, O.R. II, vol. 7, 591; William Richardson to William Hoffman, Nov. 15, 1864, O.R. II, vol. 7, 1069.

108. Wm. S. Pierson to Col. William Hoffman, Oct. 26, 1863, O.R. II, vol. 6, 423.

109. Chas. W. Hill to Capt. A. N. Mead, June 12, 1864, O.R. II, vol. 7, 228.

110. Chas. W. Hill to Col. William Hoffman, Aug. 7, 1864, O.R. II, vol. 7, 562.

111. A. W. Persons, as per Jas. C. Sellman Jr., Andersonville, Mar. 9, 1864, O.R. II, vol. 6, 1028.

112. R. B. Winder to Maj. A. M. Allen, Mar. 4, 1864, O.R. II, vol. 6, 1017–18.

113. R. B. Winder to Maj. F. W. Dillard, Aug. 19, 1864, O.R. II, vol. 7, 624–25.

114. Special Orders No. 209, Adjutant and Inspector General's Office, Sept. 3, 1863, O.R. II, vol. 7, 754–55.

115. Melossi and Pavarini, *The Prison and the Factory,* 158–59.

116. "The American War," Richmond correspondence of the *London Times* in *Cincinnati Enquirer,* Mar. 10, 1864.

3. Regulating Operation

1. "Second Minority Report on the Management of Castle Thunder," O.R. II, vol. 5, 923.

2. W. Hoffman to Col. R. C. Buchanan, Apr. 17, 1863, O.R. II, vol. 5, 487.

3. Michel Foucault, *Discipline and Punish: The Birth of the Prison,* trans. Alan Sheridan (New York: Vintage Books, 1995), 304.

4. Dumm, *Democracy and Punishment,* 118.

5. Lewis, *From Newgate to Dannemora,* 119.

6. Beaumont and de Tocqueville, *On the Penitentiary System in the United States,* 60–62; Kimmel, *Manhood in America,* 14, 17. Sociologist Michael Kimmel notes that "a man was independent, self-controlled, responsible." During the market revolution, the self-made man exhibited "success in the market, individual achievement, mobility, wealth," but economic autonomy was accompanied by "anxiety, restlessness, [and] loneliness."

7. Friedman, *Crime and Punishment,* 27.

8. Application of Richard Armstrong for position of penitentiary keeper, 1816, Virginia Penitentiary, *Penitentiary Papers, 1796–1865,* Subseries C, LVA; Benj. L. Bohrer and Go. A. Bohrer to Inspectors Penitentiary D.C. Washington (on behalf of Mr. H. M. Smith), July 3, 1857, and J. W. Jones, W. H. Ward, R. Clark, J. S. Miller, and Saml Bymington to Col. John B. Dade, Warden of the Penitentiary, August 25, 1845, Record Group 48, Records of the Office of the Secretary of the Interior, Records Relating to the U.S. Penitentiary for the District of Columbia, 1826–65, Miscellaneous Records, 1829–62, Entry 470, Box 2 and 1 (respectively), NARA II.

9. Lewis, *From Newgate to Dannemora,* 119.

10. Michael Gray, in his study of Elmira Prison, notes that "prison camp officers were considered gentlemen and behaved that way." Gray, *The Business of Captivity,* 126.

11. Keve, *History of Corrections in Virginia,* 27.

12. Prior to the Civil War, Alexander served in the U.S. Navy. He resigned when war broke out and joined the Confederate Navy. In 1862, federal forces captured Alexander, indicted him for treason and piracy, and sentenced him to execution. Alexander awaited his fate at Fort McHenry, but outsmarted his captors, escaped, and fled to Richmond. There he became assistant provost marshal and later commandant of Castle Thunder. For information on Alexander's naval service, capture, imprisonment, and escape, see Casstevens, *George W. Alexander and Castle Thunder,* 7–57.

13. Andrea Nicole Mitchell, "The Georgia Penitentiary at Milledgeville" (MA thesis, Georgia College and State Univ., 2003), 38.

14. No. 380, "An Act to Reform the Penal Code of this State," 588.

15. *First Annual Report of the Board of Managers of the Prison Discipline Society,* 32.

16. Keve, *History of Corrections in Virginia,* 30–32; discussion of creation of Interior Guard in Virginia General Assembly, Penitentiary Institution, 1846, VHS.

17. Prison populations rose as follows: Ohio Penitentiary: 215 in 1832; 461 in 1842; 503 in 1852. Virginia Penitentiary: 158 in 1817; 181 in 1839; 313 in 1857. D.C. Penitentiary: 42 in 1833; 84 in 1843; 114 in 1854. Zombek, "Transcending Stereotypes," Appendix.

18. "Salaries of Government Officers at the District Penitentiary, *Washington (D.C.) Evening Star,* May 5, 1854, 2.

19. *Coshocton (Ohio) Democrat,* Aug. 25, 1858, 1.

20. "Legislature's Proceedings Thursday March 22, 1860," *Cincinnati Enquirer,* Mar. 23, 1860, 3; "From Columbus, Progress of Legislative Business," *Cincinnati Enquirer,* Mar. 17, 1864, 2.

21. Sean Wilentz has noted the general shift toward factory labor in the mid-nineteenth-century United States. The development of prisons fell in line with this shift as punishment became centralized at the state level and prison guards oversaw prison labor. Guards can be considered laborers themselves. Similarities between prison guard duty and factory work are evident. As Charles Sellers notes, early manufacturing workers labored for twelve to fourteen hours a day, were isolated from rural culture, and conducted repetitive labor. Sean Wilentz, *Chants Democratic: New York City and the Rise of the American Working Class, 1788–1850* (New York: Oxford Univ. Press, 1984), 12–13; Charles Sellers, *Market Revolution* (New York: Oxford Univ. Press, 1992), 28. Numerous scholars have noted men's increasing participation in political and civic affairs throughout the first half of the nineteenth century. Prison rules forbidding political discussions must have stifled the individuality of guards as civilians became increasingly attuned to politics. Glenn A. Altschuler and Stuart M. Blumin, *Rude Republic: Americans and Their Politics in the Nineteenth Century* (Princeton: Princeton Univ. Press, 2000); Mary Ryan, *Civic Wars: Democracy and Public Life in the American City during the Nineteenth Century* (Los Angeles: Univ. of California Press, 1998).

22. H. Exec. Doc. No. 45, 33rd Cong., 1st sess., 5.

23. Ohio Penitentiary, *Report of the Directors of the New Penitentiary, 1834,* 10–11, WRHS; Ohio Penitentiary, *Annual Report of the Director and Wardens . . . , 1855,* 47, OHS.

24. "Message from the President of the United States transmitting the Annual Report of the Inspectors of the Penitentiary in the District of Columbia," H. Exec. Doc. No. 46, 21st Cong., 1st sess. (Feb. 1, 1830), 8–9, NYPL.

25. C. P. Sengstack to Mr. Daniel McGiven, Dec. 20, 1860, dismissal of Daniel McGiven, Record Group 48, Records of the Office of the Secretary of the Interior, Records Relating to the U.S. Penitentiary for the District of Columbia, 1826–65, Miscellaneous Records, 1829–62, Entry 470, Box 3, NARA II.

26. "Court Martial," *Richmond Daily Dispatch,* Mar. 11 1863, http://dlxs.richmond.edu/d/ddr.

27. For all of Elliot's orders, see Lieutenant Colonel Elliott, "General Orders No. 3," Dec. 15, 1863, Henry Thweatt Owen Papers, 1825–1920, Section 4, VHS.

28. David Tod, "Special Orders No. 212," Mar. 2, 1862, O.R. II, vol., 3, 344–45.

29. For all of Richardson's directives, see R. Lamb, "Instructions to Prison Guards" by command of Colonel Richardson, Apr. 1, 1864, O.R. II, vol. 7, A01.

30. Castle Thunder's rules from "Rules and Regulations for the Government of Castle Thunder, 1863," Broadside, LVA. Michael Gray notes that at Elmira, the procedures for serving meals "resembled those in a factory" as officers took roll call, ward sergeants marched men to breakfast in two lines, and systematically filed into

the dining area, where they took assigned seats. Officers at other prisons probably used similar strategies. Gray, *The Business of Captivity,* 32.

31. A. W. Persons, General Orders No. 6, Mar. 15, 1864, O.R. II, vol. 6, 1054; R. D. Chapman, General Orders No. 37, May 23, 1864, O.R. II, vol. 7, 159.

32. Roger Pickenpaugh notes that Union guards experienced the same conditions—cold weather, poor quarters, illness, and boredom—as did Confederate inmates. Pickenpaugh, *Captives in Gray,* 132–34. Clayton Newell and Charles Shrader note that recruiting for the Regular Army was a challenge by 1864, and that Regular regiments were "depleted to the point where they had to be withdrawn from the field to perform such noncombat missions as guarding prisoners or quelling riots." Newell and Shrader, *Of Duty Well and Faithfully Done,* xiv.

33. David Tod to William Hoffman, July 10, 1862, O.R. II, vol. 4, 164.

34. Henry B. Carrington to Adjutant General Thomas, May 28, 1862, O.R. II, vol. 3, 605.

35. H. M. Lazelle to William Hoffman, July 13, 1862, O.R. II, vol. 4, 199.

36. Gustav C. E. Weber to W. A. Hammond, Aug. 14, 1862, O.R. II, vol. 4, 389. I assume that the guard force was eleven hundred. The National Park Service lists the strength of one regiment as ten companies, or eleven hundred officers and men. See "Gettysburg National Military Park: Army Organization during the Civil War," www .nps.gov/archive/gett/getttour/armorg.htm.

37. W. Hoffman to L. Thomas, Sept. 10, 1862, O.R. II, vol. 4, 504.

38. Population estimates are as follows: 1,600 inmates were listed on Aug. 14, 1862, and 723 inmates were listed on Oct. 27, 1862. See, respectively, Gustav C. E. Weber to W. A. Hammond, Aug. 14, 1862, O.R. II, vol. 4, 389; H. W. Freedly to William Hoffman, Oct. 27, 1862, O.R. II, vol. 4, 659–60; Guard estimate from William Hoffman to H. W. Freedly, Oct. 15, 1862, O.R. II, vol. 4, 624–25.

39. William Hoffman to H. W. Freedly, Oct. 15, 1862, O.R. II, vol. 4, 624–25.

40. H. M. Lazelle to William Hoffman, Dec. 31, 1862, O.R. II, vol. 5, 133. For information on the 88th Ohio, see Larry Stevens, "88th Ohio Infantry Compiled by Larry Stevens," www.ohiocivilwar.com cw88.html.

41. F. S. Parker to W. P. Richardson, Sept. 4, 1864, O.R. II, vol. 7, 764–65.

42. W. Hoffman to Maj. W. S. Pierson, Dec. 28, 1861, O.R. II, vol. 3, 171; Wm. Hoffman to Maj. W. S. Pierson, June 16, 1862, O.R. II, vol. 4, 89; H. M. Lazelle to Col. W. Hoffman, July 10, 1862, O.R. II, vol. 4, 167–68; W. Hoffman to Brig. Gen. L. Thomas, Nov. 11, 1863, O.R. II, vol. 6, 500.

43. Thos. P. Turner to Brig. Gen. J. H. Winder, May 25, 1864, and H. Wirz to Maj. Thomas P. Turner, May 8, 1864, O.R. II, vol. 7, 168–71.

44. R. B. Winder to A. R. Lawton, June 10, 1864, O.R. II, vol. 7, 222; J. H. Winder to General Bragg, June 20, 1864, O.R. II, vol. 7, 386; Jno. H. Winder to Gen. S. Cooper, June 24, 1864, O.R. II, vol. 7, 410–11; Jno. H. Winder, Special Orders No. 1, Jan. 2, 1865, O.R. II, vol. 8, 12; Jno. Winder to Gen. S. Cooper, Jan. 24, 1865, O.R. II, vol. 8, 126–27.

45. "Statement of Prisoners of War on hand at the Following Camp Prisons, etc., up to the latest received dates," O.R. II, vol. 8, 174; Guard Reports 1864–65, Reports for

Feb. 3, 1865, Apr. 10, 1865, and Apr. 19, 1865, Record Group 393, Pt. 4, E 2136, Nos. 311 B, 311/797 DW, NARA I.

46. Guard Reports 1864–65, Reports for Feb. 3, 1865, Apr. 10, 1865, and Apr. 19, 1865, Record Group 393, Pt. 4, E 2136, Nos. 311 B, 311/797 DW, NARA I.

47. William S. Roberts, *A Discourse, Before the Officers of the Ohio Penitentiary, On the First Sabbath in February, 1852,* WRHS.

48. Nancy Isenberg, *Sex and Citizenship in Antebellum America* (Chapel Hill: Univ. of North Carolina Press, 1998), 105; Kimmel, *Manhood in America,* 14, 17.

49. For information on Alexander's appointment, see Casstevens, *George W. Alexander,* 44. For Castle Thunder's brutal reputation, see Speer, *Portals to Hell,* 94.

50. Sandra V. Parker, *Richmond's Civil War Prisons,* 2d ed. (Lynchburg, Va.: H. E. Howard, 1990), 33; G. W. Alexander to the Honorable Committee of the House of Representatives, CSA, Apr. 13, 1863, O.R. II, vol. 5, 916; Majority Report of the Committee of Congress to Investigate the Management of Castle Thunder, May 1, 1863, O.R. II, vol. 5, 919.

51. "Castle Thunder Items," *Richmond Examiner,* June 30, 1864.

52. Philip R. Shriver and Donald J. Breen, *Ohio's Military Prisons in the Civil War* (Columbus: Ohio State Univ. Press for the Ohio Historical Society, 1964), 8; W. Dennison to Hon. Simon Cameron, Aug. 14, 1861, O.R. II, vol. 2, 42.

53. Shriver and Breen, *Ohio's Military Prisons in the Civil War,* 8.

54. Speer, *Portals to Hell,* 79–80.

55. B. F. Hoffman to Colonel Hoffman, Feb. 7, 1862, O.R. II, vol. 2, 211–12; David Tod to Hon. William Seward, Jan. 28, 1862, O.R. II, vol. 3, 219; M. Welker to Hon. Simon Cameron, Oct. 3, 1861, O.R. II, vol. 3, 48.

56. David Tod to Major General Halleck, Mar. 28, 1862, O.R. II, vol. 3, 408; David Tod to General Halleck, Apr. 8, 1862, and H. W. Halleck to Governor Tod, Apr. 8, 1862, O.R. II, vol. 3, 433.

57. C. P. Buckingham, Special Orders No. 202, Feb. 27, 1862, O.R. II, vol. 3, 334; "The Prisoners at Columbus—How They Are to Be Treated," *New York Times,* Mar. 9, 1862, 2–3; David Tod, Special Orders No. 212, Mar. 2, 1862, O.R. II, vol. 3, 344–45.

58. For Hoffman's approval and Tod's orders, see R. Jones to Brig. Gen. L. Thomas, Apr. 6, 1862, O.R. II, vol. 3, 427–29; N. A. Reed (enclosures), "To the President of the United States," Apr. 26, 1862, O.R. II, vol. 3, 498–500.

59. James B. Finley, *Memorials of Prison Life* (1853; repr., New York: Arno Press, 1974), 21.

60. Shriver and Breen, *Ohio's Military Prisons in the Civil War,* 12–13.

61. E. M. Stanton to Major General Halleck, Mar. 30, 1862, O.R. II, vol. 3, 410–11; David Tod to Edwin Stanton, Mar. 31, 1862, O.R. II, vol. 3, 412; "Colonel Moody," *Columbus Crisis,* Apr. 30, 1862.

62. H. M. Lazelle to William Hoffman, July 13, 1862, O.R. II, vol. 4, 195–208; Speer, *Portals to Hell,* 80–81.

63. H. M. Lazelle to William Hoffman, July 13, 1862, O.R. II, vol. 4, 195–208.

64. Speer, *Portals to Hell,* 137.

65. John F. Marsh to William Hardee, May 3, 1864, O.R. II, vol. 7, 108–9.

66. The Confederacy also had a commissary general of prisoners. Gen. John H. Winder held the post from November 21, 1861 until early 1864. After Winder resigned, the South's prison system deteriorated. On June 6, 1864, Lt. Col. Archer Anderson, who served as assistant adjutant general for the post of Richmond, complained about the lack of organization in the Confederacy's prison system. He noted that Winder, during his tenure as commissary general, "had a general supervision over all the military prisons of the country," a function not retained by Winder's successor, Major Carrington. Anderson noted that "nobody knows exactly how many prisoners of war we have in confinement in the different prisons," and that "no officer is charged with the management of the whole." Archer Anderson to Gen. Braxton Bragg, June 6, 1864, O.R. II, vol. 7, 206.

67. Henry T. Clark to Hon. J. P. Benjamin, Jan. 9, 1862, O.R. II, vol. 3, 767–68.

68. B. Craven to Hon. Secretary of War, Dec. 20, 1861, O.R. II, vol. 3, 758.

69. J. P. Benjamin to Capt. B. Craven, Dec. 21, 1861, O.R. II, vol. 3, 760.

70. Citations for this and the above paragraph from Henry T. Clark to Hon. George W. Randolph, May 2, 1862, O.R. II, vol. 3, 861–62.

71. James G. Ramsay to Hon. J. A. Seddon, Nov. 15, 1864, and Jno. I. Shaver et al. to Hon. James A. Seddon (enclosure), O.R. II, vol. 7, 1128–30; James A. Seddon to Hon. J. G. Ramsay, Nov. 21, 1864, O.R. II, vol. 7, 1151.

72. Isaiah H. White to Surgeon General S. P. Moore, Apr. 26, 1864, O.R. II, vol. 7, 91; Jno. Withers, Special Orders No. 100, Apr. 29, 1864, O.R. II, vol. 7, 99. Inspection reports: Howell Cobb to Gen. S. Cooper, May 5, 1864, plus enclosures, O.R. II, vol. 7, 119–21; Isaiah H. White to Captain Bowie, May—, 1864, O.R. II, vol. 7, 124–25; Thos. P. Turner to Brig. Gen. J. H. Winder, plus enclosures, May 25, 1864, O.R. II, vol. 7, 167–71; R. H. Chilton to Lt. Col. John S. Saunders, Nov. 26, 1864, O.R. II, vol. 7, 1162–63.

73. Lewis, *From Newgate to Dannemora*, 91; Cole, *A Fragile Capital*, 122.

74. Ohio Penitentiary, *Annual Report of the Director and Wardens . . . , 1840*, 14, OHS.

75. J. H. Matthews, *Historical Reminiscences of the Ohio Penitentiary: From Its Erection in 1835 to the Present Time, a Descriptive View of the Interior and Its System of Government, Modes of Punishment, Brief Sketches of the Prisoner's Life, Escapes, Noted Criminals* (Columbus, Ohio: Chas. M. Cott, 1884), 18–19, 22; H. Exec. Doc. No. 46, 21st Cong., 1st sess., Rules and Regulations (Feb. 1, 1830), NYPL.

76. McLennan, *The Crisis of Imprisonment*, 69.

77. Ohio Penitentiary, *Annual Report of the Director and Wardens . . . , 1855*, 50–51, OHS; H. Exec. Doc. No. 46, 21st Cong., 1st sess., *Duties of Convicts* (Feb. 1, 1830), NYPL; Virginia Penitentiary, *Penitentiary Papers, 1796–1865* Subseries C, Box 3, LVA. The Virginia Penitentiary did not admit visitors, since it interfered with discipline. Letters could not pass more often than three months and only through the superintendent. The Virginia prison also had a classification system that ordered prisoners' lives and afforded varying privileges. The structure of the system

resembled a grading scale used in schools. It divided inmates' sentences into thirds and encouraged prisoners to pass certain standards to advance to the next level and eventually obtain release. This classification system encouraged and rewarded good behavior by promoting convicts to the next class prior to the expiration of a third of their term of imprisonment. Officers could demote inmates a grade level for poor conduct. Prison officials also punished inmates with periods of solitary confinement, terms in the dungeon, or whippings overseen by the superintendent and administered in private. Prisoners in the lower two classes, which respectively constituted the first and second thirds of the prison sentence, could not speak with the keeper without the approval of the assistant keeper, his immediate subordinate. Prisoners of the highest class could contact the keeper, thus readying themselves for readmittance to civilian life by having the privilege of communicating with superiors restored. See Crawford, *Report on the Penitentiaries,* 108.

78. For watches cataloged at Andersonville, see Henry Wirz, receipt list from R. B. Winder, July 1, 1864, O.R. II, vol. 7, 432. For Carrington's efforts to track inmates' money, see Is. H. Carrington to Hon. James A. Seddon, July 12, 1864, O.R. II, vol. 7, 460–61. Commandant William Wood of the Old Capitol Prison was to forward civilian inmates' money to John Mulford, who manned the exchange vessel on the James River. See John E. Mulford to Col. W. Hoffman, Mar. 20, 1863, O.R. II, vol. 5, 375–76. The quartermaster stored inmates' personal items at Salisbury. See W. M. Gardner to Gen. Braxton Bragg, Oct. 14, 1864, O.R. II, vol. 7, 986–87. Quartermasters or commandants usually held inmates' private property and guards stored inmates' money unless it was a large amount, in which case guards could use it to support their army and the war effort. Flory, *Prisoners of War,* 97–98. There is no definition of what constitutes a "large amount" of money.

79. W. Hoffman to Maj. W. S. Pierson, July 2, 1862, O.R. II, vol. 4, 117; W. Hoffman to Brig. Gen. John S. Mason, July 8, 1863, O.R. II, vol. 6, 93.

80. For Old Capitol Prison record keeping, see W. Hoffman to W. P. Wood, Apr. 11, 1863, O.R. II, vol. 5, 466; William P. Wood to Col. W. Hoffman, Apr. 13, 1863, O.R. II, vol. 5, 479. For Andersonville, see, Jno. Withers, Special Orders No. 59, Mar. 11, 1864, O.R. II, vol. 6, 1038; W. S. Winder, Special Orders No. 109, June 29, 1864, O.R. II, vol. 7, 400–401.

81. Information regarding rules and regulations from David Tod, "Special Orders No. 212"; William Hoffman, "Circular April 20, 1864," O.R. II, vol. 7, 72–75; "Rules and Regulations for the Government of Castle Thunder," 186. Inmates at Johnson's Island and Andersonville were also organized into messes for roll call and ration distribution.

82. See Speer, *Portals to Hell,* 93, for divisions of inmates at Castle Thunder.

83. D. A. Mahoney, *The Prisoner of State* (New York: Carleton, 1863), 152–59.

84. Stuart Banner, *The Death Penalty: An American History* (Cambridge, Mass.: Harvard Univ. Press, 2002), 148–49; Louis Masur, *Rites of Execution: Capital Punishment and the Transformation of American Culture, 1776–1865* (New York: Oxford Univ. Press, 1989).

85. As noted in Chapter 1, Mark Neely Jr. denounced the use of "torture" at D.C. Penitentiary's Central Guard House. According to Neely, these torturous methods of punishment included hanging by the wrists in handcuffs and the shower bath. Examination of imprisonment in the antebellum period reveals that these tactics were standard. Neely Jr., *The Fate of Liberty*, 210–12. Colvin and Meranze have contended that penitentiaries were deemed crucial to democracy since they restrained state power. Colvin, *Penitentiaries, Reformatories, and Chain Gangs,* 24–25; Meranze, *Laboratories of Virtue,* 14–15.

86. McLennan contends that whipping tipped the balance of power in the guards' favor, while Goldsmith acknowledges the uneven balance of power, but contends that inmates wielded influence. McLennan, *The Crisis of Imprisonment,* 71; Goldsmith, "History from the Inside Out," 111.

87. John F. Callan, *The Military Laws of the United States, Relating to the Army, Volunteers, Militia, and to Bounty Lands and Pensions, from the Foundation of the Government to the Year 1863* (Philadelphia: George W. Childs, 1863), 190–91.

88. Walden, "History of the Georgia Penitentiary at Milledgeville" (MA thesis, Georgia State Univ., 1974), 56–57; Crawford, *Report on Penitentiaries,* 107.

89. Ohio Penitentiary, *Annual Report of the Director and Wardens . . . , 1855,* 50.

90. H. Exec. Doc. No. 49, 22nd Cong., 2d sess., 2.

91. H. Exec. Doc. No. 49, 22nd Cong., 2d sess., 6–7; H. Exec. Doc. No. 46, 21st Cong., 1st sess., *Rules and Regulations,* 3; "Message of the President of the United States, Transmitting the Seventh Annual Report of the Inspectors of the Penitentiary," H. Exec. Doc. No. 81, 24th Cong., 1st sess. (Jan. 28, 1836), 2, NYPL.

92. H. Exec. Doc. No. 81, 24th Cong., 1st sess., 5; emphasis in the original.

93. Dix, *Remarks on Prisons,* 13; emphasis in the original.

94. Ohio Penitentiary, *Annual Report of the Directors and Warden . . . , 1844,* 5–6, OHS; emphasis in the original.

95. Finley, *Memorials of Prison Life,* 106–7. For Finley's antislavery opinions, see pp. 44–45. Friedman, *Crime and Punishment,* 53. The constant supervision and physical punishment that slaves endured, according to James Horton, reminded slaves of their "inability to control [his or her] life." James Oliver Horton, "Freedom's Yoke: Gender and Conventions Among Antebellum Free Blacks," *Feminist Studies* 12, no. 1 (Spring 1986): 53; Jim Cullen, "'I's a Man Now': Gender and African American Men," in *Divided Houses: Gender and the Civil War,* ed. Catherine Clinton and Nina Silber (New York: Oxford Univ. Press, 1992), 90. Distancing the prison program from slavery by banishing whipping emphasized that convicts, although detained, were still above slaves, although both groups remained outside the body politic. Isenberg, *Sex and Citizenship,* 105. Isenberg contends that "children, blacks, slaves, infidels, Indians, resident foreigners, lunatics, convicts, and paupers" had no political value. Lorien Foote notes that officers used violence to enforce obedience on the battlefield, but that enlisted men rejected corporal punishment. Foote, *The Gentlemen and the Roughs,* 124, 127.

96. Ohio Penitentiary, *Annual Report of the Director and Wardens . . . , 1856,* 4.

97. Ohio Penitentiary, *Annual Report of the Director and Wardens . . . , 1856,* 4; emphasis in the original; Ohio Penitentiary, *Annual Report of the Director and Wardens . . . , 1858,* 11–12, 37, OHS.

98. "House Investigation of the Conditions at Castle Thunder, Testimony of Stephen Childrey," O.R. II, vol. 5, 886.

99. "Majority Report of the Committee of Congress to Investigate the Management of Castle Thunder," submitted by W. R. Smith, O.R. II, vol. 5, 919–20.

100. Simpson, "The Prisoners of the Ohio Penitentiary," 32–33; Ohio Penitentiary, *Annual Report of the Director and Wardens . . . , 1861,* 8, OHS.

101. Ohio Penitentiary, *Annual Report of the Director and Wardens . . . , 1861,* 3, OHS.

102. General Orders No. 100, Art. 77, 1863.

103. John P. Sherburne to Major Doster, May 19, 1862, O.R. II, vol. 3, 554.

104. A. M. Clark to William Hoffman, Nov. 7, 1863, O.R. II, vol. 6, 479–80; Wm. W. Orme to Edwin Stanton, Dec. 7, 1863, O.R. II, vol. 6, 661.

105. David Tod to Hon. E. M. Stanton, Oct. 21, 1863, O.R. II, vol. 6, 402; P. H. Watson to Gov. David Tod, Oct. 23, 1863, O.R. II, vol. 6, 415. Guards at the following posts also received the same number of revolvers and rounds of ammunition: Camp Chase, Camp Douglas, Camp Morton, Rock Island, and Point Lookout; see Wm. Hoffman to Hon. E. M. Stanton, Nov. 27, 1863, O.R. II, vol. 6, 584–85.

106. Peace Democrats generally opposed the war and Lincoln's suspension of habeas corpus. Ohio authorities uncovered a plot afoot among Peace Democrats in Ohio to liberate and arm inmates at Camp Chase and Johnson's Island. For information on the Peace Democrats, see Frank L. Klement, *The Copperheads in the Middle West* (Gloucester, Mass.: P. Smith, 1972); Jennifer L. Weber, *Copperheads: The Rise and Fall of Lincoln's Opponents in the North* (New York: Oxford Univ. Press, 2006). For information on the foiled Peace Democrat plot, see Angela M. Zombek, "Camp Chase Prison: A Study of Power and Resistance on the Northern Home Front, 1863," *Ohio History* 118 (Aug. 2011): 24–48.

107. A. H. Poten to W. Wallace, Jan. 17, 1864, O.R. II, vol. VI, 854.

108. W. Hoffman to E. M. Stanton, Mar. 17, 1864, O.R. II, vol. VI, 868.

109. Lamb, "Instructions to Prison Guards," A01.

110. Doc. No. 7, *Report of the Superintendent of the Penitentiary, 1863,* 7, LVA.

111. Record Group 48, MLR A1–475, *Register of Punishments, 1831–1862,* NARA II.

112. Gillispie, *Andersonvilles of the North,* 41–42.

113. Lincoln closed the D.C. Penitentiary in September 1862. Punishments and infractions at the D.C. Penitentiary are from Record Group 48, MLR A1–475, *Register of Punishments, 1831–1862,* punishments dated from Apr. 29, 1861 to July 6, 1862, NARA II.

114. The population of the D.C. Penitentiary peaked at 330 in 1862. This was greater than any year in the antebellum period. See Zombek, "Transcending Stereotypes," Appendix.

115. See, for example, James Wadsworth to superintendent of Old Capitol Prison, May 22, 1862, O.R. II, vol. III, 571; Robert H. Tyler to Col. Robert Ould, Oct. 8, 1862,

O.R. II, vol. III, 362; Treatment of Prisoners in Castle Thunder Evidence Taken before the Committee of the House of Representatives of the Confederate States to Investigate the Treatment of Prisoners at Castle Thunder, Apr. 11, 1863, O.R. II, vol. 5, 871–915. Marshall, *American Bastille*, 327; James Roberts Gilmore, *Patriot Boys and Prison Pictures* (Boston: Ticknor & Fields, 1886), 247; John L. Ransom, *Andersonville Diary: Escape and List of the Dead, with Name, Co., Regiment, Date of Death and No. of Grave in Cemetery* (1881; repr., DSI Digital Reproduction, 2003), 14, 23, 30, 42, 52, 54, 69, 77–78, 86.

116. Record Group 48, MLR A1–475, *Register of Punishments, 1831–1862,* NARA II.

117. In their assessment of masculinity in the American Revolution, Stephan Dudink and Karen Hagemann assert that American Revolutionaries fashioned themselves after "the model of the virtuous citizen-soldier who was willing to sacrifice all for his liberty and that of the republic." The republican masculinity of the militias "centered around a masculinity of independence that connected the individual citizen to the collective activities of politics and war," upholding the virtue of soldiers. Stephan Dudink and Karen Hagemann, "Masculinity in Politics and War in the Age of Democratic Revolutions, 1750–1850," in *Masculinities in Politics and War: Gendering Modern History,* ed. Stephan Dudink, Karen Hagemann, and John Tosh (New York: Manchester Univ. Press, 2004), 7–8. James McPherson asserts that Civil War soldiers enlisted and continued fighting due partly to ideals of masculinity. McPherson contends that "duty and honor were closely linked to concepts of masculinity in Victorian America" and that war was a test of manhood as soldiers desired to prove their manliness and honor under fire and were supported by civilians at home for their sacrifice. See James M. McPherson, *For Cause and Comrades: Why Men Fought in the Civil War* (New York: Oxford Univ. Press, 1997), 25, 31.

118. Record Group 48, MLR A1–475, *Register of Punishments, 1831–1862,* Box 1, Punishments 1831–47, Orders 1851–54, NARA II.

119. Cloyd, *Haunted by Atrocity,* 60.

120. Michael Kimmel notes that the self-made man was defined by "success in the market, individual achievement, mobility, and wealth," characteristics that contrasted sharply with the army's strict scheduling and discipline. See Kimmel, *Manhood in America,* 17.

121. Case No. 1073, William Fahey, Feb. 17, 1862, Record Group 48, Entry 473, Box 4, NARA II.

122. For branding example, see Case 1043, Pvt. Walter T. Bell of Co. A 1st Battalion, 11th Infantry, and Case 1042, James Rea, Dec. 10, 1862. For a list of general punishments, see Court Martial Records, RG 48, MLR A1–475, *Register of Punishments, 1831–1862,* NARA II.

123. H. Exec. Doc. No. 46, 21st Cong., 1st sess., *Rules and Regulations* (Feb. 1, 1830), 10. Specifically, see the cases of Charles F. Williams and John Thomas of Taft's 5th New York Battery, numbers 1155 and 1159 respectively, May 7, 1862. Also see Case 1057, John Harrington, Feb. 17, 1862. The order to shave Harrington's head was later rescinded. Records RG 48, MLR A1–475, *Register of Punishments, 1831–1862,* NARA II.

124. Speer, *Portals to Hell,* 148.

125. "Local Matters: The State Line Prisoners," *Richmond Daily Dispatch,* Feb. 7, 1863.

126. State of Ohio Executive Order, July 30, 1863, in "The Order for Morgan's Imprisonment," *Richmond Daily Dispatch,* Aug. 14, 1863, http://dlxs.richmond. edu/d/ddr/; Speer, *Portals to Hell,* 140–50.

127. "Outrage on Confederate Officers," *Richmond Daily Dispatch,* Aug. 6, 1863, http://dlxs.richmond.edu/d/ddr/; "Morgan in a Penitentiary," *Richmond Daily Dispatch,* Aug. 7, 1863, http://dlxs.richmond.edu/d/ddr/; "The Shaving of Heads," *Richmond Daily Dispatch,* Aug. 17, 1863, http://dlxs.richmond.edu/d/ddr/.

128. "Morgan Not Lee Treats," *Richmond Daily Dispatch,* Aug. 18, 1863, http:// dlxs.richmond.edu/d/ddr/; "Death of Col. Cluke," *Richmond Daily Dispatch,* Jan. 26, 1864, http://dlxs.richmond.edu/d/ddr/.

4. The Internal World of the Prison

1. "The Rebel Barbarities," *Boston Liberator,* Apr. 3, 1863, 3.

2. Gibson, "Global Perspectives on the Birth of the Prison," 1058–59. Pieter Spierenburg, *The Prison Experience: Disciplinary Institutions and Their Inmates in Early Modern Europe* (London: Rutgers Univ. Press, 1991), 4; Norman Bruce Johnston, *Forms of Constraint: A History of Prison Architecture* (Urbana: Univ. of Illinois Press, 2000), 2. This study is influenced by Pieter Spierenburg's work, which seeks to remedy the fact that "little is known of what actually happened in the prisons" in Europe. It seeks to remedy this problem in scholarship on American prisons. Norman Johnston calls for scholars to produce a "realistic" view of what went on in prison by ceasing to mistake the rhetoric of state officials and educated elites for administrative practice and instead "document actual prisons, their goals, their methods, and their successes."

3. Duff, *Six Months of Prison Life,* 5.

4. Mahoney, *The Prisoner of State,* 281.

5. "Federal Treatment of Prisoners. Horrible Barbarities—Statement of a Paroled Prisoner," reprinted from the *Memphis Avalanche,* Dec. 11, 1861, in *Richmond Daily Dispatch,* Dec. 19, 1861, http://dlxs.richmond.edu/d/ddr/.

6. E. C. Sanders to Maj. Gen. J. G. Foster, Apr. 24, 1863, O.R. II, vol. 5, 518–19.

7. General Churchill to Colonel Hoffman, n.d., and W. Hoffman to General Churchill, via Col. R. C. Buchanan, commanding Fort Delaware, Apr. 17, 1863, "From Gen. Churchill to Col. Hoffman," *Richmond Daily Dispatch,* May 7, 1863, http://dlxs.richmond.edu/d/ddr. Churchill was transferred from Camp Chase to Fort Delaware and voiced his complaints to Hoffman upon his transfer.

8. The inmate to whom Barbiere was referring was incarcerated at Johnson's Island. Joseph Barbiere, *Scraps from the Prison Table: At Camp Chase & Johnson's Island* (Doylestown, Pa.: W. W. H. Davis, 1868), 83.

9. "A Loyal Letter," *Washington (D.C.) National Republican,* June 4, 1863, 2.

10. "Reformed Rebels," *New York Times,* Mar. 16, 1864, 1.

11. "'Secesh' in the Ohio Legislature," reprinted commentary from the *Cincinnati Commercial* in *Memphis Daily Appeal*, Apr. 13, 1862, 1. On May 4, 1862, the *Memphis Daily Appeal* reported that Ohio Senator John Sherman presented a series of resolutions protesting against Confederate prisoners at Camp Chase being allowed to retain their slaves as servants. *Memphis Daily Appeal*, May 4, 1862, 1. The *St. Cloud Democrat* published a similar story, noting that "a growing astonishment, which will soon be indignation" was apparent among the people since Washington politicians failed to prohibit slaves in Camp Chase. "The Negro Prisoners at Columbus," *St. Cloud (Minn.) Democrat*, May 15, 1862, 2.

12. "The Treatment of Our Prisoners," reprinted from the *Vicksburg Whig* in *Memphis Daily Appeal*, Sept. 20, 1861, 1.

13. "Sent to Salisbury," 3; *Zanesville (Ohio) Daily Courier*, Feb. 25, 1865, 2.

14. Finley, *Memorials of Prison Life*, 70.

15. Entries June 12 and June 6, 1864, William T. Peabody, *Andersonville Diaries*, vol. 2, 216–17, Andersonville National Historic Site Library (hereafter cited as ANHS).

16. James M. McPherson notes that officers were generally several years older than enlisted men, were more educated, and had higher social status. McPherson, *For Cause and Comrades*, 54; According to Southern honor, Southern men hailing from the upper echelons of society were accustomed to administering justice and wielding influence over their families. Bertram Wyatt-Brown, *Southern Honor: Ethics and Behavior in the Old South* (New York: Oxford Univ. Press, 1982), 363.

17. Entry 17 Jan. Sunday (1864), Robert Bingham Papers, #3731-z, Southern Historical Collection, The Wilson Library, Univ. of North Carolina at Chapel Hill (hereafter cited as SHC UNC).

18. "A Little as to Prison Life," E. D. Dixon Recollections, #223-z, SHC UNC.

19. *New Orleans Times Picayune*, July 23, 1858, 1; "A Popular Institution," *Coshocton (Ohio) Progressive Age*, July 28, 1858, 2; notation of the seven-hundredth convict appeared in *Gettysburg Compiler*, Aug. 9, 1858, 1.

20. *New Orleans Times Picayune*, July 19, 1858, 1; "The Execution of Albert Myers, the Murderer of Richard Neville," *Coshocton (Ohio) Progressive Age*, Dec. 22, 1858, 2; *Janesville (Wis.) Weekly Gazette*, Mar. 18, 1859, 3.

21. *Baltimore Sun*, Apr. 30, 1853, 4. Smith's race was unreported.

22. Doc. No. 13, *Annual Report of the Board of Directors of the Penitentiary Institution, 1857*, xvi, 1063, LVA.

23. "Prisoners in the Virginia Penitentiary," *New Orleans Times Picayune*, Mar. 28, 1858, 6.

24. Entries May 22, 26, and 27, 1864, John Duff, *Andersonville Diaries*, vol. 1, 54, ANHS; entries May 26 and July 9, 1864, William Tritt, *Andersonville Diaries*, vol. 2, 321, 326, ANHS.

25. Entry Salisbury, N.C., Jan. 10, 1862, in the Mangum Family Papers #483, SHC UNC.

26. *Weekly Raleigh Register*, Nov. 3, 1831, 3; "Missionaries in the Penitentiary," *Boston Liberator*, Oct. 15, 1831, 3; "Interesting from the Georgia Penitentiary," *Pittsburgh Gazette*, June 8, 1832, 2.

27. "Duties of the Chaplain," Ohio Penitentiary, *Report of the Directors of the New Penitentiary, 1834,* WRHS; "Duties of the Chaplain," Ohio Penitentiary, *Annual Report of the Director and Wardens . . . , 1856,* OHS; "Duties of the Chaplain," *Rules and Regulations for the Government of the Penitentiary for the District of Columbia, Jan. 1, 1830,* RG 48, Records of the Office of the Secretary of the Interior, Records Relating to the U.S. Penitentiary for the District of Columbia, 1826–65, Miscellaneous Records, 1829–65, Entry 470, Box 1, NARA II.

28. Ohio Penitentiary, *Annual Report of the Director and Wardens . . . , 1838,* 6, OHS; Ohio Penitentiary, *Annual Report of the Directors and Warden . . . , 1840,* 4, OHS.

29. "No. 83, AN ACT," *Hamilton (Ohio) Telegraph,* May 3, 1860, 1.

30. Lewis, *From Newgate to Dannemora,* vii–ix, 231; Colvin, *Penitentiaries, Reformatories, and Chain Gangs,* 29–30.

31. "Message from the President of the United States Transmitting a Report of the Inspectors of the Penitentiary in the District of Columbia, for the Year 1836," H. Exec. Doc. No. 97, 24th Cong., 2nd sess., 6, NYPL; Lewis, *From Newgate to Dannemora,* 231.

32. De Beaumont and de Tocqueville, *On the Penitentiary System in the United States,* 91. De Tocqueville and de Beaumont noted that the penitentiary system in the United States was advantageous because "1. impossibility of the mutual corruption of the prisoners, 2. great probability of their contracting habits of obedience and industry, which render them useful citizens, 3. possibility of a radical reformation."

33. Doc. No. 13, *Annual Report, 1857,* xvi, 1063, LVA.

34. Ohio Penitentiary, *Annual Report, 1862,* OHS.

35. L. Molon to Edwin M. Stanton, Aug. 22, 1862, O.R., II, vol. 4, 423. According to John Gjerde, Protestant anti-Catholicism revolved around the fear that Catholicism held conscience in captivity through the papacy and the priesthood, which limited believers because of explained doctrine, interpreting the Bible for the laity, dispensing penance, and hearing confessions. The structure of the Church fostered the "hierarchy and authoritarianism of Europe." Jon Gjerde, *Catholicism and the Shaping of Nineteenth-Century America,* ed. S. Deborah Kang (New York: Cambridge Univ. Press, 2012), 29, 55.

36. W. Hoffman to Maj. W. S. Pierson, Sept. 8, 1862, O.R. II, vol. 4, 498.

37. R. A. Sidley to Col. William Hoffman, May 11, 1863; Wm. S. Pierson to Rev. R. A. Sidley, May 6, 1863, O.R. II, vol. 5, 594; W. Hoffman to Maj. W. S. Pierson, May 19, 1863, O.R. II, vol. 5, 663.

38. Steven Woodworth has noted that Sabbath observance was so widespread in the nineteenth century that any deviation from the norm was bound to be noticed and commented on. Steven E. Woodworth, *While God Is Marching On: The Religious World of Civil War Soldiers* (Lawrence: Univ. Press of Kansas, 2001), 79.

39. Zombek, "Camp Chase Prison," 32.

40. "Religious Services at Camp Chase," *Daily (Columbus) Ohio Statesman,* Oct. 4, 1862, 2.

41. Marvel, *Andersonville;* David R. Bush, *I Fear I Shall Never Leave This Island: Life in a Civil War Prison* (Gainesville: Univ. Press of Florida, 2012); Roger

Pickenpaugh, *Johnson's Island: A Prison for Confederate Officers* (Kent: The Kent State Univ. Press, 2016).

42. Steven Woodworth notes that religious revivals swept Union and Confederate armies in all theaters beginning in the spring of 1863. Gardiner Shattuck notes that a "Great Revival" swept through the Confederate Army in Virginia from fall 1863 through spring 1864. Woodworth, *While God Is Marching On,* 214, 229–30; Gardiner Shattuck, *A Shield and Hiding Place: The Religious Life of the Civil War Armies* (Macon: Mercer Univ. Press, 1987), 99.

43. Entries for this and the previous paragraph as follows: J. S. Joyner to Mother, Sept. 18, 1863; J. S. Joyner to Mother, Jan. 30, 1864; J. S. Joyner to Mother, June 14, 1864; J. S. Joyner to Mother, Sept. 8, 1864, in Joyner Family Papers #4428, SHC UNC.

44. Entries Feb. 8, 1865; Feb. 1, 1865; Jan. 22, 1865, in the Virgil S. Murphey Diary #534-z, SHC UNC.

45. Entries Oct. 22, 1863; Oct. 31, 1863; Nov. 1, 1863; Nov. 29, 1863, in the Robert Bingham Papers #3731-z, SHC UNC.

46. Entries Dec. 27, 1863; Dec. 31, 1863; Jan. 1, 1864, in the Robert Bingham Papers #3731-z, SHC UNC.

47. Peabody died at Andersonville on Sept. 1, 1864. Entries June 5, 1864; June 6, 1864; June 23, 1864; July 10, 1864; July 14, 1864; July 17, 1864; July 20, 1864; July 22, 1864; July 25, 1864, in *Andersonville Diaries,* vol. 2, 215–18, 220–22, 225, ANHS.

48. Entries June 26, 1864; July 3, 1864; July 10, 1864; July 17, 1864; July 24, 1864; Aug. 7, 1864, in John L. Hoster, *Adventure of a Soldier,* 91–93, 95, 97, 100, ANHS.

49. Entry June 17, 1864, James Vance Diary, *Andersonville Diaries,* vol. 3, 438, ANHS.

50. A. W. Mangum to Sister, Mar. 14, 1862; A. W. Mangum to Sister, Jan. 10, 1862; AWM to Sister, Apr. 11, 1862; unsigned to Sister, June 6, 1862, in the Mangum Family Papers #483, SHC UNC.

51. "Righteous," *Boston Liberator,* Sept. 26, 1862, 4.

52. Judith I. Madera, "Floating Prisons: Dispossession, Ordering, and Colonial Atlantic 'States,' 1776–1783," in Tarter and Bell, *Buried Lives,* 195; Daniel E. Williams, "'The Horrors of This Far-Famed Penitentiary': Discipline, Defiance, and Death during Ann Carson's Incarcerations in Philadelphia's Walnut Street Prison," in Tarter and Bell, *Buried Lives,* 207.

53. Walden, "History of the Georgia Penitentiary at Milledgeville," 38–39; Inspector Report, 1831, Board of Inspectors Reports, 1820–73, Records of the Georgia Prison Commission, 1817–1936: A Part of the Georgia Board of Corrections, Record Group 21, Archives Institute Georgia Department of Archives and History, Atlanta, Georgia (hereafter cited as GA); Report of the Committee on the Penitentiary, Georgia, General Assembly, Senate, *Journal of the Senate of the State of Georgia, 1861,* 132.

54. "Virginia Penitentiary," *Newbern Carolina Federal Republican,* June 7, 1817, 3.

55. "An Act to Provide for Obtaining Stone for the Public Buildings, and Works of the State, and for Other Purposes," *Sandusky (Ohio) Clarion,* July 11, 1845, 1; *Cincinnati Chronicle* quoted in "Ohio Penitentiary," *Alton (Ill.) Weekly Telegraph,* July 19, 1845, 2.

56. "No. 94, An Act to Provide for the Completion of the New State House," *Coshocton (Ohio) Democrat,* May 12, 1858, 1.

57. "Becoming Valuable," *Richmond Dispatch,* June 5, 1858, 1.

58. "Reports from Alexandria," *New York Times,* June 3, 1861, 1.

59. "Local Matters . . . Heavy Docket," *Richmond Dispatch,* Sept. 4, 1862, 1.

60. "A Veteran Observer," *New York Times,* Nov. 26, 1861, 2.

61. "The Rebel Prisoners on Johnson's Island—To the Editor of the *New York Times,*" *New York Times,* Nov. 18, 1863, 2.

62. "Union Prisoners at Richmond—A Narrative of Their Privations and Sufferings—Statement of Rev. Jno. Hussey, L.L.D., a Released Prisoner," *Semi-Weekly (Milwaukee) Wisconsin,* Sept. 5, 1863, 2.

63. "How the White Soldiers Suffer and Die: From the Memorial of the Thirty-Five Thousand Perishing Prisoners in the Pen of Pestilence and Famine at Andersonville, Ga.," *Cincinnati Enquirer,* Sept. 26, 1864, 1.

64. "Cut His Fingers Off to Avoid Work," *Fayetteville North-Carolinian,* Dec. 30, 1854, 3.

65. J. B. Mitchell to Father, May 4, 1864, and J. B. Mitchell to Mother, June 10, 1864, in the James B. Mitchell Papers, 1859–1913, Library of Congress, Washington, D.C. (hereafter cited as LOC).

66. "Story of His Experience as Told to Me by My Father, J. J. Sherman," John J. Sherman Papers, 1844–1922, LOC; Nathaniel Shepard Armstrong Price Papers, 1861–1910, LOC; Glenn Robins, ed., *They Have Left Us Here to Die: The Civil War Prison Diary of Sgt. Lyle Adair, 111th U.S. Colored Infantry* (Kent, Ohio: The Kent State Univ. Press, 2011), 72.

67. W. W. Day, *Fifteen Months in Dixie: My Personal Experience in Rebel Prisons. A Story of the Hardships, Privations and Sufferings of the "Boys in Blue" during the Late War of the Rebellion* (Owatonna, Minn.: The People's Press Print, 1889), 28, 34.

68. Nathaniel Shepard Armstrong Price Papers, 1861–1910, 7, LOC.

69. Entries Oct. 10, 1864, and Oct. 26, 1864, M. J. Umsted Diary, *Andersonville Diaries,* vol. 2, ANHS.

70. Entries Mar. 18, 1864, and Jan. 3, 1864, John C. Ely Diary, *Andersonville Diaries,* vol. 1, ANHS; entry July 23, 1864, Unknown Diary, *Andersonville Diaries,* vol. 3, ANHS.

71. Robins, *They Have Left Us Here to Die,* 69–70.

72. Jos. H. Saunders to Mother, Nov. 7, 1863, in the Joseph Hubbard Saunders Papers, #650, SHC UNC (1864 is in parentheses, added later by someone other than Saunders, at the top of the letter).

73. Citations from this and the previous paragraph from entries Oct. 29, 1863; Oct. 30, 1863; Jan. 23, 1864; Dec. 17, 1863, in the Robert Bingham Papers, #3731-z, SHC UNC.

74. "Prison Life on Johnsons Island by an Exchanged Prisoner," *Memphis Daily Appeal,* Apr. 29, 1864, 1.

75. Case 1059, John Nugent, Jan. 9, 1862, Record Group 48, Entry 473, Box 4, NARA II.

76. "Prisoners in the Penitentiary of the District of Columbia by Sentence of Courts-Martial: Letter from the Secretary of the Interior," H. Exec. Doc. No. 127, 37th Cong., 2d sess. (June 12, 1862), NYPL; David K. Sullivan, "Behind Prison Walls: The Operation of the District Penitentiary, 1831–1862," *Records of the Columbia Historical Society, Washington, D.C.,* vol. 71/72, the 48th Separately Bound Book (1971/1972), 265.

77. "From Cincinnati—Sentence of Court Martial Approved," *Plymouth Republican,* May 14, 1863, 2; *New York Times,* May 29, 1863, 3; "Retaliation," *Cincinnati Enquirer,* Feb. 17, 1864, 2; "Retaliatory," *Raleigh Weekly Standard,* Feb. 17, 1864, 4.

78. *Cleveland Daily Leader,* May 5, 1862, 1.

79. "A Destructive Gun—Barbarous Treatment of Rebel Deserters: A Correspondent of the *New York Herald* Who Has Been in 'Dixie' Is Now Giving the Public His Experience While There," *Milwaukee Semi-Weekly Wisconsin,* Feb. 3, 1864, 1.

80. S. Boyer Davis to Dear Friends, Feb. 16, 1865, in the Benjamin R. Smith Autograph Album, #3379-z, SHC UNC; J. B. Mitchell to Mother, Feb. 17, 1865, in the James B. Mitchell Papers, 1859–1913. LOC.

5. Life Out There

1. *Philadelphia Journal,* summarized in *White Cloud Kansas Chief,* Aug. 25, 1859, 1.

2. McLennan, *The Crisis of Imprisonment,* 47.

3. "To My Mother," *Asheville (N.C.) News,* Mar. 20, 1856, 1. Also reprinted from the *Ohio State Journal* in the *Brooklyn Daily Eagle,* May 5, 1856, 1.

4. Finley, *Memorials of Prison Life,* 95–96, 142; emphasis in the original.

5. Sarah Donnelly to George Montgomery, Feb. 5, 1856, Record Group 48, Records of the Office of the Secretary of the Interior, Records Relating to the U.S. Penitentiary for the District of Columbia, 1826–65, Miscellaneous Records, 1829–62, Entry 470, Box 2, NARA II.

6. John A. Shreene to Son, Sept. 10, 1854, ibid.

7. Samuel Burks Taylor to Sister, Oct. 17, 1863, Samuel Burks Taylor Letter, Oct. 17, 1863, OHS; Thomas W. Bullitt to Sister, New Year 1864, and Thomas W. Bullitt to Sister, Sept. 19, 1863, Helen Bullitt Papers, 1862–64, OHS.

8. P. H. Watson to Joseph H. Geiger, Mar. 22, 1862, O.R. Series II, vol. 3, 400; William Hoffman, "Circular April 20, 1864," O.R. Series II, vol. 7, 72–75; Gray, *The Business of Captivity,* 109.

9. J. B. Mitchell to Father, Mar. 8, 1864, and J. B. Mitchell to Mother, June 10, 1864, James B. Mitchell Papers, 1859–1913, LOC; emphasis in the original.

10. A. E. Bell to Wife, Jan. 3, 1864, Alfred E. Bell Papers, 1861–65, WRHS.

11. J. S. Joyner to William, Aug. 13, 1863; J. S. Joyner to Uncle, Sept. 21, 1864; and J. S. Joyner to Mother, Sept. 8, 1864, Joyner Family Papers #4428, SHC UNC.

Jos. H. Saunders to Sister, Feb. 11, 1865, Joseph Hubbard Saunders Papers, #650, SHC UNC.

12. C. B. S. to Miss Belle D. Price, June 22, 1862, Charles Barrington Simrall Papers, #1665, SHC UNC. Simrall was indeed privileged during confinement. He noted receiving parole to the city of Columbus during which time he visited the Insane Asylum. See Charles to Dear Friend, Sept. 10, 1862, Simrall Papers, SHC UNC.

13. Bell also kept track of gaps in letters from his wife, which ranged from eight days to two weeks in February, March, and April 1864. A. E. Bell to Dear Wife, Mar. 15, 1864; A. E. Bell to Dear Wife, May 3, 1864; A. E. Bell to Dear Wife, May 10, 1864;and A. E. Bell to Dear Wife, June 19, 1864, WRHS.

14. J. B. Mitchell to Brother, Feb. 9, 1865, James B. Mitchell Papers, 1859–1913, LOC.

15. James Mitchell to Father, Aug. 1, 1864. In a letter to his father, dated February 5, 1865, Mitchell noted that he received three letters from him dated November 1 and 6, 1864, and also December 23, 1864. In letters to his father, respectively dated October 17, 1864, and December 11, 1864, Mitchell complained in the former that he had not received any word from home in three months, and in the latter stated that the last letter he received was dated July 26, 1864. James B. Mitchell Papers, 1859–1913, LOC.

16. J. S. Joyner to William, Aug. 13, 1863; J. S. Joyner to Mother, Oct. 20, 1863; and J. S. Joyner to Mother, Jan. 2, 1865, Joyner Family Papers #4428, SHC UNC.

17. Jos. H. Saunders to Mother, Apr. 28, 1864; Jos. H. Saunders to Mother, Jan. 10, 1865; and Jos. H. Saunders to Sister, Feb. 11, 1865, Joseph Hubbard Saunders Papers, #650, SHC UNC.

18. Griffith, "Fredericksburg's Political Hostages," 407–8.

19. John Johnson to Gen. John H. Winder, July 4, 1863, CSA-Henrico, 1861–64, Folder 7 of 14, VHS.

20. Lt. James I. Metts, Johnson's Island, Ohio, Friday Graham, Oct. 25, 1863, My Dear Son [letter's closing is illegible]; Lt. James I. Metts Near Sandusky, Ohio, Graham, Sept. 14, 1863, My Own Dear Son [letter's closing is illegible]; Uncle to Dear Nephew, Jan. 28, 1864; and T. G. Wall to Lt. J. I. Metts, Mar. 18, 1864, James Isaac Metts Papers, #3624-z, SHC UNC.

21. Cloyd, *Haunted by Atrocity.*

22. Unidentified to Brother, Apr. 20, 1862, Camp Chase, Ohio Papers, 1862–63, Folder 1 of 12, VHS.

23. John Sullivan Healy to Julia Wheeler Healy, Jan. 6, 1865, John Healy Family Papers, WRHS.

24. Richard Stott notes that Civil War soldiers were serene and conformed with the subdued manhood in which men, by midcentury, found fulfillment in the home. Richard Stott, *Jolly Fellows: Male Milieus in Nineteenth-Century America* (Baltimore: The Johns Hopkins Univ. Press, 2009), 1, 3, 56–57, 223.

25. W. C. Cariner to Hennie, Apr. 20, 1862, Camp Chase, Ohio Papers, 1862–63, Folder 1 of 12, VHS.

26. James J. Williamson, *Prison Life in the Old Capitol and Reminiscences of the Civil War* (West Orange, N.J.: James J. Williamson, 1911), 29.

27. The all-male world of prison is akin to the predominately male world of Southern mines that historian Susan Lee Johnson describes. Johnson notes that skewed sex ratios in immigrant camps caused men to take on "tasks that their womenfolk would have performed back home." For more information, see Chapter 2: "Domestic Life in the Diggings," in Susan Lee Johnson, *Roaring Camp: The Social World of the California Gold Rush* (New York: W. W. Norton, 2000), 100.

28. Finley, *Memorial of Prison Life*, 96–97.

29. Carter M. Louthan to Sister Ella, Feb. 14, 1864, Louthan Family Papers, call MSS1 L9361A, unprocessed collection, VHS; Dix, *Remarks on Prisons*, 66.

30. Carter M. Louthan to Ella Brown, Mar. 12, 1864, Louthan Family Papers, call MSS1 L9361A, unprocessed collection, VHS.

31. Amy Murrell Taylor, *The Divided Family in Civil War America* (Chapel Hill: The Univ. of North Carolina Press, 2005), 160.

32. Jane to Dearest Father, May 30, 1862, Camp Chase, Ohio Papers, 1862–63, Folder 1 of 12, VHS.

33. Lucius Q. C. Lamar, "Rules and Regulations for the Internal Government of the Penitentiary," in *A Compilation of the Laws of the State of Georgia, Passed by the Legislature Since the Year 1810 to the Year 1819, Inclusive* (Augusta, Ga.: T. S. Hannon, 1821), 668.

34. General Orders No. 83, Oct. 9, 1864; C. Morfit to Maj. Mason Morfit, Nov. 23, 1864, O.R. vol. 7, 960, 1157–58.

35. Williamson, *Prison Life in the Old Capitol*, 74; Mahoney, *The Prisoner of State*, 167–69.

36. Governor Wise to Col. Morgan, Oct. 25, 1856, Dec. 4, 1858, and Dec. 11, 1858, Charles S. Morgan Papers, Morgan P. Robinson Collection, Old Catalogue, Folder 2, Box, 1, VHS.

37. Ann Bohlayer to Mr. Sengstack, Jan. 2, 1861, Record Group 48, Records of the Office of the Secretary of the Interior, Records Relating to the U.S. Penitentiary for the District of Columbia, 1826–65, Miscellaneous Records, 1829–62, Entry 470, Box 3, NARA II. Mark Kann notes that prison officials "who were benevolent, upright, and gentlemanly were to guide inmates through rehabilitation." See Mark E. Kann, *Punishment, Prisons, and Patriarchy: Liberty and Power in the Early American Republic* (New York: New York Univ. Press, 2005, 161.

38. Pass No. 380, Headquarters Military District of Washington, Provost Marshal's Office, June 17, 1864, Record Group 393, Pt. 4, Entry 2131: Passes, NARA I.

39. Henry B. Todd Capt. & Provost Marshal Col. M. Murphy, Adjutant to W. Wood, Supt. Old Capitol Prison Headquarters Provost Marshal's Office, Washington, D.C., Mar. 2, 1863, Record Group 393, Pt. 4, Entry 2131: Passes, NARA I; emphasis in the original.

40. Griffith, "Fredericksburg's Political Hostages," 417.

41. Browne's letter was published in the *Cincinnati Times* and reprinted in the

Richmond *Daily Dispatch*. See "Our Condition Bettered by Gettysburg," *Richmond Daily Dispatch,* Nov. 13, 1863, http://dlxs.richmond.edu/d/ddr.

42. See, for example, pass authorized by Henry B. Todd, Dec. 24, 1863, granting visitation privileges to Frank R. Smith, H. B. Todd to Mr. Wood, Dec. 16, 1863; H. B. Todd to Mr. Wood, Sept. 14, 1863; and Henry B. Todd to Mr. Wood, Aug. 24, 1863, Record Group 393, Pt. 4, Entry 2131: Passes, NARA I.

43. Organizations like the U.S. Sanitary Commission and the U.S. Christian Commission could also send packages. Flory, *Prisoners of War,* 100–101.

44. Marshall, *American Bastille,* 353.

45. Union forces suffered heavy casualties on May 26, 1864, at the Battle of New Hope Church on the Dallas Line. Entries June 6 and 7, 1864, David F. Weimer Diaries, 1839–1921; entries Sunday, May 22, 1864; Tuesday, May 24, 1864; and Thursday, May 26, 1864, Ira B. Sampson Papers, 1862–91 #3870-z SHC UNC.

46. Hines, "Thrilling Narrative of the Escape of Gen. John H. Morgan," WHRS.

47. Doc. No. 15, *Annual Report, 1848,* Virginia House Docs & Annual Reports Film 1063, Reel 2 1848–49, LVA.

48. "Pleasure Excursion," *Cleveland Daily Leader,* June 21, 1864, 1.

49. Box 1, Punishments 1831–47, Record Group 48, MLR A1–475, Register of Punishments, 1831–62, NARA II.

50. A. L. Stephens, charges against Joe Cunningham, July 12, 1859, Record Group 48, Records of the Office of the Secretary of the Interior, Records Relating to the U.S. Penitentiary for the District of Columbia, 1826–65, Miscellaneous Records, 1829–62, Entry 470, Box 3, NARA II.

51. *Cleveland Herald,* Mar. 4, 1864, Issue 52, Col. B.

52. Capt. H. M. Lazelle to Col. William Hoffman, July 13, 1863, O.R. Series II, vol. IV, 197. Similarly, at Elmira, many prisoners were not thrilled with "money being made at their expense" by visitors paying entry fees and gawking at them. Gray, *The Business of Captivity,* 24–25.

53. Capt. H. M. Lazelle to Col. William Hoffman, July 13, 1863, O.R. Series II, vol. IV, 197.

54. Ibid., 197.

55. "Rules and Regulations for the Government of Castle Thunder, 1863," Broadside, LVA; "Days of Visiting," *Richmond Daily Dispatch,* Apr. 30, 1863, http://dlxs. richmond.edu/d/ddr.

56. William Hoffman "Circular April 20, 1864," O.R. Series II, vol. 7, 72–75.

57. "Governor Tod," *Cincinnati Enquirer,* Jan. 28, 1862, 2.

58. "Returned South," *Raleigh (N.C.) Weekly State Journal,* Aug. 27, 1862, 4; "Sanitary Supplies," *Daily Milwaukee News,* Nov. 12, 1864, 1.

59. "PARDONED," *Baltimore Sun,* May 31, 1842, 1; "Correspondence of the Baltimore *Sun,* Washington April 5," *Baltimore Sun,* Apr. 6, 1858, 4; "Pardoned," *New Orleans Times Picayune,* Nov. 25, 1856, 4.

60. *Philadelphia Public Ledger,* Apr. 19, 1844, 2.

61. "Miscellaneous—Touching Incident," *Coshocton (Ohio) Progressive Age,* Apr. 7, 1858, 1.

62. "Refused a Pardon," *New Orleans Times Picayune*, Sept. 18, 1861, 2.

63. Lieber, *A Popular Essay*, 27, 38–39.

64. W. H. Lowry to Warden Sengstack, Apr. 8, 1861, Record Group 48, Records of the Office of the Secretary of the Interior, Records Relating to the U.S. Penitentiary for the District of Columbia, 1826–65, Miscellaneous Records, 1829–62, Entry 470, Box 3, NARA II.

65. Both black and white inmates received pardons for these reasons. Case of Isaac Linton, Doc. No. 1, *Message IV, Relative to Reprieves and Pardons, to the General Assembly of Virginia, December 7, 1857;* Henry A. Wise to the Senate and House of Delegates of the General Assembly of the Commonwealth of Virginia, clx-viii–clxix, LVA.

66. Papers regarding a pardon sought by Thomas Johnson, 1812–13, Virginia Penitentiary, *Penitentiary Papers, 1796–1865,* Subseries E, LVA; Case of Nelson Hooper, Doc. No. 1, *Message IV, Relative to Reprieves and Pardons, to the General Assembly of Virginia, December 7, 1857,* clxxiv; Henry A. Wise to the Senate and House of Delegates of the General Assembly of the Commonwealth of Virginia, LVA.

67. Letter B. P. Hussey to Dr. Wm. A. Patterson, Mar. 14, 1858, and Hussey to Morgan, July 3, 1858, Charles S. Morgan Papers, Morgan P. Robinson Collection, Old Catalogue, Folder 7, Box, 1, VHS.

68. Doc. No. 16, *Communication Relative to Pardons, Reprieves, etc., December 1863,* 4–5, LVA.

69. The assessment of soldiers' crimes and pardons came from the reading of Doc. No. 40, *Communication Relative to Reprieves, 1861;* Doc. No. 6, *Communication Relative to Reprieves, Pardons, etc., 1862;* Doc. No. 7, *Communication Relative to Reprieves, Pardons, etc., 1863;* Doc. No. 16, *Communication Relative to Reprieves, December 1863;* Doc. No. 35, *Governor's Communication on the Subject of Pardons, Reprieves, etc., 1864,* LVA. Specific examples of pardoning soldiers based on good conduct, being under the influence of liquor at the time of crime, and the crime being accidental can be found throughout these records.

70. Case of Charles Smith, Doc. No. 7, *Communication Relative to Reprieves, . . . 1863,* 7, and Case of Frances Marion, Doc. No. 16, *Communication Relative to Reprieves, . . . December 1863,* 3–4, LVA.

71. The assessment of common reasons for pardon came from an examination of the following documents: Doc. No. 40, *Communication Relative to Reprieves, . . . 1861;* Doc. No. 6, *Communication Relative to Reprieves, . . . 1862;* Doc. No. 7, *Communication Relative to Reprieves, . . . 1863;* Doc. No. 16, *Communication Relative to Reprieves, . . . December 1863;* Doc. No. 35, *Governor's Communication on the Subject of Pardons, . . . 1864,* LVA.

72. Friedman, *A History of American Law,* 212.

73. Dodge, *Whores and Thieves of the Worst Kind,* 36.

74. Finley, *Memorials of Prison Life,* 95–97.

75. D. R. Fletcher to Mother, Apr. 21, 1862, and John J. Guthrie to Mother, Apr. 20, 1862, Camp Chase, Ohio Papers, 1862–63, Folder 3 of 12, VHS.

76. J. S. Joyner to Uncle, Sept. 21, 1864, Joyner Family Papers #4428, SHC UNC.

77. Theodore P. Hamlin to Father, Nov. 6, 1864; Theodore P. Hamlin to Father, Jan. 11, 1865; Theodore P. Hamlin to Father, Mar. 1, 1865; Theodore P. Hamlin to Father, Feb. 17, 1865; and Theodore P. Hamlin to Sister, Mar. 16, 1865, Theodore P. Hamlin Papers, 1834–85, #304-z SHC UNC.

78. Frank W. Keyes to Hon. O.R. Singleton, Apr. 26, 1862, Camp Chase, Ohio Papers, 1862–63, Folder 5 of 12, VHS. For Camp Chase population, see Zombek, "Transcending Stereotypes," Appendix.

79. A. N. Davis to A. Lincoln, Apr. 2, 1862, O.R. II, vol. 3, 418–19.

80. J. B. Dorr, T. J. Harrison, and George Stoneman to The President of the United States, Aug. 14, 1864, O.R. II, vol. 7, 616–18.

81. C. H. Stillwell to President, Sept. 7, 1864, O.R. II, vol. 7, 783.

82. De Beaumont and de Tocqueville, *On the Penitentiary System,* 88–89.

83. George Hendricks to Pennel Hendricks, Feb. 1859, Record Group 48, Records of the Office of the Secretary of the Interior, Records Relating to the U.S. Penitentiary for the District of Columbia, 1826–65, Miscellaneous Records, 1829–62, Entry 470, Box 3, NARA II.

84. O. L. Clarke to Warden of the Penitentiary in Washington, D.C., Oct. 1859, Record Group 48, Records of the Office of the Secretary of the Interior, Records Relating to the U.S. Penitentiary for the District of Columbia, 1826–65, Miscellaneous Records, 1829–62, Entry 470, Box 2, NARA II.

85. Dodge, *Whores and Thieves of the Worst Kind,* 57.

86. Ro. S. Breckenridge to Saml. Galloway Esq., Jan. 10, 1862, Samuel Galloway Papers, 1840–95, OHS.

87. Revd. Dr. T. V. Moore to Revt & Dear Sir, Nov. 10, 1863, and William D. McKinsly etc., at enclosure, Nov. 5, 1863, Confederate States of America Army Department of Henrico Records (hereafter cited as CSA-Henrico), Records, 1861–64, Section 11, VHS; emphasis in the original.

88. James Quinn to His Grace Right Revt. Bishop McGill, CSA-Henrico, Records, 1861–64, Section 11, VHS.

89. Robert R. Collier to James A. Seddon, Dec. 22, 1862, O.R. II, vol. 5, 791–92.

90. Thomas A. Jones to Mr. J. Dent, Nov. 18, 1861, O.R. Series II, vol. 2, 869–70; Kate Parr to Hon. William H. Seward, Jan. 3, 1862, O.R. Series II, vol. 2, 1287–89. Paul Anderson acknowledges that Union soldiers could shame Southern manhood by overpowering women while men were away at war. This act could, according to Anderson, render the same effect of undercutting Southern manhood, since it stood as a public reminder that "the men could not protect their homes anyway." See Paul C. Anderson, *Blood Image: Turner Ashby in the Civil War and the Southern Mind* (Baton Rouge: Louisiana State Univ. Press, 2002), 179–80.

91. Geg. F. Harbin to William H. Seward, Dec. 6, 1861, O.R. Series II, vol. 2, 870.

92. W. H. Wadsworth to William H. Seward, Dec. 7, 1861, O.R. Series II, vol. 2, 923.

93. R. H. Hanson to Hon. Samuel Galloway, June 25, 1862, Samuel Galloway Papers, 1840–95, OHS.

94. Kann, *Punishment, Prisons, and Patriarchy,* 179.

95. Sam Milligan to James A. Seddon, Dec. 6, 1863, CSA-Henrico, Records, 1861–64, Section 1, VHS.

96. John W. Rider to Capt. William Richardson, Jan. 18, 1864, CSA-Henrico, Records, 1861–64, Section 1, VHS. Chandra Manning contends that Confederate patriotism contained an inherent tension "between the needs and interests of the Confederacy, and the needs and interests of soldiers and their families." Manning posits that "initially the tension remained latent, but as the needs of families increasingly conflicted with the demands of the Confederacy, strains became harder to ignore." Rider's case provides a good example of this tension. See Chandra Manning, *What This Cruel War Was Over: Soldiers, Slavery, and the Civil War* (New York: Vintage, 2007), 217. Similarly, Paul Anderson contends that the "home stood as a profound symbol of patriarchy and protection," and that "to cow a man at his front door was to degrade him and his family in the most public way imaginable." See Anderson, *Blood Image,* 179–80.

97. Levi Bennett to Brig. Gen. J. H. Winder, Jan. 11, 1864, CSA-Henrico, Records, 1861–64, Section 1, VHS.

98. Jno. A. Carper to General Winder, June 18, 1863, CSA-Henrico, Records, 1861–64, Section 1, VHS. Victoria Bynum contends that "to be poor, female, and without the guardianship of a white male figure was to be without honor or worth in the antebellum South." I believe that this standard applied during wartime. See Victoria Bynum, *Unruly Women: The Politics of Social and Sexual Control in the Old South* (Chapel Hill: Univ. of North Carolina Press, 1992), 7–8.

99. Nina Silber contends that "it was far more common among Confederates to meld the personal and political, indeed to make the private obligation stand in for a larger ideological motive. While Unionists, at times, did the same . . . it was far more common for them, especially in their private explanations of why they fought, to separate the private and the political." Nina Silber, *Gender and the Sectional Conflict* (Chapel Hill: The Univ. of North Carolina Press, 2008), 12–13.

100. H. D. Crockett et al. to Judge Key, Sept. 13, 1861, O.R. Series II, vol. 3, 40.

101. B. F. Hoffman to Col. [William] Hoffman, Feb. 7, 1862, O.R. Series II, vol. 2, 211–12.

102. Information from this and the above paragraph from B. F. Hoffman to Col. [William] Hoffman, Feb. 7, 1862, O.R. Series II, vol. 2, 211–12; W. Hoffman to W. Richardson, Oct. 1, 1864, O.R. Series II, vol. 7, 907; D. C. Buell to General Halleck, July 1, 1862, O.R. Series II, vol. 4, 109; William Wood to Gen. E. A. Hitchcock, Oct. 5, 1863, O.R. Series II, vol. 5, 775.

103. The case of Ann Bohlayer, discussed earlier in this chapter, also provides a good example. William Boyd to Wife, Mar. 28, 1860, and Mrs. Bohlayer to Mr. Sengstack, Jan. 2, 1861, Record Group 48, Records of the Office of the Secretary of the Interior, Records Relating to the U.S. Penitentiary for the District of Columbia, 1826–65, Miscellaneous Records, 1829–62, Entry 470, Box 3, NARA II.

104. Nash's petition is undated. William Nash et al. to his Excellency the Governor and Council of State, undated, Virginia Penitentiary, *Penitentiary Papers, 1796–1865,* Subseries D, LVA.

105. Jas. P. Couthouy to B. R. Wellford, Feb. 9, 1863, O.R. II, vol. 5, 828–30.

106. Chas. Dunham to John H. Winder, May 7, 1863, CSA-Henrico, Records, 1861–64, Section 3 A-C, VHS.

107. J. T. Kirby to J. H. Winder, May 1, 1863, CSA-Henrico, Records, 1861–64, Section 3 A-C, VHS; emphasis in the original.

108. From the 1790s to the 1850s, Ayers argues that there were "Southerners who argued that the penitentiary constituted an essential part of any enlightened government [while] other Southerners warned that the penitentiary posed a real and direct threat to American freedom and to the ideals of the American Revolution." Ayers, *Vengeance and Justice,* 35. Hindus argues that the institution of slavery, as opposed to the penitentiary, maintained order in the South and contends that this system kept Southern patriarchs in power. Hindus, *Prison and Plantation,* 253.

109. For more general information on the Confederate government's centralized power and its detention of political prisoners, see Neely, *Southern Rights.*

6. Shifting Power Dynamics

1. "Breaking Prison," *New Orleans Times Picayune,* June 14, 1843, 2; "Desperate Efforts of Rebel Prisoners at Camp Chase to Gain Their Liberty," *Daily Milwaukee News,* July 13, 1864, 4. The paper did not give the number of men who attempted escape.

2. Meranze, *Laboratories of Virtue,* 222; Lewis, *From Newgate to Dannemora;* McLennan, *The Crisis of Imprisonment;* Goldsmith, "History from the Inside Out."

3. Goldsmith, "History from the Inside Out," 110, 120–21.

4. McLennan, *The Crisis of Imprisonment,* 45; Dix, *Remarks on Prisons,* 81–83.

5. Crawford, *Report on the Penitentiaries,* 102–3.

6. Box 1, Punishments 1831–47, Orders 1851–54, Record Group 48, MLR A1–475, *Register of Punishments, 1831–1862,* NARA II.

7. Simpson, "The Prisoners of the Ohio Penitentiary, 1883," 26–27; Finley, *Memorials of Prison Life,* 48–49, 345.

8. "Dangerous Prisoner," *Philadelphia Public Ledger,* Dec. 27, 1837; "Murder in the Ohio Penitentiary," *Baltimore Sun,* June 16, 1841, 2; *Baltimore Sun,* May 18, 1843, 2.

9. Doc. No. 8, *Annual Report of the Board of Directors of the Penitentiary Institution, 1847,* 5–6, LVA.

10. Crawford, *Report on the Penitentiaries,* 102, 109; Box 1, Punishments 1831–47, Orders 1851–54, Record Group 48, MLR A1–475, *Register of Punishments, 1831–1862,* NARA II; Ohio Penitentiary, *Annual Report of the Director and Wardens . . . , 1856,* 15, OHS.

11. Johnston, *Forms of Constraint;* Goldsmith, "History from the Inside Out."

12. Box 1, Punishments 1831–47, Record Group 48, MLR A1–475, *Register of Punishments, 1831–1862,* NARA II.

13. Cases of the Barkers and Brown from ibid. Austin Reed, prisoner at New York's Auburn Penitentiary, noted that rules forbade convicts from passing food to

each other. Officers punished this offense with whipping. Austin Reed, *The Life and the Adventures of a Haunted Convict,* ed. and with an intro. Caleb Smith (New York: Random House, 2016), 144.

14. "Message from the President of the United States transmitting the Annual Report of the Inspectors of the Penitentiary in the District of Columbia," H. Exec. Doc. No. 29, 30th Cong., 2d sess., *Warden's Report* (Jan. 16, 1849), NYPL.

15. Box 1, Punishments 1831–47, Record Group 48, MLR A1–475, *Register of Punishments, 1831–1862,* NARA II.

16. Ibid.

17. Box 1, Punishments 1831–47, Record Group 48, MLR A1–475, *Register of Punishments, 1831–1862,* NARA II.

18. Goldsmith, "History from the Inside Out," 120; Dodge, *Whores and Thieves,* 31.

19. Regarding female criminals in the antebellum period, Nicole Hahn Rafter notes that because "true women were considered the guardians of morality, when a woman transgressed she seemed to threaten the very foundations of society . . . this early view of the female criminal as beyond redemption was related to the archetype of the Dark Lady, a woman of uncommon strength, seductive power, and evil inclination." Nicole Hahn Rafter, *Partial Justice: Women, Prisons, and Social Control,* 2d ed. (New Brunswick, N.J.: Transaction Publishers, 1990), 49.

20. Record Group 48, MLR A1–475, *Register of Punishments, 1831–1862,* NARA II.

21. "Terrible Affair in the Ohio Penitentiary," *New York Times,* Aug. 6, 1859.

22. Col. H. B. Carrington, "Attempted Revolt of Confederate Prisoners of War at Camp Chase, Ohio," June 1, 1862, OHS.

23. Speer, *Portals to Hell,* 223. Inmates' escape attempts at this time coincided with a plot hatched by the followers of Peace Democrat Clement Vallandigham, specifically state school commissioner Charles W. H. Cathcart, and fellow conspirators Nathan Cressup, Mr. Slade (a cutter in a local clothier), and Dr. Lazelle (a Rebel surgeon on parole). Union authorities detained these men, who planned to release the nearly three thousand Confederate inmates at Camp Chase, supply them with arms, and then release Confederate general John Hunt Morgan from the Ohio Penitentiary and march for the South, destroying everything in their wake. See Zombek, "Camp Chase Prison," 24–48.

24. *Daily Milwaukee News,* Dec. 25, 1864, 1.

25. "The Ringleader," *Richmond Daily Dispatch,* Dec. 29, 1862, and "Attempt to Blow up a Building," *Richmond Daily Dispatch,* Nov. 3, 1862, http://dlxs.richmond.edu/d/ddr.

26. *Hagerstown (Md.) Torch Light and Advertiser,* Aug. 19, 1823, 2; "Virginia Penitentiary," *Raleigh (N.C.) Southern Weekly Post,* Dec. 16, 1854, 2; "Fire in the Virginia Penitentiary," *Milwaukee Weekly Wisconsin,* Dec. 20, 1854, 2.

27. Andrea Nicole Mitchell, "The Georgia Penitentiary at Milledgeville" (MA thesis, Georgia College and State Univ., 2003), 53–54, 51; Walden, "History of the Georgia Penitentiary at Milledgeville, 1817–1868," 46; "Attempt to Burn a Prison," *Philadelphia Public Ledger,* Aug. 28, 1838, 2.

28. "Miscellaneous Items," *Raleigh (N.C.) Register,* July 6, 1861, 3. Gov. John Letcher, in his annual message, noted that all buildings had been reconstructed, and that nearly all machinery in the ax factory had been replaced and would soon resume operation. He, however, regretted that the machinery in the weaving department would take quite some time to resume operations. The loss to the state amounted to between $10,000 and $12,000. "Governor Letcher's Message," *Richmond Dispatch,* Dec. 2, 1861, 5.

29. Thomas Thornley to Board of Inspectors, May 1, 1856, Record Group 48, Records of the Office of the Secretary of the Interior, Entry 466, Misc. Letters to the Board of Inspectors and Warden, Box 1, NARA II.

30. Goldsmith, "History from the Inside Out," 113.

31. *Warden's Report,* Jan. 1, 1854, Record Group 48, Records of the Office of the Secretary of the Interior, Records Relating to the U.S. Penitentiary for the District of Columbia, 1826–65, Miscellaneous Records, 1829–62, Entry 470, Box 2, NARA II.

32. Office of the Board of Inspectors of U.S. Penitentiary D.C., Mar. 22, 1861, To the Honorable Caleb B. Smith, Secretary of the Interior, Record Group 48, Records of the Office of the Secretary of the Interior, Entry 466, Miscellaneous Letters to the Board of Inspectors and Warden, Box 1, NARA II.

33. Finley, *Memorials of Prison Life,* 206.

34. "Local Matters . . . Escaped from Prison," *Richmond Dispatch,* Sept. 5, 1854, 4; W. Maxwell to Mr. Sengstack, Mar. 11, 1861, Record Group 48, Records of the Office of the Secretary of the Interior, Records Relating to the U.S. Penitentiary for the District of Columbia, 1826–65, Miscellaneous Records, 1829–62, Entry 470, Box 3, NARA II.

35. "A Cute Trick," *Weekly Raleigh (N.C.) Register,* Mar. 6, 1840, 1.

36. It is unclear whether Savage was a member of the Union Army or Confederate Army. "Interesting Narrative of an Escaped Prisoner," *Richmond Daily Dispatch,* July 19, 1862; *Memphis Daily Appeal,* Sept. 15, 1862, 1; "Foiled in His Purpose," *Richmond Daily Dispatch,* Dec. 28, 1864, http://dlxs.richmond.edu/d/ddr.

37. "Trouble on Johnson's Island—Attempt of the Prisoners to Escape—The Attempt Discovered and Frustrated," *Nashville Daily Union,* June 9, 1864, 1.

38. Xenophon to Dear Sir, Jan. 23, 1865, in the Edward Alexander Scovill Papers, 1862–71, WRHS.

39. "Nineties" was the method that Andersonville officials used to organize inmates into detachments for ration distribution. Citations from this and the above paragraph from the following: entry July 21, 1864, James Vance Diary, *Andersonville Diaries,* vol. 3, 442; entry Monday, July 18, 1864, John L. Hoster, *Adventure of a Soldier,* 96; entry July 16, 1864, Alonzo Tuttle Decker Diary; entry May 18, 1864, John Duff Diary, *Andersonville Diaries,* vol. 1, 17, 54. All from ANHS. Entry July 17, 1864, in the Andrew G. White Papers, 1864–1905, LOC); entry June 18, 1864, in the David Weimer Diaries, 1839–1921, LOC.

40. Citations from this and the previous paragraph from Brown, *The Salisbury Prison,* 79, 82; entry Feb. 13, 1864, John C. Ely Diary, *Andersonville Diaries,* vol. 1,

85, ANHS; Robert H. Kellogg, *Life and Death in Rebel Prisons* (1865; repr., Bedford, Mass.: Applewood Books), 126–27.

41. Walden, "History of the Georgia Penitentiary," 92. Walden also notes on pp. 129–30 that by the end of 1853, the Georgia Penitentiary witnessed seventy-one escapees, forty-five of whom guards recaptured, and three of whom they killed in the act. *Weekly Raleigh Register,* Dec. 29, 1826, 3; "From the Ohio Bulletin—Ohio Penitentiary," *Wilmington (Ohio) Democrat and Herald,* Jan. 31, 1840, 3.

42. "Attempt of Rebel officers to Escape from Johnson's Island," *Janesville (Wis.) Weekly Gazette,* Jan. 1, 1864, 4. Also printed in *Reading (Pa.) Times,* Jan. 5, 1864, 3.

43. The signature line is cut off of this correspondence, but the likely author was Henry Wirz. Unknown to Gen. J. H. Winder, Sept. 16, 1862, in Record Group 109, ch. 9, vol. 199 ½, "Secretary of War Letters Confederate Military Prison Richmond, Virginia January 1862–December 1863," NARA I; "Escape of Prisoners," *Washington (D.C.) National Republican,* May 14, 1864, 2.

44. Citations from this and the above paragraph from "Miscellaneous News &c," *Cincinnati Enquirer,* Nov. 18, 1864, 3; *Salisbury Daily Carolina Watchman,* Nov. 11, 1864, 2; Brown, *The Salisbury Prison,* 52–53; "Army Newspaper Correspondents," *Times* (London), Feb. 3, 1865, 28.

45. Entries Jan. 16, 1864, and Feb. 7, 1864, in the Robert Bingham Papers, #3731-z, SHC UNC.

46. Entries written in pencil and entitled "Trading" in the Nathaniel Shepard Armstrong Price Papers, 1861–2010, LOC.

47. Peter Force, R. R. Crawford, and George Parker, to J. Thompson, secretary of the interior, Oct. 26, 1860, Record Group 48, Records of the Office of the Secretary of the Interior, Entry 466, Miscellaneous Letters to the Board of Inspectors and Warden, Box 1, NARA II.

48. Ohio General Assembly, 1864–65, "Report of the Committee on the Penitentiary," OHS.

49. W. David Lewis notes that the procedures to which penitentiary officials subject incoming convicts amounted to a "process of calculated humiliation" that ultimately began the process of negating inmates' individuality. Lewis, *From Newgate to Dannemora,* 91–92.

50. Capt. Samuel Burks Taylor to Sister, Oct. 17, 1863, Samuel Taylor Burks Letter, OHS.

51. Speer, *Portals to Hell,* 149.

52. Lewis, *From Newgate to Dannemora,* 122–23.

53. United States War Department, General Orders No. 207 (July 3, 1863), in Flory, *Prisoners of War,* 148. General Orders No. 100, The Lieber Code, Art. 77.

54. Information from this and the preceding paragraph from Ohio Penitentiary, *Annual Report of the Directors and Warden . . . , 1863,* 7, OHS.

55. Hines, "Thrilling Narrative of the Escape of Gen. John H. Morgan"; Ohio General Assembly 1864–65, *Report of the Committee on the Penitentiary, 1864,* OHS.

56. McLennan, *The Crisis of Imprisonment,* 44.

57. "The *Louisville Journal* Says of the Treatment of Morgan's Men who are Still Confined in the Ohio Penitentiary," *Fayetteville (N.C.) Observer,* Jan. 11, 1864; "Daring Rebel Plot Frustrated," *Milwaukee Daily Sentinel,* Feb. 26, 1864.

58. "Narrative of Gen Morgan's Escape," *Richmond Daily Dispatch,* Jan. 6, 1864, http://dlxs.richmond.edu/d/ddr/.

59. For further information on Morgan's visit to Libby Prison, see Frances H. Casstevens, *"Out of the Mouths of Hell": Civil War Prisons and Escapes* (Jefferson, N.C.: McFarland, 2005), 273. Col. Thomas Rose of the 77th Pennsylvania Volunteers, and Maj. Andrew Hamilton of the 12th Kentucky Cavalry secretly organized work parties to descend into the basement of Libby Prison and began to dig a tunnel behind stoves and fireplaces in the prison's kitchen. Federal soldiers dug their sixty-foot route to freedom in forty-seven days, primarily using knives, chisels, and spittoons. The ingenious inmates masked their work by spreading dirt from their digging over the cellar floor and covering it with straw. In the end, 109 prisoners escaped, 59 reached Union lines, 2 drowned, and 48 were recaptured. For information on the tunnel's excavation, see Speer, *Portals to Hell,* 231–32; for information on escape and recapture, see Blakey, *General John H. Winder,* 172–73.

60. Entries July 17, 1864; July 19, 1864; July 28, 1864; and September 19, 1864, in the Andrew G. White Papers, 1864–1905. LOC.

61. Robert Scott Davis notes that escape attempts increased, albeit slightly, as Andersonville's population climbed. The population peaked at 33,006 in August 1864, but escapes only increased from 20 in July to 30 in August. Robert Scott Davis, "Escape from Andersonville: A Study in Isolation and Imprisonment," *The Journal of Military History* 67, no. 4 (Oct. 2003): 1069.

62. Ira B. Sampson recalled that escapees were hunted by bloodhounds and that authorities found three tunnels in late June 1864. Entries June 1, 1864; June 3, 1864; and June 27, 1864, in the Ira B. Sampson Papers #3870-z, SHC UNC. David Weimer recalled that the Rebels directed four cannons toward inmates with orders to fire if they attempted escape, and that two men from his mess commenced tunneling. Entries October 23, 1864, and October 26, 1864, in the David F. Weimer Diaries, 1839–1921, LOC. John H. Winder to Gen. S. Cooper, Aug. 13, 1864, O.R. II, vol. 7, 588–89. Entry Aug. 9, 1864, in the Alonzo Tuttle Decker Diary, *Andersonville Diaries,* vol. 1, 18, and entry Aug. 28, 1864, in the James Vance Diary, *Andersonville Diaries,* vol. 3, 446, ANHS.

63. "Washington City Items," *Baltimore Sun,* Mar. 17, 1840, 2; Thornton, *A Complete Guide,* 56–57; H. Exec. Doc. 49, 22d Cong., 2d sess., *Journal and Reception of Convicts* (Jan. 19, 1833).

64. Ohio Penitentiary, *Annual Report of the Directors and Warden . . . , 1839,* 5–6, OHS.

65. Ohio Penitentiary, *Annual Report of the Directors and Warden . . . , 1860,* OHS.

66. Keve, *The History of Corrections in Virginia,* 26; "Postscript," *Weekly Raleigh (N.C.) Register,* June 25, 1803, 3.

67. Virginia General Assembly, *Report of the Joint Committee to Examine the Penitentiary, 1840–1841,* Jan. 30, 1841, VHS.

68. For the number of black inmates at the Virginia Penitentiary, see Zombek, "Transcending Stereotypes," Appendix; Doc. No. 14, *Annual Report of the Board of Directors of the Penitentiary Institution, 1851,* 18, LVA; "By Telegraph to the *Daily Eagle*—From Virginia," *Brooklyn Daily Eagle,* Dec. 28, 1853, 3.

69. The Georgia Penitentiary held 214 inmates at the end of October 1861. Walden, "History of the Georgia Penitentiary," 144; *New Orleans Times Picayune,* Aug. 6, 1861, 2.

70. For population totals throughout the war, see Doc. No. 6, *Annual Report of the Board of Directors of the Penitentiary Institution, Year ending September 30, 1862,* 5; Doc. No. 66, *Report of the Joint Committee on the Penitentiary, March 1862,* 3; Doc. No. 9, *Annual Report of the Board of Directors of the Penitentiary Institution, Year Ending September 30, 1863,* 18; Doc. No. 12, *Annual Report of the Board of Directors of the Penitentiary Institution, Year Ending September 30, 1864,* LVA.

71. Doc. No. 1, *Message of the Governor of Virginia and Accompanying Documents,* x, 19.

72. Doc. No. 12, *Annual Report of the Board of Directors of the Penitentiary Institution, Year Ending September 30, 1864,* 6, LVA.

73. Rebecca McLennan makes this assertion regarding a prison break at New York's Sing Sing prison in 1913. Security was high at the prison during that year, but prisoners nonetheless used their numbers to their advantage and effected escape. During the nineteenth century, particularly during wartime, military prison and penitentiary officials worried about the prospect of inmates' revolt or escape. McLennan, *The Crisis of Imprisonment,* 1.

74. "Arrival from Camp Chase," *Wilmington (N.C.) Journal,* Nov. 12, 1863, 4; *White Cloud Kansas Chief,* Mar. 17, 1864, 2.

75. For information about the Canada plot, see "Prisoners on Johnson's Island," "More Stuff," and "More about the Plot—Buffalo," *Dayton Daily Empire,* Nov. 12, 1863, 4; "By Telegraph" and "Johnson's Island," *Washington (D.C.) National Republican,* Nov. 13, 1863, 2; "The Rebel Plot in Canada," "Further Particulars of the Rebel Plan to Escape," and "More Preparations for Defense," *Washington (D.C.) National Republican,* Nov. 14, 1863, 1. Report from propeller captain from "Buffalo, November 13," *Janesville (Wis.) Weekly Gazette,* Nov. 20, 1863, 1. Entry Nov. 11, 1863, in the Robert Bingham Papers, #3731-z, SHC UNC.

76. Citations from this and the above two paragraphs from entry Jan. 1, 1864, in the E. D. Dixon Recollections, #223-z, SHC UNC; entries Jan. 4, 1864, and Jan. 6, 1864, in the Robert Bingham Papers, #3731-z, SHC UNC; entries Jan. 21 and 22, 1864, in the Virgil S. Murphey Diary, #534-z, SHC UNC.

77. A. W. Mangum to Sister, Mar. 11, 1862, in the Mangum Family Papers #483, SHC UNC. J. A. Lowry to Mother, July 20, 1862, in the James Addison Lowry Letters #5196, SHC UNC.

78. *Raleigh (N.C.) Weekly Standard,* Oct. 28, 1863, 3; *New York Times,* Nov. 1, 1863, 3.

79. Jno. H. Gee to J. H. Winder, Dec. 15, 1864, in United States War Department, *The War of the Rebellion: A Compilation of the Official Records of the Union and Confederate Armies,* Series II, vol. 7, 1230, O.R.

80. Peter Zinn to Maj. Joseph Darr Jr., Nov. 21, 1862, O.R., Series II, vol. 5, 139.

81. For the cases of Cloyd, Rutter, and Hurst, see W. Richardson to Col. W. Hoffman, July 19, 1864, and W. Richardson to Col. W. Hoffman, July 19, 1864 (two separate letters), O.R., Series II, vol. 7, 474–75.

82. Inmates understood that the punishment for approaching windows was close confinement. See Marshall, *American Bastille,* 325–26; Griffith, "Fredericksburg's Political Hostages," 416–17, 422.

83. All stories found in the *Richmond Daily Dispatch:* "Escape of a Condemned Man," Oct. 21, 1862; "Escape from Castle Thunder," Feb. 17, 1865; Webster's account found in "Attempted Escapes," Mar. 30, 1863, and "Execution of Captain Webster," June 1, 1863, http://dlxs.richmond.edu/d/ddr.

7. Fallen from Grace

1. "New Prisons," *Dayton Empire,* reprinted in *Dawson's Fort Wayne Weekly Times,* May 1, 1864, 2.

2. Dodge, *Whores and Thieves of the Worst Kind,* 12.

3. Ibid., 13.

4. Ayers, *Vengeance and Justice,* 62; Rafter, *Partial Justice,* 10.

5. Edith Abbott, "The Civil War and the Crime Wave of 1865–1870," *Social Science Review* 1, no. 2 (1927): 215.

6. Estimate of the number of women confined in Castle Thunder in Parker, *Richmond's Civil War Prisons,* 25.

7. Kristen L. Streater, "'She-Rebels' on the Supply Line: Gender Conventions in Civil War Kentucky," in *Occupied Women: Gender, Military Occupation, and the American Civil War,* ed. LeeAnn Whites and Alecia P. Long (Baton Rouge: Louisiana State Univ. Press, 2009), 98; LeeAnn Whites, "'Corresponding with the Enemy': Mobilizing the Relational Field of Battle in St. Louis," in Whites and Long, *Occupied Women,* 111; Dodge, *Whores and Thieves of the Worst Kind,* 12. For an excellent study of women's prisons in the postwar West, see Anne M. Butler, *Gendered Justice in the American West: Women Prisoners in Men's Penitentiaries* (Urbana: Univ. of Illinois Press, 1997).

8. Rafter, *Partial Justice,* xii.

9. Deborah Gray White, *Ar'n't I a Woman?: Female Slaves in the Plantation South* (New York: W. W. Norton, 1999), 15, 30–31; Lewis, *From Newgate to Dannemora,* 158.

10. Bynum contends that women, particularly poor white and free black women in the South, needed the state to exercise patriarchal control since they typically had no other form of male protection. Isenberg, *Sex and Citizenship,* xii, 28–29, 87; Bynum, *Unruly Women,* 57.

11. Percentages derived from available statistics. *Ohio Statesman,* quoted in the *Huntington Indiana Herald,* Nov. 7, 1860, 3. In D.C., the black female population was eleven and the white one in 1850. This was the largest difference between black and white female inmates. In Virginia, black women outnumbered white women by fourteen in 1855 and 1856. Zombek, "Transcending Stereotypes," Appendix.

12. Citations from this and the previous paragraph from No. 380, "An Act to Reform the Penal Code of This State, and to Adapt the Same to the Penitentiary System," Penal Code 1816, in Lamar, *A Compilation of the Laws of the State of Georgia,* 668; "The Georgia Penitentiary," *Georgia Journal,* quoted in *Raleigh (N.C.) Minerva,* Nov. 29, 1816, 3; "Georgia Penitentiary," *Baltimore Sun,* Dec. 22, 1847, 4; Mitchell, "The Georgia Penitentiary at Milledgeville," 65; Walden, "History of the Georgia Penitentiary," 31, 116–17.

13. Rafter, *Partial Justice,* xxx.

14. Silber, *Gender and the Sectional Conflict,* 40–41.

15. Keve, *The History of Corrections in Virginia,* 26.

16. Proceedings of the Monthly Visitors Monday Morning, Oct. 30, 1811, Virginia Penitentiary, *Penitentiary Papers, 1796–1865,* Subseries C, LVA.

17. Citations from this and the above paragraph from *Pittsburgh Gazette,* Aug. 5, 1833, 2; "Female Convicts," *Lynchburg Express,* quoted in *Salisbury Carolina Watchman,* Dec. 25, 1851, 3; "A Fact for the Ladies," *Richmond Enquirer,* quoted in the *Raleigh (N.C.) Southern Weekly Post,* Oct. 8, 1853, 4.

18. "From the *Ohio Bulletin*—Ohio Penitentiary," *Wilmington (Ohio) Democrat and Herald,* Jan. 31, 1840, 3; "Ohio Penitentiary," quoting from the *Cincinnati Republican* in *Alton (Ill.) Telegraph,* Feb. 5, 1842, 3. I am unsure, given the available data, whether these women were white or black.

19. Ohio Penitentiary, *Annual Report of the Director and Wardens . . . , 1855,* 5, OHS.

20. Finley, *Memorials of Prison Life,* 60–61.

21. Ibid., 99.

22. Ibid., 136.

23. Box 1, Punishments 1831–47, Record Group 48, MLR A1–475, *Register of Punishments, 1831–1862,* NARA II.

24. Rafter, *Partial Justice,* 7.

25. Finley, *Memorials of Prison Life,* 322.

26. Isenberg, *Sex and Citizenship in Antebellum America,* 7–8, 44.

27. Dix, *Remarks on Prisons,* 48.

28. Ohio Penitentiary, *Annual Report of the Director and Wardens . . . , 1855,* 47, OHS.

29. H. Exec. Doc. No. 45, 33rd Cong., 1st sess. (Jan. 16, 1854), 4, NYPL.

30. *Matron's Report, Oct. 1, 1855,* in *Warden's Report, 1855,* RG 48, Records of the Secretary of the Interior, Records Relating to the U.S. Penitentiary for the District of Columbia, 1826–65, Miscellaneous Records, 1829–62, Entry 470, Box 2, NARA II.

31. In the antebellum period, there were never more than three white women at the Virginia Penitentiary, four white women at the D.C. Penitentiary, and three

white women at the Ohio Penitentiary. Alexis de Tocqueville noted that the United States had one white woman in confinement for every one hundred prisoners, while Europe had twenty in one hundred. De Beaumont and de Tocqueville, *On the Penitentiary System,* 99. For the female population of the Virginia, D.C., and Ohio penitentiaries, see Zombek, "Transcending Stereotypes," Appendix.

32. Thornton does not list the specific date of Bryant's imprisonment, but she does note that Bryant was held during Thomas Thornley's term as warden (1853–59). See Thornton, *A Complete Guide,* 35. Thornton does not list the population of the female department during this time. My best guess, judging from the 1852 annual report, is that it was around eight. See *Warden's Report,* "Message from the President of the United States transmitting the Annual Report of the Inspectors of the Penitentiary in the District of Columbia," H. Exec. Doc. No. 41, 32d Cong., 2d sess. (Feb. 10, 1853), NYPL.

33. Bynum, *Unruly Women,* 112.

34. Ohio Penitentiary, *Annual Report of the Director and Wardens . . . , 1861, 1862,* and *1863,* OHSy; Doc. No. 13, *Annual Report . . . , 1861;* Doc. No. 9, *Annual Report . . . , 1863;* Doc. No. 7, *Report of the Superintendent, 1863;* and Doc. No. 12, *Annual Report . . . , 1864,* LVA.

35. Doc. No. 7, *Report of the Superintendent . . . , 1863,* 7, LVA.

36. Mitchell, "The Georgia Penitentiary," 67.

37. In her study of women's sphere in American society, Nancy Cott notes that common female domestic duties included sewing shirts and other articles of clothing, ironing, washing, and spinning. See Nancy Cott, *The Bonds of Womanhood: Woman's Sphere in New England, 1780–1835,* 2d ed. (New Haven: Yale Univ. Press, 1997), 41.

38. Historian Melinda Lawson explains the origin of Soldiers' Aid Societies as follows: American women, as early as the 1790s, had been "forming charitable societies and auxiliaries to male societies as a means of combating the poverty and vice that they saw around them. With the firing on Fort Sumter on April 12, 1861, these women's organizations . . . voluntarily reconfigured themselves as soldiers' aid societies" that gathered material support for the Union troops. See Melinda Lawson, *Patriot Fires: Forging a New American Nationalism in the Civil War North* (Lawrence: Univ. Press of Kansas, 2002), 22. The Sisters of Charity were a Catholic religious order founded by Elizabeth Seton in Emmitsburg, Maryland, in 1809. During the 1840s, the order became affiliated with the French Daughters of Charity, headquartered in Emmetsburg, Pennsylvania. This order specialized in nursing, and its adherents both provided supplies for Union troops and nursed wounded soldiers in many areas of the North and the South. For a history of the Sisters of Charity, see Sisters of Charity of Cincinnati, "Our History," http://srcharitycinti.org/ about/ history.htm. For information on the Daughters of Charity, their expertise in nursing, and their activity in the South, see Virginia Gould, "'Oh, I Pass Everywhere': Catholic Nuns in the Gulf South during the Civil War," in *Battle Scars: Gender and Sexuality in the American Civil War,* ed. Catherine Clinton and Nina Silber (New York: Oxford Univ. Press, 2006), 41–60.

39. Ohio Penitentiary, *Annual Report of the Director and Wardens . . . , 1861, 1862,* and *1863,* OHS.

40. It is unclear from the evidence whether these women were committing prostitution and other crimes with civilians or with soldiers. Examples of quoted cases can be found in "Going Away," *Richmond Daily Dispatch,* Dec. 12, 1862, and "Incident on the Cars," *Richmond Daily Dispatch,* May 23, 1863. I searched the entire newspaper from 1861 through 1865 to determine cause of arrest, and I searched Series II of the Official Records to obtain a summary of crimes.

41. To gain this information, I searched Series II of the *Official Records* for information on Camp Chase and Old Capitol Prison.

42. "Prison Record," *Richmond Daily Dispatch,* July 9, 1863; Edwin Stanton to Col. Ludlow, June 30, 1863, and Edwin Stanton to Major Turner, June 30, 1863, O.R. Series II, vol. 6, 62–63.

43. "Arrest of Ladies," *New York Herald Washington Correspondence* in the *Cincinnati Enquirer,* May 31, 1862, 2.

44. *New York Times,* June 21, 1862, 8; "Signaling Prisoners," *Washington (D.C.) National Republican,* Apr. 11, 1863, 3.

45. Saml. Galloway to L. C. Turner, Apr. 23, 1863, O.R. II, vol. 5, 514–15; *Memphis Daily Appeal,* Apr. 24, 1863, 1.

46. Jno. Mason to William Hoffman, Apr. 23, 1863, O.R. Series II, vol. 5, 511.

47. "Washington, October 30," *Janesville (Wis.) Weekly Gazette,* Nov. 7, 1862, 1.

48. "Miscellaneous News Items," *Memphis Daily Appeal,* Apr. 10, 1864, 1; "News from Washington," *New York Times,* Sept. 23, 1864, 1.

49. Wilson Barstow to Brig. Gen. Wadsworth, Apr. 1, 1862, O.R. Series II, vol. 2, 577.

50. C. P. Wolcott to Brig. Gen. Wadsworth, Aug. 7, 1861, O.R. Series II, vol. 4, 310.

51. "The Female Traitors," *New York Times,* Jan. 22, 1862, 2.

52. "A Furious Female Secessionist," *Zanesville (Ohio) Daily Courier,* Jan. 10, 1862, 1.

53. Bynum, *Unruly Women,* 57.

54. *Cincinnati Enquirer,* Jan. 28, 1863, 3; "Women and Children Sent from Their Homes," *Richmond Daily Dispatch,* June 1, 1863.

55. Edward Ayers contends that the antebellum South's honor system "offered women nothing except prestige by association with a male relative." With male relatives absent, women often fell from grace and needed the state to ensure virtue. Ayers, *Vengeance and Justice,* 29. Victoria Bynum offers a similar analysis in her discussion of poor white and free black women. Bynum contends that these women, "lacking identification with a powerful class of white males either as wives or slaves, they posed a potential threat to the social harmony of a community" and therefore "the state assumed the role of patriarch in the lives of such women." Bynum, *Unruly Women,* 57.

56. For Victorian attitudes toward incarceration, see Elizabeth D. Leonard, *All the Daring of the Soldier: Women of the Civil War Armies* (New York: Penguin Books, 2001), 44. Bertram Wyatt-Brown claims that "Honor and interest combined to repress feminine lustfulness" and that men, "as proprietors and protectors of female

virtue . . . were brought to public shame by the tarnished woman." Wyatt-Brown, *Southern Honor,* 294.

57. "Caged Camp Followers," *Richmond Examiner,* July 19, 1864, http://www .mdgorman.com/Written_Accounts/Examiner/1864/richmond_examiner_719 1864.htm; Kann, *Punishment, Prisons, and Patriarchy,* 81.

58. Stephanie McCurry, *Confederate Reckoning: Power and Politics in the Civil War South* (Cambridge, Mass.: Harvard Univ. Press, 2010), 25.

59. Joan Scott notes that Natalie Davis suggested that historians should seek to understand "the range in sex roles and in sexual symbolism in different societies and periods, to find out what meaning they had and how they functioned to maintain the social order or to promote its change." The discrepancy between Confederate officials' interpretations of female soldiers and those of journalists provide a good example of a society very much in transition in terms of acceptable female behavior. Joan Scott, "Gender," in *Gender and the Politics of History* (New York: Columbia Univ. Press, 1988), 29.

60. Drew Faust, *Mothers of Invention: Women of the Slaveholding South in the American Civil War* (Chapel Hill: Univ. of North Carolina Press, 1996), 220.

61. Loreta Janeta Velazquez, *The Woman in Battle: A Narrative of the Exploits, Adventures, and Travels of Madame Loreta Janeta Velazquez, Otherwise Known as Lieutenant Harry T. Buford,* ed. C. J. Worthington (Richmond, Va.: Dustin, Gilman & Co., 1876), 177–81; "Documenting the American South," http://docsouth.unc.edu/ fpn/velazquez/velazquez.html.

62. Velazquez, *The Woman in Battle,* 278–79.

63. Ibid., 279.

64. Ibid., 281. According to Velazquez, Winder assigned a member of the North Carolina Militia to arrest her and frame her for disloyalty, but she outsmarted the ruse.

65. "City Intelligence—The Female Lieutenant, 'Lt. Buford,'" *Richmond Examiner,* June 11, 1863, Issue 113, Col. D.

66. DeAnn Blanton and Lauren M. Cook, *They Fought Like Demons: Women Soldiers in the American Civil War* (Baton Rouge: Louisiana State Univ. Press, 2002), 57, 123, 129, 148, 150.

67. "Female Soldiers," *Richmond Whig,* Oct. 31, 1864, http://www.mdgorman .com/Written_Accounts/Whig/1864/richmond_whig,_10_31_1864.htm. Anne Butler contends that "the penitentiary symbolized the most extreme penalty for breaking the covenants of society in regard to gender place." My hypothesis about Castle Thunder's female inmates' interpretation of their prison sentences stems from this assertion. Butler, *Gendered Justice,* 228; Blanton and Cook, *They Fought Like Demons,* 154.

68. In his analysis of the Richmond Bread Riot, Michael Chesson demonstrated how young, attractive women with good reputations often received favorable legal treatment and favorable reviews in the press. Michael B. Chesson, "Harlots or Heroines?: A New Look at the Richmond Bread Riot," *Virginia Magazine of History and Biography* 92, no. 2 (Apr. 1984): 163, 166.

69. "The News: Female Spy Arrested in Richmond," *Semi-Weekly Raleigh Register*, July 22, 1863.

70. Allan's case provides one counterpoint to Victoria Bynum's contention that if a woman misbehaved, even wealth could not prevent her plunge in status. Allan was, however, the exception to this rule. Bynum, *Unruly Women*, 45.

71. Sally A. Brock, *Richmond during the War: Four Years of Personal Observation by a Richmond Lady* (New York: G. W. Carleton & Company Publishers, 1867), 249–50.

72. Wilson Barstow to Brig. Gen. Wadsworth, Apr. 1, 1862, O.R. Series II, vol. 2, 577.

73. Dr. Mary E. Walker received her MD from Syracuse Medical College. During the Civil War, she volunteered as a Union physician, particularly in the Western theater. She received the Congressional Medal of Honor for her wartime service. For this and further information on Walker, see, Elizabeth D. Leonard, "Mary Walker, Mary Surratt, and Some Thoughts on Gender in the Civil War," in *Battle Scars: Gender and Sexuality in the American Civil War*, ed. Catherine Clinton and Nina Silber (New York: Oxford Univ. Press, 2006), 104–9; and Catherine Clinton, "'Public Women' and Sexual Politics during the American Civil War," in Clinton and Silber, *Battle Scars*, 70–74.

74. Faust, *Mothers of Invention*, 101, 109, 112.

75. "From Southern Papers," *New Haven Daily Palladium*, May 6, 1864, Issue 134, Col. A.

76. "Female Yankee Surgeon," *Richmond Sentinel*, Apr. 22, 1864, http://www.mdgorman.com/Written_Accounts/Sentinel/1864/richmond_sentinel,_4_22_1864.htm; "Female Yankee Surgeon," *Richmond Whig*, Apr. 22, 1864, http://www.mdgorman.com/Written_Accounts/Whig/1864/richmond_whig,_4_22_1864.htm.

77. Dodge, *Whores and Thieves of the Worst Kind*, 30.

78. "Epitome of the Week," *Frank Leslie's (New York) Illustrated Newspaper*, July 16, 1864, Issue 459, Col. A, 259.

79. "Miss Walker, The Yankee Surgeoness," *Richmond Examiner*, June 29, 1864, http://www.mdgorman.com/Written_Accounts/Examiner/1864/richmond_examiner_6291864a.htm. Since the Emancipation Proclamation was in effect and African Americans served in the Union Army, Southerners considered Walker guilty of miscegenation, most commonly defined as relations between white women and black men. Bynum, *Unruly Women*, 96.

80. Walker's reported pleas prove contrary to Blanton and Cook's claim that "the majority of female POWs, Union and Confederate, accepted their fate as a misfortune of war just as their male comrades did." Blanton and Cook, *They Fought Like Demons*, 87.

81. "Dr. Mary E. Walker," *Richmond Whig*, May 2, 1864, http://www.mdgorman.com/Written_Accounts/Whig/1864/richmond_whig,_5_2_18642.htm.

82. "Miss Walker, the Yankee Surgeoness."

83. "City Intelligence," *Daily Richmond Examiner*, July 27, 1864.

84. Central Intelligence Agency, "Intelligence Collection—the North," https://www.cia.gov/library/publications/additional-publications/civil-war/p11.htm.

85. "Wants to Go Home," *Richmond Enquirer,* June 10, 1864, http://www.md gorman.com/Written_Accounts/Enquirer/1864/richmond_enquirer_61064.htm; Mrs. T. Webster to Jefferson Davis, Oct. 13, 1862, O.R. Series II, vol. IV, 917.

86. Gregory Downs contends that when women and men in North Carolina petitioned state or national authorities, they, through languages of gender, assumed the "mantle of the needed" and emphasized their powerlessness. This tactic tied the legitimacy of authority to the "leader's gentlemanly obligations to weak and dependent women" as women and men used gendered appeals to achieve their own ends. The same pattern is here evident in Richmond. Gregory P. Downs, *Declarations of Dependence: The Long Reconstruction of Popular Politics in the South, 1861–1908* (Chapel Hill: Univ. of North Carolina Press, 2011), 6; Central Intelligence Agency, "Intelligence Collection—the North."

87. Antonia Fort to dear Ma, Carroll Prison Sunday (n.d.) and poem Written in Prison by Antonia Fort to her mother in Willard Family Collection, Part I, Containers 170 and 173, LOC.

8. War's Legacy

1. "A Soldier's Reply," *Daily Milwaukee News,* June 28, 1865, 5.

2. Abbott, "The Civil War and the Crime Wave of 1865–1870," 233–34.

3. Lincoln designated the Albany Penitentiary (New York) the state prison at Clinton, New York, the Ohio Penitentiary, the Penitentiary at Jefferson City, Missouri, and "other prisons as the Secretary of War may designate" as military prisons. Abraham Lincoln, "Order Concerning Prisoners," Feb. 15, 1865, http://quod.lib.umich .edu/cgi/t/text/text-idx?c=lincoln;rgn=div1;view=text;idno=lincoln8;node=lincoln 8%3A627.

4. Dabney, *Richmond: The Story of a City,* 200.

5. "Herold's Confession Sent to Europe," *Daily Milwaukee News,* May 12, 1865, 1. Prior to their execution, federal officials held conspirators Mary Surratt and Dr. Samuel Mudd in the Old Capitol prison, and the six others on the ironclad ships *Montauk* and *Saugus.* Before the trial, federal authorities moved the conspirators to the penitentiary and shackled David Herold, Lewis Powell, Edman Spangler, and George Atzerodt to balls and chains. Doug Linder, "The Trial of the Lincoln Assassination Conspirators," 2009, http://law2.umkc.edu/faculty/projects/ftrials/lincoln conspiracy/lincolnaccount.html.

6. *Cincinnati Enquirer,* Mar. 27, 1865, 3; "Notice by the War Department," *Cincinnati Enquirer,* Apr. 10, 1865, 3; "Release of Prisoners," *Daily Milwaukee News,* June 9, 1865, 1; "Dispatches to the Associated Press Washington, Thursday June 29," *New York Times,* June 30, 1865, 1; "Under Sentence," *Philadelphia North American and United States Gazette,* Aug. 25, 1865.

7. "Old Capitol Prison at Auction," *Cleveland Daily Leader,* June 28, 1865, 1; *Daily Milwaukee News,* July 7, 1865, 1; E. D. Townsend to Maj. Gen. C. C. Augur, Nov. 29, 1865, O.R. Series II, vol. 8, 819; "Old Capitol Prison to Be Vacated and

Closed. Disposition of Prisoners Preparatory to the Restoration of the Writ of Habeas Corpus," *Washington (D.C.) National Republican,* Nov. 30, 1865, 2; "America from an American Correspondent," *Times* (London), Dec. 15, 1865, 6.

8. "Ex Governor John Letcher," *Washington (D.C.) Daily National Intelligencer,* July 12, 1865; *Montpelier Vermont Watchman and State Journal,* Nov. 17, 1865; *Cincinnati Enquirer,* May 20, 1865, 1; "The Arrest of Governor Vance," *New York Times,* May 22, 1865, 1; "Governor McGrath," *Daily Milwaukee News,* June 7, 1865; "Miscellaneous News, New York July 11," *Daily Milwaukee News,* July 13, 1865, 1. Colonel Harrison, Jefferson Davis's private secretary, was also lodged in the Old Capitol, according to the *Janesville Daily Gazette.* "The Prisoners," *Janesville (Wis.) Daily Gazette,* May 29, 1865, 1. The *National Republican* carried details of Wirz's execution, describing the scaffold scene and the request of his confessor, Father Boyle, for the body. "Reports on Behalf of Wirz," *Washington (D.C.) National Republican,* Nov. 10, 1865, 2. John Gee arrived at the Old Capitol in November 1865 and his sentence was commuted. "Afternoon Telegraph," *Cincinnati Enquirer,* Nov. 25, 1865, 1. For an excellent study of Gee's trial, see Guénaël Mettraux, "A Little-Known Case from the American Civil War: The War Crimes Trial of Major General John H. Gee," *Journal of International Criminal Justice* 8 (2010): 1059–68.

9. "From Telegraph Report," *New Orleans Times Picayune,* July 12, 1865, 2. For accounts of the fall of Richmond, see Emory M. Thomas, *The Confederate State of Richmond: A Biography of the Capital* (Baton Rouge: Louisiana State Univ. Press, 1971), and Ernest B. Furgurson, *Ashes of Glory: Richmond at War* (New York: Vintage Books, 1996).

10. "From Richmond," *Milwaukee News,* Apr. 12, 1865; "News of the Day: General News," *Richmond Republic,* quoted in *New York Times,* May 29, 1865, 4; "Castle Thunder," *Richmond Daily Dispatch,* Dec. 12, 1865.

11. *Daily Milwaukee News,* Apr. 7, 1865, 1; *New Orleans Times Picayune,* Apr. 11, 1865, 4; "Castle Thunder," *Richmond Daily Dispatch,* Dec. 12, 1865, http://dlxs.richmond.edu/d/ddr/; "Multiple News Items," *Chillicothe Scioto Gazette,* Jan. 9, 1866; *Gettysburg Adams Sentinel,* Dec. 5, 1865, 4.

12. "From Richmond," *Milwaukee News,* Apr. 12, 1865; *New Orleans Times Picayune,* Apr. 11, 1865, 4. This list of crimes was compiled from an examination of the collection "Papers Relating to Citizens, 1861–1867," National Archives and Record Administration, Record Group 109, www.fold3.com. The exact total number of inmates, however, remains unknown.

13. *Richmond Daily Dispatch,* general search conducted between the dates cited in the text, http://dlxs.richmond.edu/d/ddr/.

14. "Military Rule in Richmond" by a "Correspondent of the New York *World,*" *Milwaukee News,* July 21, 1865, 4.

15. Survey of crimes compiled from Virginia Penitentiary, *Prison Register and Indexes, 1865–1980,* Prison Register No. 1, LVA, and from a general newspaper search: "Local Matters: Sentence of the Prisoners," *Richmond Daily Dispatch,* Dec. 21, 1865; "Multiple News Items," *Denver Daily Rocky Mountain News,* June 19,

1875; *St. Louis Globe-Democrat,* Oct. 10, 1875, Issue 144, Col. C, 11; "Latest News Items," *San Francisco Daily Evening Bulletin,* July 13, 1876; "Horrible Affair at Canton, Ohio," *Columbus Crisis,* Oct. 16, 1867; "Multiple News Items," *St. Louis Globe-Democrat,* Jan. 4, 1876; "Military Prisoners Ledged in the Ohio Penitentiary," Oct. 19, 1865; "From Columbus Senate Proceedings—Penitentiary," Jan. 19, 1866; "Neighborhood News Special Reports," Feb. 8, 1866; "Local News," May 16, 1866; "Rebel Spy Released from the Ohio Penitentiary," July 21, 1866; "Multiple News Items," Oct. 11, 1866; "Local News," July 9, 1867; "News of the Day," Dec. 24, 1868, all from *Daily Cleveland Herald.*

16. Eric Foner notes that the Supreme Court's decision in *Ex Parte Milligan* threw into question Reconstruction policies, specifically martial law and Freedmen's Bureau courts, that congressional Republicans championed. The Reconstruction Act of 1867 divided the eleven Confederate states (except Tennessee) into five military districts to protect freedmen's rights and outline steps by which Confederate states could be recognized by Congress. Eric Foner, *Reconstruction: America's Unfinished Revolution, 1863–1877* (New York: HarperCollins, 1989), 272, 276.

17. "The Case of W. J. Brennan. Important Decision—Military Tribunals Unconstitutional," *Augusta Chronicle,* quoted in the *Atlanta Constitution,* Nov. 25, 1868, 2; emphasis in the original.

18. "Latest News—Our Richmond Correspondence," *Petersburg (Va.) Progress Index,* Feb. 19, 1866, 3; "Augusta Circuit Court," *Staunton (Va.) Spectator,* June 5, 1866, 3; "State News . . . Horse Thief Sentenced," *Petersburg (Va.) Progress Index,* May 29, 1868, 2.

19. "A Visit to the Penitentiary," *Petersburg (Va.) Progress Index,* July 7, 1868, 1.

20. The paper did not note how many inmates were involved in the affray. "Threatened Mutiny," *Raleigh (N.C.) Daily Standard,* Dec. 5, 1865, 1. The story was also printed in *Edwardsville (Ill.) Madison County Courier,* Dec. 7, 1865, 1.

21. *Gettysburg Adams Sentinel,* Dec. 26, 1865, 1; "From Columbus . . . Prisoners Confined in the Penitentiary," *Cincinnati Enquirer,* Jan. 11, 1866, 3.

22. "Cincinnati, April 23," *Alton (Ill.) Weekly Telegraph,* Apr. 28, 1865, 1; "Chicago—The Chicago Conspirators. CHARLES WALSH PARDONED—THOMAS B. PAYNE IMPRISONED—INDICTMENT OF THE SONDS OF LIBERTY," *Wilmington (N.C.) Herald,* July 4, 1865, 1; "A Traitor Unbosoms Himself," *Alton (Ill.) Telegraph,* June 8, 1866, 1; Foner, *Reconstruction,* 272.

23. "General Intelligence," *Elyria (Ohio) Independent Democrat,* July 5, 1865, 2; "Military Prisoners Ledged in the Ohio Penitentiary," *Daily Cleveland Herald,* Oct. 19, 1865.

24. "News of the Day," *Daily Cleveland Herald,* May 19, 1866.

25. "Rebel Spy Released from Ohio Penitentiary," *Daily Cleveland Herald,* July 21, 1866; *Raleigh (N.C.) Weekly Progress,* July 28, 1866, 2.

26. Information from this and the above paragraph from "A Good Resolution," *Cincinnati Enquirer,* Mar. 1, 1869, 4; "Ohio Legislature," *Coshocton (Ohio) Democrat,* Mar. 2, 1869, 1. Zombek, "Transcending Stereotypes," Appendix; *Washington (D.C.) National Republican,* Mar. 10, 1870, 1.

27. De Beaumont and de Tocqueville, *On the Penitentiary System in the United States,* 60–62; Kimmel, *Manhood in America,* 95; Kuntz, *Criminal Sentencing in Three Nineteenth-Century Cities,* 299.

28. James McPherson asserts that Civil War soldiers enlisted and continued fighting due partly to ideals of masculinity. McPherson contends that "duty and honor were closely linked to concepts of masculinity in Victorian America," and that war was a stern test of manhood, as soldiers desired to prove their manliness and honor under fire and soldiers were supported by civilians at home for their sacrifice. See McPherson, *For Cause and Comrades,* 25, 31. After the war, many veterans experienced a crisis of manhood. Nina Silber notes that as soldiers, veterans were the "pride and hope of the nation," but during the 1860s and 1870s, the volatile economy undermined masculine duty to provide for their families. Union veterans formed organizations like the Grand Army of the Republic to preserve their identity and establish their image of "manly heroism" in the United States. Nina Silber, *The Romance of Reunion: Northerners and the South, 1865–1900* (Chapel Hill: The Univ. of North Carolina Press, 1993), 58, 169.

29. McLennan, *The Crisis of Imprisonment,* 140.

30. "Prison Statistics," *Milwaukee Daily Sentinel,* Mar. 2, 1869; "By Telegraph from Washington," *Macon Georgia Weekly Telegraph and Georgia Journal & Messenger,* Dec. 14, 1869.

31. "Multiple News Items," *Chillicothe (Ohio) Scioto Gazette,* May 15, 1866; To His Excellency Gov. G. C. Walker, Governor of Virginia, Feb. 19, 1870, and Petition on behalf of Henry R. Jones, Mar. 21, 1870, *Penitentiary Papers, 1867–1897,* Subseries VI, Folder 1: Applications and Recommendations 1870, 1872, 1874, LVA.

32. Keve, *The History of Corrections in Virginia,* 70. Although the federal garrison left Richmond, Radical Republicans and President Ulysses S. Grant exerted heavy influence on the South in the early 1870s, particularly through the Enforcement Acts. For disfranchisement of former Confederates during congressional Reconstruction and the Enforcement Acts, see Foner, *Reconstruction,* 253–61, 454–59, and Michael Fitzgerald, *Splendid Failure: Postwar Reconstruction in the American South* (Chicago: Ivan R. Dee, 2007), 72, 89.

33. "The News Telegraphic Summary," *Milwaukee Daily Sentinel,* Mar. 10, 1869.

34. Information about Wardwell and his appointment from Scott Reynolds Nelson, *Steel Drivin' Man: John Henry, The Untold Story of an American Legend* (New York: Oxford Univ. Press, 2006), 59, 65, 66.

35. Ibid., 68; Alex Lichtenstein, *Twice the Work of Free Labor: The Political Economy of Convict Labor in the New South* (London: Verso, 1996), 51.

36. *Report of the Board of Directors of the Virginia Penitentiary, with Accompanying Documents, for the Year Ending Sept. 30, 1871* (Richmond: B. F. Walker, Supt. Public Printing, 1871), 25–26, 28–29, LVA. (These reports cited hereafter as *Report of the Board of Directors of the Virginia Penitentiary,* followed by the report date.)

37. Fitzgerald, *Splendid Failure,* 118.

38. In 1869 the U.S. House of Representatives released Report No. 45, which challenged the idea that the Northern refusal to continue prisoner exchanges in

1863 directly caused suffering and death in Northern and Southern prisons. Sanders Jr., *While in the Hands of the Enemy,* 310.

39. "A Singular and Gratifying Scene.—Rebel Soldiers Paying a Tribute to a Union Man from Maine," *Bangor Daily Whig & Courier,* July 2, 1868.

40. "State News," *Petersburg (Va.) Progress Index,* Apr. 23, 1868, 1; "State News," *Petersburg (Va.) Progress Index,* May 7, 1868, 3; "Sent to the Pen," *Petersburg (Va.) Progress Index,* May 25, 1868, 3; "Our Richmond Letter," *Petersburg (Va.) Progress Index,* Nov. 14, 1868, 1.

41. "'The Fourth' at the Pen," *Richmond Examiner* and *Enquirer* reprinted in *Petersburg (Va.) Progress Index,* July 6, 1868, 2.

42. Lichtenstein, *Twice the Work of Free Labor,* 25–26.

43. Dabney, *Richmond,* 216; for population totals, see Zombek, "Transcending Stereotypes," Appendix.

44. "Georgia Legislature—Senate—Wednesday July 29, 1868," *Atlanta Constitution,* July 30, 1868, 1; *Milledgeville Recorder,* quoted in *Atlanta Constitution,* June 3, 1869, 1.

45. For bills regarding convict leasing proposed, opposed, and authorized, see "Georgia Legislature—Senate—Thursday January 28, 1869," *Atlanta Constitution,* Jan. 29, 1869, 1; "Georgia Legislature—Senate—Monday March 8, 1869," *Atlanta Constitution,* Mar. 9, 1869, 1; "Georgia Legislature—Senate—Monday March 15, 1869," *Atlanta Constitution,* Mar. 16, 1869, 1. For information about the number of convicts leased in early May, see *Atlanta Constitution,* May 13, 1869, 1. News on the act that authorized the farming out of convicts found in "Official Executive Department, Atlanta, Georgia, July 21, 1869," *Atlanta Constitution,* July 24, 1869, 3. Principal keeper's report in "The Penitentiary," *Atlanta Constitution,* Aug. 23, 1870, 2.

46. *New Orleans Times Picayune,* Mar. 12, 1865, 8; *Sandusky Register,* quoted in the *New York Times,* Apr. 15, 1865, 4.

47. Citations for this and the preceding paragraph included here. For the stipulations of Johnson's Proclamation, see "President Johnson's Amnesty Proclamation," *New York Times,* May 30, 1865; *Janesville (Wis.) Weekly Gazette,* June 8, 1865, 4; "Camp Chase Items," *Cincinnati Enquirer,* May 27, 1865, 1. Penitentiary officials created a prison fund from a portion of the revenue generated from prisoners' labor and from money collected from incoming prisoners. Military prison authorities likewise created prison funds from the money collected from incoming inmates. These funds were used to address prisoners' needs, like transportation home and money to hold individuals over until they could find gainful employment; the latter applied mostly to penitentiary inmates while the former applied to both military prison and penitentiary inmates.

48. "Letter from a Rebel Officer," *Boston Journal,* printed in *Daily Milwaukee News,* May 16, 1865; The War Department ordered all POWs below the rank of colonel released upon taking the oath. War Dept., Adjutant General's Office: General Orders No. 85, May 8, 1865, *O.R.,* Series 2, vol. 8, 538; release of POWs below captain: Andrew Johnson, Executive Order—General Orders No. 109, June 6, 1865, "The American Presidency Project," http://www.presidency.ucsb.edu/ws/index.php?pid=72212.

49. "Pardoned," Macon reports summarized in the *Atlanta Constitution,* Sept. 19, 1869, 2.

50. "House of Representatives. Morning Session," *Cincinnati Enquirer,* May 13, 1868, 3. On June 3, 1870, the *Coshocton Tribune* reported that there were 1,016 inmates in the Ohio Penitentiary. *Coshocton (Ohio) Tribune,* June 3, 1870, 1; "General News," *Elyria (Ohio) Independent Democrat,* Aug. 3, 1870, 2.

51. "Our Richmond Letter," *Petersburg (Va.) Progress Index,* Aug. 3, 1868, 2.

52. "Execution of Oliver and Hartup—Retribution for Murder," *Elyria (Ohio) Independent Democrat,* Sept. 13, 1865, 3; "The Marion County Tragedy," *Cincinnati Enquirer,* Jan. 24, 1867, 1.

53. *Cincinnati Enquirer,* June 13, 1866, 2.

54. "Thirty-Ninth Congress, Second Session," *Washington (D.C.) Daily National Intelligencer,* Feb. 7, 1867; "Washington: The Registration Bill Passed," *Daily Cleveland Herald,* Mar. 20, 1867; *Bangor Daily Whig & Courier,* Mar. 21, 1867, Issue 68, Col. G.

55. Carla Yanni highlights how insane asylums expanded after the Civil War. As population increased, officials shifted their emphasis away from moral reform and toward regimentation. Carla Yanni, *The Architecture of Madness: Insane Asylums in the United States* (Minneapolis: Univ. of Minnesota Press, 2007).

56. *Janesville (Wis.) Daily Gazette,* May 4, 1865, 1.

57. Angela M. Zombek, "Paternalism and Imprisonment at Castle Thunder: Reinforcing Gender Norms in the Confederate Capital," *Civil War History* 63 no. 3 (Sept. 2017).

58. "Sale of Salisbury Prison Lot," *New Bern (N.C.) Times,* Sept. 29, 1866, 1; *Raleigh (N.C.) Sentinel,* Oct. 24, 1866, 2; "North Carolina News," *Wilmington (N.C.) Daily Dispatch,* Nov. 6, 1866, 1. Hinton R. Helper contended that slavery hindered the South's economic progress and that nonslaveholding whites should overthrow the planter aristocrats in his self-published work, *The Impending Crisis of the South* (New York: Burdick Brothers, 1857).

59. "To the Prisoners of War and of Arbitrary Arrests in the United States of America," *Columbus Crisis,* Sept. 25, 1867.

60. All information regarding the congressional investigation from *Report of the Treatment of Prisoners of War, by the Rebel Authorities, during the War of the Rebellion: To Which Are Appended the Testimony Taken by the Committee and Official Documents and Statistics, etc.,* H. Exec. Doc. 45, 40th Cong., 3rd sess. (Washington, D.C.: Government Printing Office, 1869), 5–7.

61. Ibid., especially 5–27.

62. "From the *Pioneer,*" *Raleigh (N.C.) Daily Standard,* June 26, 1866, 2.

63. "A Penitentiary," *Raleigh (N.C.) Sentinel,* Nov. 24, 1866.

64. "A Penitentiary," *Charlotte (N.C.) Democrat,* Dec. 25, 1866, 3.

65. North Carolina Department of Public Safety, "History of the North Carolina Correction System," http://www.doc.state.nc.us/admin; "State Penitentiary" and "For the *Journal,*" *Wilmington (N.C.) Journal,* July 31, 1868, 4.

66. "State Penitentiary," *Greensboro (N.C.) Patriot,* Aug. 13, 1868, 1.

67. "For the *Standard*—Salisbury Offers a Site for the Penitentiary Free," *Raleigh (N.C.) Daily Standard,* Jan. 19, 1869, 2.

68. "Senate, Monday, April 5, 1869," *Wilmington (N.C.) Journal,* Apr. 9, 1869, 3.

69. "The Penitentiary," *Salisbury (N.C.) Daily Carolina Watchman,* Apr. 9, 1869, 3; "The Penitentiary," *Charlotte (N.C.) Democrat,* Apr. 13, 1869, 3; Jason Tomberlin, "This Month in North Carolina History: January 1870—North Carolina State Penitentiary Opens," http://www2.lib.unc.edu/ncc/ref/nchistory/jan2007/index.html.

70. "Penitentiary Contracts—North Carolina Mechanics Ignored," *Tarborough (N.C.) Southerner,* Apr. 28, 1870, 2; "Governor's Message," *Winston-Salem (N.C.) People's Press,* Nov. 25, 1870, 2; *Brooklyn Daily Eagle,* Nov. 28, 1870, 1.

71. Tomberlin, "North Carolina State Penitentiary Opens"; "Prison Horror," *Raleigh (N.C.) Tri-Weekly Era,* Feb. 27, 1872, 2, emphasis in the original; "The North Carolina Penitentiary," *Raleigh (N.C.) Daily Era,* Oct. 31, 1872, 2.

Conclusion

1. McKelvey, *American Prisons,* 70, 88–89; E. C. Wines, *Report on the International Penitentiary Congress of London,* Held July 3–13, 1872, to Which Is Appended the Second Annual Report of the National Prison Association of the United States, Containing the Transactions of the National Prison Reform Congress, held at Baltimore, Maryland, January 21–24, 1873 (Washington, D.C.: Government Printing Office, 1873).

2. McKelvey, *American Prisons,* 91, 95.

3. "Christianity Behind the Bars—the Lecture by Mr. James Trimble at Temperance Hall No. 184 Superior Street," *Cleveland Morning Herald,* Oct. 27, 1871.

4. Enoch Wines to Gov. Walker, Sept. 27, 1869, enclosure July 1869: Office of the Prison Association of New York, Virginia Penitentiary, *Penitentiary Papers 1867–1897,* Call 25299, LVA.

5. F. H. Wines, *Punishment and Reformation,* 79.

6. Ibid., 6.

7. Patricia O'Brien notes in her study of France that the four major "spurts of penal reforms directly followed the four revolutions . . . in 1789, 1830, 1848, and 1871." Patricia O'Brien, *The Promise of Punishment: Prisons in Nineteenth-Century France* (Princeton, N.J.; Princeton Univ. Press, 1982), 20. Thomas Dumm notes that, after the revolution, the "establishment of a disciplinary society in the United States was the restless end of a quest to ensure the safety of the subjects of the liberal democratic state." Dumm, *Democracy and Punishment,* 146.

8. Foner, *Reconstruction,* 25. Rebecca McLennan also notes that the Union victory inspired a burst of reform activity. McLennan, *Crisis of Imprisonment,* 90–91.

9. Colvin, *Penitentiaries, Reformatories, and Chain Gangs,* 2.

10. E. C. Wines, *Report of the International Penitentiary Congress of London,* 93.

11. George F. Root composed this song in 1863 and it was published in 1864.

12. "Grand Excursion to Columbus," *Newark (Ohio) Advocate,* June 22, 1877; "Another Excursion to Columbus," *Newark (Ohio) Advocate,* July 6, 1877.

13. E. C. Wines, *Report of the International Penitentiary Congress of London,* 45, 88; Bureau of Justice Statistics, "Reentry Trends in the U.S.: Recidivism," http://www.bjs.gov/content/reentry/recidivism.cfm.

Bibliography

Andersonville National Historic Site Library, Andersonville, Georgia (ANS)

Andersonville Diaries Vols. 1–3.
Hoster, John L. *Adventure of a Soldier.*

Georgia Department of Archives and History, Atlanta, Georgia

Inspector Report, 1831. Board of Inspectors Reports, 1820–73. Records of the Georgia Prison Commission, 1817–1936: A Part of the Georgia Board of Corrections, Record Group 21.

Library of Congress, Washington, D.C. (LOC)

Mitchell, James B. Papers, 1859–1913.
Price, Nathaniel Shepard Armstrong. Papers, 1861–1910.
Sherman, John J. Papers, 1844–1922.
Weimer, David F. Diaries, 1839–1921.
White, Andrew G. Papers, 1864–1905.
Willard Family. Collection, Part I, Containers 170 and 173.

National Archives and Records Administration, Washington, D.C. (NARA I); College Park, Maryland (NARA II)

Record Group 48: MLR A1–475 *Register of Punishments, 1831–1862.* NARA II.
Record Group 48: Records of the Department of the Interior, Entry 473, Box 4. NARA II.
Record Group 48: Records of the Office of the Secretary of the Interior, Entry 466, Miscellaneous Letters to the Board of Inspectors and Warden, Box 1. NARA II.
Record Group 48: Records of the Office of the Secretary of the Interior, Records Relating to the U.S. Penitentiary for the District of Columbia, 1826–65, Miscellaneous Records, 1829–62, Entry 470, Boxes 1–3. NARA II.

Record Group 109: "Papers Relating to Citizens, 1861–1867." NARA I.

Record Group 109: Ch. 9, Vol. 199 ½, "Secretary of War Letters Confederate Military Prison Richmond, Virginia January 1862–December 1863." NARA I.

Record Group 249: Entry 131, Box 1. NARA I.

Record Group 393, Pt. 4: Headquarters Military District of Washington, Provost Marshal's Office, Entry 2131. NARA I.

New York Public Library, New York, New York (NYPL)

Penitentiary in the District of Columbia. *Annual Report of the Inspectors of the Penitentiary in the District of Columbia, 1829–1862*. Washington, D.C.: Government Printing Office, 1830–62.

Ohio Historical Society, Columbus, Ohio (OHS)

Bullitt, Helen. Papers, 1862–64.

Burks, Samuel Taylor. Letters, 1863.

Carrington, Col. H. B. "Attempted Revolt of Confederate Prisoners of War at Camp Chase, Ohio."

Galloway, Samuel. Papers, 1840–95.

Gray, R. M. *Civil War Reminiscences*. Civil War Collection, Reel 2.

Ohio General Assembly. "Report of the Committee on the Penitentiary," 1864–65.

———. "Report of the Standing Committee on the Penitentiary, Mr. Kirtland from the Standing Committee on the Penitentiary," 1831–32.

Ohio Penitentiary. *Annual Report of the Director and Wardens of the Ohio Penitentiary to the Governor of Ohio, 1835–1880*.

Southern Historical Collection, The Wilson Library, University of North Carolina at Chapel Hill (SHC UNC)

Bingham, Robert. Papers, #3731-z.

Dixon, E. D. Recollections, #223-z.

Hamlin, Theodore P. Papers, 1834–85, #304-z.

Joyner Family. Papers, #4428.

Lowry, James Addison. Letters, #5196.

Mangum Family. Papers, #483.

Metts, James Isaac. Papers, #3624-z.

Murphey, Virgil S. Diary, #534-z.

Sampson, Ira B. Papers, 1862–91, #3870-z.

Saunders, Joseph Hubbard. Papers, #650.

Simrall, Charles Barrington. Papers, #1665.

Smith, Benjamin R. Autograph Album, #3379-z.

Library of Virginia, Richmond, Virginia (LVA)

Doc. No. 1. *Message IV, Relative to Reprieves and Pardons, to the General Assembly of Virginia, December 7, 1857.*

Doc. No. 1. *Message of the Governor of Virginia and Accompanying Documents.* Richmond: William F. Ritchie, Public Printer, 1862.

Doc. No. 6. *Annual Report of the Board of Directors of the Penitentiary Institution, Year Ending September 30, 1862.*

Doc. No. 6. *Communication Relative to Reprieves, Pardons, etc., 1862.*

Doc. No. 7. *Communication Relative to Reprieves, Pardons, etc., 1863.*

Doc. No. 7. *Report of the Superintendent of the Penitentiary, 1863.*

Doc. No. 8. *Annual Report of the Board of Directors of the Penitentiary Institution, 1847.*

Doc. No. 9. *Annual Report of the Board of Directors of the Penitentiary Institution, Year Ending September 30, 1863.*

Doc. No. 12. *Annual Report of the Board of Directors of the Penitentiary Institution, Year Ending September 30, 1864.*

Doc. No. 13. *Annual Report of the Board of Directors of the Penitentiary Institution, 1857.*

Doc. No. 14. *Annual Report of the Board of Directors of the Penitentiary Institution, 1851.*

Doc. No. 15. *Annual Report of the Board of Directors of the Penitentiary Institution, 1848.*

Doc. No. 16. *Communication Relative to Reprieves, Pardons, etc., December 1863.*

Doc. No. 35. *Governor's Communication on the Subject of Pardons, Reprieves, etc., 1864.*

Doc. No. 40. *Communication Relative to Reprieves, Pardons, etc., 1861.*

Doc. No. 66. *Report of the Joint Committee on the Penitentiary, March 1862.*

Report of the Board of Directors of the Virginia Penitentiary, with Accompanying Documents, for the Year Ending Sept. 30, 1871. Richmond: B. F. Walker, Supt. Public Printing, 1871.

"Rules and Regulations for the Government of Castle Thunder, 1863."

Virginia Penitentiary. *Penitentiary Papers, 1796–1865.*

———. *Penitentiary Papers, 1867–1897.*

———. *Prison Register and Indexes, 1865–1980,* Prison Register No. 1.

Wise, Henry A., to the Senate and House of Delegates of the General Assembly of the Commonwealth of Virginia.

Virginia Historical Society, Richmond, Virginia (VHS)

Camp Chase, Ohio. Papers, 1862–63.

Confederate States of America, Army, Department of Henrico. Records, 1861–64.

Louthan Family. Papers, Call MSS1 L9361A, unprocessed collection.

Owen, Henry Thweatt. Papers, 1825–1920.

Robinson, Morgan P. Collection, Old Catalogue, Folder 2, Box, 1.

Virginia General Assembly. Joint Committee on the Penitentiary. *Report of the Joint Committee on the Penitentiary, 1835.*

———. Joint Committee on the Penitentiary. *Report of the Joint Committee to Examine the Penitentiary, 1840–1841.*

———. *Penitentiary Institution, 1846.*

Western Reserve Historical Society, Cleveland, Ohio (WRHS)

Bell, Alfred E. Papers, 1861–65.

Healy, John. Family Papers, 1865.

Hines, Thomas H. "Thrilling Narrative of the Escape of Gen. John H. Morgan, from the Ohio Penitentiary." N.p.: O. P. Print, 1887.

Ohio Penitentiary. *Report of the Directors of the New Penitentiary, 1834.*

Roberts, William S. *A Discourse, Before the Officers of the Ohio Penitentiary, on the First Sabbath in February, 1852.*

Scovill, Edward Alexander. Papers, 1862–71.

Simpson, Harry G. "The Prisoners of the Ohio Penitentiary, 1883."

Newspapers

Alton Telegraph (Alton, Ill.)

Asheville News (Asheville, N.C.)

Atlanta Constitution (Atlanta, Ga.)

Bangor Daily Whig & Courier (Bangor, Maine)

Bloomsburg General Advertiser (Bloomsburg, Pa.)

Brooklyn Daily Eagle (Brooklyn, N.Y.)

Carolina Federal Republican (New Bern, N.C.)

Carolina Watchman (Salisbury, N.C.)

Charlotte Democrat (Charlotte, N.C.)

Cincinnati Enquirer (Cincinnati, Ohio)

Cleveland Daily Leader (Cleveland, Ohio)

Cleveland Morning Herald (Cleveland, Ohio)

Columbus Crisis (Columbus, Ohio)

Coshocton Democrat (Coshocton, Ohio)

Crisis (Columbus, Ohio)

Daily Carolina Watchman (Salisbury, N.C.)

Daily Cleveland Herald (Cleveland, Ohio)

Daily Dispatch (Richmond, Va.)

Daily Empire (Dayton, Ohio)

Daily Era (Raleigh, N.C.)

Daily Evening Bulletin (San Francisco, Calif.)

Daily Milwaukee News (Milwaukee, Wis.)

Daily National Intelligencer (Washington, D.C.)

Daily Ohio Statesman (Columbus, Ohio)

Daily Richmond Examiner (Richmond, Va.)

Daily Rocky Mountain News (Denver, Colo.)

Daily Standard (Raleigh, N.C.)

Dawson's Fort Wayne Weekly Times (Fort Wayne, Ind.)

Democrat and Herald (Wilmington, Ohio)

Elyria Independent Democrat (Elyria, Ohio)

Emporia Weekly News (Emporia, Kans.)

Evening Post (New York, N.Y.)

Evening Star (Washington, D.C.)

Examiner (Richmond, Va.)

Fayetteville Observer (Fayetteville, N.C.)

Frank Leslie's Illustrated Newspaper (New York, N.Y.)

Georgia Weekly Telegraph and Georgia Journal & Messenger (Macon, Ga.)

Gettysburg Compiler (Gettysburg, Pa.)

Greensboro Patriot (Greensboro, N.C.)

Hamilton Telegraph (Hamilton, Ohio)

Huron Reflector (Norwalk, Ohio)

Indiana Herald (Huntington, Ind.)

Janesville Weekly Gazette (Janesville, Wis.)

Liberator (Boston, Mass.)

Madison County Courier (Edwardsville, Ill.)

Mecklenburg Jeffersonian (Charlotte, N.C.)

Memphis Avalanche (Memphis, Tenn.)

Memphis Daily Appeal (Memphis, Tenn.)

Milwaukee Daily Sentinel (Milwaukee, Wis.)

Milwaukee News (Milwaukee, Wis.)

Nashville Daily Union (Nashville, Tenn.)

National Republican (Washington, D.C.)

Newark Advocate (Newark, Ohio)

New Bern Daily Progress (New Bern, N.C.)

New Bern Times (New Bern, N.C.)

New Haven Daily Palladium (New Haven, Conn.)

New York Times (New York, N.Y.)

North American and United States Gazette (Philadelphia, Pa.)

North-Carolinian (Fayetteville, N.C.)

People's Press (Winston-Salem, N.C.)

Pittsburgh Gazette (Pittsburgh, Pa.)

Portsmouth Daily Times (Portsmouth, Ohio)

Progress Index (Petersburg, Va.)

Progressive Age (Coshocton, Ohio)

Public Ledger (Philadelphia, Pa.)
Raleigh Minerva (Raleigh, N.C.)
Raleigh Register (Raleigh, N.C.)
Raleigh Sentinel (Raleigh, N.C.)
Reading Times (Reading, Pa.)
Richmond Dispatch (Richmond, Va.)
Richmond Enquirer (Richmond, Va.)
Richmond Examiner (Richmond, Va.)
Richmond Sentinel (Richmond, Va.)
Richmond Whig (Richmond, Va.)
Sandusky Clarion (Sandusky, Ohio)
Santa Cruz Weekly Sentinel (Santa Cruz, Calif.)
Scioto Gazette (Chillicothe, Ohio)
Semi-Weekly Wisconsin (Milwaukee, Wis.)
Southern Weekly Post (Raleigh, N.C.)
St. Cloud Democrat (St. Cloud, Minn.)
St. Louis Globe-Democrat (St. Louis, Mo.)
Sun (Baltimore, Md.)
Tarborough Southerner (Tarborough, N.C.)
Times (London, Greater London, England)
Times Picayune (New Orleans, La.)
Tioga Eagle (Wellsboro, Pa.)
Torch Light and Advertiser (Hagerstown, N.C.)
Tri-Weekly Era (Raleigh, N.C.)
Vermont Watchman and State Journal (Montpelier, Vt.)
Washington Post (Washington, D.C.)
Weekly Progress (Raleigh, N.C.)
Weekly Standard (Raleigh, N.C.)
Weekly State Journal (Raleigh, N.C.)
Weekly Wisconsin (Milwaukee, Wis.)
Wellsboro Gazette (Wellsboro, Pa.)
White Cloud Kansas Chief (White Cloud, Kans.)
Wilmington Daily Dispatch (Wilmington, N.C.)
Wilmington Herald (Wilmington, N.C.)
Wilmington Journal (Wilmington, N.C.)
Wisconsin Tribune (Mineral Point, Wis.)
Zanesville Daily Courier (Zanesville, Ohio)

Published Primary and Secondary Sources

Abbott, Edith. "The Civil War and the Crime Wave of 1865–1870." *Social Science Review* 1, no. 2 (1927): 212–34.

Adshead, Joseph. *Prisons and Prisoners*. London: Longman, Brown, 1845.

Altschuler, Glenn A., and Stuart M. Blumin. *Rude Republic: Americans and Their Politics in the Nineteenth Century*. Princeton, N.J.: Princeton University Press, 2000.

Anderson, Paul C. *Blood Image: Turner Ashby in the Civil War and the Southern Mind*. Baton Rouge: Louisiana State University Press, 2002.

Andrzejewski, Anna Vemer. *Building Power: Architecture and Surveillance in Victorian America*. Knoxville: University of Tennessee Press, 2008.

Ayers, Edward L. *Vengeance and Justice: Crime and Punishment in the Nineteenth Century American South*. New York: Oxford University Press, 1984.

Bangert, Elizabeth C. "The Press and the Prisons: Union and Confederate Newspaper Coverage of Civil War Prisons, 1861–1865." MA thesis, William and Mary, 2001.

Banner, Stuart. *The Death Penalty: An American History*. Cambridge, Mass.: Harvard University Press, 2002.

Barbiere, Joseph. *Scraps from the Prison Table: At Camp Chase & Johnson's Island*. Doylestown, Pa.: W. W. H. Davis, 1868.

Barksdale, K. T. "Francis H. Pierpont (1814–1899)." *Encyclopedia Virginia*. www .EncyclopediaVirginia.org/Pierpont_Francis_H_1814–1899.

Beaumont, Gustave de, and Alexis de Tocqueville. *On the Penitentiary System in the United States and Its Application in France*. Carbondale: Southern Illinois University Press, 1964.

Beeghley, Leonard. *Homicide: A Sociological Explanation*. New York: Rowman & Littlefield, 2003.

Blakey, Arch Frederic. *General John H. Winder, C.S.A.* Gainesville: University of Florida Press, 1990.

Blanton, DeAnn, and Lauren M. Cook. *They Fought Like Demons: Women Soldiers in the American Civil War*. Baton Rouge: Louisiana State University Press, 2002.

Bonner, James C. *Milledgeville: Georgia's Antebellum Capital*. Athens: The University of Georgia Press, 1978.

Brock, Sally A. *Richmond during the War: Four Years of Personal Observation by a Richmond Lady*. New York: G. W. Carleton & Company Publishers, 1867.

Brown, Louis A. *The Salisbury Prison: A Case Study of Confederate Military Prison*. Wendell, N.C.: Avera Press, Broadfoot's Bookmark, 1980.

Bureau of Justice Statistics. "Reentry Trends in the U.S.: Recidivism." www.bjs.gov /content/reentry/recidivism.cfm.

Bush, David R. *I Fear I Shall Never Leave This Island: Life in a Civil War Prison*. Gainesville: University Press of Florida, 2012.

Butler, Anne M. *Gendered Justice in the American West: Women Prisoners in Men's Penitentiaries*. Urbana: University of Illinois Press, 1997.

Bynum, Victoria. *Unruly Women: The Politics of Social and Sexual Control in the Old South*. Chapel Hill: University of North Carolina Press, 1992.

Callan, John F. *The Military Laws of the United States, Relating to the Army, Volunteers, Militia, and to Bounty Lands and Pensions, from the Foundation of the Government to the Year 1863*. Philadelphia: George W. Childs, 1863.

Casstevens, Frances H. *George W. Alexander and Castle Thunder: A Confederate Prison and Its Commandant*. Jefferson, N.C.: McFarland, 2004.

——. *"Out of the Mouths of Hell": Civil War Prisons and Escapes*. Jefferson, N.C.: McFarland, 2005.

Central Intelligence Agency, "Intelligence Collection—the North." www.cia.gov/library /publications/additional-publications/civil-war/p11.htm.

Chesson, Michael B. "Harlots or Heroines?: A New Look at the Richmond Bread Riot." *Virginia Magazine of History and Biography* 92, no. 2 (April 1984): 131–75.

Clavin, Matthew J. "'The Floor Was Stained with the Blood of a Slave': Crime and Punishment in the Old South." In Tarter and Bell, *Buried Lives*, 259–81.

Clinton, Catherine. "'Public Women' and Sexual Politics during the American Civil War." In Clinton and Silber, *Battle Scars*, 61–77.

Clinton, Catherine, and Nina Silber, eds. *Battle Scars: Gender and Sexuality in the American Civil War*. New York: Oxford University Press, 2006.

——. *Divided Houses: Gender and the Civil War*. New York: Oxford University Press, 1992.

Cloyd, Benjamin G. *Haunted by Atrocity: Civil War Prisons in American Memory*. Baton Rouge: Louisiana State University Press, 2010.

Coffman, Edward M. *The Old Army: A Portrait of the American Army in Peacetime, 1784–1898*. New York: Oxford University Press, 1986.

Cole, Charles C., Jr. *A Fragile Capital: Identity and the Early Years of Columbus, Ohio*. Columbus: Ohio State University Press, 2001.

Colvin, Mark. *Penitentiaries, Reformatories, and Chain Gangs: Social Theory and the History of Punishment in Nineteenth Century America*. New York: St. Martin's Press, 1997.

Constitution of the Confederate States. March 11, 1861. http://avalon.law.yale.edu/ 19th_century/csa_csa.asp.

Cott, Nancy. *The Bonds of Womanhood: Woman's Sphere in New England, 1780–1835*. 2d ed. New Haven: Yale University Press, 1997.

Crawford, William. *Report on the Penitentiaries of the United States*. With a new introduction by Norman Johnston. 1835. Reprint, Montclair, N.J.: Patterson Smith, 1969.

Cullen, Jim. "'I's a Man Now': Gender and African American Men." In *Divided Houses: Gender and the Civil War*, edited by Catherine Clinton and Nina Silber, 76–91. New York: Oxford University Press, 1992.

Dabney, Virginius. *Richmond: The Story of a City*. Charlottesville: University Press of Virginia, 1990.

Dale, Elizabeth. *Criminal Justice in the United States, 1789–1939*. Cambridge: Cambridge University Press, 2011.

Dalsheim, Stephen. "The United States Penitentiary for the District of Columbia, 1826–1862." *Records of the Columbia Historical Society, Washington, D.C.*

Vol. 53/56. The 42nd Separately Bound Book. Washington, D.C.: Columbia Historical Society, 1953–56.

Davis, Robert Scott. "Escape from Andersonville: A Study in Isolation and Imprisonment." *The Journal of Military History* 67, no. 4 (October 2003): 1065–82.

Day, W. W. *Fifteen Months in Dixie: My Personal Experience in Rebel Prisons. A Story of the Hardships, Privations and Sufferings of the "Boys in Blue" during the Late War of the Rebellion.* Owatonna, Minn.: The People's Press Print, 1889.

Derden, John K. *The World's Largest Prison: The Story of Camp Lawton.* Macon, Ga.: Mercer University Press, 2012.

Dix, Dorothea Lynde. *Remarks on Prisons and Prison Discipline in the United States.* 2d ed. With a new Introduction by Leonard D. Savitz. 1845. Reprint, Montclair, N.J.: Patterson Smith, 1967.

"Documenting the American South." http://docsouth.unc.edu/fpn/velazquez/velazquez.html.

Dodds, Gilbert F. *Camp Chase: The Story of a Civil War Post.* Columbus, Ohio: The Franklin County Historical Society, a Civil War Centennial Project, n.d.

Dodge, L. Mara. *Whores and Thieves of the Worst Kind: A Study of Women, Crime, and Prisons, 1835–2000.* DeKalb: Northern Illinois University Press, 2002.

Downs, Gregory P. *Declarations of Dependence: The Long Reconstruction of Popular Politics in the South, 1861–1908.* Chapel Hill: University of North Carolina Press, 2011.

Doyle, Robert C. *The Enemy in Our Hands: America's Treatment of Enemy Prisoners of War from the Revolution to the War on Terror.* Lexington: The University Press of Kentucky, 2010.

Dudink, Stephan, and Karen Hagemann. "Masculinity in Politics and War in the Age of Democratic Revolutions, 1750–1850." In Dudink, Hagemann, and Tosh, *Masculinities in Politics and War,* 3–21.

Dudink, Stephan, Karen Hagemann, and John Tosh, eds. *Masculinities in Politics and War: Gendering Modern History.* New York: Manchester University Press, 2004.

Duff, W. H. *Six Months of Prison Life at Camp Chase, Ohio.* 3rd ed. Clearwater, S.C.: Eastern Digital Resources, 2004.

Dumm, Thomas L. *Democracy and Punishment.* Madison: University of Wisconsin Press, 1987.

Dynes v. Hoover, 61 U.S. 65, 15 L. Ed. 838 (1857).

Dzurec, David. "Prisoners of War and American Self-Image during the American Revolution." *War in History* 20, no. 4 (November 2013): 430–51.

Faust, Drew. *Mothers of Invention: Women of the Slaveholding South in the American Civil War.* Chapel Hill: University of North Carolina Press, 1996.

Finley, James B. *Memorials of Prison Life.* 1853. Reprint, New York: Arno Press, 1974.

First Annual Report of the Board of Managers of the Prison Discipline Society, Boston, June 2, 1826. Boston: T. R. Marvin, Congress Street, 1827.

Fitzgerald, Michael. *Splendid Failure: Postwar Reconstruction in the American South.* Chicago: Ivan R. Dee, 2007.

Flory, William E. S. *Prisoners of War: A Study in the Development of International Law*. Washington, D.C.: American Council on Public Affairs, 1942.

—— *Punishment and Reformation: A Study of the Penitentiary System*. 1895. Reprint, Memphis: General Books, 2010.

Foner, Eric. *Reconstruction: America's Unfinished Revolution, 1863–1877*. New York: Perennial Classics, 1988.

Foote, Lorien. *The Gentlemen and the Roughs: Manhood, Honor, and Violence in the Union Army*. New York: New York University Press, 2010.

Foucault, Michel. *Discipline and Punish: The Birth of the Prison*. Translated by Alan Sheridan. New York: Vintage Books, 1995.

Friedel, Frank. *Francis Lieber: Nineteenth-Century Liberal*. 1947. Reprint, Clark, N.J.: The Lawbook Exchange, 2003.

Friedman, Lawrence M. *A History of American Law*. 3rd ed. New York: Simon & Schuster, 2005.

——. *Crime and Punishment in American History*. New York: Basic Books, 1993.

Furgurson, Ernest B. *Ashes of Gory: Richmond at War*. New York: Vintage Books, 1996.

Garland, David. *Punishment and Modern Society: A Study in Social Theory*. Chicago: University of Chicago Press, 1990.

Georgia General Assembly, Senate. *Journal of the Senate of the State of Georgia, at the Annual Session of the General Assembly, Begun and Held in Milledgeville, the Seat of Government, in 1861*. Milledgeville, Ga.: Boughton, Nisbet & Barnes, State Printers, 1861.

——. *Journal of the Senate of the State of Georgia, at the Annual Session of the General Assembly, Begun and Held in Milledgeville, the Seat of Government, in 1862*. Milledgeville, Ga.: Boughton, Nisbet & Barnes, State Printers, 1862.

"Gettysburg National Military Park: Army Organization during the Civil War." www .nps.gov/archive/gett/getttour/armorg.htm.

Gibson, Mary. "Global Perspectives on the Birth of the Prison." *American Historical Review* 116, no. 4 (October 2011): 1040–63.

Gillispie, James M. *Andersonvilles of the North: The Myths and Realities of Northern Treatment of Civil War Confederate Prisoners*. Denton: University of North Texas Press, 2008.

Gilmore, James Roberts. *Patriot Boys and Prison Pictures*. Boston: Ticknor and Fields, 1866.

Gjerde, Jon. *Catholicism and the Shaping of Nineteenth-Century America*, edited by S. Deborah Kang. New York: Cambridge University Press, 2012.

Goffman, Erving. *Asylums: Essays on the Social Situation of Mental Patients and Other Inmates*. Garden City, N.Y.: Anchor Books, 1961.

Goldsmith, Larry. "History from the Inside Out: Prison Life in Nineteenth-Century Massachusetts." *Journal of Social History* 31, no. 1 (1997): 109–25.

Gorman, Mike, ed. *Civil War Richmond*. www.mdgorman.com/Written_Accounts /Enquirer/1862/richmond_enquirer,_12_10_1862.htm.

Gould, Virginia. "'Oh, I Pass Everywhere': Catholic Nuns in the Gulf South during the Civil War." In Clinton and Silber *Battle Scars*, 41–60.

Gray, Michael. *The Business of Captivity: Elmira and Its Civil War Prison*. Kent: The Kent State University Press, 2001.

Griffith, Lucille, ed. "Fredericksburg's Political Hostages: The Old Capitol Journal of George Henry Clay Rowe." *The Virginia Magazine of History and Biography* 72, no. 4 (1964): 395–429.

Gross, Kali. *Colored Amazons: Crime, Violence, and Black Women in the City of Brotherly Love, 1880–1910*. Durham: Duke University Press, 2006.

Guardino, Peter. "Gender, Soldiering, and Citizenship in the Mexican-American War of 1846–1848." *The American Historical Review* 119, no. 1 (February 2014): 23–46.

Helper, Hinton R. *The Impending Crisis of the South*. New York: Burdick Brothers, 1857.

Hesseltine, William B. *Civil War Prisons: A Study in War Psychology*. 1930. Reprint, Columbus: The Ohio State University Press, 1998.

Hindus, Michael Stephen. *Prison and Plantation: Crime, Justice, and Authority in Massachusetts and South Carolina, 1767–1878*. Chapel Hill: University of North Carolina Press, 1980.

Hooper, Osman Castle. *History of the City of Columbus, Ohio: From the Founding of Franklinton in 1797, through the World War Period, to the Year 1920*. Columbus: Memorial Publishing, 1920.

Horton, James Oliver. "Freedom's Yoke: Gender and Conventions Among Antebellum Free Blacks." *Feminist Studies* 12, no. 1 (Spring 1986): 51–76.

Ignatieff, Michael. *A Just Measure of Pain: The Penitentiary in the Industrial Revolution, 1750–1850*. New York: Pantheon Books, 1978.

Isenberg, Nancy. *Sex and Citizenship in Antebellum America*. Chapel Hill: University of North Carolina Press, 1998.

Jacobs, James B. *Statesville: The Penitentiary in Mass Society*. Chicago: University of Chicago Press, 1977.

Janofsky, Jennifer Lawrence. "'Hopelessly Hardened': The Complexities of Penitentiary Discipline at Philadelphia's Eastern State Penitentiary." In Tarter and Bell, *Buried Lives*, 106–23.

Johnson, Andrew. Executive Order—General Orders No. 109, June 6, 1865. "The American Presidency Project." www.presidency.ucsb.edu/ws/index.php?pid=72212.

Johnson, Susan Lee. *Roaring Camp: The Social World of the California Gold Rush*. New York: W. W. Norton, 2000.

Johnston, Norman Bruce. *Forms of Constraint: A History of Prison Architecture*. Urbana: University of Illinois Press, 2000.

Kann, Mark E. *Punishment, Prisons, and Patriarchy: Liberty and Power in the Early American Republic*. New York: New York University Press, 2005.

Kellogg, Robert H. *Life and Death in Rebel Prisons*. 1865. Reprint, Bedford, Mass.: Applewood Books, 2008. Keve, Paul W. *The History of Corrections in Virginia*. Charlottesville: University of Virginia Press,1986.

Kimmel, Michael S. *Manhood in America: A Cultural History*. 2d ed. New York: Oxford University Press, 2006.

King, John Henry. *Three Hundred Days in a Yankee Prison: Reminiscences of War Life, Captivity, Imprisonment at Camp Chase, Ohio*. Atlanta, Ga.: Jas. P. Daves, 1904.

Klement, Frank L. *The Copperheads in the Middle West*. Gloucester, Mass.: P. Smith, 1960.

Kuntz, William Francis. *Criminal Sentencing in Three Nineteenth-Century Cities: A Social History of Punishment in New York, Boston, and Philadelphia, 1830–1880*. New York: Garland Publishers, 1988.

Lamar, Lucius Q. C. "Rules and Regulations for the Internal Government of the Penitentiary." In *A Compilation of the Laws of the State of Georgia, Passed by the Legislature Since the Year 1810 to the Year 1819, Inclusive*. Augusta, Ga.: T. S. Hannon, 1821.

Lawson, Melinda. *Patriot Fires: Forging a New American Nationalism in the Civil War North*. Lawrence: University Press of Kansas, 2002.

Leonard, Elizabeth D. *All the Daring of the Soldier: Women of the Civil War Armies*. New York: Penguin Books, 2001.

———. "Mary Walker, Mary Surratt, and Some Thoughts on Gender in the Civil War." In Clinton and Silber, *Battle Scars*, 104–19.

Levine, David. "Sing Sing Prison, Ossining, New York: A History of Hudson Valley's Jail up the River." *Hudson Valley Magazine* (September 2011). www.hvmag.com/Hudson-Valley-Magazine/September-2011/Sing-Sing-Prison-Ossining-NY-A-History-of-Hudson-Valleys-Jail-Up-the-River/index.php?cparticle=1&siarticle=0#artanc.

Levinson, David, ed. *Encyclopedia of Crime and Punishment*. Vol. 3. Thousand Oaks, Calif.: Sage Publications, 2002.

Lewis, W. David. *From Newgate to Dannemora: The Rise of the Penitentiary in New York, 1796–1848*. Ithaca, N.Y.: Cornell University Press, 1965.

Lichtenstein, Alex. *Twice the Work of Free Labor: The Political Economy of Convict Labor in the New South*. London: Verso, 1996.

Lieber, Francis. *A Popular Essay on Subjects of Penal Law, and on Uninterrupted Solitary Confinement at Labor as Contradistinguished to Solitary Confinement at Night and Joint Labor by Day in a Letter to John Bacon, Esquire. President of the Philadelphia Society for Alleviating the Miseries of Public Prisons*. Philadelphia: Published by Order of the Society, 1838. http://books.google.com/books?id=-iHINIeYa9UC&pg=PP13&dq=lieber+popular+essay+on+subjects+of+penal+law&hl=en&sa=X&ei=CoQxVKr6NJTDggSMtIGICQ&ved=0CFAQ6AEwBg#v=onepage&q=lieber%20popular%20essay%20on%20subjects%20of%20penal%20law&f=false.

———. *General Orders no. 100*. The Avalon Project. http://avalon.law.yale.edu/19th_century/lieber.asp#sec1.

Lincoln, Abraham. "Order Concerning Prisoners." February 15, 1865. http://quod.lib.umich.edu/cgi/t/text/text-idx?c=lincoln;rgn=div1;view=text;idno=lincoln8;node=lincoln8%3A627.

Linder, Doug. "The Trial of the Lincoln Assassination Conspirators." 2009. http://law2.umkc.edu/faculty/projects/ftrials/lincolnconspiracy/lincolnaccount.html.

Madera, Judith I. "Floating Prisons: Dispossession, Ordering, and Colonial Atlantic 'States,' 1776–1783." In Tarter and Bell, *Buried Lives*, 175–202.

Mahoney, D. A. *The Prisoner of State*. New York: Carleton, 1863.

Manion, Jen. *Liberty's Prisoners: Carceral Culture in Early America*. Philadelphia: University of Pennsylvania Press, 2015.

Manning, Chandra. *What This Cruel War Was Over: Soldiers, Slavery, and the Civil War*. New York: Vintage, 2007.

Marshall, John A. *American Bastille: A History of the Illegal Arrests and Imprisonment of American Citizens during the Late Civil War*. Philadelphia: Thomas W. Hartley, 1869.

Marvel, William. *Andersonville: The Last Depot*. Chapel Hill: The University of North Carolina Press, 1994.

Masur, Louis P. *Rites of Execution: Capital Punishment and the Transformation of American Culture, 1776–1865*. New York: Oxford University Press, 1989.

Matthews, J. H. *Historical Reminiscences of the Ohio Penitentiary: From Its Erection in 1835 to the Present Time, a Descriptive View of the Interior and Its System of Government, Modes of Punishment, Brief Sketches of the Prisoner's Life, Escapes, Noted Criminals*. Columbus, Ohio: Chas. M. Cott, 1884.

McCurry, Stephanie. *Confederate Reckoning: Power and Politics in the Civil War South*. Cambridge, Mass.: Harvard University Press, 2010.

McKelvey, Blake. *American Prisons: A History of Good Intentions*. Montclair, N.J.: Patterson Smith, 1977.

McLennan, Rebecca M. *The Crisis of Imprisonment: Protest, Politics, and the Making of the American Penal State, 1776–1941*. New York: Cambridge University Press, 2008.

McPherson, James M. *For Cause and Comrades: Why Men Fought in the Civil War*. New York: Oxford University Press, 1997.

Melossi, Dario, and Massimo Pavarini, *The Prison and the Factory: Origins of the Penitentiary System*. Translated by Glynis Cousin. Totowa, N.J.: Barnes & Noble Books, 1981.

Meranze, Michael. *Laboratories of Virtue: Punishment, Revolution, and Authority in Philadelphia, 1760–1835*. Chapel Hill: University of North Carolina Press, 1996.

Mettraux, Guénaël. "A Little-Known Case from the American Civil War: The War Crimes Trial of Major General John H. Gee." *Journal of International Criminal Justice* 8 (2010): 1059–68.

Mitchell, Andrea Nicole. "The Georgia Penitentiary at Milledgeville." MA thesis, Georgia College and State University, 2003.

Morris, Norval, and David J. Rothman, eds. *The Oxford History of the Prison: The Practice of Punishment in Western Society*. New York: Oxford University Press, 1998.

Neely, Mark E., Jr. *The Fate of Liberty: Abraham Lincoln and Civil Liberties*. New York: Oxford University Press, 1991.

——. *Southern Rights: Political Prisoners and the Myth of Confederate Constitu-tionalism*. Charlottesville: The University Press of Virginia, 1999.

Neff, Stephen C. *Justice in Blue and Gray: A Legal History of the Civil War*. Cam-bridge, Mass.: Harvard University Press, 2010.

Nelson, Scott Reynolds. *Steel Drivin' Man: John Henry, The Untold Story of an American Legend*. New York: Oxford University Press, 2006.

Nelson, Scott Reynolds, and Carol Sheriff. *A People at War: Civilians and Soldiers in America's Civil War, 1854–1877*. New York: Oxford University Press, 2007.

Newell, Clayton R., and Charles R. Shrader. *Of Duty Well and Faithfully Done: A History of the Regular Army in the Civil War*. Lincoln: University of Nebraska Press, 2011.

No. 380, "An Act to Reform the Penal Code of This State, and to Adapt the Same to the Penitentiary System." Penal Code 1816. In Lucius Q. C. Lamar, Esq., *A Com-pilation of the Laws of the State of Georgia, Passed by the Legislature Since the Year 1810 to the Year 1819, Inclusive*. Augusta: T. S. Hannon, 1821.

North Carolina Department of Public Safety. "History of the North Carolina Correc-tion System." www.doc.state.nc.us/admin.

O'Brien, Patricia. *The Promise of Punishment: Prisons in Nineteenth-Century France*. Princeton, N.J.: Princeton University Press, 1982.

O'Donovan, Susan. "Universities of Social and Political Change: Slaves in Jail in An-tebellum America." In Tarter and Bell, *Buried Lives*, 124–48.

Parker, Sandra V. *Richmond's Civil War Prisons*. 2d ed. Lynchburg, Va.: H. E. How-ard, 1990.

Patrick, Leslie. "Afterword." In Tarter and Bell, *Buried Lives*, 282–84.

Paulson, Linda Dailey. "Leavenworth Federal Penitentiary." In *Encyclopedia of Crime and Punishment*, vol. 3, edited by David Levinson, 1008–09. Thousand Oaks, Calif.: Sage Publications, 2002.

Pickenpaugh, Roger C. *Captives in Blue: The Civil War Prisons of the Confed-eracy*. Tuscaloosa: The University of Alabama Press, 2013.

——. *Captives in Gray: The Civil War Prisons of the Union*. Tuscaloosa: The Uni-versity of Alabama Press, 2009.

——. *Johnson's Island: A Prison for Confederate Officers*. Kent, Ohio: The Kent State University Press, 2016.

Rafter, Nicole Hahn. *Partial Justice: Women, Prisons, and Social Control*. 2d ed. New Brunswick, N.J.: Transaction Publishers, 1990.

Ransom, John L. *Andersonville Diary: Escape and List of the Dead, with Name, Co., Regiment, Date of Death and No. of Grave in Cemetery*. 1881. Reprint, DSI Digital Reproduction, 2003.

Reed, Austin. *The Life and the Adventures of a Haunted Convict*. Edited and with an introduction by Caleb Smith. New York: Random House, 2016.

Report of the Treatment of Prisoners of War, by the Rebel Authorities, during the War of the Rebellion: To Which Are Appended the Testimony Taken by the Com-mittee and Official Documents and Statistics, etc. H. Exec. Doc. 45, 40th Con-gress, 3rd session. Washington, D.C.: Government Printing Office, 1869.

Robins, Glenn, ed. *They Have Left Us Here to Die: The Civil War Prison Diary of Sgt. Lyle Adair, 111th U.S. Colored Infantry*. Kent, Ohio: The Kent State University Press, 2011.

Rothman, David J. *The Discovery of the Asylum: Social Order and Disorder in the New Republic*. Boston: Little Brown, 1971.

——. "Perfecting the Prison: The United States, 1789–1865." In *The Oxford History of the Prison: The Practice of Punishment in Western Society*, edited by Norval Morris and David J. Rothman, 100–116. New York: Oxford University Press, 1998.

Ryan, Mary P. *Civic Wars: Democracy and Public Life in the American City during the Nineteenth Century*. Los Angeles: University of California Press, 1998.

Sanders, Charles W., Jr. *While in the Hands of the Enemy: Military Prisons of the Civil War*. Baton Rouge: Louisiana State University Press, 2005.

Scott, Joan. "Gender." In *Gender and the Politics of History*. New York: Columbia University Press, 1988.

Second Annual Report of the Board of Managers of the Prison Discipline Society, Boston, June 1, 1827. Boston: Perkins and Marvin, 1829.

Sellers, Charles. *Market Revolution*. New York: Oxford University Press, 1992.

Shattuck, Gardiner. *A Shield and Hiding Place: The Religious Life of the Civil War Armies*. Macon, Ga.: Mercer University Press, 1987.

Shriver, Philip R., and Donald J. Breen. *Ohio's Military Prisons in the Civil War*. Columbus: Ohio State University Press for the Ohio Historical Society, 1964.

Silber, Nina. *Gender and the Sectional Conflict*. Chapel Hill: The University of North Carolina Press, 2008.

——. *The Romance of Reunion: Northerners and the South, 1865–1900*. Chapel Hill: The University of North Carolina Press, 1993.

Sisters of Charity of Cincinnati. "Our History." http://srcharitycinti.org/about/history.htm.

Speer, Lonnie R. *Portals to Hell: Military Prisons of the Civil War*. Mechanicsburg, Pa.: Stackpole Books, 1997.

Spierenburg, Pieter. *The Prison Experience: Disciplinary Institutions and Their Inmates in Early Modern Europe*. London: Rutgers University Press, 1991.

Stevens, Larry. "88th Ohio Infantry Compiled by Larry Stevens." www.ohiocivilwar.com/cw88.html.

Stott, Richard. *Jolly Fellows: Male Milieus in Nineteenth Century America*. Baltimore: Johns Hopkins University Press, 2009.

Streater, Kristen L. "'She-Rebels' on the Supply Line: Gender Conventions in Civil War Kentucky." In Whites and Long, *Occupied Women*, 88–99.

Sullivan, David K. "Behind Prison Walls: The Operation of the District Penitentiary, 1831–1862." *Records of the Columbia Historical Society, Washington, D.C.* Vol. 71/72. The 48th Separately Bound Book, 1971/1972.

Tarter, Michele Lise, and Richard Bell, eds. *Buried Lives: Incarcerated in Early America*. Athens: The University of Georgia Press, 2012.

Taylor, Amy Murrell. *The Divided Family in Civil War America*. Chapel Hill: University of North Carolina Press, 2005.

Thomas, Emory M. *The Confederate State of Richmond: A Biography of the Capital*. Baton Rouge: Louisiana State University Press, 1971.

Thornton, Mary C. *A Complete Guide to the History and Inmates of the U.S. Penitentiary District of Columbia, 1829–1862*. Bowie, Md.: Heritage Books, 2003.

Tomberlin, Jason. "This Month in North Carolina History: January 1870—North Carolina State Penitentiary Opens." http://www2.lib.unc.edu/ncc/ref/nchistory/jan2007/index.html.

Twenty-Second Annual Report of the Board of Managers Prison Discipline Society, Boston, May 1847. Boston: Damrell and Moore, stereotyped at the Boston Type and Stereotype Foundry, 1848.

Twenty-Third Annual Report of the Board of Managers Prison Discipline Society, Boston, May 1848. Boston: T. R. Marvin, stereotyped at the Boston Type and Stereotype Foundry, 1848.

Twenty-Fourth Annual Report of the Board of Managers Prison Discipline Society, Boston, May 1849. Boston: T. R. Marvin, stereotyped at the Boston Type and Stereotype Foundry, 1849.

United States War Department. *The War of the Rebellion: A Compilation of the Official Records of the Union and Confederate Armies*. Vols. 1–8. Washington, D.C.: Government Printing Office, 1880–1900. http://ebooks.library.cornell.edu/m/moawar/waro.html.

Velazquez, Loreta Janeta. *The Woman in Battle: A Narrative of the Exploits, Adventures, and Travels of Madame Loreta Janeta Velazquez, Otherwise Known as Lieutenant Harry T. Buford*. Edited by C. J. Worthington. Richmond, Va.: Dustin, Gilman & Co., 1876.

Walden, Mary Patricia. "History of the Georgia Penitentiary at Milledgeville, 1817–1868." MA thesis, Georgia State University, 1974.

Weber, Jennifer L. *Copperheads: The Rise and Fall of Lincoln's Opponents in the North*. New York: Oxford University Press, 2006.

White, Deborah Gray. *Ar'n't I a Woman?: Female Slaves in the Plantation South*. New York: W. W. Norton, 1999.

Whites, LeeAnn. "'Corresponding with the Enemy': Mobilizing the Relational Field of Battle in St. Louis." In Whites and Long, *Occupied Women*, 103–16.

Whites, LeeAnn, and Alecia P. Long, eds. *Occupied Women: Gender, Military Occupation, and the American Civil War*. Baton Rouge: Louisiana State University Press, 2009.

Wilentz, Sean. *Chants Democratic: New York City and the Rise of the American Working Class, 1788–1850*. New York: Oxford University Press, 1984.

Williams, Daniel E. "'The Horrors of This Far-Famed Penitentiary': Discipline, Defiance, and Death during Ann Carson's Incarcerations in Philadelphia's Walnut Street Prison." In Tarter and Bell, *Buried Lives*, 203–30.

Williamson, James J. *Prison Life in the Old Capitol and Reminiscences of the Civil War*. West Orange, N.J.: James J. Williamson, 1911.

Wines, E. C. *Report of the International Penitentiary Congress of London, Held July 3–13, 1872, to Which Is Appended the Second Annual Report of the National Prison Association of the United States, Containing the Transactions of the National Prison Reform Congress, held at Baltimore, Maryland, January 21–24, 1873*. Washington, D.C.: Government Printing Office, 1873.

Wines, Frederick Howard. *Punishment and Reformation: A Study of the Penitentiary System*. 1985. Reprint, Memphis: General Books, 2010.

Witt, John Fabian. *Lincoln's Code: The Laws of War in American History*. New York: Free Press, 2012.

Woodworth, Steven E. *While God Is Marching On: The Religious World of Civil War Soldiers*. Lawrence: University Press of Kansas, 2001.

Wyatt-Brown, Bertram. *Southern Honor: Ethics and Behavior in the Old South*. New York: Oxford University Press, 1982.

Yanni, Carla. *The Architecture of Madness: Insane Asylums in the United States*. Minneapolis: University of Minnesota Press, 2007.

Zombek, Angela M. "Camp Chase Prison: A Study of Power and Resistance on the Northern Home Front, 1863." *Ohio History* 118 (August 2011): 24–48.

——. "Citizenship—Compulsory or Convenient: Federal Officials, Confederate Prisoners, and the Oath of Allegiance." In Paul J. Quigley, ed., *The Civil War and the Transformation of Citizenship,* edited by Paul J. Quigley. Forthcoming.

——. "Paternalism and Imprisonment at Castle Thunder: Reinforcing Gender Norms in the Confederate Capital." *Civil War History* 63, no. 3 (September 2017).

——. "Transcending Stereotypes: A Study of Civil War Military Prisons in the Context of Nineteenth-Century Penitentiaries and Penal Development at the Ohio, Virginia, and D.C. Penitentiaries and at Camp Chase, Castle Thunder, and Old Capitol Military Prisons." PhD diss., University of Florida, 2012. http://ufdc.ufl.edu/UFE0044907/00001.

Index